We struck the home trail now and in a few hours were in
that astonishing Chicago—a city where they are always rubbing
the lamp and fetching up the genie and contriving and achieving
new impossibilities—It is hopeless for the occasional visitor to try
and keep up with Chicago—She outgrows his prophecies faster
than he can make them—She is always a novelty! For she is never
the Chicago you saw when you passed the last time.

Mark Twain 1883

Chicago in

Remember

a Time of C

Neal Samors

Introduction by Bob Sirott

the Sixties

ing

hange

Frontice
"Loyalists Shouting 'We Want Daley' at Democratic
National Convention." As published in the *Chicago
Daily-News.* Photographer: Edward DeLuga.
Copyright by *Chicago Sun-Times,* August 30, 1968.
Reprinted with permission.

First Edition, October, 2006
Second Edition, November, 2006

Edited by Neal Samors and Jennifer Samors
Produced by Neal Samors
Designed by Sam Silvio, Silvio Design, Inc.
Printed in Canada by Friesens Corporation

ISBN: 0-9788663-0-4 (Softcover)
ISBN: 0-9788663-1-2 (Case)

Front Cover:
Michigan Avenue, Looking North, 1964.
(Photograph by Eric Bronsky)

Back Cover:
State Street, Looking South from Lake Street, 1960.
(Photograph courtesy of *Chicago Sun-Times)*
Copyright, 1960 by *Chicago Sun-Times,* Inc.
Reprinted with permission.

Inside Back Cover:
(Photograph by Richard Lang)

For more information on this book
as well as author's other works visit my website:
www.chicagosbooks.com
Email: NSamors@comcast.net

Table of Contents

Preface

Chicago in the Sixties: Remembering a Time of Change is a book that combines the memories of 80 current and former Chicagoans with over 150 black and white photographs. The interviewees include: individuals who grew up in the 1930s and 1940s, lived through the Great Depression, fought in World War II, and returned to build families and careers; ones born in the early to mid '40s, grew up in the 1950s, went off to college, got married and found jobs during the 1960s; and, finally, individuals born in the '50s, experienced the challenges of their teenage years in the '60s, and saw careers begin to take shape in the 1970s. Thus, the book's interviewees provide the reader with a broad range of perspectives about the many changes that occurred throughout the '60s.

I was born in 1943 on Chicago's Far North Side, went to high school from 1957 to 1961, was in college, undergraduate and graduate, throughout much of the 1960s, and was a college teacher from 1968 to 1974 before beginning a 25-year career in educational testing. For me, the 1960s were a dynamic, challenging and fascinating period of history, and one of the most memorable decades of the twentieth century.

The book begins with stories from the '60s about life in city and suburban neighborhoods as diverse as West Rogers Park, Albany Park, Old Town, Lawndale, Austin, Bronzeville, Little Italy, Hyde Park, and Bridgeport, nearby cities of Harvey, Cicero, and Joliet, and suburban neighborhoods from Evergreen Park and Oak Lawn south and southwest of Chicago, Oak Park and Glen Ellyn to the west and Skokie, Palatine, and Glencoe to the north. Although some of those neighborhoods experienced more changes than others, the lives of all of the area's city and suburban residents were influenced in some ways by the powerful events of the decade.

For many Chicagoans, sports served as a welcome distraction from the onslaught of political and social changes taking place. Sporting events became an important part of Chicagoans' memories of the '60s especially since it was a rare period of successful seasons for most of the city's professional and college teams. These included the 1961 Stanley Cup-winning Blackhawks, the 1963 NCAA Championship Loyola Ramblers, and the 1963 NFL Champion Bears. In addition, the White Sox and Cubs both came close to experiencing their own championship seasons. For example, the White Sox ended the 1964 season within one game of the eventual American League pennant winners, the New York Yankees. And, of course, Cubs fans remember, with fondness and sadness, the 1969 team which was in first place in the National League East most of the season. However, in August, the Mets charged past the Cubs and won the NL East, and, eventually the World Series. Also, in 1967, a new NBA team, the Chicago Bulls, was introduced to the city's professional basketball fans.

Chicago politics during the decade were dominated by one individual: Mayor Richard J. Daley. His so-called "Machine" maintained a continuous influence over city, county, and state politics and government. In fact, the "Machine" was so successful in its ability to deliver the Democratic vote that Mayor Daley has often been credited with playing a key role in ensuring the election of John F. Kennedy to the presidency in 1960. A separate result of that election was the defeat of Republican Cook County State's Attorney, Benjamin Adamowski, who served only one four-year term from 1956 to 1960.

As for the physical growth of the city, the mayor and his administration, with financial support by the state and federal governments, were instrumental in supporting the construction of such major urban projects as McCormick Place, O'Hare Airport, the new University of Illinois-Chicago campus on the city's Near West Side, modern Interstate highways, and the John Hancock Building. Then, of course, there was the memorable snowstorm of January 1967 when over 20" of snow brought Chicago to a standstill and led to the city purchasing modern snow removal equipment that enabled it to deal more effectively with future snowstorms.

During the decade, the Loop began to reflect the racial shifts happening across several of the city's neighborhoods. In addition, there continued to be a steady outward migration to suburbia that had begun in the late '50s and accelerated through out the 1960s. One of the results was that many Chicagoans shopped less often at Loop stores as they shifted to nearby suburban malls. Those new malls offered many of the same stores located downtown but with the lure of free parking. To a lesser degree, there was a much slower but steady development of upscale stores along North Michigan Avenue.

These changes also caused a decline in the number of people staying in the Loop after work hours as well as on weekends. This trend affected not only shopping but also the numbers of Chicagoans who visited Loop restaurants and movie houses on or near State Street. At the same time, the Near North Side experienced a major growth spurt that increased the popularity of Rush Street and Division Street bars and restaurants, and Old Town (along with Wells Street and Second City). Some Chicagoans who wanted to continue living near the downtown discovered the advantages of renting in the newly built Sandburg Village apartments and townhouses.

During the '60s, Chicagoans reacted to numerous national and local political and social events that impacted their lives in many ways. Beginning with Kennedy's election in 1960, there were a series of crises ranging from the trauma of JFK's assassination in November 1963, the ensuing Johnson presidency, and the dramatic increase in American military presence in Southeast Asia. The year 1968 became a significant watershed for most Americans because people were faced with the impact of the assassinations of Dr. Martin Luther King and Senator Robert Kennedy. The King assassination in April 1968 brought a profound sense of grief that also erupted into riots, burning, and looting in some of Chicago's predominantly African American neighborhoods. Then, in August 1968, the Democratic National Convention was held at the city's International Amphitheater. It attracted numerous activists to the city, and their presence led to violent confrontations between anti-war protesters, police, and National Guardsmen in Lincoln Park and in front of the Conrad Hilton Hotel on Michigan Avenue. Soon after, there was the famous "Conspiracy Seven" trial, followed in 1969 by the Weathermen Underground's "Days of Rage" when protesters rampaged across the Near North Side and into the Loop only to come face-to-face with Chicago police. Despite all

these traumatic events, the decade actually ended on a more positive note when Americans first walked on the moon. Overall, during the second half of the '60s, it was difficult to catch one's breath and be able to react to the next political or social change.

Throughout the decade, there were also significant shifts in music and entertainment. During the early '60s, WLS and WCFL were the dominant rock and roll, AM radio stations that played popular music from a broad range of performers including Bobby Darin, Sonny and Cher, the Kingston Trio, Peter, Paul and Mary, Chubby Checker, and Joey Dee and the Twist. That was followed by the rapid rise in popularity of the Beatles who arrived in America, and Chicago, in the middle of the decade as part of the so-called "British Invasion." Music tastes continued to shift dramatically after 1966 influenced by the expanding "drug culture" and anti-Vietnam War feelings. It led to the rise in popularity of such performers as Janis Joplin, The Who, and Jim Morrison and the Doors. Also, Hugh Hefner and his *Playboy* Magazine and Playboy Clubs contributed to what became known as the "sexual revolution."

Meanwhile, there were innovations in local television. These included more sophisticated ways of presenting news, weather, and sports programming in color and the introduction of the very popular children's show, Bozo's Circus, on WGN-TV. During much of the decade, although Chicagoans continued to have four daily newspapers, they slowly changed to watching television as a preferred way of following news events. Members of the media. Like many others, they saw the decade as encompassing two distinct time periods: the first, a continuation of the 1950s lasting until the mid '60s; and the second, a distinctly new time period that seemed to begin in 1965 and continue throughout much of the 1970s. Then, in the late '60s and throughout the 1970s, Chicago regional theater companies rose to national prominence with the growth of such venues as Goodman Theater, Hull House Theater, Steppenwolf Theater, Remains Theater, and Victory Gardens Theater.

Many observers have expressed the view that the 1960s was probably one of the most significant decades of the twentieth century and was clearly "A Time of Change."
Neal Samors

For Freddi and Jennifer

Acknowledgments

I want to express sincere gratitude to Bob Sirott for writing the excellent introduction to this book. It provides the necessary framework for understanding life and growing up during the 1960s.

Also, special acknowledgment to the organizations and individuals that provided access to their outstanding photo collections. They include Ron Theel and Trina Higgins of the *Chicago Sun-Times,* Hugh Hefner, Teri Thomerson, Bonnie Jean Kenny, and Marcia Terrones of *Playboy* Magazine, Julia Bachrach of the Chicago Park District, Bruce Moffat and Joyce Shaw of the Chicago Transit Authority, and the staff of the Chicago Historical Society (now Chicago History Museum). In addition, my deepest thanks to Bob Adamowski, Bob Sirott, Clark Weber, Newton and Jo Minow, Erin McCann, Eric Bronsky, Glenn Hall, Jack Rosenberg, Joyce Sloane, Tom Dreesen, Kent Beauchamp, Harry Volkman, Frank Mathie, Joel Daly and Walter Jacobson for providing photographs from their personal collections. Also, special thanks to Bob Sirott, Jim O'Connor, Bill "Red" Hay, Jerry Petacque, Lee B. Stern, Sandy Pesmen, Jack Rosenberg, Carmen Salvino, Robert Adamowski, Joe Levinson, Clark Weber, Tom Dreesen, Joyce Sloane, and Frank Mathie for connecting the author with other interviewees for this book.

The author wants to express deepest appreciation and acknowledgment to the following individuals whose oral histories provided the author with the rich details concerning their memories of life in Chicago during the 1960s. Their remembrances are personal, poignant, vibrant, and humorous and provide the depth of experiences described in this book. They include: Robert Adamowski, Leonard Amari, Jon Anderson, U.S. District Judge Marvin Aspen, Kent Beauchamp, Arthur Berman, Shelley Berman, Trudy Bers, Dick Biondi, Eric Bronsky, Alderman Edward M. Burke, Truda Chick, Richard Christiansen, Joel Daly, U.S. Representative Danny Davis, Leon Despres, Anna Marie DiBuono, Tom Dreesen, Cook County Circuit Judge Richard Elrod, Robert Feder, Rick Fizdale, John Gorman, Jackie Grimshaw, Jon Hahn, Al Hall, Glenn Hall, Bill "Red" Hay, Hugh Hefner, Ken Holtzman, Reverend Jesse Jackson, Walter Jacobson, Bill Jauss, Marilyn Katz, Johnny "Red" Kerr, Nick Kladis, U.S. District Judge Charles Kocoras, Rick Kogan, Bill Kurtis, Jim Landis, Richard Lang, Joe Levinson, Ramsey Lewis, Gene Mackevich, Joe Mantegna, Norman Mark, Frank Mathie, Erin McCann, Jim McDonough, Jo Baskin Minow, Newton Minow, Mike Nussbaum, Jim O'Connor, Sheldon Patinkin, Sandy Pesmen, Jerry Petacque, William Petersen, Charles "Arch" Pounian, Mike Pyle, Harold Ramis, Ronnie Rice, Jimmy Rittenberg, Jack Rosenberg, Carmen Salvino, Warner Saunders, Gale Sayers, U.S. Representative Jan Schakowsky, Raymond Simon, Gary Sinise, Bob Sirott, Bill "Moose" Skowron, Joyce Sloane, Lee B. Stern, Harry Volkman, Clark Weber, Joel Weisman, Lois Wille, Harvey Wittenberg, Bruce Wolf, and Steve Zucker.

Introduction

In one of Sam Cooke's hit records from the summer of 1962, "Having A Party," the lyrics included this line: "The Cokes are in the ice box, and the popcorn is on the table." Parties in the early 1960's didn't require much more than that and a record player or radio. (Cooke's song also mentions calling in requests to the deejay.)

It was a simple, innocent time. But by the end of that decade, the music would reflect an angry and cynical youth culture, where parties still included coke—but not the kind you drank. It was one decade divided in two, by a war in Southeast Asia and assassinations. The music and movies of the time were, as always, perfect reflections of what was going on in our culture. You could see both moods of the '60s on The WLS "Silver Dollar Surveys." In October of 1961 "Lets Get Together" by Haley Mills, from the Disney movie "The Parent Trap," was the number one record in Chicago. By the summer of '68, it was Simon and Garfunkel's "Mrs. Robinson" from "The Graduate" topping the charts.

We had a lot of "friends" growing up with us on local TV back then, including *Garfield Goose* with Frazier Thomas, Elmer The Elephant and his pal John Conrad, *Serial Theatre* with Chuck Bill, *Shock Theatre* ("Hello I'm Marvin"), and Terry Bennett. Real, live, actual humans kept us company-not just cartoons and puppets. There weren't a lot of channels to choose from, but it forced us to watch programs we might not have chosen had MTV or HBO been around. One of my father's favorite shows was the highbrow Omnibus with Alistair Cooke. I watched it with him on Sunday afternoons, since there wasn't much else to choose from, and besides, we only had one TV. Now we have video on demand, specialized cable channels, and niche formats of music, so nobody has to be exposed to anything they aren't interested in watching. WLS-AM used to play everything from Lawrence Welk to The Kingston Trio. If enough people were buying a song, it got on their play list, regardless of genre. I think the result was a generation of listeners who were exposed to a variety of records, and to this day appreciate more than just one type of music.

We didn't have the Internet, so the newspapers were our most complete source of topical information at home. My parents always had the *Tribune, Sun-Times, Daily News,* or *Chicago Today (Chicago American)* around the kitchen table. In the pre-Googling era, you read about subjects you didn't request. I think we were the better for it. We would become interested in articles we weren't intending to read and were fascinated by topics in which we thought we had no interest. Today's generation of computer-users miss out on that bit of unexpected education.

By the time we were teens and getting out of the house, there was plenty to do, including The Rainbow Rink, Bounceland, and Buffalo's Ice Cream Parlor (when The Good Humor Man wasn't coming down the street any time soon). In the early '60s, my north side, Albany Park neighborhood was filled with Cubs fans who used to populate the Wrigley Field grandstands or the bleachers back when so few people went there that the Cubs rarely opened their upper deck. Over at Comiskey Park, the White Sox had better teams through most of the decade, and were regularly outdrawing the hapless Cubs until around 1967. But day baseball was a magnet for kids on summer vacation and a relief for parents who would be nervous letting their children take the bus or "L" to see the Sox at Comiskey Park, especially at night. ("Parents, it's the 10:30, curfew time. Do you know where your children are?"—Remember those TV and radio announcements?) Then, as now, two worlds existed in Chicago—one north of Madison Street, the other south. Ignorance bred prejudice, as it unfortunately still does.

Baseball was our game in the summers of the '60s. Softball diamonds were always busy. We played touch football in the street in the fall right after listening to Jack Brickhouse and Irv Kupcinet describe Bears games on radio. Most of their home games were not televised back then. We even followed the Blackhawks closely, in large part because so many of their games were televised on Channel 9 and Lloyd Pettit provided the play-by-play. (Do you understand that Bill Wirtz?)

About the time our interests turned to girls, we enjoyed a new weekend pastime. Teen clubs offered non-alcoholic drinks and live bands with the city's popular radio DJs like Clark Weber, Dick Biondi, Ron Britain, Art Roberts, or Barney Pip emceeing, all for a two dollar admission. Dex Card's "Wild Goose," "The Cellar," and "The Kinetic Playground," were among the most popular teen clubs around Chicago. After the Beatles invaded America, groups like The Buckinghams, New Colony Six, Cryin' Shame, Ides Of March, and Shadows Of Knight performed at the local clubs, made records, and were played on WLS, WCFL, as well as radio stations across the country when some of their songs became national hits on "The Billboard Top 100" list.

In the era before the Walkman, the only portable entertainment "to-go" was the transistor radio. Without computers, VCRs, and video games, the voices on the radio were much more important to us. Whether it was Jack Quinlan, Vince Lloyd, Bob Elson, Lloyd Pettit, or Red Rush describing sports events, or Clark Weber, Dick Biondi, Ron Riley, Jim Stagg, and Joel Sebastian playing the hit music of the day, we spent more time with the people on the air, and cared about them in a way future generations would find hard to understand with their myriad choices of after-school entertainment. Not only did we feel "close" to our favorite radio personalities, we could see them up close too. WLS Radio, then at 360 North Michigan Avenue, had a viewing room for those of us who were devoted fans of the deejays. At Marina City, the studios of WCFL featured a "VIP Room" where visitors could watch their heroes do their shows, and occasionally mingle with visiting rock stars.

In 1964, a 15 year-old boy, bitten with the broadcasting bug, took the Ravenswood "L" from his neighborhood Kimball station to the Merchandise Mart studios of NBC's WMAQ-TV and Radio on a Saturday night. Nothing was open to the public, but a few of the friendly staff announcers on duty that evening (who did everything from music shows, station breaks, and commercials, to news, weather, and traffic reports) kindly showed the earnest young man around and answered his many questions about their work. Yes, that was me. On a recent Saturday night at the NBC Tower, as I was preparing to co-anchor the evening's 10:00 pm news, I flashed back to that time more than 40 years ago and remembered what it felt like—the excitement, the dreams that seemed so far from my reality, and the warmth and wisdom of the great old pros like Jim Hill, Ed Grennan, John Doremus, and "Officer Vic" Petrolis, whose kind words and gentle encouragement I will never forget, and hope to pass on to today's young visitors to NBC.

My favorite place in the world is still my old neighborhood. I grew up on Ridgeway between Argyle near Eugene Field Park. When I go back there, I like to sit on the steps of the old Field House and contemplate life today, and yesterday. Now I can also do that by going through the pages of this book. I hope you'll join me and enjoy a few contemplative moments of your own as we sit on the steps and remember the '60s together. **Bob Sirott**

This was taken in April 1962 of 5035 N. Ridgeway in front of the apartment where I grew up. That's Eugene Field Park a block north behind us. I'm riding on Scott Berman's bike. I have my crew-cut and am 13 years old in the photo. Scott Berman is the son of Maury Berman who created "Superdawg."

Life in City Suburban Neighborh

and

oods

Marlin Perkins at Buckingham Fountain, 1961. (Courtesy of Chicago Park District)

Truda Chick

I was born in Chicago on June 14, 1943. My family had a beautiful, spacious apartment on Monticello and Wilson Avenues in Albany Park where we lived until I was ten years old. I have positive memories of growing up in that neighborhood, but since my parents always wanted to own a house, we moved to one in West Rogers Park on Fitch, between Rockwell and Washtenaw. My parents thought that the new house was going to be wonderful, but soon after our move, several developers built huge apartment buildings next to our house. We were upset because those structures blocked our views and gave us a loss of privacy.

While we lived in Albany Park, I attended Haugan Elementary School, but when we moved in 1953, my new school was Rogers Elementary School where I made a whole new group of friends. However, at that time, Rogers was very insular, the kids appeared to be quite snobby regarding social interrelationships, and there were strong cliques. Even though Haugan was a very good school, Rogers was a challenge for me because it was a step up, academically. Upset about moving to the new neighborhood, I soon became acclimated to it.

Downtown was a great place to go and my memories are very clear about going to State Street each year to see the ornately decorated windows of Marshall Field's and Uncle Mistletoe. It was a big part of my life when I was young, and every Saturday my mother, my sister, and I would go downtown. We would have lunch at the Walnut Room in Marshall Field's, and we also ate at De Mets, which owned candy stores and restaurants, Johnnies, a coffee shop, and Paulsen's. Sometimes we would window shop along Michigan Avenue, and I remember taking singing lessons downtown and performing in plays.

The same social pattern I experienced at Rogers was repeated in Sullivan High School, which provided me with clear academic challenges in some of my courses. Science and math were not my strong subjects, but I did better in the Social Sciences and English. My social life at Sullivan was affected by the high school cliques, although I ended up developing some very good friendships there. High school life was bittersweet, and, looking back, some people tend to "sugar coat" their memories of growing up. However, rather than fool myself about the pluses and minuses, there were clearly some negative memories about high school as well as positive ones, which included being at the famous Ashkenaz Delicatessen on Morse Avenue, either eating inside or standing outside talking to friends, even if it was freezing cold. I was selected to join the Elites, a social club, during my junior year, and many of us used to go to the Granada a lot during high school, as well as to other neighborhood movie theaters like the Nortown, the Howard, and the Adelphi.

When we lived in West Rogers Park, my parents would take the family, including my grandmother, to restaurants on Sundays, at such local favorites as the Pekin House on Devon (as well as restaurants in Chinatown) because they enjoyed Chinese food. They were fond of the Black Angus on Western near Touhy and the Gold Coin on Howard and Clark. Since my mother didn't drive, my parents would eat at restaurants that were within walking distance, including the Pickle Barrel at Howard and Western. On occasion, they would go to Chicken in the Rough and Fritzels located downtown.

Rock and roll music was a big part of being a teenager, although Elvis was not one of my favorite singers. The most popular deejay in the '50s in Chicago was Howard Miller on WIND-AM radio, and on Saturday nights, I enjoyed taking long, hot baths, turning on the hi-fi in my bedroom and listening to Johnny Mathis. After starting high school in the late '50s, I would come home and watch "American Bandstand" as a way of unwinding. Then, in the '60s, my favorite group was the Beatles, whose music was great to listen to on the radio or on my record player.

During high school, I found a job working downtown at Mary Ann's, a women's apparel store and was working there on Monday and Thursday nights and Saturdays. The salary was commission-based, but there was a woman who worked full-time and would take my customers, enabling her to make the sales instead of me. After work in the evenings, when the downtown stores were open late, my father would pick me up after I took the "L" from the Loop to the Howard Street station. Then they shifted me to the Mary Ann store on Devon Avenue. My mother liked to shop downtown at Field's, the Fair Store, Wieboldt's, and Chandler's Shoe Store, and she preferred them over the stores at the suburban shopping centers that were just being built. She would also go to the Maller's Building at 5 N. Wabash and buy things for my father's business.

My father sold apparel to people who worked at the racetracks. Many of them tended to gamble away their money, and they would ask my father to pawn their things and give them the money. As a result there were a lot of objects from these people around our house before my father sold them.

My sister, Sharon, is five years older than me, and she attended Roosevelt High School in Albany Park before we moved. Sharon didn't want to change high schools, so, my father drove her to Roosevelt every morning until she graduated.

Although my choice for college would have been to attend a Big Ten school, I ended up going to Chicago Teachers College, which later changed its name to Northeastern Illinois University. In hindsight, I realize that it was my parents' influence that caused me to attend the school that they selected, and become a teacher. Perhaps my career should have focused on utilizing my writing skills or becoming a social worker. I quickly finished my courses at Chicago Teacher's College, assisted by the fact that we were on a trimester plan that influenced me to attend school all year round. Without my own car, I would take public transportation or get a ride from my uncle who had a store on Bryn Mawr Avenue. Ironically, getting through college quickly only meant my rushing to make $5,300 a year as a teacher in Chicago.

After graduation from college, my teaching assignment was in Chicago schools located in some of the city's toughest neighborhoods. My student teaching was completed at Wicker Park Elementary School on the northwest side near Humboldt Park. In the mid-'60s, it wasn't a very safe neighborhood. From there I was sent to Mulligan Elementary School, located close to the area where the "L" begins to become the subway near Fullerton and there were a lot of young teachers working at the school. As an FTB (full-time basis) teacher, it meant that the Chicago Board of Education hadn't found a permanent position for me. From there, it was on to Richard E. Byrd School and the difficult task of teaching third grade. At Mulligan, the students had been multicultural, while at Byrd School, located in the Cabrini-Green projects off Division Street, the students were almost all African American. During my last year of full-time teaching in 1968, my class at Byrd included a group of educationally mature girls. They could handle more advanced work so we went on a field trip to the nearby Chicago Historical Society to learn details about Chicago history. Looking back on my teaching experiences during 1968, the year was fulfilling and, regrettably, teaching would have been a happier experience if there were more years in classrooms like that one. After that year, I decided to become a substitute teacher.

I had met Jerry, my husband-to-be, as a result of being fixed up with him by his mother. During my visits every Saturday to a beauty shop on Touhy Avenue, west of California in West Rogers Park, I would use my time marking papers while sitting under the hair dryer. There was a regular patron who was very friendly, and one Saturday she asked me, "How would you like to go out with my son?" It didn't seem like a very good sign, and that increased my hesitancy. She said to me, "He has lots of girlfriends, but he went off to the Army for six months, and lost contact with many people." My response was, "Do you have a picture of him?" She showed me his picture, and it struck me that I had seen him at the Granada years before while attending the movies with friends. So, changing my mind about a possible date, I said to her, "Ask him to call me." After approximately 18 months of dating, we were married.

Jerry worked as a traveling salesman for Bobbie Brooks, the women's clothing company. Since he was on the road quite often, we didn't know where we were going to live, so we decided to rent a furnished apartment in the Belmont Hotel on Belmont and Sheridan. During the mid- to late-'60s, Jerry was in the National Guard and stationed at the Northwestern Armory. He was called into duty during the 1967 riots and was shot at while driving telephone operators to their communication centers since phone lines had been cut. During the riots, he went into a phone booth to call his mother and let her know what was going on. She heard shooting in the background and thinking that he might have been shot, she fainted. I also remember bringing corned beef sandwiches to him when he was on duty at the Armory. The memories of those times are both bitter and sweet because things were changing so quickly, much of it due to the Vietnam War, the assassinations, the various protests, and the Democratic National Convention. During the late '60s, it seemed that certain areas of Chicago were like war zones.

Since we lived in the city, we didn't have to rely on a car to get us downtown. Some of our favorite nearby restaurants included R.J. Grunts, the Tree Room in the Belden Stratford Hotel, and the Claim Company, where we loved their Mother Lode hamburgers. We enjoyed the whole Lincoln Park scene, but we also went downtown, eating at Fritzel's, going to the Chicago Theater for movies and, later, for stage productions.

The 1960s bring back a series of mixed memories. Many of us hated to see what was happening to certain areas of the city toward the end of the decade. Perhaps that reaction was influenced by my experiences teaching in the inner city and my husband's service in the National Guard and the riots. The day that we got married, in 1966, there were riots in Cicero against Reverend Martin Luther King. Jerry had to convince his captain, with the offer of free liquor, to let him get married that day. Also there was a Montgomery Ward's warehouse near my school and some of my young students took various objects out of that place during the rioting and looting. That was a shock to me. All of those events were so stunning, and after a while, I couldn't even go into those neighborhoods to teach. Cooley High School was also near Byrd School, and, one day when my new 1965 red Chevrolet was parked in front of the school, the kids from the high school were throwing rocks and stones at it. Each night, coming home from teaching, my mother had no realization what a horror it was to deal with driving on the expressways and facing the tensions caused by my teaching. Looking back, since there was an opportunity in those years to earn less money by teaching in the suburbs, my decision to remain as a teacher in the Chicago schools is regrettable.

Howard Street and Hermitage, 1964
(Courtesy of CTA)

John Gorman

Born in 1944, I grew up in Edgewater after living for a short time in Rogers Park at Touhy and the Lake. We had moved to an apartment near Newgard and North Shore in St. Ignatius Parish. My strongest memories are of going to St. Gertrude's at Granville and Glenwood and growing up around there. We had a group of about 15 of us who hung out at Lakewood and Devon at a corner drugstore. The memories are of the nuns, playing basketball, football, and line ball at Hayt Elementary School in the gravel schoolyard. We also played football at Senn, and that was where my grammar school team practiced.

We used to go downtown regularly to the movie theaters. I was in 7th or 8th grade when we went to the United Artists to see a movie, and I lost my wallet. I had to go back in the theater to look for the wallet, but didn't find it and it was a loss of $7. I wasn't aware of race as an issue when I grew up in the city because there weren't any black people in my neighborhood. You were either Irish or, if you went to the public schools, chances are you were Jewish. There were a few Italians and Germans, but my friends' names were all Irish, and it was a little Irish ghetto. I can remember going to the Sox games and seeing blacks on the "L" once you were south of downtown but we were largely unaware of African Americans.

In high school, although I went to Loyola Academy in Wilmette, my memories are mostly of living in Chicago. There actually was a school bus that picked us up across the street to take us back and forth to high school. I took the bus during my freshman and sophomore years before I started getting a ride to school with a kid from the neighborhood named Dickie Devine, the same Richard A. Devine, I now work for in the State's Attorney's office. We would get in his old, beaten up Studebaker, drive up Touhy to the Edens Expressway where he would have to put the car into overdrive in order to speed up fast enough to merge into the Edens traffic.

During our junior and senior years, all the members of the basketball team formed a car pool. We played Catholic League teams in basketball, including Gordon Tech, Weber, St. George, De La Salle, and Brother Rice. Loyola Academy was ranked first in the state in March 1962 with a 21-1 record before we played Gordon Tech for the Catholic League championship, a team we had beaten twice by 12 and 13 points. But we lost to them at the old DePaul Alumni Gym by four points. Then, we went to the Chicago Stadium and played for third place and managed to lose to Marshall in overtime by two points. So we ended our season with a 21-3 record, which is still the best record that a Loyola Academy basketball team ever had.

Summertime in high school included playing something we called "L" tag. Somebody would say "you're it," and you would tag them as if you were running around the school playground. Then somebody would chase you, tag you, and run through the train cars to get away from them. It was all dangerous stuff, and although we were mindful of the third rail, we played the game nonetheless. We also spent a lot of time down at the beaches on the lake at Devon and at Granville. I was probably the last guy in my group of friends to start drinking in high school, but we used to go do that at the beach. I remember the Sovereign Hotel because that's where Bill Wade of the Bears lived, and he used to occasionally walk around the neighborhood. He was a nice guy and would always give us an autograph and talk to us.

After graduation, I went to Xavier University, majored in history, and played for the school on a basketball scholarship. I played during my sophomore, junior, and senior seasons, but between my junior and senior year I had a motorcycle accident and cut up my leg. I was injured, so I played on and off during senior year and averaged only seven points a game after averaging 14 points a game as a junior.

In the summers between my years at Xavier, my friends and I would go down to Rush Street and hit the bars. I worked at the Zoo, one of the Near North bars, with a bunch of buddies from the neighborhood who also worked there. At the end of my senior year in college, I hurt my back, had a back operation, and recuperated by going swimming because I could barely walk. I went to the Sovereign Hotel because they had a swimming pool.

During those years, you weren't a real Chicagoan if you weren't cognizant of the racial changes that were going on in the city beginning in the late '60s. I remember going into bars on Wells Street when I was around 21 years old and having no problems. But, after the riots started in the mid-1960s, including the ones at Cabrini-Green, I remember being told that the blacks were coming east on Division Street and that we better get out of there. The threat wasn't true, but the racial situation in the city just changed so much in a matter of years. I also knew that the city was going through major changes because some of my relatives, who had lived on the South Side in Visitation Parish, kept moving from the city to the suburbs, including Oak Lawn and Evergreen Park. These were people who had continued to sell their houses as they moved further and further southwest in their flight to the suburbs.

In August 1968, when the convention was happening, a buddy of mine was a precinct captain. He lived just east of Senn High School on Rosedale, and he called up one day and asked me, "How would you like to go to the convention?" It was the Thursday night of the convention when Humphrey was going to deliver his acceptance speech. We got those tickets because so many delegates had left early, and Daley was going to be damned if he was going to let the cameras show an empty Amphitheater. He sent school buses to the neighborhoods to pick up Daley supporters, like myself, who filled up the Amphitheater.

When we arrived there, they put little buttons on us that said "I'm Proud of Chicago." Those buttons indicated to the security people that we were one of Daley's guys, and they directed us to sit in some of the empty seats. After the convention, my buddy and I went down to the Boul Mich and ran into David Condon of the Tribune, who was a Notre Dame graduate, and Tom Powers, who was a Tribune reporter. We started talking to them, and Condon asked me where I went to school. I told him Xavier, and he said,

"Geez, you went to four years of school and never got an education, huh, kid." Years later, in 1974, I ended up working with Tom Powers at the Tribune and became friendly with him many years later.

I graduated from Xavier in 1968, rather than '66, because my back operation had forced me to drop out of school for a couple years. I was still living at 1343 W. Granville and didn't move out of there until after I graduated from college and joined the Peace Corps. I went to India and arrived there on January 30, 1969. I helped work on an irrigation program in India and wound up doing a lot of surveying for a hydrology study. I lived about 110 miles north of Delhi. Although I went to India weighing 254 lbs., by the time I returned I only weighed 178 lbs. After completing my Peace Corps service, I traveled for a couple of years. I lived and worked in Australia for a while, came back to Asia, and went across to Africa and to South Africa where I worked as a bartender, just as I had done in Sydney. I came back to Chicago after being gone for three years and by the time I returned, my parents had moved two blocks away to Greenview and Glenlake.

After I returned from the Peace Corps, I enrolled in graduate school for a semester before being offered a job at City News Bureau which I took and stayed for 20 months. I was hired by the Tribune in May 1974 and stayed until June 2000. I was a general assignment reporter at the paper for my first five years, an assistant city editor for the next five years, and then I switched and went to the business section for three years. Then Jack Fuller snatched me out of the business section and sent me over to the Federal Building where I was for three years. Next, I was given an option to go to the suburbs, but my children were young at the time, so the idea of a short commute from Lake Forest appealed to me and I went out to the Tribune's Lake County bureau for my last 10 years. I have been working for Dick Devine in the State's Attorney's Office for six years as Director of Communications/Press Secretary.

I think that calling the 1960s in Chicago as the "decade of change" is a very apt description. The difference between Chicago in 1960 and when I left town in 1969 was profound, and the changes were racial and driven by the events of the times. The effect on the city was to divide it between blacks and whites. I think that the South Side had more houses while the West Side had more apartment buildings. So, the black South Side seemed more stable than the black West Side. I think that the poor, black people from the South moved into the West Side, and after King's assassination, they burned down much of their neighborhood as things seemed to be changing on a weekly basis. In the '60s, I don't remember being aware or concerned about going to the Chicago Stadium even though it was in a black neighborhood. But, when I went to work for the City News Bureau in the '70s, you were very aware where you were going when you attended a Bulls or Blackhawks game at the Stadium.

Bus passengers boarding at
Lane Tech High School, 1964
(Courtesy of CTA)

Logan Square, 1966
(Courtesy of CTA)

Fullerton and Sheffield, 1960
(Courtesy of CTA)

Bob Sirott

When I was an 11-year-old teenager in the 1960s, my family lived in a second-floor apartment in a two-flat building in Albany Park. Just opening the window and looking outside was my version of "going on line." I would see who was out there and what was going on in the neighbor-hood, surveying the block and looking for any kids who were around. In those days I remember yelling out, "Hey, does anybody want to go to the park and play?" The center of my universe was Eugene Field Park, a hub of activity for the neighborhood kids all year round.

In the summer, we played 16-inch softball and hardball, only sometimes in organized leagues. We played all day during the summer and the four hours after school in the afternoons and early evenings during the school year. In the fall and winter months, we were out there playing touch or tackle football, usually just in pick-up games. There was a field house at Eugene Field Park with a gymnasium, a woodshop, and a game room, and, on Friday evenings during the school year, the gymnasium was opened for something they called "open gym," a "do what you want" night. Believe it or not, we used to line up early on Friday evenings just to receive numbers because they couldn't accommodate all the kids in the gym at one time.

I attended Volta Elementary School and, despite the fact that it was one of Chicago's better schools, classes were crowded. I think that in the '50s and '60s, Volta was similar to other city elementary schools: crowded classrooms; an older, brick building; and a mix of old and young teachers. In those years, there were primarily two-parent households and, in general, mothers didn't work outside the home. Albany Park, in the '60s, was still mostly a Jewish community with a very strict emphasis on education, so I think that it was comparable to what you see in the suburbs now, rather than in most of today's city neighborhoods.

Like other neighborhoods, we had our own community institutions, including the local hot dog stand. In Albany Park, ours was Maury's at Lawrence and Lawndale, owned and operated by Maury Andes. When we walked in, since Maury knew what each of us usually ordered, he would look at his customers and might say, "Two hot dogs with mustard and pickle—right?" And, he knew it. We went there not only for hot dogs, but for a chance to be part of a social network. Over the years, many former residents returned to Maury's with their kids. Maury was the one guy who knew where everybody had moved because everybody kept in touch with him, and he was much more than the proprietor of a hot dog stand. He served as counselor, reunion organizer, and somebody you could always talk to. In general, I think that the decade of the '60s was probably the end of a great many places like that.

During the '60s, we had several focal points in addition to the Eugene Field Park field house, and Maury's hot dog place. There were also a couple of pizza places, including Napoli's and Marie's on Lawrence Avenue, and the Rollaway Bowling Alley on Pulaski. Most of these were "ma and pa" places, and none survived into the 1980s. If you talked to someone else who grew up when I did in Chicago, they would tell you about their local hot dog stand, park, bowling alley, and pizza places.

The music of the '60s was another important aspect of our lives. Until the Beatles came to America, we still had teen idols and very simple songs. Then, with the so-called "British invasion" in 1964, everything started to get a little more complicated, and that led right into the mid-'60s when the Vietnam War expanded and the protests and the music took on a tougher edge. By the late '60s, everything was exploding, and you can probably track it to the changes in music since that was a reflection of the way we were, instead of the other way around. There probably is not a lot of difference between life in the '50s during the Eisenhower years and recollections of the 1960s, up to 1964. After the assassination of JFK in November 1963, and the arrival of the Beatles in the winter of '64, all hell seemed to break loose and continued into the radical changes that were going on across society, including fashion and politics.

In January 1963, I began my freshman year at Roosevelt High School in Albany Park. I remember that on my first day, incoming students were required to gather in the school's huge assembly hall for orientation. I was in the last class at Roosevelt that graduated in the middle of the school year, in January. After that, they only had June graduations. It was very intimidating when I first got to Roosevelt because it was such a huge school to me. A lot of the kids who had been with me at Volta had moved to the suburbs by then, so I didn't know many of the people in my freshman class. And, strangely enough, among the three guys whom I met at Roosevelt and who have become lifelong friends, none of them had gone to Volta. They all went to elementary school at Haugan, and I met them on my first day of high school.

While I was at Roosevelt, kids usually smoked cigarettes in the bathrooms, rather than marijuana. I look back on high school in the early '60s as a pretty benign time in terms of what we did there, how we behaved, and the level of attention to our studies. It was the last period before Vietnam, so we were still focusing on traditional high school activities like joining clubs and teams and participating in Homecoming dances. While I was at Roosevelt, it was a very traditional high school and there was still a tremendous amount of interest in those kinds of activities and high school events. As for me personally, I didn't do too much in high school because my hangout was the park, so I was not in a lot of high school clubs. In fact, the best description of my life in high school happened during my senior year when I ran into an English teacher at Roosevelt whom I had for homeroom. I never was in any of his classes, but, he stopped me and said, "Sirott, when are you going to start doing something around here?"

A key memory for me from the '60s was going downtown regularly with my dad, who was a furrier and worked in the Mallers Building at 5 South Wabash. Downtown was always magical to me, and as I got older, I would go to the Loop with my friends. When I would go with my father, I didn't find that time spent in his fur showroom was very exciting. So, I just wandered around the Loop. My favorite places included Marshall Field's, the Treasure Chest on Randolph, and the WLS studios at Michigan and Wacker. I loved to walk around Field's since it was the store with great toy and book departments, and they were still making the Frango mints to sell at the store. So, it was more than just the name and the memories: Marshall Field's was still a very unique place during those years. I would also go to Randolph Street where the Treasure Chest was located. It was a fantastic place, and they had wonderful novelties that included the ability to print a newspaper with a phony headline. It was just a great, great little store that was always teeming with kids.

Then, there were the rock and roll radio stations. My favorite, of course, was WLS-AM where Dick Biondi was "king" and on the air from 9:00 pm to midnight. Dick really was a key to why the station was so popular with the kids of that era, and we were really into him and the music that he and the other disc jockeys played. Today, it is difficult to fully grasp the popularity of Biondi and WLS, because now, nighttime radio struggles to survive against television. But, in those days, there were a limited number of radio and television stations, and you didn't have other sources of entertainment like the Internet, computer games, and video games. Biondi really talked the kids' language, and you could call him at night in his studio before he went on the radio. Word got out that if you called WLS between 7:00 pm and 9:00 pm, you could talk to the "wild Italian" and he would say hello to you. In fact, when word got out that he would take your call, something bizarre happened with the telephone company. You would get a busy signal, but between the beeps of the busy signal, you could talk to other kids. The telephone lines were so screwed up that it became known as the "beep line." Word spread at school that if you called and got the busy signal, you should try to talk between the beeps. That was a wild phenomenon!

Things changed for all of us after the Kennedy assassination in 1963 and the expansion of the war in Vietnam by 1965. In truth, the war never went well for America, and that had a tremendous impact on the '60s. I didn't really get drawn into it directly since I had a student deferment when I attended Columbia College for four years to get my bachelor's degree. After college, I was in the draft lottery and I still remember the impact of that annual event.

I would sit around with my friends listening to the radio when they announced results of the lottery. You realized that your life was at stake. I had a high number, so, by chance, I wasn't drafted, but I remember being with friends when somebody's birthday would come up, they would get a low number, and just experience a "mock faint." The ones with low numbers would just fall over backwards, while those who had high numbers would jump up and wave their fists in the air. It was something! I did have several friends who were drafted and went to Vietnam, and a couple people I knew died there.

The war was also directly related to the establishment of the '60s drug culture. In 1967, around the time I was graduating from Roosevelt, America dramatically increased its involvement in Vietnam and that contributed to the beginning of a greater use of drugs. I also remember the 1968 Democratic Convention, even though I didn't go down to the Hilton. But, since a friend of mine and I had motorcycles, we went for a ride up north along Sheridan Road during August 1968, and ended up on the Northwestern University campus. All of a sudden we were in the middle of a giant protest. But, overall, we were generally apolitical, or at least, non-activists.

My personal introduction to a career in radio and television began when I was hired for a part-time job as a page at NBC-TV during my senior year of high school. At the time, NBC was in the Merchandise Mart, sharing studios with NBC Radio on the 19th floor of the building. I was at NBC from about 1966 until 1971, before moving into radio production and public affairs doing a lot of writing for programs. In 1971, I got my first on-air job at WBBM-FM doing weekends and fill-in, and, at the end of that summer, I was either rewarded or punished, I'm not sure which, by being given the Monday through Friday morning drive show on WBBM-FM. I say that I'm not sure if I was rewarded or punished, because nobody back then listened to FM radio, especially in the morning, and almost nobody had an FM radio in their car. In 1973, I went to WLS and I always told people that I had to leave FM to go to work for WLS so I could afford an FM radio in my car.

Bob Sirott at WLS-AM studios
during 2-6 pm show. June, 1974.
(Courtesy of Bob Sirott)

Bob Sirott presented with an
award from Chicago Heart Association
by Fahey Flynn. February, 1969.
(Courtesy of Bob Sirott)

Jon Hahn

Nothing ages you faster than to pick up one of those *"Chicago, Then and Now"* publications and realize that you grew up in the "Then" era. Chicago of the 1950s and 1960s was my Chicago, my coming-of-age home town, where neighborhoods and parishes and politics and sports were constants, like the Chicago Cubs won-loss records or Democratic machine politics or fireflies in summertime evenings.

We thought the Prudential Building was one helluva skyscraper. We believed that Wrigley Field would never have night games. We hoped gasoline price wars and cheap draught beer would always be just down the street and around the corner.

Cheap (less than $100) college tuition got me and anyone else into the Navy Pier ("Harvard on the Rocks") branch of the University of Illinois, before anyone dreamed of Chicago Circle. The Pier expelled me like so much academic vomitus after one excruciating semester, the start of a very informal work-study path through several colleges and universities as well as shoveling dirt at Montrose cemetery, window decorating at Wieboldt's, raking moss out of North Shore lawns for an Evanston landscaper, installing rain gutters for a Chicago roofing contractor, and hustling bedpans as an orderly at Illinois Masonic Hospital where I fell in love with Maggie, a willowy, red-haired student nurse.

But that was "Then," when my own little world was changing so much and so fast that I lacked the perspective to see the city changing around me.

I saw deteriorating neighborhoods throughout the city. But more often and everywhere, I saw older homes and whole blocks of homes and commercial buildings being restored. New picture windows were facing the street, showcasing elaborate Polk Brothers table lamps. Dormers were added almost overnight to bungalow attics, adding mother-in-law apartments of uncertain legal status. (I knew two Chicago firefighters who, on a single 48-hours-off-shift, could frame-out a bungalow attic to a small apartment).

Upwardly-mobile in 1960s Chicago didn't mean a Gold Coast condo; young people with good jobs and more young families with working wives moved to new subdivisions in new suburbs that seemed to spurt out of what used to be cornfields and pumpkin patches. Their parents, unable or unwilling to transplant, put more money into their homes in the Old Neighborhood. Hey, the kids were raised and off on their own, we took our one trip to 'Vegas and another to the islands, now maybe we can afford to get rid of the Harvest Gold refrigerator and stove and maybe even put a knotty-pine rec room with a wet bar in the basement.

And the city, who would have thunk it, seemed to be paying attention to the neighborhoods, even to the point of taking back the night with mercury vapor lights in the alleys and new paving. Many blue collar neighborhoods seemed to look better, but maybe that was just the bricks-and-mortar equivalent of blue-tinted gray hair. At any rate, someone was paying attention. Maybe not resisting change, but trying to stay ahead of the inevitable.

Change was more obvious in commercial and industrial areas, where everything from big factories to mom-and-pop grocery stores closed their doors for good. My great-grandfather, a blacksmith, used to shoe draught horses (there's a pun here somewhere) for many of the North and Northwest Side breweries. I helped drain the last bit of Sieben's Beer from that venerable Near North Side brewery in the late 1960s. The beer garden on N. Larabee Street was not far from the old Lane Technical High School, which was transplanted decades earlier.

During the early 1960s, I finished my undergraduate degree at Urbana-Champaign and stretched a master-degree program two years (journalism) so I could stay close to another Northwest Side girl. We married in '63 and then lived two years in Michigan before returning to Chicago in '66, when we bought a home in Wauconda (Remember the driving-on-the-beach scene in "The Blues Brothers" filmed at a beach on Wauconda's Bangs Lake). For two years, I drove from Wauconda to a reporting job at the *Evanston Review* and watched the farm fields fill up with new subdivisions and shopping malls and pavement. Toward the end of the 1960s, I migrated downtown to the *Chicago Daily News,* one helluva

commute through ever-increasing traffic. Mostly, I drove major arterials—Rand Road, Elston, Clybourn, or Milwaukee Avenue—along which I could see the evolution of neighborhoods.

Names changed on the awnings of display windows of businesses along the arterials as the ethnic fabric of the communities changed. Alas, sometimes there appeared steel accordion security fences on storefronts. And, of course, a bumper crop of parking meters and parking-restriction signs.

Wauconda used to be an hour drive northwest of Chicago and, for 12 years I watched the inevitable encroachment of shopping malls that seemed to dwarf Old Orchard, and fledgling communities along the Northwest Tollway, Tri-State, and the arterials. We mourned the closure and demolition of Riverview Amusement Park and relocation of the Logan Square eagle column while we celebrated the extension of the "L" along the Kennedy (for which I give grudging acknowledgment to Richard J. Daley's vision).

We couldn't know then, in the 1960s, that there would be no more Polk Brothers, Goldblatt's and Wieboldt's. I mean, it wasn't like we didn't know that roller derby and Rainbow Arena wrestling would eventually pass, but no one could foresee the replacement of the main Chicago Public Library building at Randolph (I used to buy roses for my downtown dates in the 1950s, from a vendor set up in the alleyway behind that library building). Neither did we think that the Lake Shore Drive "S" curves might any day soon disappear, or the Grant Park band shell would be replaced and the underground garage expanded, as something called progress made the crooked straight and the rough places plain.

Chicago in the 1960s really was changing, faster than any of us might've imagined, I remember scoffing at Richard J. Daley's prognosis of people catching fish in the Chicago River. I sorta wish he'd lived to see that.

Western, Lincoln and Lawrence, 1960
(Courtesy of CTA)

Division and Hoyne, 1962
(Courtesy of CTA)

Rick Kogan

In 1960, I was nine years old when we lived in Old Town, at 1715 N. North Park, in a second floor apartment. I shared my bedroom with my younger brother, Mark. My father, Herman, had his book-filled, crowded office at the front of the apartment, and it overlooked the street. One of my first memories was the sound of dad's typewriter in that office. That was where he wrote his books on the weekends. When we moved into our apartment in the early '50s, rent was $75 a month, and it was not chic and it was not hip and it was not cool to live in Old Town. Wells Street was nothing but a couple of antique stores and a couple of clubs. Sandburg Village had not yet been built. I think they started tearing down Clark Street around 1960, but before that it was really a bizarre skid row with brothels and nasty night clubs. I did a little newspaper that I published in those years called *The Old Town News,* and there was a cover story titled "Clark Street Falling Down" which was about the demolition of all the buildings on Clark Street.

There were a lot of interesting people who lived in the neighborhood, and one of them was Alderman Paddy Bauler, a Chicago politician from the old school. As it turned out, my first brush with local politics was through Paddy, who ran the ward from his saloon/office at 403 W. North Avenue, just off Sedgwick. My best friend, growing up, all through the '50s and '60s, was Mathias "Ty" Bauler, who was Paddy's grandson. Once a month or so, when we needed money, we would wander over to Paddy's place.

He was a very large man, and it was like walking into the office in "The Godfather." Paddy would be sitting there, just a fat guy, surrounded by other fat guys, and I really got the sense that he didn't like kids at all. But, we would sit there, and he would say to us, "How's school, kids?" and "How you doing in school?" Ty would say, "Really good, grandpa," and I would say, "Really good, Alderman Bauler." And, we would shoot the crap for a few more minutes. He would add, "You kids play baseball?" and then he would give each of us a dollar and tell us to go buy ice cream at John Merlo's, the ward committeeman, who ran an ice cream parlor east on North Avenue. But, we would take the money and not go to Merlo's because we really didn't want ice cream.

One day, Ty and I were playing golf at Waveland when we were 14 or 15 years old in the mid '60s. We were on the 7th hole at Waveland and screaming down the fairway at full speed toward us was a Chicago Police car. We are trying to figure out what we had done. The cops jumped out and said, "Any of you kids Bauler?" Ty said, "Yeah, I'm Bauler." They said, "Get in the car!" We asked, "What's the matter?" Their response was, "Your grandpa says the blacks are rioting at Cabrini-Green and you've got to get home." So, the cops drove us back to Old Town and they told us that Paddy, as goofy and addled as he was, was sitting in his saloon with a shotgun in his lap, facing the window waiting the inevitable riot. But it never happened, although even if the Cabrini-Green projects weren't in his ward, they were close enough for him to be fearful.

I first started at LaSalle School at Sedgwick and Eugenie in the 1950s, but so many people of that era began to move to the suburbs so their kids could have a better education than they perceived was available in the Chicago Public Schools. I was in 7th grade, and my brother, Mark, was in 6th grade, when our parents enrolled us at the Latin School, a private school at 65 E. Scott Street. When I first went to Latin, there was a large group of kids coming to the private schools from the public schools. That was one of the white motifs of the '60s: where are you going to go to high school? I would walk to Latin from our apartment, and it was jarring for me because all the students wore coats and ties, which wasn't part of my experience. Yet, I liked going to Latin School, and, in retrospect, it was a great education. I went there through high school and graduated in 1969. I made lifelong friends, and my senior class was so small that we only had 38 co-eds graduating that year.

I started my writing career at Latin, and the first thing I remember composing was a description of my feelings when Kennedy was shot in 1963. I was in 7th grade and my teacher, Mrs. Graham, decided to highlight the paper at our weekly Monday morning chapel in the assembly hall. Everyone at the school was there when Mrs. Graham announced that she wanted to read a paper from one of her students. It was my paper and I think the gist of it was that, intellectually, I felt that I should be crying, but that I was incapable of such an emotional reaction to the assassination. That was the first public reading of a Rick Kogan story, and it was one of my most embarrassing moments because I thought, "Don't do this. I'm new here, so just don't do this to me." But, she did!

When we graduated, everyone went on to college—except me. I went to UIC for about a week, but it was a shock to walk into my first lecture hall with 300 people and then be told to read *The Red Badge of Courage,* a book I had been assigned as a freshman at Latin. My father, who was incredibly supportive, accepted it when I said to him, "I don't think that I am going to learn anything there." He was a three-year Phi Beta Kappa from the University of Chicago during the Depression who worked midnight to 8:00 am for the City News Bureau, and he could have "guilt-tripped" me back to school in five seconds. But he said, "What do you want to do?" I said, "I am going to drive a cab." He said, "Well, go ahead." He always thought I would go back to school, but I kept getting different jobs.

Dad had gone to the *Daily News* in the early '60s to start Panorama. I assume that on one level I understood being a newspaper man was not a terribly lucrative kind of thing, but to hang out at the paper as a kid was a wonderful experience. I was lucky to be surrounded by books, and our apartment was always filled with such creative people as Studs Terkel, Nelson Algren, Willard Motley, Jim Jones, and Mort Sahl. Creativity was nurtured in my house, and I was always reading books.

In the late '60s, Old Town was transforming into an incredibly colorful place. However, those of us who had grown up in Old Town were neither afraid nor wowed with the changes because they happened so slowly. We knew enough people, like the older brothers and sisters of people from Old Town who had become part of that whole culture, so it was never scary to us. What my friends Ty and Ralph and I used to do was, when we sensed that something was up and people were parking on our streets, we would carry a brick in our hands and approach people parking on North Park, St. Paul or Eugenie Streets. We would say to them, "It's a dollar to park here." If they said to us, "F—k you," we would run. But a surprising number said, "Okay." And, we would always walk Wells Street later at night and wait for guys who seemed to be really drunk. Then we would approach them and just simply ask them for $5 without any kind of intimidation. It was true that, on Friday and Saturday nights, it was difficult to walk down the sidewalks on Wells because it had become a tourist attraction. What started the downward move in Old Town happened when a young couple from the suburbs was shot and killed in the neighborhood. That event terrified suburbia, and, at the same time, some of the real estate people started rent gouging. As a result, many of the unique stores left the area.

During the summer of 1968, I was working as a copy boy in the basement of the Conrad Hilton during the Democratic Convention answering phones for the *Daily News* and the *Sun-Times.* I remember when Abra Anderson, a friend of my father, took me to the Convention. At the Amphitheater, I saw the armed camp that was set up outside the place and had never seen anything like that. I was at the Hilton when the events happened across the street, and that was another powerful moment for me. It was terrifying, gut-wrenching, and very ugly. Everybody was scared, including the cops and the kids, and there was just this unbelievable tension on the streets. It was a clear clash of cultures, and I think that the fear came from a lack of knowledge and communication. I have always appreciated the chance to grow up the way I did because I was never afraid to explore the city.

In the early '70s, I was driving a cab to save up money to go on a European adventure. I finally wound up taking that trip when I was 20 years old in 1971-72 and I stayed there for about a year. I lived in Spain, wrote horrible short stories, but was always, always, always drawn back to Chicago. My father was awfully good about supporting what I did, and although he was a great journalist, I never thought about making that my career. However, I did feel that there was something terribly romantic about the business. When I came back from Europe in the early '70s, Jon and Abra Anderson were starting a magazine called *The Chicagoan.* I was looking for a summer job and went in to apply because I knew them as well as Dick Christiansen, the magazine's editor.

Marshall Rosenthal, who had been editor of *The Seed,* interviewed me, and I was ready to take any job there. The only pieces I could bring in were a story I wrote for the Latin school paper about why the students should support the school football team, another one which was a review of Tom Wolfe's *The Electric Cool Aid Acid Test* that I also wrote for the Latin paper, and a travel story that I had written in Spain that had been published by the *Tribune.* Marshall, in his infinite wisdom, said to me, "We'd like to hire you as a reporter." I said, "That's great." But, I went home terrified and said, "Dad, they offered me a job as a reporter." He said, "That's great." I answered, "Well, I don't know how to do this." And, in his wonderful way, he mentioned the names of five reporters who I knew and who were goofs. He said, "If they can do it, don't you think you can do it?" It was such an empowering comment, so I said to him, "My god, of course I can do it!"

The Earl of Old Town, Northeast Corner
of Wells and North Avenue, 1973
(Courtesy of Chicago Historical Society, ICHi-32102).

Southwest corner of North Sedgwick and
West North Avenue, May 27, 1967
Photographer; Sigmund Osty
(Courtesy of Chicago Historical Society, ICHi-26950).

Jon Anderson

I arrived in Chicago on June 15, 1963 from Montreal, Canada, where I was working for *Time* Magazine. I wanted to get an assignment to Paris, France, but they said, "No. We are an American magazine, and you should go to the United States for one year and then we will send you to Paris. Chicago is the most representative city in the country since it has such a wide variety of things going on." When we arrived in Chicago, they put my family and me up at the Park Dearborn Hotel, at Goethe and Dearborn, on the Gold Coast. A while later, we moved into an apartment in a wonderful place called Crilly Court, which was two blocks of homes from Wells Street to North Park, just north of North Avenue.

Crilly Court was four stories high with big back balconies. There was also a long row of townhouses. Old Town was just starting to become popular. Everything was kind of new and coming up from the ground. The balconies were so wide that to some, it looked like "Catfish Row." The rent for my apartment, with four bedrooms and a fireplace, was $225 a month, and that was considered outrageous since we had neighbors who had paid $175 a month only a few years before we moved there.

Everybody could go from balcony to balcony and talk. In our building, living on the first floor was Henry Rago, the editor of *Poetry* Magazine. He and his wife, Juliette, would go to Europe every summer and come back and talk about their trip. On the next floor was Virginia Kay, a writer for *Chicago's American* and later on a columnist in the *Chicago Daily News,* and Norton Kay, the political editor of *Chicago's American*. The other way, there was a writer for the 1930's radio show "Vic and Sade." In addition, we had Hoke Norris, a famous Southern writer, and, the other direction, Herman Kogan. Of course, he attracted everyone to his back porch. So, we used to have these magical parties.

We had the Old Town Art Fair that highlighted quality artists and attracted real neighborhood people. The other big neighborhood event was the Old Town Garden Walk when everyone placed hanging plants on their balconies. The artists were the early "settlers" of the area. They moved into Old Town, got it all set up, including the cafes, and, when the rental prices went up too much, they moved to New Town near Broadway and Belmont before going to other neighborhoods.

In the mid '60s, I left *Time* and worked for Second City, in management. Bernie Sahlins was moving the operation to a new location in Pipers Alley and wanted to add a complex called the Second City Center for the Public Arts. The idea was to have a kind of storefront Lincoln Center in Piper's Alley. The cabaret was open and that was about it. I went to work for the *Chicago Sun-Times* just in time to cover the riots of 1967.

In those years, the *Sun-Times* was the best paper in town. It was a sharp, young publication, just like *Newsweek* was the sharp newsmagazine at the time. The *Sun-Times* had good reporters out on the street covering everything while the *Tribune* was going through a kind of stodgy period. There were also two afternoon papers, the *Daily News* and the *American.* But the *Sun-Times* was the hot newspaper in the '60s. Kup was at the height of his power. He had his television program that everybody watched on Saturday night. It began at 10:30 pm and would continue until every guest finished talking. It was like a saloon with no closing time.

In the late '60s, I was a features writer but sometimes they drafted me to write "running" coverage of an event from the news desk. When the Martin Luther King riots broke out in April 1968, I had the opportunity to cover it out in the field. The day after Dr. King's assassination, I went over and walked west on Division Street. A girl, about 15, came up to me and said, "If I was you, I'd get my ass out of here!" I said to her, "Madam, I think you're right." It was like a thunderstorm, things were ready to explode. I went back to the office and became anchorman at the newspaper. The shooting started. Everything became chaotic as the riots began on the West and South sides. People were just stunned. They had no way to put the events in some context, and it took years to rebuild those neighborhoods.

The Democratic Convention in August 1968 was totally confusing. Mayor Daley was proud to have the convention in his city and in his neighborhood. So, the people who were coming in to mess it up were not looked on with any favor. The Yippies really knew how to use the media to publicize their goals, and they would stage events to get television coverage. During the convention, my assignment was to cover the events at the Conrad Hilton. I was the pool-reporter covering Vice President Humphrey when he was in his suite, and I was there when he was nominated for President. By tradition, the presidential nominee didn't go to the hall, but remained at his hotel. When Muriel Humphrey's picture appeared on television, he got up, walked across, and kissed the screen, and I got to report that to the world. I was also in the suite when the demonstrators were chanting "Dump the Hump!" from below on Michigan Avenue. He had just won the nomination, but you could tell that he was really caught in a bind. He couldn't disavow Lyndon Johnson's position on the Vietnam War. Yet, he was caught up in the vortex of all the opposition that had formed outside the hotel.

Unlike *Time, Newsweek* was out on the street with the Civil Rights struggle and the Vietnam protests. It was the same thing at the Convention. The people who really covered it were out there moving with the demonstrators. The Daley people didn't seem to know how to handle the situation. At the time of the convention nobody quite knew what forces were behind the demonstrations. The city was afraid that there might also be a race riot. But the focus was mainly anti-war.

The "Conspiracy Seven" trial was a total debacle from beginning to end. Judge Julius Hoffman was the wrong jurist to handle that trial. A lot of the conspirators had never met each other before the trial. That undercut the charge of conspiracy. Hoffman seemed to be socially ambitious. He used to save the first row of seats for society friends to whom he presented himself as the person saving the nation from chaos. These were the same people who were outraged by the play *Hair*. They saw Judge Hoffman as a bulwark of stability. He would actually keep relatives of the defendants out of the courtroom because there were only so many seats. Yet, he would be certain to save the front row for society ladies from the Gold Coast and Lake Forest.

The 1960s did divide up into very different eras. From 1960 to 1963, until the Kennedy assassination, was one distinct period. Then, from 1963 to 1965, there was Lyndon Johnson behaving like a social activist President and beginning his Great Society. Meanwhile, the Vietnam War was slowly building and exploded after the Gulf of Tonkin "incident." I actually went to Vietnam for a week in January 1965. On a trip for *Time*, I dropped into Saigon. There were 20,000-30,000 American advisors in the country, as well as all sorts of "consultants." The consultants came from "think tanks" and lived in nice houses with servants and their families. At that time, the war hadn't really picked up the pace. There was a lot of Vietnamese student opposition. The Buddhist monks had begun to oppose the war. In January 1965, the main priority of the Vietnamese students was to study for their baccalaureate exams.

In Chicago, people began to take strong positions for and against Mayor Daley. They were either wildly for him or against him. Richard J. Daley did a lot to build the physical plant in the city, with new buildings, expressways, and a new university campus for the University of Illinois-Chicago. He brought many different people into City Hall, but he was viewed by many as a "plantation boss." If you were in with The Boss, it was great; if you weren't, it wasn't so great. Yet, he was quite an amiable guy if you met him at a public event. He had a kind of presence which he created. He wasn't as simple a person as the media tried to portray him. He deliberately stayed in his Bridgeport neighborhood, in a small bungalow, his whole life. Nobody in Lake Forest could understand that. Daley was very much a neighborhood person. That was part of his power.

The 1960s were a decade of change. New expressways allowed people to move to the suburbs and quickly get in and out of the central city. Also, there was a kind of diffusion of the energy out of the Loop. It used to be that, in the '50s, people came downtown to movie theaters and restaurants. In the mid- to late-'60s, the Loop movie theaters began to get tacky or go out of business. In turn, Rush Street was doing very well in the '60s, and Old Town had its period of great renewal. What with the troubles and unrest at the end of the decade, some suburbanites stopped coming downtown for fun. One great new draw—North Michigan Avenue—was yet to come.

Jerry Petacque

We were still living on the northwest side of Chicago in 1955 when I graduated from the University of Illinois Law School, passed the Bar exam, and began to practice law. At that time, Alderman Tom Keane, the alderman of the 31st Ward, whose father had been a friend of my dad, was one of the city's power brokers. One day, I received a call at home from the alderman, and he said, "Jerry, this is Alderman Keane. Are you interested in politics?" I said, "I'm not too sure." He said, "I'll tell you what I will do. We'll start off by putting you in the Corporation Counsel's Office." Our discourse was very minimal as he told me about his plans for my political career. He also asked me to be active in his ward and become a precinct captain, and then he said that I could look forward to a bright political career and he was certain that someday I would be a judge. So, it perpetuated the long term relationship between the Petacque and Keane families.

In the early '60s, I got a call from a friend who was a judge. He said, "Jerry, the mayor's looking for a blue ribbon judicial system. I think that you are a good candidate, in terms of your reputation, ethics, and intellect." I quickly became aware that I was being considered for a judgeship. I discussed the situation with my brother, Art, the award-winning reporter at the *Chicago Sun-Times*, and Art thought that it was a good idea. The net result was that through political channels I was being proposed as a judicial candidate for the Circuit Court of Cook County. In order for that to happen, I had to go through the political hierarchy. I was called by Mayor Richard J. Daley's office and told to appear before a meeting of the Democratic Party at the LaSalle Hotel. Mayor Daley came to me, shook my hand and he said, "Jerry, I'm proud to have you a part of our team. This is for the Circuit Court only, but based on your reputation, career, and legal ability, it is only a stepping stone. Eventually, you will become a federal judge."

Then, his contact man informed me that I would need to speak to the Democratic Party and tell them exactly what I intended to do as a judicial candidate. During my presentation, I thought that I was offering academic babble to the committee, but since they clapped I figured I had done a good job. That night, I get a phone call from my brother, Art, who had a lot of political influence, and he told me, "Jerry, my friend Marshal Korshak called and said, 'I understood what your brother is saying, but all my other fellow members want to know what the heck was your brother talking about?'" They just didn't understand my presentation.

Despite the confusion generated by my speech, I was approved by the Democratic Party, as well as the Chicago Bar Association. So, I sat back and became very introspective as I thought about what salary I was making as a lawyer, what it meant to have two kids in school, and that I was struggling to build a financial base. On the other hand, I didn't think that I wanted the judicial position and I made the decision not to take the job. I called the mayor on the phone, and he wasn't too happy with me. When I saw him again, he said hello but it was obvious that he was displeased that I had turned down the judicial appointment and it did affect our future dealings.

My impression of Richard Daley was that he had developed a "radiance" of personality, was omnipresent in a social situation, even though he didn't articulate it, and you were completely aware of his presence. He oozed power and that was interesting because, in the way he stood and in his body language, he controlled his environment.

But I felt that even though he was a dominant, controlling figure and took his space, he did not displace you. The mayor actually pulled you toward him, and he was, psychologically, a very complex man.

When I got married, we lived at 19 E. Pearson in a duplex apartment. My wife was an artist at the Art Institute. I started taking some lessons there, and, eventually, I expanded my horizons and became a sculptor while I was also practicing law. So, art fairs became significant to our lives. We were selling our art at several of the city's major art fairs, including the Old Town Art Fair, Hyde Park Art Fair, and Gold Coast Art Fair. I got into a couple of major shows as well as a major gallery on Michigan Avenue.

In the early '60s, my wife needed a studio to do her art and we were about to have a child. As a result, we began looking to try to find a new place to live. We saw a co-op that I liked on Dearborn, and the agent at that time was a friend of mine. He said, "Well, Jerry, it is a quota building. Your wife is blue-eyed and blonde, and she doesn't look Jewish. But, I will try to get you into this co-op." I told him no, I'm not going to assimilate. So, that ended our interest in cooperatives. Our next option was to build a new house on a vacant lot we found at 309 W. Eugenie. It became the first new house in Old Town in many years. It was unusual architecture that was featured in newspapers.

The Old Town Art Fair was the place to be for artists and the neighborhood was very much like Greenwich Village in terms of its orientation. There were a lot of rooming houses in the area, and when we built our house, we had trouble getting a mortgage. However, a friend of mine, Albert Hannah who was a developer, got us a mortgage. The neighborhood at that time included a lot of struggling as well as some affluent artists. There was a local grocery store on the corner, but there were no Walgreens or Treasure Island stores. It was a multi-flavor neighborhood, but as time went on, Wells Street became a flourishing nightclub area, along with jazz and folk venues.

What was good about Old Town was that it was a neighborly community where everybody knew each other. However, later, when it became a concrete jungle of condos and new architecture, the artists had to move out because of rental increases, and, as a result our little grocery store closed. Clark Street was being torn down in those days, the skid row was no longer there, and they were starting to build Sandburg Village. The Compass Players started in the neighborhood, and it was a neighborhood of warmth, pseudo-culture, and a nice place to live.

Since Old Town was centrally located and near downtown, it was the perfect place to live. By the mid '60s, the area began to prosper, and on Saturday nights you couldn't walk or drive down Wells Street.

Suburbanites began coming into Chicago because they had a wide spectrum of things to do and places to go in Old Town like La Strada, a great Italian restaurant, Earl of Old Town, a folk place, and Barbara's Bookstore. So, it was semi-garish, but not like Rush Street became in the end. The current era of Wells Street is that it has become a pseudo-Walton Street with fancy boutiques and chauffeur-driven men and women. It is no longer an artsy-craftsy neighborhood, but an area with people who put up huge houses, and, as a result, it has lost its flavor. As time went by, people started remodeling and renovating houses in the area because it became economically productive to do that. Old Town was near transportation and downtown Chicago, and you could see the Loop from the neighborhood.

In 1963, a group of us wanted to become restaurateurs, so just about the time we were building our new house, four other lawyers and I got together and opened up a place called Rigoletto's Opera Café at 1448 N. Wells Street. It was a unique place where you could eat great Italian food and listen to live opera singers. For a while, it was mentioned in the newspapers and we got a lot of press, so it was an exciting time for us. The café was open from 1963 to 1965, but rents became prohibitive, there were murders of suburbanites near Old Town, and we had to close the café. People from the suburbs stopped coming into Old Town due to their concern for security because Wells Street was not too far from Cabrini-Green and there was a lot of paranoia about the projects. But Cabrini-Green never bothered me and I had positive interactions with African Americans who lived there. Although the projects were the other side of the world, it was an exciting and dynamic place and interesting to see how other people lived in a different social structure.

As time went on, the Old Town Art Fair was a delight with a lot of local artists and very few from out of state, but, in later years, the Art Fair was dominated by artists from outside of Illinois. In terms of my experience as an artist, I was totally untrained as a sculptor. I got some dental wax and started doing organic shapes and forms, and exhibited at the Old Town Art Fair for about 25 years. At one time, the Art Institute had a sales and rental gallery, and that was a high priced place where people of national significance would show their works. Luckily, they exhibited some of my work and it became an ego trip.

There also was the Benjamin Gallery on Michigan Avenue, which had works by Henry Moore and other people of significance in her gallery. For some reason, after seeing my work at the Old Town Art Fair, she liked it. As a result, I was in the Benjamin Gallery for a number of years.

During the '50s and '60s, most of my peer group lived in Chicago and had not begun their move to the suburbs. However, when they all began to raise their kids, they decided that they weren't going to let their children attend Chicago Public Schools and made the determination to move to the northern suburbs. Our viewpoint was that we wanted our kids exposed to the bigger social structure and people from different racial and religious backgrounds. But, the irony was that we sent our kids to the Latin School because it became a question of the security in the Chicago Public Schools, which seemed to be infested with gangs.

My kids went to the Latin School for their education. I was a city liberal, and my wife and kids wanted to be exposed to the social stratification of today's society. I didn't want to move to the suburbs because that represented one group,

and I wanted my kids to have a different experience since my wife and I had grown up with multi-cultural and multi-racial experiences. We interviewed at Latin School and Francis Parker, the two closest private schools. We visited Parker in the late '60s at the time that Eugene McCarthy was running for President, and the headmaster was articulating how liberal the school was and the flexibility encouraged at the school. It seemed to us that Parker had an intellectual snobbishness and liberal affectation while Latin School had an economic affectation. So, I think that we just flipped a coin and our kids went to Latin. But, in retrospect, Parker would have probably been a better way to go.

I thought that Latin School was a more formalistic place, supposedly ranked higher than Parker. Most of our kids' peer group seemed to live on or near Astor Street in the Gold Coast. On the other hand, we lived "across the tracks" on Eugenie, west of Wells Street, and our kids had difficulty being assimilated into the "Astor Street crowd." Those kids flew to Cannes, France during spring break and were dropped off at Latin in their chauffeur-driven Mercedes, and I used to call that daily event the "waltz of the Mercedes."

Old Town Art Fair
(Courtesy of Eric Bronsky)

Eric Bronsky

I was born in 1951 and lived in Garfield Park until 1955 when we moved to the North Town neighborhood on the city's Far North Side. My family lived on the top floor of a three-flat apartment on Washtenaw, near Granville, and I attended kindergarten and early grade school at Clinton Elementary School on Fairfield Avenue. The school's population grew rapidly, and since they were not well equipped to deal with that many students, they had to have two tiers of classes. They didn't build temporaries, so each section would meet for only half a day, morning or afternoon. It got to the point where my parents felt that I was not getting a good education at Clinton so they transferred me to Harris School, a coed private school in the Lake View area at Lake View and Wrightwood.

Harris was operated like an old British academy and with a headmaster who was in charge of the school. We had to wear uniforms each day: the boys wore navy blue blazers with the school's logo embroidered on the pocket, a tie and grey slacks. I liked going to Harris and I remember that on Wednesday afternoons the students were divided up so they could participate in extracurricular activities that included a variety of sports, as well as theater and cooking. Since I wasn't that interested in sports, I preferred the classes on theater.

One of my favorite pastimes at that time was model building, and I had a couple of friends at Harris who also enjoyed building model trains. I used to visit two wonderful hobby shops downtown at the time: the Hobby Service and Supply located above the Walgreens at the corner of Randolph and State; and, the best of them all, the All Nation Hobby Shop at 220 W. Madison.

I was 11 years old in 1962, when we moved to 511 Brompton, which was actually part of the 3520 N. Lake Shore Drive building. We only lived there for two years because the building had been poorly maintained and there was a lack of security. I had my bicycle stolen, and when we replaced it, the new bicycle was also stolen. Anybody could go into the building through the service entrance since it was never locked up. With coal furnaces still used at that time, there was a haze in the air and my mother always complained that she just couldn't keep our apartment clean.

When our lease came up, my parents decided not to renew it. We had heard about Sandburg Village, which was being developed by Arthur Rubloff, and had been under construction in 1962. The area around Sandburg looked very nice, and what was unique was that the place was designed for middle-class residents. Up to that point, nothing like Sandburg Village had been designed or created at any earlier time in Chicago's history. I think that when we moved into our two-bedroom apartment in 1964, the rent was around $240 a month which my parents considered affordable.

Initially, Sandburg Village covered two blocks with four high-rise apartment buildings designated by letters of the alphabet: A, B, C, and D; and townhouses. Later, they assigned names of poets to the buildings: Alcott, Bryant, Cummings, Dickinson, and then the E building, which went up in early '64 and later became known as Eliot House. That was where we rented a unit on the third floor. We had a view overlooking Goethe Street and the old St. Paul Lutheran Church, which during the time we were living there was torn down and the old church was replaced with a brand new one. Although Sandburg Village was located between Clark and LaSalle, the official address of the buildings was Sandburg Terrace. Whenever people asked me for directions, I invariably told them Sandburg Terrace, quickly adding the phrase, "between Clark and LaSalle."

I went to high school at a boarding school away from Chicago, but with my various winter, spring, and summer vacations, I was actually living at Sandburg Village for almost five months a year. When I was home, whichever direction I walked in the neighborhood included a variety of interesting things to see. There was a lot of change, and, perhaps the thing that made the area most exciting to live in was the diversity. In the early '60s, if you crossed Clark Street, there were still a few businesses remaining from the days when Clark Street was a Skid Row with numerous "single resident occupancy" buildings.

Further north was Lincoln Park and if you went directly east you were in the Gold Coast, including the famous Ambassador East and West Hotels. Division Street was a very lively and thriving commercial district, even before Sandburg Village. There were a number of businesses and restaurants there that I remember. First and foremost, there was an old fashioned ice cream parlor called Ting-A-Ling. They had wood booths and a tile floor, and it was very much like the old Buffalo Ice Cream parlor located on Irving Park and several others that I remember. There were a few neighborhood Chinese restaurants too. The ones that I recall and that were both located on Division Street, were Ding Ho and China Doll. Those restaurants were there for a number of years, open well into the '70s. Also, at the corner of State and Division was a coffee shop called Mitchell's, and on Dearborn Street, just north of Division, there was an English pub called Ballantine's. It later became Oliver's and was a pub where patrons could throw peanut shells on the floor. Division Street had not became known for singles' bars at that time, so the area was more geared to neighborhood residents than to young people or singles.

The most interesting area of all was Wells Street, which became known as Old Town. In the '60s, we saw it blossom and really thrive. The original Piper's Alley was not duplicated by the development that replaced it and that would include Second City. One of the most memorable restaurants on Wells Street was That Steak Joynt that opened in the 1960s and was adjacent to Second City. It was great entertainment just to walk the streets, do people-watching, see the hippies, and go into the "head shops" with the black light posters and the psychedelic strobe lights. It was very colorful and a very exciting place to be at the time.

Sandburg Village was built in a neighborhood that had deteriorated and a lot of the buildings were neglected and needed to be rehabbed or torn down. I believe that developers started purchasing the area, piece by piece, but I am uncertain if any portion of the property was acquired by the city through eminent domain, or if it was, in fact, bought up directly by developers. However, it was remarkable foresight on somebody's part. Sandburg Village was located in an area of the city that would become a buffer zone and serve as a link between some very interesting neighborhoods. Sandburg was actually built over a large, underground, parking garage that served the high rise buildings on the blocks, while the individual townhouses had their own carports facing the driveway going to LaSalle Street. So, Sandburg Village proper was actually raised a few feet, and, as you entered the block, you would walk up a few steps. It was a nicely landscaped area, and there were kiosks that had travel posters and night lighting mounted on them. Those kiosks actually masked the ventilation ducts from the underground garage. Sandburg Village turned condo in 1979.

One of the things that made the complex so unique was that it was a somewhat self-contained community. They had their own commissary, later replaced by the Sandburg Supermart, just south of the Latin School at North and Clark. There was a barber shop, a restaurant on the first floor of one of the towers, a pharmacy, and even a monthly newsletter in a semi-magazine format. The newsletter included a gossip column and a discussion of neighborhood events, brief articles about local places, cultural events and activities. And, there were even some clubs for residents. I was a member of the Sandburg Camera Club, and they met in a room on the first floor of the Bryant House at 1355 Sandburg. They had a darkroom, but it was more of a social kind of thing which meant that we would take photos, bring them to our next meeting, compare each other's photos, and socialize.

Sandburg Village was probably not replicated anywhere else in Chicago. The timing for building it and the location was right. It really appealed to a lot of people, and it didn't take long for the concept to catch on and for people to move there. The complex provided an opportunity for people to remain in the city, especially those who might have contemplated moving elsewhere. This all happened during a time when there was a lot of suburban flight, and most new residential developments were either new high rises located near north or along the lakeshore, or large residential communities being built in the suburbs. People could work downtown and get home quickly, and there was a variety of transportation available to the residents.

In 1969, we moved to a townhouse in Sandburg Village because we needed more space. It was really much more like living in a home. I had lived in apartment buildings all my life, so it was quite unique. The townhouse was also rental that included superb maintenance and building services. If you had a problem and something broke, somebody would be there, usually the same day, to repair it.

In retrospect, I think that the neighborhood and adjoining communities were in transition, just like the 1960s.

Sandburg Village (Courtesy of Eric Bronsky)

Tearing down buildings before
construction of Sandberg Village, c. 1960
(Courtesy of Eric Bronsky)

Streetcars on Clark Street, pre-Sandberg Village
(Courtesy of Electric Railway Historical Society)

Erin McCann

I was born on February 6, 1949 in Chicago and grew up at 85th and Justine, in St. Ethelreda parish. I went to the parish grammar school, then to Mother McAuley High School in the fall of 1963, and, after high school, to Loyola University. My neighborhood was predominantly Irish Catholic, although my particular block was very much a "United Nations." We had a lot of immigrants after World War II from Austria and Germany, as well as Irish, Poles, and Swedes, and my block was much more diverse than the neighborhood.

The area was called Brainerd, and Foster Park was our park that was located about a block away. The neighborhood was primarily made up of bungalows, although there were some apartment buildings which meant that big families were often raised in apartments. On Ashland Avenue, one block west, there were a group of stores that made up the shopping district, including a butcher, a grocery store, a tavern, a hardware store, and a florist. My sister and I were two of seven children in our family. We were "latch key" kids because our mother was a legal secretary who worked downtown.

My father, John L. Sullivan, was a lieutenant in the Chicago Police Department, and he was acting captain of the Deering District that covered Bridgeport and Comiskey Park for some years when the captain retired. He ran the 9th District that is located down the street from Mayor Richard J. Daley's house in Bridgeport. My father loved being in the police department, and he was there for 33 years until his retirement in 1962. He then became chief security officer for the Metropolitan Sanitary District until he was 75.

Foster Park was important to us because my mother wanted to make certain that my sister and I didn't get into any trouble when we got home from school. So, she signed us up for tap and ballet lessons, and we were at the park four days a week. They had a big, beautiful field house with boys' and girls' gymnasiums, as well as a woodworking shop down in the basement. I remember when I was three years old they had square dancing outside for the neighborhood residents in the summer. It was a great park and a positive influence on the neighborhood environment. You could go there and borrow a bat and ball or a tennis racket and tennis balls. That was my first introduction to the concept of collateral, because in order to borrow sports equipment, you had to leave something of value like a watch or a ring. It was like a "poor men's country club," and since my school didn't have a gym, we would go to Foster Park to use the gymnasium equipment.

Downtown was a great adventure. I remember when my girlfriend and I would get on the train and go downtown in grammar school and get off at the old LaSalle Street Station. I loved the station, and we would take the escalators up to the street level. They even had a booth there for making records, and my girlfriend and I "cut" a record called "Winter Wonderland" in the booth. I also did some of my Christmas shopping downtown and recall my older cousin taking us to Marshall Field's to eat under the tree and to see Santa Claus every Christmas.

We moved from the neighborhood in 1968 because the makeup of the community was changing and that affected all of our neighbors, even the kids. My parents made certain that I grew up knowing survival skill, street smarts, and also how to navigate the Southwest Side. We didn't go into "bad" neighborhoods if we could avoid it, and we didn't travel alone. I grew up using public transportation because most of the time my father didn't have a car. I remember that for a few years my friends talked about moving, but nobody wanted to leave the neighborhood because it represented so many memories for all of us and had been the center of our lives. Although some neighbors moved to nearby neighborhoods, they weren't ready to go to the suburbs.

All of the disruption in our lives seemed to be related to racial change, and I think that one of the prevailing issues was a sense of fear: fear for our own security; fear of losing what we had; fear of financial loss; and, fear of loss of familiarity. I think that emotions ran high in those years, and there was a clear sense of loss of the past. Our neighborhood and parish was an ethnic enclave that was just developing and hadn't matured enough to appreciate what a neighborhood could be. There were a lot of factors at work, but this change in racial makeup was something that was foisted upon us and we weren't prepared for it. To this day, people look back on the late '60s as a time of sadness. It was a world gone away for a lot of people who moved from the South Side. And, it wasn't just the Irish who were affected. It was the Italians, the Poles, the Greeks, and the Jewish community in South Shore. I think that a lot of people lost their religious centers after they left the neighborhood, and when they moved to the suburbs, there were a lot of good things that happened to them. They had bigger and nicer houses with more room and new prosperity. But, I think that a lot of them tried to recreate in the suburbs what they had in the city and never could quite do that.

There was "block-busting" going on in our area. We got called all the time by real estate companies and they would ask, "Do you want to sell your house? Are you aware that your neighbors are selling their homes?" My parents always said no. The joke on the Southwest Side was that once "block-busting" started, you knew that the neighborhood was going to have rapid changes because, inevitably, those people who started "block clubs" to maintain the neighborhood were usually the first ones to sell. These were blue-collar families, and finances were always foremost in their minds.

Their homes were their major investments, and they had to protect that investment. As I recall it, our neighborhood was more than half black before my parents moved. We twice had incidents when police officers chased black offenders through our particular gangway and that was scary, especially when you had four sisters.

I remember developing survival-skill type habits at night when I learned to drive. One of my older sisters had a car and she'd let me take it out, but I always kept the car doors locked when I pulled up in front of the house. Then, I would take out my house key before I unlocked the car door. The old joke was that you never locked a door behind you unless you saw an open door in front of you. I can remember jumping out and scrambling up the front steps of my house with front porch lights that never worked. So, it was dark on the front porch. I think that the potential for crime in those days was a combination of real as well as imagined fears, and I think that white people living in changing neighborhoods had developed a fear of being a victim of crime.

In St. Sabina Parish, which bordered my parish/neighborhood, the issue became the killing of a 16-year old kid named Frank Kelly. There was an incident on a Sunday night at a dance there, and he was with some kids who had exchanged taunts with some black kids. One of the black kids took out a gun and shot and killed Kelly in front of the St. Sabina gym in August 1965 where there was a dance. That event electrified the parish. Despite all the changes, people claimed that they were going to stay in their neighborhoods and work it out. But, after that incident, it changed the whole feeling about how people perceived the neighborhood. People started leaving soon after, and they were actually moving out at night. You would see trucks that would advertise being "night movers." It was done at night because neighbors didn't want to tell others they were moving or that they had sold their home to a black family. There were neighbors who would never talk to each other again after that happened, and they were viewed as disloyal to the neighborhood. The downside of the situation was intolerance and lack of accepting other kinds of people, but comfort level was important. These people were first and second generation immigrants, including Irish, Germans, and Swedes, and a lot of them felt comfortable and identified with the neighborhood. But, we did have some white neighbors who stayed and refused to move.

I remember being at Loyola University at the downtown campus in April 1968 when we heard that there was rioting on the South and West Sides after the King assassination. I used to take the "L" to school every day, and I did take it that day. I was in a dilemma, and I had friends on the North Side who offered me the opportunity to stay at their homes. I figured I had two options: I could either take the chance and ride the "L" home or go to one of my friends' houses. As a kid, being the youngest of seven, I was very independent. I had always taken the "L" and learned to exercise caution. I was a little nervous about going home that day, but I got on the "L" and when I got off at the "L" station, there wasn't anyone else going my way. I had heard that they were burning down buildings on the West Side. I remember going down the stairs and hoping I could catch a bus right away at the 63rd Street station. There was one lone policeman standing at the bottom of the steps from the "L," and he looked at me and said, "What are you doing here? There is rioting on 63rd Street. I said, "Officer, I'm just trying to get home." So, I hopped on a Marquette Park bus that swung over to 67th Street and I got off at Ashland in order to get another bus to get home to 85th Street.

I was standing there for what seemed like an eternity. I was thinking, "This is really not a good situation, and there is no bus coming." I saw a car going by with four National Guardsmen in it with their rifles pointed out the window of the car, and they were patrolling Ashland Avenue. I realized that it was definitely not a good sign. I stood there for what seemed like an hour, until, finally a car with two women pulled up and they said, "Oh, you shouldn't be standing there by yourself on the corner. Do you need a ride?" I said, "Sure do." And they said, "Which way are you going?" I said, "I'm going south on Ashland." They said, "Oh, sorry, we're going west." They pulled away because they were afraid and I thought that was my last chance to find a way home. But, eventually, the bus came heading south and I got on it and made it home. The interesting thing is that when I got home I don't recall if I mentioned this experience to my parents, or even if they expressed concern about how I got home that day. You were expected to navigate on your own, and they just figured that their kids would find a way home and be able to solve their own problems. I know they worried about us, but showing it wasn't really the style of the day, nor was it the style of the Irish.

Senator Everett Dirksen,
President Dwight Eisenhower and
Acting Captain John L. Sullivan, 1961.
(Courtesy of Erin McCann).

Acting Captain John L. Sullivan
with Chicago Police assigned to Comiskey Park, c. 1960
(Courtesy of Erin McCann).

Eric McCann

Anna Marie DiBuono

My neighborhood is called Little Italy, which is a name that has also been given to other Italian neighborhoods in Chicago, like Grand Avenue, Ogden and Racine, and 24th and Oakley. There were five different Italian neighborhoods in Chicago, and each one included people from various regions of Italy. For example, people who resided in my neighborhood on the Near West Side came from such places as Naples, Calabria, Bari, and Abruzzo, Italy.

During the 1960s, the defining event for the neighborhood happened when Mayor Richard J. Daley decided to build a new campus for the University of Illinois at Chicago and move it from Navy Pier. The city was considering our Italian neighborhood on the Near West Side or Garfield Park, but the mayor wanted the campus to be situated on the Near West Side because that would place the university adjacent to the expressways. In addition, he thought it would be the best location because it was near downtown and that would enable students to get jobs in the Loop. When the city announced its choice, there was much opposition vocalized to City Hall by local residents and politicians. In the early '60s, the city began boarding up neighborhood buildings, including houses and stores, and they were getting ready to tear down much of the neighborhood. At that time, I didn't realize the impact of the event, but it was sad to think that so many of the neighborhood people had to leave. They moved out to a variety of western suburbs including Berwyn, Cicero, Hillside, Maywood, and Broadview, although some did move north. There was much anger in the community, and the opposition to it was led by my dear friend, Florence Scala. She fought very hard to stop it from happening, and she put all her heart and soul into the fight. But, the city establishment won out. I was too young to get involved in the dispute, but we all have great appreciation for what Florence tried to do and how she represented our feelings about the decision.

I clearly remember when the neighborhood was being torn down, and it was very difficult to see all these things that meant so much to you coming down. I have so many memories of the people who lived here, especially since I personally knew who resided in each house. Most of the old timers are all dead, and the younger generation just went on to different lives in different areas, but, as for my own house, I feel blessed that it wasn't selected for demolition. From Racine to Carpenter, both sides of Carpenter remained intact, but a section of it included an empty lot at Vernon Park that was already vacant. For a while, until they did build townhouses there, that property remained empty.

They did tear down Miller and Polk Streets, and even from Morgan Street to Taylor Street. I remember Taylor and Halsted with Chesrow's Drugstore on the northwest corner, and Lezza's Pastry on the southeast corner. Then, across the street was Salvino's Liquor Store, and then, next door, on Taylor Street, was the original Ferrara Pastry Shop. The Salerno Funeral Parlor was across the street from the drugstore, and I have wonderful memories of all those places.

I was pleased when, later, they did build some new houses on those streets. The Newman Center was erected on Vernon Park and Morgan, and Catholic students go there to study and attend Mass. Father Pat Marshall has done a wonderful job there. But, I think back now and it seems like the neighborhood went through its changes so long ago, while, in a way, it seems like it was just yesterday.

I loved Chicago in the '60s because the restaurants were wonderful and there was just so much happening for me at that time in my life. There was the Chez Paree, Fritzels, Shangri-La, and my all-time favorite restaurant: the Imperial House on Walton. The decade of the '60s, except for the demolition, was just a nice time for me. In those years, I was going to the Loop everyday because I worked there and shopped on Michigan Avenue. In fact, one of the things that I remember was that Saks and Bonwit Teller were closed on Saturdays in the summer. Then, before you knew it, with the competition from other stores across the city and suburbs, they were open on Saturday and then on Sunday. That was also when the malls, like Old Orchard in Skokie, were first starting, and many people stopped coming downtown to shop as often as they had. However, before that all happened, I remember the late '50s and early '60s as a nicer, more elegant time in Chicago. I was working at LaSalle and Madison for an insurance company, and it was a nice part of the Loop for me because I was working across the street from St. Peter's Church, which meant that I was able to go there regularly for Mass. On Tuesdays, they had a novena to St. Anthony, and it was nice for me because I liked going into St. Peter's.

My neighborhood was going through major changes in those years. All of a sudden the supermarkets, like Dominick's and Jewel, were getting more popular, while, earlier, we had primarily mom and pop stores. We didn't go very far for our shopping because we could buy everything we wanted at our neighborhood stores. And, then before you knew it, the stores were closing because the University was being built.

At the triangle on Blue Island, Halsted and Harrison Streets, the Greek stores were moving further north closer to Van Buren, Jackson, Adams and Monroe, because of UIC and the Congress Expressway. The Greek bakeries and grocery stores had to close as the impact of the University spread across a variety of Near South and Near West neighborhoods. We were just happy to be in our own neighborhood, despite the changes, and our church, Our Lady of Pompeii, remained the center of our lives. But, when many of the parishioners moved away, it affected the churches in the neighborhood including Notre Dame and Our Lady of Pompeii.

Happily, the changes had no negative affect on my family's restaurant, Tufano's. It was and still is a neighborhood restaurant. I have nostalgic memories of all those events, but I have to admit that the university has done a good job of taking care of the grounds located around and near the campus, and, in the long run, UIC added a lot to the neighborhood. One of the hardest things for me was to see my grandma and grandpa's bakery and the original house where we had lived being torn down. Thus, the '60s were the end of an era for me, my family, and our neighbors and friends. It affected my mother because she had come from Italy and had struggled much of her life, and, all of a sudden, it was gone. My family is very close and they have kept the restaurant going all these years. So, the changes in the neighborhood led to progress at a major price.

previous page
"Street Scene in Little Italy, near Taylor and Halsted."
As published in the *Chicago Daily-News*. Photographer: Edward De Luga.
Copyright, 1963, by *Chicago Sun-Times*, Inc.
Reprinted with permission.

"Torn Down Buildings in Little Italy for UIC with Philip DeRosa, 7,
and his sister, Doren, 3, and Goodrich School in background."
As published in the *Chicago Daily News*. Photographer: Edward De Luga.
Copyright, 1963, by *Chicago Sun-Times*, Inc.
Reprinted with permission.

"Cafeteria at the new University of Illinois Chicago campus."
As published in the *Chicago Sun-Times*. Photographer: Howard Lyon.
Copyright, 1965, by *Chicago Sun-Times*, Inc.
Reprinted with permission.

Anna Marie DiBuono

Gene Mackevich

My connection with Maxwell Street began when my grandfather, Isador, came to Chicago from Russia in the early 1900s, without any money. He was forced to leave Russia at the age of 14 because the government wanted to put him in the army. He had a cousin somewhere in America, but he did not know exactly where. As it turned out, his cousin lived in a place called Menominee, Michigan with just five Jews in the town. As the story goes, supposedly my grandfather arrived in America with 14 cents in his pocket, found his cousin, and stayed there for a very short period of time because he did not like it there. Since he had another relative in Chicago, he came to live here.

Most of the Jews in those years lived on the West Side, and none of them had any money. My grandfather chose to live on the North Side and opened a railroad salvage store in the Maxwell Street area. He worked extremely hard seven days a week. His first real estate purchase was at 719 W. Maxwell with no money down. He loved owning property, and he loved the tumult of the area. After a couple of years, he had enough money from selling railroad salvage items, and moved across the street to 712 Maxwell, sometime between 1908 and 1911. The name of his store was I. Mackevich.
My grandfather was a very smart businessman who had handshake contracts with most of the major railroads that came into Chicago, including the Milwaukee Road, the Penn Central, Illinois Central, and any railroad that had more than one box car.

His deal with the railroads was that any time there was a wreck involving spoilage, or any time smoke came in and rusted a cab, he would buy it. He would walk into a warehouse or cars that were completely dark and purchase the entire contents without knowing what was there or what it would cost him. It was really "blind man's bluff," but that was how he made his living. My grandfather continued to build his business through World War II. After WWII, the cost of processing and conditioning salvage merchandise became excessive. Even though he had an exclusive contract with many railroads on their salvage, he began to ease out of the business. True, everyone in the world thought salvage would make them a fortune. But as others came in, he left. "Railroad salvage" became a buzz word to get rich fast, but my grandfather saw the "writing on the wall."

Before he left the salvage business, he developed a retail department store. For example, if he purchased a carload of luggage, all of a sudden we had a luggage department. If he got a carload of groceries as a staple from the old A&P Company or Kroger's, he would fit the merchandise into our grocery department. In addition, he had his own sources of products, such as flour and sugar, delivered to him in his own proprietary bags.

The business continued to grow until the middle of World War II, when my dad, Ira, took over. My grandfather got sick and died in 1948. But, before his death, he had established a foundation of a business that would continue for years.

My grandfather was known to everybody as "Mr. Mackevich." He was barely five feet tall, rarely drank, and never smoked. We had an Italian store manager, Jim Gozzola, who was treated like a member of our family. Mackevich's had approximately 40,000 square feet of selling space, a warehouse, and one of the largest parking lots on the West Side attached to any business area. All of the policemen who went to the Police Academy at the old Foster School parked in our lot. We had shipping and receiving, and, later on, when I got into the business, we had the first self-service supermarket, the first self-service meat store, the first lobster tank, and the first self-service produce in the Midwest. And, yes, all on Maxwell Street.

In addition, we had men's, ladie's and children's clothing stores that were all part of the complex of buildings that made up Mackevich's. We had luggage, a liquor store (no drinking, just package goods), jewelry, small appliances, 12,000 sq. feet of furniture and major appliances, a small loan department, a discount acceptance corporation, and a travel agency. We advertised that people should come to Mackevich's for one-stop shopping, all in one store. They could walk into our store, and there was nothing, except submarines and aircraft, that they couldn't buy. It all started with railroad salvage. The products and services offered were endless. We were called the "Marshall Field's" of the Near West Side both for the African American community, and later the Hispanic community.

I am so blessed, and I had the best of all worlds. I had a good education, good parent support, and training on Maxwell Street that taught me about people. I learned humility and not just how to sell somebody something, but to recognize where they were coming from. In one second, you were talking to an African American gentleman who wanted one product, a Polish person wanting something else, and a very wealthy gentleman from Highland Park who was "slumming" on a Sunday morning coming down to show his son what Maxwell Street was all about. You had to talk to all of them and put yourself in their shoes and see where they were coming from. Our operation was very unique. At that time, Maxwell Street was the second largest business community in the Chicago area, outside of State Street. On a weekend, we had the biggest store with the greatest amount of traffic in the whole area.

When the University of Illinois-Chicago came in, they had a master plan to build the university all the way over to the University of Illinois Medical Center and the Veterans Hospital on Racine. They wanted to have a medical center that would continue all the way south to Michael Reese Hospital. The politicians knew if they did not give us the proper support in terms of police protection and sanitation services, that over a period of time, people would not want to come to the area, which is exactly what happened. In my opinion, this was the city and the university's master plan to take over control of the area. They wanted the land where Maxwell Street was located, but it took longer than they thought to force us out because many of the businesses just refused to leave.

I received my first notification of urban renewal in October 1966. Thirty-five years later and nine law firms employed by the University of Illinois, I was still telling the city that their offers for the property were highly undervalued. I finally settled with the University on May 15, 2003, but they had me in a bind for 37 years before finally achieving their purpose. I believe that the city wanted the tax dollars from a clean, fresh new area, a new neighborhood, and the elimination of the eyesore that was Maxwell Street.

As for my memories about the city, and especially about Maxwell Street, in the 1960s it was booming. During the weekends, from Friday at 3:00 pm to Sunday at 4:30 pm, we had over a million people on Maxwell Street. Not everyone came there to shop because some came there to show their grandchildren what it was all about. Maxwell Street adjusted to the changing racial conditions in the city. If we had to go from the African American client to the Hispanic client, or to what I would call the United Nation clients, the merchants were so down to earth, so real, so practical, so human that they could handle anything and anybody. The average person who worked in those stores could speak six, seven or even eight languages. I was on the street from June 10, 1953 to January 10, 1972, and, in that period of time, the biggest thing that I took away was the understanding of people, how to get along with them, and how to be tolerant of everybody. We saw thousands and thousands of families seeking to live the American dream, and they started with nothing, including my own family. Working there was the greatest education in the world.

Maxwell Street market, Jefferson near 12th Street, 1959.
Photograph by Clarence W. Hines.
(Courtesy of Chicago Historical Society, ICHi 34437.)

Maxwell Street market, 1959. Photograph by Clarence W. Hines.
(Courtesy of Chicago Historical Society, ICHi 34470.)

U.S. District Judge Charles Kocoras

I was born in 1938 and during the '40s and '50s lived at 7105 S. Lafayette. I attended Parker High School from 1952 to 1956 and then Wilson Junior College from '56 to '58 before transferring to DePaul. I received a BA in Commerce with a major in Accounting at DePaul in 1961, and, in 1965 went to law school there at night, graduating with my J.D. in 1969.

During the late 1950s, my neighborhood was undergoing a considerable amount of racial change, which led to "white flight." My father had died in 1956, when I was 18 and the third oldest among four kids. It meant that I had responsibility for my widowed mother and one sister who was still living at home. We decided not to move even though the neighborhood had gone through rapid change, but, after a while, we were the only white family on the block. The actual cause of our move was when the city built the Dan Ryan Expressway and we lost our home to eminent domain.

The county only offered us $18,000 for our large frame house, and there wasn't any way that we could duplicate it with another house for that amount of money. We weren't smart enough to hire lawyers, so, I became the family's representative in negotiations with Cook County. I decided to visit the county offices in order to seek more money for our house. There were three people at the meeting, and in my full naiveté, I attempted to make a case for more money. As a result of my persuasive entreaties, they increased their generous offer by $100, to $18,100. That increased offer just about paid for my carfare back home.

We had seen some new homes in the southwest suburb of Evergreen Park, and since there were other Greek families living there as well as former neighbors, it seemed like a decent place for us to live. We moved there and bought a newly constructed three-bedroom bungalow. It was nothing fancy and was on a small lot, but it wasn't too far from where we had lived and was close to Evergreen Cemetery where my father was interred. We squeezed together in the house, and since one sister was married by then, and another was about to get married, there were basically three of us, including my mother, my youngest sister, and myself.

During the late '50s, I worked at Continental Bank after junior college but decided that the banking business was not what I wanted for a career. While everybody in my family was impressed that I graduated from high school and had a wonderful job in banking, little did they know that it was menial work at a very low pay. There was no college tradition in my family, since both of my parents were immigrants from Greece, so, the idea of college wasn't something that was regularly discussed. Luckily, I did receive encouragement from my mother about going to college.

In 1961, after finishing my undergraduate degree at DePaul, I joined the National Guard and went into military service. I did my basic training at Ft. Leonard Wood, Missouri, and then went to Ft. Knox, Kentucky. While I was there, the Berlin Wall was built and all of the Reservists and National Guard people thought that we were going to be called up to active duty and go to Europe. Luckily, that never materialized, but for almost the entire time I was in the Service, our concern was focused on what was going to happen in Germany. As it turned out, there was no armed confrontation between the United States and Russia, although there continued to be lot of uncertainty at the time. After I completed my active duty, I remained in the National Guard for another five years while I began working full-time as an IRS Revenue Agent.

When President Kennedy was assassinated in 1963, I was working for the IRS in Harvey, Illinois. It was shocking news that was difficult to absorb and understand, and I felt numb from his death. At first, we didn't know if the President had died, but within a half hour of the shooting we learned it was true. That November weekend, all of America stopped whatever it was doing and it became one of the most sobering times in American history. I adored Kennedy because I thought that he was such a gifted person, and I appreciated the fact that he was glib, funny, young, and dynamic. I listened to his debates with Richard Nixon on the radio in the fall of 1960 and was so excited because I knew that the first debate was going to be important. When I heard the debate on radio, I knew that Kennedy had gotten the better of Nixon, and was very excited about it. I was a Kennedy guy and wanted him to be elected, and his assassination took a long time to feel real. I remember walking around in a daze that weekend.

I had a similar reaction when Robert Kennedy was assassinated in June of 1968. I had wanted him to be president, although I didn't think that he had the experience or depth of his brother, Jack. Upon hearing the news on the radio the morning after the assassination, I thought that it was more than anybody could be expected to endure. Ironically, by that June, I had come to the conclusion that Bobby did have the ability and capacity to lead the country.

One of the most vivid memories I have of that time was April 4, 1968 when Martin Luther King was assassinated. Although it had been five years since the JFK assassination, it seemed close in time and had a similar effect on the quality of people's lives. I was just overwhelmed by the event with sadness and grief and wondered what was happening in our country and the way that people resolved differences by killing our leaders. I was young and in law school and quite interested in politics and the workings of society and government. I knew that when I came home from law school that night I wouldn't have anyone to talk to about the assassination to release my emotions. Some mutual friends had given me the phone number of a woman who was also unattached, and that night I decided to call her even though we hadn't met.

I poured out my soul to her and even had the nerve to ask her if she would be willing to move to an island in Greece with me. I didn't even ask her for a date during that call. She said no to the move to Greece, but she had been similarly affected by the King assassination. We agreed to go out that weekend and went to a show downtown even though the city was erupting and we were somewhat concerned about our safety. Most people were staying home and not going out for any reason. As it turned out, we had a pleasant evening, saw the movie "The Graduate," and hit it off as we discussed our mutual despair over the state of the country. Happily, we ended up marrying six months later in September 1968.

When the Democratic convention happened in August that year, I managed to get some tickets to attend it with my wife to-be. Those were the days of rioting in Chicago, the country and city seemed to be up for grabs, and there was chaos everywhere. However, in the middle of all that, the political process fascinated me. I was told that I could go to the convention and sit in a certain section, but had to attend with representatives of the mayor's 11th Ward, even though I didn't live there. I wasn't politically active just interested. My wife and I went to someplace in the 11th Ward, around 35th and Halsted. They had buses there for the 11th Ward people because the galleries were "packed" to provide support for Mayor Daley, and we were part of the "packing."

We got in the bus, and they drove us to the Amphitheater which wasn't too far away. There wasn't a lot of room for spectators because of all the delegates, but we had a section where we were supposed to sit. Of course, at that point, Vice President Hubert Humphrey was going to get the nomination and I think that we also heard Senator Edmund Muskie, Humphrey's vice presidential choice, speak to the convention. He was very good, but although we didn't hear Humphrey speak, the Democratic Party showed a tribute to Bobby Kennedy.

In general, I was aware of what was going on at the Hilton and the problems happening in the city. The whole thing was upsetting, but I don't know if I particularly took sides. If I did, I probably favored the police because of all these long-haired people who had come to Chicago to mess up my city. Yet, I was deeply opposed to the Vietnam War, and I knew that the protesters had a cause. People had a right to speak, but some went beyond the bounds of free speech, and Chicago was probably "spoiling for a fight" anyway. The mayor certainly was, and the country was split. It was his city and he wasn't going to tolerate any interference, especially with the convention happening here and it was going to be his big "plum." He had everything at stake, he was a determined man, he had a strong mind set, and there wasn't much "give" in him.

The year of 1969 was eventful for me because I graduated from law school, passed the Bar, left the IRS, got a new job with a small law firm, and our first son was born. I wanted to get into a courtroom and see if I could be a trial lawyer since doing tax work for people wasn't bringing me an enormous amount of satisfaction. I applied to the U.S. Attorney's Office where Tom Foran was the U.S. Attorney. Tom was on his way out because the Republicans had won the 1968 election, but he was in the middle of trying the "Conspiracy Seven" case. I had a very brief interview with his first assistant, Jack Schmetterer, and he told me that they didn't have the power to hire since after the trial was over they were going to be leaving office. He promised to pass my application on to the successors, and, as it turned out, I did join the U.S. Attorney's Office in 1971 as an Assistant United States Attorney. I remained there from '71 to '77, and when, Jim Thompson, who had been the U.S. Attorney for Northern Illinois and whom I had served under for about four years, became governor, he offered and I accepted a position in state government as chairman of the Illinois Commerce Commission. I left that in early '79 after Thompson won his re-election and went into private practice for two years. In late 1980, I was selected to the Federal bench when Jimmy Carter appointed me at the recommendation of Senator Adlai Stevenson, with the support of Senator Chuck Percy.

Jeffrey and 71st, 1969
(Courtesy of CTA)

Ashland and 79th
(Courtesy of CTA)

Alderman Edward M. Burke

I grew up on the city's Southwest Side and attended DePaul University from 1961 to 1965. I was always involved in politics through my father, Alderman Joseph Burke (14th Ward).
Thus, the political world was like the family business. Those late '50s and early '60s were a time when we still had a neighborhood/parish focus in Chicago.

Since I went to college in the city, I was a commuter college student, and because I stayed in the city, much of my focus in those days was studying for my college classes.

Racial changes in the neighborhoods and parishes were starting on the South Side in the early 1960s. Our neighborhood/parish was Visitation with boundaries of 52nd Street on the north, 59th Street on the south, the Pennsylvania Railroad tracks on the east, and Loomis Avenue on the west, and, in those days, it was one of the largest Catholic parishes in America. Racial changes led to panic selling among the area residents, and it became a major tragedy because the changes seemed to happen overnight. The families who owned those homes had virtually their entire net worth tied up in that little 25-foot piece of real estate, and they envisioned losing the whole value of their major asset. Essentially, these people were pushed to get out, and nobody wanted to be the last one on board a "sinking ship."

My family didn't move out. We stayed in our home at 5240 S. Sangamon Street until 1970, and by then, south of Garfield Boulevard had become primarily African American. The area north of the boulevard was also beginning to change, and all of our neighbors were moving southwest; most making the big leap to Evergreen Park and Oak Lawn, and some even as far as Orland Park. There are many people living in the Southwest suburbs today who grew up in Visitation parish. Looking back, I thought all the changes of the early 1960s were profoundly sad. When you think about growing up in an area where you knew everybody on the block, belonged to the church where you made your First Communion and Confirmation and went to grammar school at the parish school, it was a tragedy to see it all unravel in a few years. Several generations of people lived within blocks of one another, creating a little village. The changes which began before 1965 just speeded up as the years went on.

In the 1960s, there had been no real downtown development for 20+ years, and the last big skyscraper was built before World War II. The first major building after that was the Prudential Building on Randolph and Michigan. Randolph Street, west of State Street, was pretty seedy, including the Greyhound Bus Terminal and the movie palaces that began showing black exploitation movies. Those deteriorating conditions kept some people from coming into certain parts of the Loop. The Daley Center had not been built, but the First National Bank building went up where the Morrison Hotel had stood. I think that a lot of the construction that began to occur was based on the business community's confidence in Mayor Richard J. Daley. Of course, in the early '60s, he was only in his second term of office since he had first been elected in 1955. I remember how contentious it was when the mayor decided to build the new campus of the University of Illinois-Chicago that resulted in the tearing down of whole sections of the Italian neighborhood around Taylor Street, southwest of the Loop.

As for my direct involvement in politics, I would do precinct work and poll work for my father during his election campaigns for alderman. I became more intimately involved when my father became ill in January of 1968. I became a policeman in 1965 and went through the West Side riots as well as the unrest that took place during the 1968 Democratic Convention. It was a very unusual time, not only in Chicago, but all across the country. As a policeman, I was on duty at the International Amphitheater where it was much quieter than in Grant Park or in front of the Hilton Hotel where the violence occurred.

I believe that one of the reasons the phrase "police riot" was applied to what happened during the convention in Chicago was due to a lack of communication. Today, everyone automatically assumes that there is two-way radio communication immediately available to all police officers because they carry a radio on their belt and have a microphone that's clipped to their jacket or shirt. But, back in 1968, if the policeman was out of the squad car, he had no radio and no communication with supervisors. The only portable radio in those days was a big backpack radio that was carried by a patrolman who accompanied the First Deputy at incidents occurring on the street. There was no handheld radio in 1968, and police had to use call boxes to report incidents. When I patrolled my first beat as a foot patrolman, I covered the area from Michigan Avenue to Clark Street on both sides of Van Buren, and I didn't have a radio for use in communications with my district police station. You made a pull in the call box and then hoped that somebody at the station would answer the call. If you were in trouble, you were on your own, and you just hoped that some citizen would call the police. We walked one-man beats in those days and had no partners with us. Although I was covering a kind of seedy area, it was a relatively quiet assignment for me. Once in a while, one of the plainclothes cars would stop and pick me up to take me for a cup of coffee.

At the end of 1968, I left the police force. However, in the fall of 1965, I had been assigned to the State's Attorney's Office as an investigator and spent most of my time on the West Side at 26th and California. Dan Ward was State's Attorney at that time, and I was originally assigned to his office. Ward later became an Illinois Supreme Court Justice and was replaced as State's Attorney by John Stamos, Ward's first assistant. In 1968, Stamos was dumped by the slate makers and replaced with Edward V. Hanrahan.

I was elected Ward Committeeman following my father's death in 1968, and the aldermanic seat remained vacant until a special election in 1969. The procedure was different then since the mayor did not appoint a successor. The first time I ran for the office of Alderman of the 14th Ward, I was elected, even though I was only 24 years old, and that was 38 years ago.

Wentworth and Cermak, 1961
(Courtesy of CTA)

Stony Island and 63rd, 1962
(Courtesy of CTA)

St. Basil's Bus, 1961
(Courtesy of CTA)

Trudy Bers

I was born in 1942 and grew up in Elgin, Illinois. Since my father was a psychiatrist on the staff of the Elgin State Hospital, that became my neighborhood. After going to grammar school and high school in Elgin, in 1960, it was time for me to go to college. I chose the University of Illinois at Champaign-Urbana, and as soon as I began there I was certain I had come to the right place. As I remember it, I was the only person I knew who was never homesick in four years of college. Many of my friends used to call home crying to their parents about how lonely they were, but I didn't understand their reaction.

was at the University of Illinois from 1960 until 1964, and during those four years, I was in the Alpha Epsilon Phi sorority, president of Pan-Hellenic, and involved in student government, as well as being a good student. At that time, sorority life was highly regulated; we had hours and rules about social and dating behavior. There was also a myth that sorority girls had to wear skirts to class. We were told we could not wear slacks on campus unless the Dean of Women called to say it was so cold that we were allowed to wear slacks. I found out later that there was no such rule, but for four years, we wore skirts no matter how cold it was. We were pampered, and we sometimes took cabs to class when it was really cold or rainy.

I began with a major in journalism when I got to the university. I went to see an advisor, and he told me that everybody who majored in journalism needed to take four Division of General Studies classes. I didn't want to do that, so I determined that I would be classified as "undecided" on a major. I remember meeting some people whom I thought were "neat" and found out they took a lot of classes in political science in Lincoln Hall. After taking some classes in that subject, I realized that I could do well in political science, and that was how it became not only my major but also the later focus of my doctorate. On November 22, 1963, I was at Gregg Hall just walking down the hall when somebody said that Kennedy was shot. I saw Roger Ebert, whom I knew, and he told me this was true. I remember staying on campus that weekend and watching all of the events on television at the sorority house.

I graduated from the University of Illinois in 1964, went to Columbia University in New York for my master's, and got married in the summer of 1965. We lived in an apartment in Rogers Park on Pratt between Clark and Ashland. The rent was $145 a month, and we bought a horrible gold and speckled rug for $25 from the people who lived there before us. We had a one-bedroom apartment in a three-story, courtyard building. The thing that made it tolerable was the apartment had a big eat-in kitchen, along with one bathroom, one bedroom, and parking spaces in the rear of the building.

Back in Chicago, I got a job through an employment agency, but it was not a good fit for my interests or skills, so I stayed one month. The position was at a publishing company where I was to help write teachers' guides for elementary school text books. I had finished all the coursework for my master's degree and was working on the M.A. Thesis. Since we had a good friend who worked for the Chicago's War on Poverty, he got me an interview and I was hired. Officially, I worked for the city of Chicago. The job was at 1 N. Wacker across from the Lyric Opera House, and I found myself in a job, along with other 23-year-olds, who knew nothing about fighting the War on Poverty. The key lesson I learned while working in that bureaucracy was to understand the sources of the money for the program because it gave me practical insights into the operation of government. That was absolutely a critical lesson: always know the source of the funds.

There was a certain naiveté about poverty since there was a basic unawareness that people's economic and social problems were truly multi-faceted. Towards the end of my stay there, I worked on a project where we were going to have a work-training program and we developed a very elaborate schedule of what was going to happen. It didn't occur to anybody that people couldn't get to the agency on time because they didn't have the skills to set alarm clocks to wake up to get to the bus to get to where they were supposed to be.

My memory is that the city and the downtown were still vibrant with life in the mid-to late-'60s, at least during weekdays. We didn't tend to stay downtown in the evenings or the weekends. I think that the Loop was already fading in popularity as it began clearing out in the evenings. I remember walking to Marshall Field's at lunchtime a lot because I had worked at Field's book department in the summer between undergraduate and graduate school. I had been employed in the research department, which meant taking special orders. They gave me a shopping cart, and I wheeled it around filling orders for those who had phoned in their requests. And, if I had a question, I used to go in the back and call Kroch's and Brentano's and pretend to be a customer.

As for our social life in those years, my husband, Howard, and I would visit friends at their apartments because nobody had a house. Rogers Park still had a large Jewish population in those years, although the neighborhood was in transition. Congregation B'Nai Zion, a large synagogue, was located two blocks east of our apartment. There was no expectation among our friends that anyone would remain in the city, but, instead, that they would soon move out to the suburbs. At that time, Howard was working in the financial aid office at UIC, and we had a car that his parents gave us for a wedding gift. The Vietnam War was at its height, and we were terrified that he was going to be drafted. We heard that there was an opening in the National Guard at the Madison Street Armory. Without giving it a lot of

consideration, he immediately signed up. Then he had to go to basic training in New Jersey, in the winter of 1967. The big blizzard hit in late January 1967. At that time, I would stay in the city during the week, and on weekends, take the train from downtown out to Elgin where my parents lived because I didn't want to stay home alone.

I woke up the morning of the storm, went outside to wait for the bus to take me to the "L," and, not too soon, realized that nothing was moving on the streets. There were no tire tracks on this white, expansive snow that covered Pratt Boulevard, and no one walking anywhere. But, since I thought that I should get downtown to my job, I walked four or five blocks to the "L" at Morse Avenue and boarded the train to go downtown so that I could get to my office. I walked to the office in the snow and got there about two hours late. I was one of only a few people who showed up that day, and it finally occurred to me that we were in the middle of a massive snowstorm. I had left our car parked in front of the apartment on Pratt, and it remained there for two months until we could dig it out.

When the National Guard was called up during the 1967 riots, I drove Howard down to Lake Shore Drive so he could take a bus to the Armory. He needed some things from home later in the week, so I took the Madison Street bus to the Armory, but was smart enough to ask a colleague at work to ride with me for protection. In August of 1967, we left Chicago to go back downstate again to attend graduate school to begin Ph.D. programs at the University of Illinois. Howard was reassigned to the Champaign National Guard unit. During the late '60s, he was called up several times because of all the political and social turmoil in the country.

We returned to Chicago in 1970 because Howard had taken a job at the University of Illinois-Chicago, while I got a job at the new Oakton Community College. I didn't want to come back to Chicago, but that was where the jobs were. That summer, Howard had to attend his last summer camp in the National Guard. I had heard that there was a house for rent in Park Ridge, which we thought might be nice since we didn't want to live on the North Shore. We didn't know anything about Park Ridge, but I came to see the house with my mother and our daughter, Jenny. I drove down the street and pulled up in front of the house, went up and knocked on the door, and said that I wanted to rent it, although I had never seen the inside of the place. We lived in that house for 2 1/2 years, and then decided to stay in Park Ridge and buy a home there.

Leonard Amari

I was born in June 1942, and by the time I was in grammar school, we were living in an apartment in a 12-flat in the DePaul neighborhood at 2231 N. Bissell. It was a lower middle-class neighborhood with a wide variety of ethnic groups, including German, Italian, and Irish immigrants. I attended St. Vincent DePaul Elementary School at Webster and Kenmore until about 7th grade, and then went to Our Lady of Lourdes parish in the Fighting 47th Ward. We moved from a primarily immigrant neighborhood to an established, Irish neighborhood with a strong parish structure.

During Mayor Richard J. Daley's first administration, from 1955 to 1959, things were pretty "open" in Chicago, and my father, who was a bookie at the time, made a lot of money during those four years—the only four years of his life he ever made money. When the mayor won his second term, everything shut down, and in 1964, bookmaking became a felony. It meant my father had to stop being a minor, "underworld" person, and, instead, he began tending bar. His financial situation really impacted my life. During the mid- to late-50s, when I was in high school, we moved from our apartment into our first home located in Ravenswood Manor at 2903 W. Giddings. At that point, my father was struggling financially and that led to us moving to Morton Grove at 7800 Linder, at Oakton, in a smaller house. I was away at college during those years, so I really didn't have the benefit or the experience of living in the suburbs, especially after having been a city kid my entire life.

I attended Northern Illinois University in DeKalb from 1960 to 1964, and it was a new experience because I met kids from different ethnic and racial backgrounds, some from small towns across Illinois. College was like living in a cocoon, and I felt protected from many of the events sweeping American. I also had to scrape by financially by living off-campus in unapproved housing. I had no money because my father was broke again, and it meant that I got jobs like delivering pizzas at night and working construction during the summer. Overall, the 1960s were a growth period for me socially, economically, and politically because when I grew up in the Lathrop Homes in Chicago there were no minorities, including African Americans or Hispanics living in the Near North neighborhood.

During the '60s, I think we spent most of our time and energy avoiding the draft without necessarily doing something illegal. Even today, in hindsight, people are almost completely against what our country did in Vietnam. I received deferments because I was in college, and an entire culture developed to help us avoid the draft. These included law firms specializing in getting draft deferments for guys my age. However, if you received an academic deferment, your eligibility went from age 26 to age 35. People avoided the draft for a wide variety of personal reasons, not the least being that kids were dying in Southeast Asia in large numbers.

Drugs became popular later in the '60s. When I was in college at Northern, I don't remember kids talking about taking drugs and it just wasn't part of the culture at my university. However, by the mid- to late-'60s drugs like marijuana, cocaine, and LSD became popular. I didn't get exposed to drugs until '67 or '68, and then, all of a sudden everybody was getting high. I'm not just talking about kids from tough neighborhoods, but also those from the North Shore and Chicago's Near North Side. The people in my social circle became lawyers, professional people, and teachers, but that didn't preclude them experimenting with drugs. However, it rarely became a permanent part of their lives.

When I went to law school, I lived in Morton Grove and took the Skokie Swift downtown to John Marshall Law School. But, I was isolated during those years from what was going on in the city. One of the changes in professional schools during the '60s was that all of sudden, women were starting to go to law school. In 1965-66, when I was a freshman at John Marshall, we had two women in my class and maybe three or four blacks. It was an era of discovery for me and my generation. I came from an Italian house where women stayed "barefoot and pregnant" in the kitchen.

At law school then, as now, I was consumed by studying. I watched the most significant parts of the 1960s on television as an observer, and I had final exams when there were the demonstrations in front of the Conrad Hilton Hotel in 1968. I did do some protesting and discovered liberalism. The '60s were an era of freedom and discovery, although most kids of my generation were observers rather than active participants in the political and social changes.

I opened up my own law practice on LaSalle Street at Adams and LaSalle, right out of law school. In those days, there weren't a lot of opportunities for kids who weren't part of the legal network and weren't children of lawyers. This was especially true if you went to John Marshall Law School because it was called the "last ditch" law school. The large firms didn't interview John Marshall, Kent, or DePaul kids in those days, and that fact limited my opportunity to practice law with a major firm. I was the first one to graduate from law school in my family, and that became a double-edged sword. For one thing, my family didn't have any connections to get me into the professional mainstream. On the other hand, I had a plethora of clients because I was the only lawyer that anybody ever knew. I opened up my own law practice right away and took in any case that became available to me. In the late '60s, there were only about 21,000 lawyers in the state of Illinois, so it was easy to become a lawyer. In the '60s, there was such civility among lawyers, but, today, everybody is your adversary.

The key element of the '60s was a strong sense of idealism that had been initiated with the presidency of John F. Kennedy and the era of Camelot. There was much optimism and a thirst for opportunity, but much of that was lost when Kennedy was assassinated.

U.S. Representative Jan Schakowsky

One of the best summers of my life was the summer of 1961 when I took eight hours of French at Mundelein College. I was there most of the day because it was a pretty intensive course, and most of the other students were nuns. This Jewish girl loved going to Mundelein, appreciating its calm and supportive atmosphere, walking into the building and saying, "Good morning, Sister. Good morning, Sister. Good Morning, Sister." I had this marvelous teacher, and I can still say the Lord's Prayer in French.

It was a wonderful summer. Then I went to the University of Michigan for a year and a half, and the university refused to give me credit for those eight hours of French. But, when I transferred back to the University of Illinois, I found myself with eight extra hours from my Mundelein summer. I went to Illinois for another year and a half and graduated. I rushed right through by taking a heavy load of courses, including a summer public speaking course at Roosevelt University in Chicago in which I did very poorly. So, I completed my college education by the time I was 20, and got married in February 1965.

My first job was to teach at Nettlehorst School at Broadway and Belmont. For a couple of years, I taught first grade, as my mother did, and, during the summer, I was a teacher in one of the first Head Start programs. We actually canvassed the neighborhood looking for kids for the program and went door-to-door to recruit our own students.

When I was first married, we lived west of St. Scholastica High School on Oakley in West Rogers Park, near where I had grown up. I stopped teaching when my son was born in July 1967, and we moved out to the Northwest suburbs for a few years. My daughter was born in 1968, and I stayed home with the kids. My participation in the culture of the '60s consisted of dressing the part with long straight hair and occasional hippy clothing, and flashing peace signs. But, essentially I watched the Vietnam War and the 1998 Democratic Convention in Chicago on television, being supportive but not actively involved in the politics of the time.

My manifestation of the '60s activism began in 1969 when I became part of and a leader of a small group that was fighting to get freshness dates on food packaging. We were authentic suburban polyester-wearing housewives, and our group, all six of us, created what we ambitiously called National Consumers United. It was a time when Ralph Nader was first getting started, and he took a little bit of an interest in what we were doing. We took on the food industry, and although we knew little about that industry, about organizing or public relations, what we lacked in expertise we made up in enthusiasm and determination. At that point, my great aunt, who was an immigrant from Russia, was living with me and helping to take care of the children, yet often I would take the kids with me to our store inspections where we would check for outdated food. We cracked thousands of food codes, and our "high-tech" method was to get the stock boys to tell us how they knew to put the old stuff in the front of the shelves. They'd say, "Oh, well, you have to add the outer two numbers and the inner two numbers and get the month and the day and that's how we know." We found food that was days, weeks, months, and even years beyond the date the manufacturer or retailer said it should be sold. Baby food and infant formula were among the worst offenders. We published an NCU (National Consumers United) Code Book, and sold 25,000 of them from our recreation rooms.

I first connected with this group of crusading housewives at my local National Tea Company Store. There was a heated discussion going on in the back of the store, and when I went back there discovered a woman arguing with the butcher. He was yelling at her that, "As far as you are concerned, that code means 'jingle bells' and if you ask me any more questions I am going to throw you out on your fanny, you geek!" I thought, "Wow, this is exciting." Earlier, the week before, I had asked the butcher the age of a particular cut of meat and he refused to tell me. So, I thought, "I'm going to get involved in this issue." We were a small group that declared ourselves to be a national organization. Of course, we won.

We had a great time, and we would call each other in the morning and say, "Meet me at the National when the kids get up from their nap." It was kind of wild and wooly, because National Tea Company hired lawyers from Kirkland and Ellis to look into the lives of a couple of the women in our group. The lawyers sought to intimidate their husbands by asking if they knew what their wives were doing, called the head of Baxter where one of the women's husband worked, and threatened to arrest us.

Our response was that we had to get our kids home for their naps, so, no thank you, we can't get arrested at this time and we would leave. We became shareholders and attended their shareholder meetings. One took place at Edens Plaza, and we nominated Mike Royko to the board of National. Many of those present asked for their proxies back because they wanted to vote for him. Then, the president of National got up and said, "I don't know who you women are. Are you Communists or spies from Jewel?" It was on national television. Two days later, he died from a heart attack and I've always felt a little guilty.

When I was living in the northwest suburbs, I played Mah Jongg once a week and enjoyed it and we had a big yard for the children, but much of the time I felt disconnected living out there after growing up in the city. I also felt disoriented because those suburbs seemed to consist of cul-de-sacs and no street corners. I was used to telling people to meet me at the corner of Touhy and California or Howard and Western. I was a "fish out of water," and we stayed there until we were able to afford a move back. It was just too expensive to buy a house near Chicago, so we kept looking further and further northwest to find a house we could afford. But, much of what was familiar living in the city, including the corner drugstore or deli, was not there. While living there, we had to drive some

distance to the grocery store and for other shopping, and there was certainly no public transportation. Most of the women were home with their kids, and it was a very atomizing and somewhat alienating experience for me. I felt much more a sense of community in Chicago than I ever did in the suburbs, and, also, there weren't any institutions that would bind people together. It was not nearly as comfortable as being back in the city close to my family. When my son was ready for kindergarten, we came back to Evanston and found a house there.

During high school, the Civil Rights movement had begun and I had become somewhat involved in racial issues, though Sullivan High School was nearly 100% white and mostly Jewish as I am. Our next door neighbors at our summer cottage in Michigan City had friends who had African American twins my age that lived in South Shore. We would get together occasionally back home, and I went to Woodlawn once a week to tutor a young student. I remember going downtown to a meeting about sit-ins at Walgreens, and my mother didn't want me to go. Then, at the Jewish Community Center on Touhy, some of the Freedom Riders visited and talked to us about the racial issues. I was deeply moved by them. Also, while I was in high school, there was a group called STEPS (Start To End Personal Prejudice) that I joined, but we were focusing on the relationships between Jews and Christians.

I have wondered about the roots of my passions for social justice. My parents weren't very involved, and I didn't come from a political family. I do remember being invited to go to SDS and SNCC meetings while I was at the University of Michigan, but I really didn't get very involved. Actually, one of the things that I was involved in when I was living in the suburbs in 1969 was the Grape Boycott and Cesar Chavez. I participated on some picket lines and in the very first Women's Equality Day on August 26, 1969. But, it was really the consumer movement and our freshness dating campaign that eventually brought me into politics.

When I returned to Evanston, I became involved in electoral politics, participating a bit in the campaign of Congressman Abner Mikva, and getting really active starting in 1980, trying to re-elect President Jimmy Carter. Activism and politics gave new meaning to my life. I grew up in a world of women in transition. I was a young mother with two small children, inspired by the modern women's movement that was encouraging young women like me to step out and address issues of inequality and justice. My embrace of community organizing, along the style of the father of community organizing, Chicagoan Saul Alinsky, marked the beginning of my long journey that carried me eventually to the U.S. House of Representatives.

Jim O'Connor

In the summer of 1960, I had just finished Harvard Business School and begun a three-year tour of active duty with the Air Force in Washington, D.C. At that time, John F. Kennedy was running for president. He had enormous charisma. In the early part of the '60s, other than the Cuban Missile Crisis in October 1962, it was kind of a continuation of the 1950s where young people were viewed as the "Silent Generation." There was a lot of respect for the military and for authority. I believe that President Kennedy's assassination, the escalation of the war in Vietnam, and the close attention to civil rights issues had a major impact on the disruption of a lot of the traditional lines of authority.

When I was growing up, my generation really knew very little about drugs, and I never knew a person at my high school or college who ever used them. The main vices that people my age in the '50s had were cigarettes and beer. With the skyrocketing rise in crime statistics there was a growing acceptance of the idea of defying authority. It was also the beginning of the so-called "me too" generation, and the rise of the individual. The traditional institutions were faced with a tremendous amount of pressure in the '60s, especially universities, where sit-ins were occurring with great regularity.

I began my rather traditional career in 1963 as a trainee at Commonwealth Edison. Everything in my life seemed to be pretty much in order and I had no great concerns, at that point, beyond raising a young family and just trying to make a living. We had moved to Evanston by then, and, after growing up on Chicago's Southwest Side, there were two things that caused us to go north. First, my wife, Ellen, had been raised in the Boston area and loved being near water since she grown up close to the ocean. Initially, we lived on the southeast side of Evanston, right off of Sheridan Road in two different second floor walk-ups, relatively small apartments. And, second, there were many young families raising children in our Evanston neighborhood during those years. My wife loved walking 100 yards to take the children to the beach, and for my purposes, our apartment in Evanston was within a 20-25 minute drive of my job in downtown Chicago. Since my work hours were such that I was seldom home in time for dinner, my priority was to have Ellen in a place where she felt comfortable and happy.

In April 1968, the King assassination had a great impact on the city. I was assigned to be part of Commonwealth Edison operations on the city's West Side in the wake of the riots. I was dispatched to coordinate Edison's activities with the police and the fire departments. It was interesting because each department had different objectives: the police department wanted us to restore service as quickly as possible to get people back in their homes; the fire department wanted us to be ultra-conservative in the way we approached things to make certain that there was no further danger that was presented to the firemen who were working in that area. They wanted us to keep large parts of the affected neighborhoods out of service while they made certain that the cleanup work was completed. There was some damage to Commonwealth Edison facilities, including the poles, but the main concern for the West Side was the homes that were burning and the businesses that were being shut down or looted. There was quite a wide swath of destruction occurring on Madison Street.

My role was to coordinate many of the services between the city government and our company. I was still relatively new to the company, and I was working for Morgan Murphy, who was the chairman of the executive committee of Commonwealth Edison at the time, and whose son later became a U.S. Congressman. That was a real learning experience for me, and throughout the '60s, I became aware that Mayor Richard J. Daley was in charge of the city. He was extremely strong and unbelievably aware of the details of almost everything happening in the city. I had more than a few occasions when I communicated with his office, and sometimes directly with him. I was very impressed by the people he had placed in key positions including Corporation Counsel, Ray Simon, head of Streets and Sanitation, Jim McDonough, and Director of Planning, Lew Hill. They were all smart, hard-working people who worked well as a team.

The mayor was a great listener and had a capacity to absorb, retain, and remember even the smallest details. He had a sense of what was needed to get things done and to get them done quickly. He was impatient. The mayor had an unbelievable level of energy, and I never saw him when he didn't look alert. He was always on his toes, always involved and interested, and, seemingly committed to whatever was being discussed. Most people believed that his agenda was both to build Chicago and to urge legislation at the federal level that would help urban America. Of course, he still carried the reputation that he had delivered the presidency for John F. Kennedy, and even when Johnson became president, Daley influenced their legislative agendas.

Mayor Daley retained enormous respect in Washington, and everybody felt that he could pick up the phone at any minute and get the president on the line, and I think that was probably true. People also thought of him as a neighborhood person. He and his family lived in the same house on Lowe Street in Bridgeport all those years. The business community had great confidence in Daley, believing that it was his goal to help the city grow. He had a way of rallying business people to be supportive of things that were important to the city.

Changes were happening so fast during the '60s, and when the Vietnam War really expanded after 1965, a lot of people had mixed emotions about the war and what was going on, and it was a difficult political period.

During the '60s, Chicago went through a major building boom, including the construction of Lake Point Tower, a 70-story building on Lake Michigan, and the John Hancock Building on Michigan Avenue. New highways continued to be constructed, including the Dan Ryan Expressway and the Congress Expressway, which later became known as the Eisenhower Expressway. However, when the city encouraged the development of a new campus for the University of Illinois-Chicago, it led to the displacement of families on the Near West Side. Families in this neighborhood had lived there for generations, and they were justifiably upset. But, I do think that if you apply the standard of the greatest good for the greatest number, that standard was met with the construction of UIC.

As for the displacement of families to build the highways, if you try to imagine what Chicago would be without the arteries that we have coming into the city, we couldn't survive as a major business or transportation center.

Commonwealth Edison was very much into nuclear energy at that time. We had built and started up the first privately financed, large scale, nuclear plant in the country down in Morris, Illinois back in the early 1960s. And, during the '60s, we announced the construction of a number of other new sites, and started the construction of those sites up at Zion, Illinois, out at Quad Cities off the Mississippi River, and two more units down near Morris, Illinois at Dresden. We had six large nuclear units that were under construction during that period, and if we hadn't introduced nuclear energy plants, we would today be dependent on coal-based electricity. In the '60s, coal was the enemy, and I can recall rallies in the Loop against pollution and in favor of cutting down on the dust in the air. Power plants were named as the principal culprit.

In terms of my business career, and as a relatively new kid on the block in the business community, I had tremendous bosses at Commonwealth Edison, including Tom Ayers, Morgan Murphy, and Harris Ward, who was the chairman for most of the '60s. I could not have asked for better people to work for. Mentoring was a very important part of a business leaders' role. Throughout my life, I was blessed because there was always someone to help me. I think that reaching out and helping is the greatest legacy that you can leave to people, and I had three mentors who were just terrific in letting me be a part of the scene at Commonwealth Edison.

The '60s were an exciting time. We were transitioning from the orderly period of the 1950s into a frenetic society faced with a wide array of differing and often opposing agendas. One could argue that the 1960s had the most dramatic changes taking place of any decade in the latter half of the twentieth century.

Evanston/Linden Yards, c. 1965 (Courtesy of CTA)

Bruce Wolf

In 1958, we had moved to Skokie when I was five years old after first growing up on the West Side of Chicago, then on the South Side at 8430 S. Kenton, in the Scottsdale neighborhood. Skokie really didn't feel different from Scottsdale except that our house was bigger. We moved out of the West Side because of the changing neighborhood, the turnover, and the "white flight" phenomenon, but we first moved south instead of north. Since I was so young, my recollections of the West Side were all pleasant. My father owned several hardware stores in that part of Chicago, and, later on, owned one at Fullerton and Clark for 30 years.

The difference between the South Side and Skokie was clearly that Skokie seemed very Jewish. As I remember it, we lived next door to the Iran-Hebrew Congregation on Main Street and East Prairie. I heard a story that may have been apocryphal involving a Jewish dentist who wanted to build a big home on that corner despite the fact that the neighbors across the street opposed it. There was an overtone of anti-Semitism involved in the disagreement, so the dentist responded by turning over the land to the Iran-Hebrew Congregation, an Orthodox temple, and really gave the neighbors the "shaft." We lived next to that temple, and I was bar mitzvahed there when I was 13 years old.

I went to elementary schools in District 73 1/2 and then to Oakview Junior High at East Prairie Road and Oakton. I remember playing Whiffle ball and other sports in the summers. We would leave the house at 8:00 am and come home at 9:00 pm, and parents never asked what we had been doing or where we were for the day. The neighborhood was teeming with kids, and, for me, a long trek was to walk a block and a half. I went to Camp Hastings YMCA summer camp when I was 13 years old, but got in trouble there over the selection of my daily prayers. At Camp Hastings, you were required to say a pre-meal prayer and could pick any of eight Christian prayers or one Jewish prayer. There were a lot of Jewish kids going to that camp, and they would often select the Jewish prayer. You were also allowed to make up your own prayer. The prayer I made up was, "God bless this blessed food, and God forgive these cooks for they know not what they do." In response, the counselors wanted to punish me, even though they knew I was a very sarcastic kid. My parents had a great sense of humor, enjoyed a good laugh, and appreciated comedy like Mel Brooks' "Two Thousand Year-Old Man."

During the years when we grew up in Skokie, we would never walk to Old Orchard Shopping Center but would take the bus there just to play "hide and seek". Or, we would pretend that we were James Bond and go up and down the escalators in Marshall Field's and hide around the store and the shopping center. We would also walk to Main and Crawford where there were businesses like Musket and Henrikson Pharmacy, the Noshery Restaurant, and the Hobby Shop where I once stole a little police badge, but my mother made me bring it back.

I began going to Cubs games at Wrigley Field with friends when I was 12 or 13 years old. We would take the #97 bus to Howard Street and then the "L" to the Addison station. We would also go downtown until, at the age of 14, I was nearly mugged in the mid-'60s on the Chicago River bridge going toward Marina City. These kids hurt my friend, but I ran from them and ended up spending time bowling in Marina City. I don't think that the city was changing or that we had any bad luck, except for that day.

I was a big Blackhawks fan, and remember seeing Tex Evans of the Blackhawks jump over the boards with about three seconds left in a 1961 game against the Detroit Red Wings during the season they won the Stanley Cup. I thought, "Well, we won the Cup now and they probably won't win it again next year," and they haven't won it since. In 1961, we actually went to the Uptown, Nortown, or Granada Theaters to see the Stanley Cup playoffs on closed circuit television. To this day, I think those were the most exciting places I have ever seen sporting events, with 500 people in a crowded theater watching and listening to Lloyd Pettit describe end-to-end action. People actually got up to sing the National Anthem in a movie theater when everyone at the Chicago Stadium was asked to rise. That was a dream to actually be at the game even though we were watching it on closed circuit. Yet it was just like seeing the game in person.

When we got Blackhawks season tickets in 1968, I went to a Hawks game with my cousin on Thanksgiving Day and sat in the Club Circle, about 10 rows up. Jim Pappin of the Hawks hit a slap shot, I reached up to try to catch the deflected shot, and it almost took my thumb off. My hand was wet from the puck, it swelled up, and the puck ended up in another fan's hands a couple of rows higher. In 1969, Tony Esposito was a rookie goalie after the team had finished last the year before, and when Esposito began playing for the Blackhawks, they became terrific. The 1969-1970 season was the last time there were six teams in the division. The Hawks won the division that year, and it was the last time no Canadian team made the playoffs.

The White Sox were always my favorite baseball team. Yet, hockey remains my key spectator sport and Bobby Hull is my all-time favorite athlete. In the '60s, the White Sox challenged year-in and year-out and almost won the pennant in '64. I remember seeing Jim Landis play when my father took me and two of friends to a Sox game against the Baltimore Orioles in the early '60s. We had seats down the third base line in the left field upper deck, and Jim Landis hit a homerun in the bottom of the ninth to win the game 1-0. He was a great centerfielder, and what a thrill it was to see that game.

On April 4, 1968, when Martin Luther King was assassinated in Memphis, there was rioting across the country, including Chicago. We were at home with family friends who, like my father, had stores on the West Side. My dad called up the hardware store that night, but a looter picked up the phone, left it off the hook and we heard the looting going on in the store. My parents and friends had "gallows humor" and were laughing about what the looters were doing to the store. I am sure that my father had some insurance, but not too much. He had another store at Gladys and Crawford that also got looted and driven out of the business, and I was saddened by the event. His other store was called Harry's Hardware (not my father's name) on 16th and Springfield right next to Penn School. It was a one aisle store, and I remember being there on November 24, 1963, two days after Kennedy had been assassinated. We were watching the events on television when my father said, "I think that Oswald is going to get killed," and it actually happened about a half hour later.

It was obvious that the city was going through major changes, and, although I wasn't downtown during the '68 Convention, I remember watching ABC broadcaster Howard K. Smith moderating a debate between William F. Buckley and Gore Vidal. Vidal called Buckley a "post crypto-Nazi" and Buckley, with all of his verbal skills, could only respond to Vidal with, "I'm going to punch you in your God damned face!" I was 14 by the time of the convention and was attending Niles East High School. In 1967, we had moved to a bigger, split-level house at Kostner and Cleveland that cost about $34,000, but the basement still flooded.

It was dangerous times in terms of how the various changes on Chicago's West Side affected my family's livelihood. Since I was just a teenager, I didn't realize the full impact of the events on my family and our lives. I graduated from Niles East in 1971 before going to Northwestern University.

Skokie Swift at Dempster, 1965 (Courtesy of CTA)

Robert Feder

I was born on May 17, 1956 in Chicago, and we lived at 1247 W. Marquette Boulevard on the South Side. I have no recollection of living there, so all of my memories start in Skokie where we moved in August 1957, living on Central Park Avenue between Main and Dempster Streets. It was a typical Skokie suburban upbringing.

Most of the people who moved to Skokie in the '50s and '60s probably thought that they had died and gone to heaven since the suburb offered everything, including good schools, good parks, backyards, and, in many cases, garages. I also remember that Skokie had two claims including that it was by its own description, "The World's Largest Village." That was the motto on all the street signs as you entered Skokie. The claim was based on the fact that, with 60,000-70,000 residents, it had the largest population for a municipality that was under the village manager form of government. Somehow they believed that qualified them for being the world's largest village.

The second claim was that Skokie was a predominantly Jewish suburb. Ironically, in the late '70s, we learned that it wasn't the case and the suburb was never more than 40% Jewish. In actuality, Skokie was primarily Catholic and Protestant and the two groups made up 60% of the population. But, you never would have known it based upon growing up in Skokie.

My earliest memories of Skokie in the '60s include having a lot of freedom, being very safe, going out on endless summer days, and playing with friends in unsupervised and unorganized activities. We would do whatever we wanted and with whomever we wanted to play. I don't recall ever getting in trouble. It seemed like there were kids our age everywhere, and we were never lacking for people with whom we could play. I also had the sense that the community was very homogenous and assumed that all of my friends and neighbors had common experiences. Skokie was a very safe, idyllic place to live and grow up. Everything was geared to kids, and everything was about education, giving us the best and striving for excellence, and a premium was put on that. Even if we didn't appreciate it at the time, it was clear that the whole community was geared to raising and nurturing children to be successful.

I attended John Middleton School that had been named for the first president of District 73 1/2 School Board. The "half" is an interesting thing too, because it speaks to the "Baby Boom" and the expansion of the suburb. The schools were exploding so rapidly that they ran out of numbers and had to resort to halves to squeeze in additional school districts. It also speaks to the politics of the community and how significant it was to have extreme local control. Most other townships had consolidated elementary school districts, but Niles Township, which included Skokie, Lincolnwood, parts of Morton Grove, and Niles, had six different elementary school districts all feeding into one high school district.

From a management efficiency point of view, it was pretty wasteful because the amount of overhead was insane. Each school district had its own administration, which included a superintendent and a separate board of education. But, it gave the impression that you were so close that the superintendent, literally, could be on a first name basis with every family. Niles East was the high school for School District 73 1/2, and there were three Niles Township High Schools attended by kids from all of the various elementary schools. The opening of Niles North in the mid '60s, just west of Old Orchard Shopping Center, was a big deal. The building was air conditioned and had modern facilities. Niles West High School opened in 1958, and Niles East was the original high school, an art deco masterpiece that had been built as a WPA project in the late 1930s.

There weren't that many homes in Skokie that had concrete paved alleys. Those homes that did have alleys usually had them covered with gravel. We were lucky because we had an assessment among the neighbors on our block to pave our alley with concrete. It meant that we could play all different kinds of games and sports behind our houses, including baseball and kick ball. I assumed that everyone had an alley. It was only when I would venture out into exotic places like nearby Lincolnwood that once in a while would see that they had their garbage cans placed in front of their houses. I would wonder to myself, "Why are they putting their garbage cans in front? That doesn't look nice." But, it was because they didn't have an alley.

Traditional Judaism was at that time a phenomenon born in suburbia during the '50s. Essentially, it was Orthodox Judaism, except that men and women sat together at services and they used microphones on the Sabbath. My family kept kosher, celebrated the holidays, and was among the most observant in the neighborhood. We walked to our synagogue, Skokie Valley Traditional Synagogue, which was at Dempster and East Prairie. I was bar mitzvahed there, and so were my three older brothers, and we were all married by Rabbi Milton Kanter. The synagogue was very much the focus of our family and our lives.

I vividly recall going to Comiskey Park on August 20, 1965 to attend the Beatles' concert. I was 9 years old. My brother had won tickets that morning from a radio contest, and he invited me to go along. That was an incredible experience, and it was the one and only time I ever "felt" sound because the roar of the crowd was so deafening. I didn't realize that a sound could be so loud and so sustained that it cancelled itself out and I really heard none of the Beatles' songs. I could physically feel a wave pushing against me, and I've never felt anything like that before or since. There would be a single note, and that would be the last thing that you would hear while the rest of it was just one loud noise. It truly was about

being part of an experience and being there because it wasn't about hearing music.

When I was in elementary school, I was eager to be part of a bigger world. I found myself kind of bored through most of school, but I was fascinated by radio and television. I became enthralled at a very early age with the news media, especially Walter Cronkite, who became a focus of my life. He was my lifelong hero and my role model.

When JFK was killed, I was in 2nd grade and just seven years old but it was a defining moment for me. It was right after 1:00 pm that Friday afternoon, November 22, 1963, when our teacher came into the room and said that the president had been shot. The teacher was called out again, and the principal announced on the public address system that the president was dead and we were all sent home early. It left an indelible impression on me. And, somewhere in the back of my mind was another stream of thought, and it was, "What's happening on television?" And, there was Cronkite just barely holding it together but telling us what was going on.

I started at Niles East High School in 1970. The war in Vietnam and what was going on in the rest of the world had a tremendous impact. There was a feeling that manifested itself in a growing sense of empowerment among young people, and they would express it in different ways: fashion, music, and politics. It was clear that an attitude and mood was filtering down from older siblings to younger ones. On college campuses, it really was playing out and many guys were being drafted and dying in Vietnam. I think that the impact of those events filtered down through younger siblings, so that at the high school level, there was a growing radicalism. But, too often, in our high school, it wasn't really about life and death issues. Instead, the focus was placed on whether there should be an open campus and whether students should strike because they couldn't go out to lunch. In addition, some kids wanted to establish a smoking lounge and there were discussions about the impact of smoking marijuana and whether the drinking age should be lowered to 18 years old. While there was a different magnitude to the issues, we were aware that many things were changing and that we had the power to influence those changes.

The only thing that ever brought worldwide attention to Skokie didn't occur until 1977 and 1978 when the American Nazi Party threatened to march in the suburb. By that time I was a journalist working for the *Skokie Life,* a Lerner newspaper. Interestingly enough, it was because of Skokie's Jewish image and identity that caused it to become a worldwide controversy. It was the event which demonstrated that Skokie was never really a majority Jewish population, although the suburb had a very high proportion of Holocaust survivors living there.

Sandra Pesmen

When I graduated from the University of Illinois at Urbana in 1952 with a degree in journalism and mass communications, I landed a job with the World Book as a proofreader. Within three weeks, I got a call from Earl Bush about a job with his Radio and Community News Service. The office was located atop the IAM Temple across from City Hall. Earl hired young, inexperienced (and inexpensive) people like me to cover news at the City Hall, County Building, Board of Education, and Illinois Commerce Commission beat, as well as other stories that happened in the Loop. I earned $30 a week.

I would come back with my notes, type up stories, make 20 copies, and mail them to all the community papers that were his clients. The office was a tiny cubbyhole above the temple with a ticker tape and one desk. It was so filthy that when he interviewed me there for the job, I said, "I don't know if I can work in such a dirty place." His response was, "I keep it like this because there's no news in here. You've got to get your ass out on the street and find some."

One day, in July 1952, when I was still new to the job, I told Earl that my husband-to-be, Hal, and I were getting married and I needed time off to go to the County Building and get our wedding license. Earl said, "I'll take you over to see Dick Daley, the County Clerk. He's special buddy of mine." Clerk Daley chatted with Hal and me, congratulated us, and gave us our wedding license. As we left the building, Earl turned to us and said, "Dick Daley's going to be the next mayor of the city of Chicago, and I'm going to put him there." And, in 1955, that's exactly what happened. Earl Bush became Mayor Daley's campaign manager, and later, his press secretary. I left Earl a year later to work for Lerner's Chicago North Side Newspapers because reporters there belonged to the Chicago Newspaper Guild, and my salary was raised to $75 a week.

We moved from Chicago to Detroit in 1956. I had quit working when our daughter was born the year before and my husband, who worked as a salesman for Continental Can Company, was transferred there to become Midwest Vending Manager. Then, in 1963, Hal was promoted to District Manager in Chicago, and we returned home. We looked at houses in Skokie and Lincolnwood, which were considered the "hot new suburbs," but most were too expensive for us to buy. An old friend, Dick Rose, of Footlik-Rose Architects, told us about a subdivision of mid-sized homes he had recently designed in Northbrook, just off Pfingsten Road. Northbrook was a small suburb then, with only 10,000 residents. Dick said, "The model house is sitting alone on the lot because nobody wants to buy there. Everyone thinks it's the 'wrong side' of Northbrook."

We bought that model for $30,900 and still live there. The area west of Pfingsten Road boomed and our home recently was appraised for almost twenty times the original purchase price. The area was originally farmland, and the young daughter of one farmer rode her horse across the area behind our yard every afternoon. Several of the men living in our subdivision worked for IBM and Allstate, and, although they were happy to take promotions that kept them moving, we had missed our extended families and decided to never move away again.

During that decade, all of our lives focused on our children. We became far more involved in school and village activities than our parents had been. In addition to Little League and park district activities that were just beginning to develop, our children played baseball in unorganized games. Since we were among the first residents in our subdivision, there was lots of space, and we had an empty lot next to our house. One summer, our son and his pals used hand mowers to mow grass and weeds in that lot, and then ground up chalk sticks to draw baseball lines. They used pillows for bases and played on that "field of dreams" all summer. No one even thought about sending them to camp. The same boys also played unsupervised hockey on a duck pond located on the farm across Pfingsten Road in winter.

During the '60s, most married women did not work outside the home. They spent their time caring for their children and houses, and their leisure hours were spent shopping, or playing cards. Working as a reporter, I had never done those things. When we returned to Chicago seven years later, I went back to Lerner part time. I covered local police departments once a week and attended regular Northbrook, Glenview, Deerfield, and Niles village hall meetings. I also covered the local school boards and such groups as the League of Women Voters. On Thursday and Friday, the weekly deadline days, I went to the Lerner office on Howard Street in Rogers Park to turn in my stories and help write the Women's section.

Being a reporter was an important part of my identity, and I enjoyed maintaining it. But it didn't seem normal to my suburban neighbors in the 1960s. When I met new people at parties and we got around to what I did all day, they would look at me as if to say, "What's wrong with your husband that you have to work?" My husband and I decided to ignore that because it was their problem—not ours.

While covering those village board meetings in the 1960s, I heard members constantly discussing ways to expand parking facilities at the train commuter stations, so there would be "an extra lane for Mama to pick up Papa in the evening and drop him off in the morning." They called it the "Park and Kiss" lane, assuming only men would commute.

Then, in 1969, a colleague, Diane Monk, called to tell me she had suggested my name for a new job as family living features writer at the *Chicago Daily News*. When I was hired, I realized I would be driving to the "Park and Kiss" lane each morning myself. In those days, all the suburban train stations were filled with men going to and from work. I didn't socialize with them because they were my neighbors' husbands. Most wore three-piece suits, fedora hats, and Florsheim winged-tip shoes, and the place reeked of Old Spice. A decade later, when women started traveling downtown too, we added Tabu and Chanel to the air.

At that time, Northbrook operated a small shuttle bus to pick up commuters and take them to the station because the parking lot was inadequate. One day, when I climbed aboard, I was surprised to see another woman sitting there. Her name was Jean Fonner. She was the married mother of two young children and had just taken a job as administrative assistant to the managing partner of Lord Bissell & Brook law firm. We became, and remain, great friends. Together we gathered several other neighbors into a "train gang" that rode downtown together for more than 20 years. We had coffee in Union Station every morning before work, and those commuters often gave me excellent story ideas about their lives and views that found their way into *The Chicago Daily News* and later into *Crain's Chicago Business* where I worked after the *Daily News* folded.

As for safety and security in the suburbs, we didn't lock the doors and we let the kids ride alone on the trains to go downtown without any fearful thoughts. On school holidays, my children would ride their bikes to the train station, get on with their friends, ride the upper deck to Union Station, and then walk to the *Chicago Daily News*. They would ride up the elevator to my office, and I would give them money to go across the street to buy lunch at the IBM cafeteria. They'd come back, stroll up and down Michigan Avenue, visit Marshall Field's, and then return to get me at 4:00 pm to go home.

The sexual revolution erupted in the suburbs too. We were amazed when we heard of parties where people threw their house keys into a bowl and went home with people whose keys they picked up. We had friends in a nearby suburb that gave an annual Christmas party, and in the late '60s, their guests seemed to lose their minds. They started dancing, hugging, and kissing each other's mates. I think it happened because after sitting in their kitchens cooking, cleaning, and watching kids for so many years, the women suddenly discovered they were young and attractive enough to look at people of the opposite sex with lust, and suddenly they were being told they had permission to do so. I think *Playboy* had a huge impact on everyone's lives and behavior at that time, as did the pill that gave women who always feared an unwanted pregnancy their real first protection against it.

Sports: A D

of Champi

Near Cham

and a New

Basketba

ecade

ons,

pions

NBA

Team

Bill Jauss

During the 1960s I was active in sports as a writer for the *Chicago Daily News*. As a general assignment writer, I focused particularly on college sports. The '60s was the Golden Age of college sports in Chicago when Illinois went to the Rose Bowl and Loyola won the NCAA Championship in basketball as the first Division I school from the state to have done that, both happening in 1963. The Bears won the NFL Championship in December, 1963. Illinois' Big Ten title and the Bears NFL victory both had some relationship to the impact on Americans following the assassination of President John F. Kennedy on November 22, 1963.

My most vivid memories of those days were related to two events that concerned Dick Butkus, star football player at the University of Illinois. The president was assassinated on a Friday, and the NCAA and its various conferences couldn't decide whether to cancel football games scheduled for that weekend. As it turned out, the University of Oklahoma played because Bud Wilkinson, the Oklahoma coach, talked to Bobby Kennedy who said that Jack would have wanted them to play. Michigan State had a game scheduled with the University of Illinois in East Lansing that was for the Big Ten Championship, and, as of late Friday afternoon, they hadn't decided whether or not to play the game. Bill Reed was the Big Ten Commissioner at that time, and we were supposed to drive to East Lansing to cover the game. Reed told us, "You better go there because the game might be on."

We drove to Michigan that evening, stayed overnight in Kalamazoo, and the next day, we pulled into the stadium in East Lansing at the same time the University of Illinois team was arriving. As it turned out, overnight, Governor George Romney of Michigan had received a huge pile of letters from his constituents demanding that Michigan State not play the game out of respect for the president. Illinois didn't know this and they were flying in to East Lansing. Butkus was surly most of the time anyway, and especially later in a week when he had a football game. He was really seething that these universities chose to play football at a time when the country was mourning the president. I said, "Dick..." He replied, "Don't talk to me!" He was just mad, and, as it turned out, the game was postponed, and only the Oklahoma game was played and maybe one or two others.

The other vivid memory I have of Butkus occurred at the hotel where the University of Illinois was staying before the Rose Bowl game. Butkus was sitting in the hotel lobby watching an American Football League playoff game. He was so intent on watching the game that when his wife, Helen, came by and said, "Dick, I'm going shopping with some of the other girls," Butkus just lifted his arm like he was going to belt her. I thought, oh my God, I may have to jump in and break this up. But, Helen gave me a signal not to interfere. She said to me, "Come over here. It was my fault. My husband is in his 'office' now. He is not to be disturbed." That's how serious the man was.

On another occasion, during high school when Dick was dating Helen, he was at a Chicago Vocational High School football practice and she was waiting for him in some guy's car because there was inclement weather. When Butkus saw where she was, he didn't like it at all. He came running over to make a tackle on the sidelines and kept right on going, dived right through the car's open window, and tried to nail this guy. So, yes, he was an intense person.

I remember when Ara Parseghian, who had become head football coach at Northwestern in 1956, took the Wildcats out of nowhere in the early '60s and turned them into a good football team. In late 1963, Ara decided to take the head coach job at Notre Dame and in his first year there, he took the team from 3-7 the previous season to a record of 9-1. The Fighting Irish were playing Southern Cal for the national championship in the last game of the season, but lost.

Then, in 1966, Notre Dame played Michigan State for the national title in a game that has been tabbed the "game of the century." They were both unbeaten teams and at the top of the rankings, and the game was probably as fierce, clean and hard hitting a football game as I've ever seen on any level. It was outstanding and the teams, combined, had about half a dozen players selected as All-Americans that year. Duffy Daugherty was the Michigan State coach at that time, and the end of the game was bizarre because Notre Dame had the ball. The Fighting Irish was stalling, not throwing the ball, and running out the clock, while the Michigan State players were on defense and calling timeouts with the hope of getting the ball back for one more series of plays. The game for the national championship ended in a 10-10 tie. After the game, I asked Duffy, "What do you think about having a playoff?" He responded, "Tee up the ball, and we'll go out there right now." People were so bewildered at the strange ending.

But Ara had his reason. His best back, Nick Eddy, had been injured before the game and couldn't play at all. Bubba Smith of Michigan State had squashed the Notre Dame quarterback, Terry Hanratty, and the second string quarterback, Coley O'Brien, was a diabetic and needed to control his sugar level. Notre Dame's best receiver, Jim Seymour, was limping on an injured leg. It was Michigan State's final game of the season, while Notre

Dame had one more to play in its schedule with USC. So, Ara figured that if he could get out of the game with a tie, then, if they beat USC, they would be national champions. As it turned out, Notre Dame won the game with USC by a score of 51-0 and won the national championship. To this day, the Michigan State guys have never conceded that Notre Dame won the national championship. Ara was logical and pragmatic, but it wasn't like Notre Dame or like Ara to play for a tie.

My favorite story and the highlight of the sports I covered in the 1960s was the Loyola victory in the national championship in 1963. It was such an unlikely story. In 1963, Loyola was playing as an independent, and during the NCAA tournament, they defeated the University of Illinois, the Big Ten champion, and then went to the Final Four where they defeated Duke from the ACC, then Cincinnati, the defending champion, for the title. Cincinnati was a giant team, and since there was no shot clock at that time, they would stall by just passing the ball around the court. The Ramblers were down 15 points with just 10 minutes to play in the game, but they scratched and clawed their way back and ended up winning the game and the NCAA Championship. All five Loyola starters played the entire 45 minutes in a 60-58 overtime victory. I have always considered that game to be one the greatest moments in Chicago sports history.

I also covered the Blackhawks in 1961 when they won the Stanley Cup. I remember Bobby Hull getting bashed in the eye, and the owner, Jim Norris, was involved in boxing. He looked at Bobby's eye in the locker room and said, "I've never seen a boxer with an eye like that." What was interesting was that the stars of the Blackhawks, Stan Mikita and Bobby Hull, would help the locker room attendant pick up dirty towels and jock straps after a game and throw them in the basket. I don't remember the Chicago fans being very sophisticated hockey fans, not at the level of Detroit, Montreal, or Toronto, but they loved the Blackhawks. Many of them were just there to scream and go crazy for Bobby Hull and see him score goals. I remember being with Glenn Hall, the Blackhawks goalie, waiting for a flight out of Detroit during the playoffs one night. He was standing at a bar, having a quick beer, and he looked at me and he said, "Do you know how insane I am to do this job? I get sick to my stomach every game and I don't wear a mask."

I reported on the Bears throughout the 1960s, and most of the good Bears teams were powerful on defense along with a good quarterback like Billy Wade and good running backs. In the championship game against the New York Giants in 1963, I was out at the Rose Bowl and watched the game on television along with Alex Agase, the Northwestern head coach who had replaced Ara Parseghian. It was fascinating because Alex had played football against some of these guys at the University of Illinois or in pro ball, notably Y.A. Tittle, the Giant quarterback. In World War II, he was in one of those Marine units that trained at Purdue, so he played for both Purdue and Illinois. When he came back from the war, he was on the University of Illinois team in the first Big Ten Rose Bowl game. It was fascinating watching the game with him.

As for the Cubs, Leo Durocher was the catalyst when the team started winning in 1967. He was devious and self-centered and ego driven, but it was just the right thing for the Cubs at that time. It culminated with the 1969 season, and what I remember most about that were the peddlers in the clubhouse, the ones who had deals with the players and were promoting members of the team. I would say that those peddlers made the future Bears' Super Bowl shuffle look mild by comparison. They were there all the time, but I don't believe that it was the Cubs' lack of concentration on baseball that cost them the pennant. I think that issue has been greatly overdone, as is clubhouse chemistry. If you can play ball, then you can hit, field, and pitch. You can have a bunch of "boy scouts" on a team, but I will take a team with reprobates and win the championship every time. The Cubs clubhouse was like a carnival, with Santo clicking his heals, and Aquirre and Selma in the

bullpen leading cheers with the "Bleacher Bums" in the left field stands. After the games, Fergie Jenkins, the great Cubs pitcher, along with other Cubs, went over to Ray's Bleachers, now Murphy's. Interestingly, after Fergie was traded to the American League and was away from Chicago for about six years, he came back to the Cubs. And, as a force of habit, he started going over to the corner of Waveland and Sheffield. But, the old Bleacher Bums said, "No, no, Fergie, we don't go there anymore. We go to Bernie's." So, 1969 was a carnival and a circus, and, in retrospect, I think that the Cubs got more recognition for losing than if they had won. I know that Ron Santo would argue for hours with me for making that case. I would have to say that the Mets won the pennant rather than the Cubs lost the pennant. The Mets had a pitching staff that included Nolan Ryan, Tom Seaver, and Jerry Koosman, and they won something like 80% of their games from August on. As for the Cubs, the Bleacher Bums were really interesting characters, including Mike Murphy, a student from Southern Illinois University, who blew on his bugle, Ron Grousl, sort of the unofficial leader, and Ma Duncan. They were long time Cubs fans and were later memorialized by Joe Mantegna in his play "The Bleacher Bums." A few years later, into the early '70s, the team started to get older, and Durocher outlived his usefulness. Looking back, it was a great run while it lasted and the Cubs had the whole city involved.

Chicago is a unique sports town with special teams and players, and that was exemplified in the 1960s. The fans are very loyal in this town. It was a decade of championship and near championship teams, and it was a magical age across sports, politics, and life in general. It was a glamorous time to be alive, be a sports fan, and be a Chicagoan.

Things are starting out pretty jolly at the Milwaukee Inn on the Cubs' promotional tour. Photo includes (from l to r), Ernie Banks, George Altman, Billy Williams, Ron Santo, Leo Durocher and Charley Grimm at the piano. As published in the *Chicago Daily News*. Photographer: Bob Daley. Copyright, 1966, by *Chicago Sun-Times*, Inc. Reprinted with permission.

Dick Drott Baseball Clinic, 1967
(Courtesy of Chicago Park District)

Jack Rosenberg

The 1960s was a vibrant time at WGN-Television & Radio.
We started with a broadcast first – an interview with President Kennedy on the "Lead-Off Man." It was the Presidential Opener in Washington in 1961. Vince Lloyd did the honors before the White Sox-Senators game. He and I were surrounded by the Secret Service, and Vince wasn't sure how to get rid of his trademark cigar.

In the early '60s, WGN moved from Tribune Tower into new studios at 2501 W. Bradley Place in Chicago. It was a warm, wonderful, and exciting place to work. "Bozo's Circus" started about then, and at times there was an eight-year wait for tickets. Ward Quaal was company president—the best in the business—and we had this great bastion of sports announcers—Jack Brickhouse, Vince, Lou Boudreau, Jack Quinlan, Lloyd Pettit, and more. We televised both the Cubs and Sox. Color television came into prominence. We went to video tape instead of film. And, in '62, we originated the first trans-Atlantic telecast to Europe—the early moments of a Cubs-Phillies game.

In '63, I recall that Jack Brickhouse, Lou Boudreau, Harry Creighton, and I visited Hall of Famer Rogers Hornsby at Northwestern Memorial Hospital. He had just undergone eye surgery. In those days, I occasionally wrote features for the *Chicago Tribune Sunday Magazine*. I had done a piece sometime earlier about Hornsby, the greatest right-handed hitter ever—lifetime .358. When we walked into his hospital room, Hornsby, in his typical blunt fashion, pointed at me and said: "Jack, that's the best magazine article anybody ever wrote about me. To pay you back, I'm going to give you the best story I ever gave anybody—but I don't want to tell it with anybody else around."

I was the youngster of that visiting group, so naturally I was very flattered. This was a Friday afternoon, and I said, "Thanks, Rog. How about if I come back on Monday by myself? Hopefully, you'll feel stronger by then and we'll talk." He agreed. But on Saturday morning, I turned on WGN and learned that Hornsby was dead. As the years went by, his widow would visit Wrigley Field occasionally and she and I always would speculate on the story he never told.

I have vivid recollections of the assassination of President Kennedy on Friday, November 22, 1963. I was in the news department when the bulletin came in from Dallas. Immediately, Ward Quaal summoned all department managers to discuss the station's broadcast strategy for the weekend and beyond. He asked me about the sports schedule. I said, "We have Illinois at Michigan State for the Big Ten football championship on Saturday and the Bears at Pittsburgh on Sunday." Ward said, "How do you feel about it?" I said: "I don't think that this country will be in any mood for football this weekend." He said, "I agree with you but you have signed the contracts. For starters, let's put the onus on the Big Ten. If they play the game—which would be a mistake— we're obligated to do it. And let's hold off on the Bears' game."

That Friday afternoon, Jack Brickhouse, Jack Quinlan, and I drove to O'Hare Field in a driving rainstorm for the flight to Lansing, Michigan. We arrived at the airport in time to learn the flight had been cancelled because of the weather. In those days, I always carried plane and train schedules with me.

I knew there was a train to Lansing that was leaving from Union Station at 6:00 pm. The three of us hailed a cab, sped downtown, and just made the train. The silence in the dining car was deafening the entire trip. Early the next morning, the Michigan State people informed us the game was being postponed until the following Thursday, Thanksgiving Day. Illinois wound up winning that game 13-0, and going to the Rose Bowl.

WGN also wound up pulling out of the Bears at Pittsburgh broadcast that November Sunday—the only Bears' game we didn't air over a span of 24 years. That happened to be Mike Ditka's greatest game as a Bear. On one memorable play, Ditka caught a pass, shook off six Steeler tacklers and scored the touchdown that helped bring a 17-17 tie. The Bears went on to win the division, then beat the New York Giants, 14-10, for the NFL Championship at Wrigley Field on December 29, 1963. The payoff to each Bears' player was $6,000. I still remember that Sid Luckman, the perennial all-pro Bears' quarterback of yesteryear and in '63 an assistant coach, gave his $6,000 to the pool so that each Bear would get a few dollars more.

Cubs' spring training at Mesa, Arizona in 1965 stirs sad memories. Jack Quinlan had been playing golf with Lou Boudreau. While returning to the team hotel, Jack drove into the back of a semi-truck and died instantly at the age of 38. He already was considered one of the best announcers ever. His death was a crushing blow to all of us. We created the Jack Quinlan Memorial Golf Tournament in his honor. The tournament was to last 34 years and benefit the Chicago Boys and Girls Clubs. I wrote the eulogy that appeared in the annual program. It ended with the words of Rudyard Kipling: "When earth's last picture is painted, and the tubes are twisted and dried; when the oldest colors have faded, and the youngest critic has died. We shall rest and faith we shall need it, lie down for an eon or two; until the Master of all good workmen, shall put us to work anew." I concluded the eulogy with this line: "If, in fact, the Master of all good workmen has created a play-by-play job in the Great Beyond, those who have known Jack Quinlan are positive he is the man behind the microphone."

Later in 1965, Gale Sayers, the Kansas Comet, broke in with the Bears. People have asked me over the years about my favorite sports recollections, and I have many. But I think that December day, when the rookie Sayers ran for six touchdowns against the San Francisco 49ers' is my most memorable sports moment. Never have I seen one player have such an incredible day.

In 1966, the Cubs moved their spring training base to Long Beach, California. Their expectations of better weather fizzled and the experiment lasted only one season before the return to Arizona. That also was the year the late and great Leo Durocher took over as manager of the Cubs and promised they would not be an 8th place team. He was right. They finished 10th.

The year 1968 was one of the more tumultuous of that or any decade. In April, Dr. Martin Luther King was assassinated and Chicago's West Side almost immediately was engulfed in flames. Jack Brickhouse and I were at the WGN studios preparing for a sports show which also involved Wendell Smith, who was on our staff. Wendell had been a sports columnist in Pittsburgh in his earlier days and was one of the people, along with Branch Rickey, who was instrumental in choosing Jackie Robinson to break baseball's color barrier. On this particular night, Wendell arrived at WGN from home at about 8:30. Brickhouse asked: "How bad are the fires?" And Wendell said, "I don't know. I was driving 120 miles an hour!"

The collapse of the '69 Cubs has been well-chronicled over the years. They led the NL pennant race by 9 1/2 games in August, then buckled beneath a torrid stretch drive by the eventual world champion New York Mets. Even though they faded big-time, the '69 Cubs to this day remain one of this city's favorite teams. They had a certain love affair with the fans that has endured through the years.

Among the many highlights in '69 was the first of Kenny Holtzman's two no-hitters. He beat the Atlanta Braves 3-0 on August 19th without recording a strikeout. Ron Santo's three-run homer in the first inning took care of the offense. I once invited Kenny to a Passover Seder at our home. He accepted and then asked: "Are you going to line me up with a date?" I said: "Holtzman, you've got girls coming out of your ears. You don't need me to fix you up." Said Kenny: "I'm coming either way but you seem to know everybody. If you know anyone I might like, that would be great." So I invited my neighbor's daughter, Michelle Collons. She was the right girl. They were married some months later.

Major league baseball commemorated its 100th anniversary with a luncheon in Washington, D.C. in 1969. I took my wife, Mayora, and our two children, David and Beth, who were 11 and 10, respectively, at the time. We also had the privilege of spending an hour with the Speaker of the House, Rep. John McCormack of Massachusetts, during our trip. As we were leaving, the Speaker asked, "Do you have any questions before you leave?" I said, "Yes, sir, Mr. Speaker. What's the best advice you can give my son David if he aspires to one day become Speaker of the House?" Speaker McCormack put his hand on David's shoulder and said, "David, there are three things to remember always. One, obey your parents. They're the best friends you will ever have. Two, work hard. The work ethic is what got America where it is today, the greatest country on earth. And three, always vote Democratic!"

Jack Brickhouse, Leo Durocher,
Ken Holtzman, Willie Mays and
Jack Rosenberg, c. 1969
(Courtesy of Jack Rosenberg)

Vince Lloyd, Jack Rosenberg,
Lou Boudreau, Bud Solk, and
Jack Brickhouse at Boudreau's induction
into Baseball Hall of Fame, c. 1970
(Courtesy of Jack Rosenberg)

Irv Kupcinet, Essie Kupcinet,
Mayor Richard J. Daley,
Nelda Brickhouse, Jack Rosenberg,
and Jack Brickhouse, c.1965
(Courtesy of Jack Rosenberg)

Wendell Smith, Ernie Banks and fan, c.1965
(Courtesy of Jack Rosenberg)

right
Ernie Watches His Second Homer.
As published in the *Chicago Sun-Times.*
Photographer: Gary Settle.
Copyright, 1968 by the *Chicago Sun-Times,* Inc.
Reprinted with permission.

Glenn Hall

I came to the Blackhawks in 1957 and thought it was great to be in Chicago and play in the Chicago Stadium. At that time, it wasn't a good team and they weren't drawing many fans. I was just there to play hockey and was happy to go to a team that wanted me instead of playing for the Red Wings who didn't want me. I get a little upset with players who get traded and don't like the trade. For me, the move to the Blackhawks was perfect, and since I knew some players in Chicago, I looked forward to it. I came over from Detroit with Ted Lindsay after we both got in a little trouble with the Red Wings boss, Jack Adams, and he wasn't one of our favorite people.

When I came to Chicago, we really began to improve. A few players on the Blackhawks were in favor of having a players' association, including Jimmy Thomson, Tod Sloan, and Dollard St. Laurent who were being punished for being in the association. The Blackhawks had improved their farm team (junior team), and they brought Bobby Hull up from the minors that year. We realized from the start that he was going to be a great, great hockey player, and, then, a few years later, they brought up Stan Mikita.

During our Stanley Cup year of 1960-61, I remember how good it was to win the Cup. We had a good team, although I think we had better teams in later years. We weren't as successful after 1961, and it was obvious that the opposition had better teams too. I think that with the addition of such players as Bill "Red" Hay, Stan Mikita, Reggie Fleming, and Murray Balfour we had a lot of guys who had come in and played very well that year. I think that, if anything, the team that gets along together does well. During that season we were a team that worked well together and were closer than at any other time, and when one of us went one direction, we all went in the same direction. Most of us lived in Chicago's western suburbs like Berwyn and Bellwood with our families who were very close to each other.

In 1960-61, the Blackhawks finished the season in third place, and at that time, in the playoffs, the first place team played the third place team, and the second place team played the fourth place team. It never made much sense to me since you would have thought that the first place team would have played the fourth place team. In the first round, we defeated the Montreal Canadiens, and then we played the Detroit Red Wings for the Stanley Cup. Montreal had been the dominant team all those years, yet we always believed we could beat them. If you don't believe that you can defeat the opposition, don't get dressed. We knew that they were tough, had played against them 14 times in the regular season, and I'm sure that we were able to beat them some of the time. So, if you can beat them some of the time, you can beat them all of the time if you put your mind to it, things break the right way for you, and you play to the best of your ability.

I remember playing very well against Montreal, and I always liked the challenge of playing against good teams. You got more satisfaction in beating a good team than beating a team that you should beat. So, there was a lot of satisfaction in defeating the Canadiens. As it turned out, that was the only Stanley Cup team I was on during my career, although I was the backup goalie to Terry Sawchuck when the Detroit Red Wings won the Cup In the '50s, and my name was on the Cup as the goal keeper coach in Calgary in 1989.

After we beat Montreal, we had to face Detroit in the finals of the Stanley Cup. I can remember the last game of the series, and I believe that the Blackhawks were down 1-0 in the game when Reggie Fleming got a short-handed goal and Kenny Wharram got a couple goals, including the fifth goal late in the third period that clinched the victory and the Cup. It was a very special feeling to win the Stanley Cup. The Blackhawks had good teams throughout the 1960s even though we didn't win another Stanley Cup. We were better offensively than we were defensively. If you take a look at Montreal, they were the dominant team because they were so good offensively and defensively, while the Toronto Maple Leafs were the best defensive team and we were close to Montreal as an offensive team. I have always had a special feeling about my opportunity to play in the National Hockey League with the quality of players who were in the NHL.

Throughout my years in Chicago, I never wore a face mask, although I wore one during my last 2+ years when I played for the St. Louis Blues. It was quite scary to play without a face mask, so I played the game a little bit differently. You held your hand up, you made sure that you saw the puck, and you encouraged your defensemen not to deflect the puck at you and to let you see the puck. As long as you saw the puck, you were generally in a position to kick it out of the way. I was more concerned about getting out of the way than getting in the way while stopping the puck because I wanted to stay alive and avoid major facial injuries, which were the major puck-related injuries for goalkeepers at that time. I think that I got hurt bad three times, with two of them deflections and the other one a shot that came through a screen. I also got lots of small injuries during my career. In the playoffs, you wouldn't protect yourself at the same level as you did during the regular season. You would get yourself into a locked position, but with the lock, you subjected yourself to injury and ended up sacrificing your body.

I was with the Blackhawks until 1967 when there was expansion of the NFL. I intended to retire in 1966 in Chicago, but the Blackhawks kept calling me back for another season. I didn't realize until later why they were so interested in having me back. The truth was that teams had to have an experienced NHL goalkeeper in order to make him available for the NHL draft. They really needed to "expose" me in order to keep Denis DeJordy as their goalkeeper. I think that's why the Blackhawks kept on pushing for me to come back. I really had no intention of coming back for another season, but they offered me a bunch of money. So, I went back with the intention of 1966 being my last year.

As it turned out, St. Louis was a great place for a goalkeeper to play because their style was totally different than the Blackhawks, and the Blues' style complemented the goalkeeper. I finished my career with four seasons in St. Louis, and I enjoyed playing there. The team certainly wasn't the quality of Chicago, but the style was more complementary to a goalkeeper. It also was great being there because we were a team made up of players who were old guys they felt couldn't play anymore and a bunch of young kids who would never play. Instead, we banded together and became a real good hockey team. There were two divisions after expansion, and to make the original six teams "sweat" really made me feel good because they really had to work to beat us.

In terms of my well known dislike of coming to training camp each year, there were a number of reasons. First, in those days, training camp was a focus on conditioning where you were expected to get in shape. I always felt that I kept myself in pretty good shape and I didn't need training camp. Second, there was the issue of Bobby Hull and Stan Mikita shooting the puck at four million miles an hour. That didn't make it a fun situation, and the two-a-day practices and putting on that cold, wet, sweaty equipment was not a lot of fun. I think that the biggest issue was that I didn't think I needed the training camp, and I felt that it hurt me. In fact, even today, I think that the practices hurt a lot of the players. If the team wanted me to play well, I always needed a day off.

Years later, the Blackhawks moved from the Chicago Stadium to the new United Center. My friend said to me, "Remember telling Nancy, my wife, about the noise in the Chicago Stadium." I said, "You know what, I do remember." The story was that his wife asked me, "How do you handle the noise in the Chicago Stadium?" I said, "You simply blank it out." She said, "Bulls--t, don't tell me you can blank out the noise in the Chicago Stadium!" I said to her, "Well, there was one guy I could hear." She said, "I thought so. What was he yelling?" I said, "He was yelling 'cold beer, get your cold beer!'" Obviously, I could hear what I wanted to hear. I think that the noise in the Stadium was absolutely great and I think that when they moved to the United Center, they did a reasonably good job, but the acoustics were perfect for the Chicago Stadium and it was great to play under those conditions. I was received quite well when I played goalie for the Blackhawks, as all of us were. A lot of the fans were loyal and had been there when the team wasn't doing very well. When the Blackhawks started playing well, they had something to compare it to, and it was a nice situation. Chicago was a great city, the fans were so supportive, and I really appreciated the opportunity to play with the Blackhawks.

Hall in nets as goalie for
Chicago Blackhawks.
(Photo courtesy of Glenn Hall)

Chicago Black Hawks
Stanley Cup Championship team, 1961.
(Photo courtesy of Glenn Hall)

Bill "Red" Hay

I was playing junior hockey in Regina, Saskatchewan, Canada on a team that was the property of the Montreal Canadiens. They tried to sign me, but I decided to take a different route and go to Colorado College. Tommy Ivan watched me as a junior and he followed my career through Colorado College. We won the NCAA Championship in 1957, and after graduation, I went to the Montreal Canadiens' pro camp. I was there for two weeks, but then I went home to Calgary and tried to find a job as a geologist. I had quit playing and I couldn't find a job there, so I called up a buddy who was coaching the Calgary Stampeders of the Western Pro League, which was a Chicago Blackhawks farm team. They made a deal and Montreal loaned me to Calgary for that year, and that was how Tommy Ivan of the Blackhawks picked me up.

The following year, I went to Chicago's camp and made the Blackhawks team. In those days, you didn't worry about the salary because you just wanted to play hockey. It was a thrill to be the first one to come out of college to play in the NHL for any length of time. Based on Tommy's scouting, he was able to select such good college players as Cliff Koroll and Keith Magnusen. Other NHL teams began scouting college leagues and they found a lot of hockey players, including Americans as well as Canadians.

My rookie year with the Blackhawks was in the 1958-59 season. We had some good young players who had come up through the Montreal chain including Ab McDonald and Murray Balfour. The stars of our team, at that time, were Stan Mikita, Bobby Hull, and, of course, Glenn Hall. The team also included Dollard St. Laurent, Tex Evans, Al Arbor, and Moose Vasko. We melded together, learned how to win, and became an exciting team.

Our families were living in as comfortable areas as we could find, mainly to the west of Chicago off the Congress Expressway (Eisenhower Expressway). They were new rental houses, our wives didn't know anybody, and the kids went to schools out there. We lived close, and the only entertainment or social function we had, because of our schedule, was to get together with our teammates. That was how we grew up together, and our wives raised the kids, and it was very good. We were traveling by train in those days and going out of the Dearborn Station. It wasn't an easy life on the wives, but they had each other, although their only night out was going to a hockey game. We were all raising young kids in those years, and, in those days we played games on Christmas Day and New Years Day.

Monday nights became family night for my teammates and our families, and it was our only time off during the week. The single team members were in the Loop, and they moved around a little bit, but most of my teammates and I spent our time in the suburbs. When the season ended, we all got back to Canada for our summer jobs because we needed to make money to supplement our hockey salaries. I'm glad I did because it really groomed me for my career after retirement from hockey.

My initial impression of the Chicago Stadium was that it was so much bigger and more crowded than anyplace we had played in Canada. I remember one time when Rudy Pilous, the Blackhawks coach, was talking about how much faster the Zamboni Machine was going than most of his skaters between the second and third periods. I leaned over to Bobby Hull and said, "What number is this Zamboni guy wearing? He sounds like he's having a pretty good game!" It was a big building, but it didn't take long to get used to it because we got to know people who ran the building.

The Stadium actually shook when we came up the stairs to the hockey rink. Of course, the person who contributed to the atmosphere there was the famous organist, Al Melgard. The thing that was so nice about it was that, as we began winning, the place really filled up and once it was full, it was noisy. NHL teams didn't like coming into the Chicago Stadium because it wasn't a new building, it wasn't like their buildings, and that gave us a "leg up." In fact, the Stadium rink was a little smaller in size, and that helped us against certain teams. The slap shot was just coming into its own, so the shooting power was gaining momentum and Stan and Bobby were curving their sticks. Bobby could shoot a puck from his own goal line and break the glass at the other end, and that got to be dangerous. We won close games because Glenn Hall was by far the best goal tender in the NHL and kept us in games. When we won the Stanley Cup in 1961, it was the special teams that really out performed the other teams when we beat Montreal, and then beat Detroit for the Cup.

This many years later, I meet Chicago people who still remember the Blackhawks of the '60s. They loved the NHL because there were only six teams, and they loved the Blackhawks because we played exciting hockey and had the great "Million Dollar Line." Hockey was thrilling for the fans, and they loved watching our teammates like Bobby Hull, Stan Mikita, and Glenn Hall, who were just coming into their own. It was a thrill for the fans, and hockey was affordable at that time. When we won the Stanley Cup in 1961, it helped build fan loyalty. We had winning teams throughout the decade, we had good playoffs, we were close to winning other Stanley Cups, and the people respected us for that.

In the '60s, Jim Norris and Arthur Wirtz were the owners of the Blackhawks and knew how to run an organization and manage it. They hired Tommy Ivan, and Tommy hired Rudy Pilous and they were allowed to operate the team without the interference that you see today. We developed into a pretty good team, and there was nothing finer and nothing more exciting than the '61 team that won the Stanley Cup.

The 1961 team was exciting because we were young, we were together, and could have a lot of fun on a six-pack. Nobody had agents. We grew up together, and we lived together. The wives got along very well, as did the players. Eddie Litzenberger was our captain, and he was a strong leader. We worked very, very hard, and, of course, Bobby was coming into his own and was playing with Murray Balfour and me on the "Million Dollar Line." Bobby learned how to score goals by being in the right spot. Of course, Stan Mikita, Ab McDonald, and Kenny Wharram played on another great line.

At the beginning of the '60-'61 season, we had the sense that we were a special team. We were learning how to win, and it wasn't a matter of coming in second or making the playoffs because we were seeking to win the Stanley Cup. Jim Norris, who was a grand, grand gentleman, had never won the Stanley Cup. He was a good friend of the players and treated us very, very well. And, we wanted to play for him, and we wanted to win for him. Our coach was Rudy Pilous (he left a year later), and, then, Billy Reay became the head coach of the Blackhawks.

What I remember about the '60-'61 season was seeing Bobby Hull getting 51 goals and that was the first time that had ever been done in the history of the NHL. And, our entire team developed into an offensive powerhouse while still being able to play solid defense, especially since the goal tenders on the other strong teams were so good. With the curved sticks and the way our guys started to shoot, we were able to score from out around the blue-line, and sometimes even further. So, the Blackhawks opened up the game and made it great for the fans. It was a new mentality of the Hawks. There were a lot of young guys coming in, and we didn't know how they had played before and how they lived.

We beat Montreal first in six games. We didn't let them score on the power play, and Glenn really played well. We took away their power play, and that was the strength of all those Montreal winning teams. They had won the Cup five years in a row, but in the 1960-1961 season, we developed momentum and won the Stanley Cup. I remember that during the final series in Detroit, we had a little tussle with them in the third game at home, and that got us back the momentum. And, then, we knew that we could beat them. It was very close, and once we got by Montreal, we knew that we weren't going to lose it because the year before we had come close. For several years after we came close and should have won, but we couldn't keep the team effort together as well as it should be.

Jim Landis

I was born in Fresno, California during World War II, but, since it was wartime, my dad's job brought us up to the Bay Area right above Oakland. I only got to the Midwest after I joined the White Sox organization, but, since I had grown up on the West Coast and had watched Pacific Coast League baseball, my dream was to be drafted by a West Coast team.

following page
Tommie Agee of White Sox slides into home plate. As published in the *Chicago Daily News*. Photographer: John Jaqua. Copyright, 1967, by the *Chicago Sun-Times*, Inc. Reprinted with permission.

My first year in the big leagues was with the White Sox in 1957. As for my reaction to coming to Chicago and playing at Comiskey Park, I was a young, naïve kid at the time and in awe of everything. You come up from playing baseball in minor league parks, and your dream is to play baseball in big league parks. I was probably too much in awe and I thought to myself, "I made it! Golly gee!" Before, I was in the minor leagues for three years from Class D baseball up to Class A baseball and then to Double A in Memphis with the White Sox organization.

When I first was brought up to the majors, Larry Doby was playing in center, so I started with the White Sox in right field. I only played a few games at the position, because, after a little while, they released Doby and I became the center fielder for the team. Although Comiskey Park was a big ball field, to be honest with you, once I got over being awed and adapted to the position, I thought it was one of the greatest ball parks to play centerfield. The dimensions may have been big, but there were no tricky corners to deal with, and both the right and left field fences met out in center. To play centerfield was great because you had a very clear idea where everything was located.

During my years with the White Sox, we lived on the South Side at the Hyde Park Hotel at 51st and Hyde Park Boulevard, close to the Museum of Science and Industry, and, for at least a year, we hardly went downtown. Then, as we got a little more adapted to Chicago, we went downtown on a regular basis. We liked the city and the fact that we lived close to the ballpark, and that made it convenient for us. There were at least seven White Sox ballplayers and their families living at the hotel during the regular season so that helped us feel bonded to each other, our wives, and kids.

When I got to the White Sox, I didn't have any particular sense that we had a team that was going to win the pennant, but, by 1958, things started to gel pretty well. One thing that you have to remember about those days was that the Yankees were very tough and they had won the pennant so many years in a row. In fact, after we won the pennant in 1959, the Yankees started winning again. We had great pitching by 1958, and a very solid defense, and it made a very interesting situation to think of the future as a winner.

I can remember one thing about 1959 was that, besides winning the pennant and going to the World Series, I was with a great group of guys. I roomed with Sammy Esposito, the utility infielder, in those years when we were traveling on the road. In the second half of the 1959 season, we felt very confident that we were going to win the pennant. We were confident in those days, but I wouldn't use the word "cocky" to describe our feelings. We knew that things were going very well and that we were playing darned good baseball. When you look back and see that three guys from that team are in the Hall of Fame (Nellie Fox, Luis Aparicio, Early Wynn), I say to myself that it was a very talented group of players. Then, when we clinched the pennant in Cleveland, we were just in awe because we played hard, knew we had a good lead, and just went in there and did the things we were supposed to do. We felt so good inside.

As for the World Series, I remember two things about it. I think that one of the things that affected our chances was that we had to wait for the playoffs in the National League before the Dodgers won it and that seemed to take a little edge off the White Sox. It also was tough to play baseball in the Coliseum since that stadium was not built for baseball. They had bad backgrounds for hitting and for fielding because they didn't have walls that had color on them, and all we saw were the shirts of the fans sitting in the stands. We played in that World Series against Sandy Koufax and Don Drysdale, and they were two of the best pitchers in baseball.

After 1959, the team was still able to challenge for the American League pennant, but, to be honest, I had a feeling that many of the players on the team weren't happy because the White Sox traded away at least six great young ballplayers in order to have more power on the team. Those players included Norm Cash, Johnny Callison, Earl Battey, and John Romano, and we traded that nucleus to establish a new ball club. I wish that we had kept the same players from the 1959 team for a few more years. I think that it demoralized the team and the system that we had developed with a focus on great defense and pitching. Those trades changed the nature of the White Sox, and even though we were still competitive, we changed the style of our ball club by getting players who seemed to focus on hitting the long ball. I think that we gave up a heck of a lot too much, and I know that some of my former teammates feel the same way.

In the early '60s, we always had a competitive ball club, but the Yankees were a dominant team once again, and there was the possibility that we got a little lucky in 1959. When I look back at the '59 team and our teams in the early '60s, the Yankees might have been a little bit better. One of my greatest memories when I was growing up concerns one of my idols, Stan Musial. In 1962, when I was selected to the American League All-Star Team, players from both teams stayed at the same hotel. I came downstairs in the hotel on the morning of the game to get on the bus, and staring me in the face was Stan Musial. I sat next to him and talked to him all the way out to the stadium and you simply don't forget moments like that. After I was with the White Sox for about nine years, they decided to trade me.

Overall, I really enjoyed my career with the White Sox since we were always in contention, played good baseball, and there is nothing better than that. I was proud winning the pennant in '59 even though we lost the World Series. I also thought that the White Sox fans were great because they were always supporting the team and rooted hard for us.

Bill "Moose" Skowron

I was born on December 18, 1930 and grew up on the Northwest Side of Chicago on Fullerton and Central. I went to St. Stanislaw Bishop in Martyr Grammar School, and from there I went to Weber High School at Division and Ashland. I played football and basketball at Weber, and since they didn't have a baseball team, I played softball during the summer in the Windy City League. I would play softball two or three times a week, and, on Sundays, I would play hardball. My dad didn't go for that too much because he played semi-pro ball here in Chicago on a team called the Cragin Merchants.

It was a semi-pro league, and my dad played about 17-18 years. After I got my start, I went to Purdue University on a football scholarship and Hank Stram, who became coach of the Kansas City Chiefs, was my baseball and football coach. I wound up winning the Big Ten batting championship, and I hit .500 in my sophomore year. I got the nickname "Moose" from my grandfather who shaved off all my hair because he did our haircuts at home. I was completely bald and when I went outside all the older guys called me Mussolini, because I looked like the Italian dictator, and that led to the name "Moose."

While I was at Purdue, I played semi-pro ball one summer in Austin, Minnesota, the home of the Hormel Meat Company. Doug Minor, a White Sox scout, and Bill Frinch, a scout for the Cubs, didn't offer me a contract. However, Joe McDermott and Burleigh Grimes, who were Yankee scouts, saw me play there. I struck out twice in one game, the catcher dropped the ball, and I beat the throw to first base. As a result, the Yankees offered me $25,000, and I quit school to play in their system.

I signed with the Yankees in 1950 when I was 20 years old, and they sent me to Puerto Rico, where Rogers Hornsby was my manager. I played shortstop, but made too many errors, so they tried me at third base and left field, and, finally, they suggested that I become a first baseman. They sent me to Arthur Murray Dance Studio to learn how to dance because I was no gazelle around first base. In other words, I was no Vic Power who, to me, was the greatest defensive player I ever played against. Then, I went to a B-level minor league team, Virginia in the Piedmont League. We won the championship, and Mayo Smith was our manager. I led the league in hitting with a .334 average, and then I went from B-ball to Triple A with the Kansas City Blues, and I was minor league player of the year. That was when the Yankees said to me, "Moose, the only way you can make the major leagues is to learn how to play first base." In '53, they sent me back to Kansas City and I developed my skills so that I could play first base. Then, Johnny Mize retired from the Yankees and Joe Collins was the regular first baseman for the team. I came to the majors in 1954, and we won 103 games, but lost the pennant to the Cleveland Indians.

I was with the Yankees from 1954 until 1962, and we won seven pennants out of nine years as well as four World Series. Then, I was traded to the Dodgers and we won another pennant and the World Series. So, I was in eight World Series in my first 10 years in baseball. However, as far as I was concerned, my big break came 1964 when I was traded to the White Sox. It had to be my most difficult year because we lost the pennant that year by one game to the Yankees. At the end of the season, we beat the Yankees four straight at Comiskey Park and Phil Linz, who was a utility player for the Yankees, started playing the harmonica. Yogi Berra, who was the manager, told Linz to stop playing the harmonica. Mickey Mantle told me the inside story of what happened that day. Mick was in the middle of the bus, and Phil Linz said to him, "Mick, what did Yogi say?" Mickey said to Linz, "Yogi wants you to play it louder." They got into a fight, and it motivated the Yankees enough so that they won 11 games in a row to end the season. The White Sox won nine games in a row, but lost the pennant by one game. If we had won the pennant, I would have been in three consecutive World Series with three different teams.

I was with the White Sox for four years from 1964 to 1967. Even though we lost the pennant by one game in '64, we remained in contention the rest of my time with the team. I got in trouble although I led the team in all offensive records for a couple of years. Gary Peters, Joel Horlen, Hoyt Wilhelm, and Eddie Fisher told me that they wanted me to play all the games. But, Tom McCraw was platooning with me, and I told my manager, Eddie Stanky, that I wanted to play and not sit on the bench. He said to me, "Moose, it's my prerogative." I didn't know what the word meant, but I got traded two days later. Stanky said to me, "Moose, you're either going to the Cleveland Indians or the California Angels." I said, "Send me to the Angels!" They had a first baseman by the name of Don Mincher whom I didn't mind playing "second fiddle" to. I just didn't like playing behind Tom McCraw, since his career batting average was only around .220 or .230.

My favorite White Sox players when I was on the team included Joel Horlen, Al Weis, my daughter's godfather, "Honey" Romano, and Pete Ward. We had a good team, but although we had great pitching, we were not very good at hitting. Our pitching staff included Gary Peters, Joel Horlen, Eddie Fisher, and Johnny Buzhardt. Comiskey Park was easy for me to hit home runs since it was a "band box" to me, in comparison to Yankee Stadium where it was 461' to dead center. So I couldn't wait to go on a road trip to Chicago. Casey Stengel said to me, "If you don't like Yankee Stadium, we can get rid of you." I said, "Oh, no. I don't want to leave New York because I had to chance to earn some extra money by playing in the World Series." As it turned out, coming back to my hometown of Chicago was a big break for me and I enjoyed playing for the White Sox. In fact, these days, I work for the White Sox speakers' bureau and do other things for the team. The people have been great to me in Chicago.

Mike Pyle

After growing up in Hubbard Woods, I graduated from New Trier in 1957 and went to Yale University. My decision to attend Yale was a very difficult one, since my father wanted me to attend Michigan State where my brother Palmer was playing football. However, Ivy League schools had contacted me and I was interested in Yale. So when I was accepted there I decided to go there. I went there without receiving an athletic scholarship, and it cost my parents the money, but they accepted my decision. When I got to college, my freshman year was very difficult because it was very unfamiliar. During my sophomore year, I was on the football team and the coach asked me to switch from tackle to center. I was the team's center in my sophomore, junior, and senior year. And, as a senior, I was named captain of the team.

In my senior year at Yale, we were lucky enough to have an undefeated, untied season, and I think we were 16th in the national polls. Our team was the first undefeated Yale team since 1923. I graduated from Yale in 1961, but I hadn't thought about playing professional football, although I was curious whether I might be drafted by the NFL. When I was selected by the Chicago Bears, I was able to make a quick decision. I had also been drafted by the New York Titans of the American Football League, and the owner, Harry Wismer, invited me to come to New York. Wismer said that he would pay me good money and was trying to encourage me to come there. But, I soon realized that his goal was to get an Ivy Leaguer to play for New York in the brand new Shea Stadium that hadn't even been finished, and wouldn't be completed until 1964.

George Allen, the personnel director for the Bears, drafted me to play center. I started the fourth exhibition game and played every play for the Bears until I got hurt in 1964. The players who were drafted in 1961 included Mike Ditka, Bill Brown, and Roosevelt Taylor, and Ditka was selected Rookie of the Year in 1961. I was invited to the All-Star game the summer of 1961, and the game scared the heck out of me because I had only played Ivy League football and had never seen players with such size and speed like the ones in the All-Star camp. The All-Stars played the Philadelphia Eagles in that game and my father invited over 100 people to the game. The Sunday morning after the game, I was going to pick up Ditka and drive him down to camp, but, sadly, Saturday night my father died. I was honored that he saw me play in the All-Star game, and his memory inspired me to make the team.

In a 1962 pre-season game, we played the Philadelphia Eagles, and Chuck Bednarik was playing middle linebacker for them. He came in on a "blitz," and I got a piece of him. He thought I held him because his foot hooked into my hand as he ran over me. So, he kicked me in the head, and I looked around to see if there was an official nearby. There was, so I jumped up, and since you can't let a guy kick you in the head without doing something, we had a very short scuffle that was broken up by the officials. After the game, we were waiting for the bus to go to the airport. Bednarik walked over to me and said, "Pyle, I'm sorry I kicked you in the head. By the way, keep up the good work. You and I are the only two Ivy Leaguers in the league." That year, the Bears had a good season and went 9-5.

The championship year of 1963 was probably my best year. In the fall of 1963, George Halas came to Mike Ditka and me and asked us if we would be the co-captains of the offensive team, along with Joe Fortunato and Larry Morris as the defensive co-captains. We had a pretty good team in 1961 and were 8-6, and the next year, we won one more game. But the Green Bay Packers had won the western conference in both of those years. In 1963, the only difference with the Packers was that Paul Hornung wasn't there because he was suspended for a year for gambling.

We played the Packers in the first game of the 1963 regular season and beat them, 10-3. Coach Halas thought that if we could beat the Packers, we had a chance to win the conference. After beating the Packers in that first game, we won two more games, and then we went to the West Coast to play the Rams and the 49ers. We beat the Rams 52-14, but lost to the 49ers, 20-14, the only game we lost that year. But, we were building a confidence level that we could win the championship. Then, in the third week of November, President Kennedy was assassinated on Friday, November 22. I think of the assassination more in personal terms than its impact on football and the Bears. There was a tremendous feeling of shock that this kind of thing could happen, and I remember hearing about it that Friday at the end of practice.

NFL Commissioner Pete Rozelle made the decision to play the scheduled games that weekend, although college football cancelled their schedules. But, the NFL also decided to not have radio or television coverage of the games. We went to Pittsburgh to play the Steelers and almost got beat. We were tied by Pittsburgh 17-17, and Ditka made the greatest run I have ever seen on a football field as he avoided one tackler after another, although he was too tired to get into the end zone.

The next game against the Minnesota Vikings also ended in a 17-17 tie. So, after two straight tie games, we were focused on playing well in our last two games. We won both games and had a final record of 11-1-2, but the tie games didn't count as losses. The last game of the season was against Detroit at Wrigley Field when Dave Whitsell intercepted a pass and ran in for the final touch-down and we won 24-14. The NFL championship game was on December 29, 1963. We beat the Giants 14-10 in the most amazing game I've ever played in Chicago. Everybody, including

the fans, was a part of the buildup for the title game because the last football championship game that was played in Chicago went back to the 1940s. December had 13 days below zero, and we weren't allowed to wear gloves, not even when we practiced the week before the game outside at Montrose Harbor because Wrigley Field was covered with a tarp. Throughout my career, whenever the ground was too wet because of the rain, we would practice in the Chicago Armory on Chicago Avenue where they also played polo, which meant dirt and horse manure. It was very cold on the day of the championship game, and by the fourth quarter, it was -15 degrees. But, everybody in Chicago was so supportive of the team, and people went all over the state to watch the game because television had blacked out coverage in the city.

Halas certainly respected the best players on the team, and although he would sometimes have battles with them, he liked the guys who stood up to him. The harder he was challenged, the more that Halas respected it, and vice versa. Coach had an unusual way of pushing guys, including going head-to-head with players like Rick Casares and Doug Atkins. If he thought that guys were running around or drinking too much, he'd lower their required weight, thinking that it might work to control their behaviors, but he hurt a couple of players with that strategy.

In 1964, Johnny Morris broke the league record for catches by tight ends with 94 receptions, and that year, the Bears were using more passing plays. Bill Wade was calling his own plays and he liked to throw the ball, and Ditka caught 78 passes. We didn't have a great running game after Willie Gallimore had died in a tragic accident. Rick Casares, the fullback, was reaching the end of his career, and we had just picked up Joe Marconi, a 10-year veteran with the Rams. Ronnie Bull had backed up Willie Gallimore in '63, and it was legend that Ronnie had carried the ball when it was -15 degrees at the end of the championship game 6 to 8 times in a row, just to keep control of the ball and for the offense to run the time out with short running plays. In '64, Green Bay won the title and the Bears' record was 5-9. The defense was good, but it wasn't overwhelming like it had been, although it still included players like Ed O'Bradovich, Doug Atkins, Bill George, and Fred Williams. Since we had won the championship in 1963, the Bears were not able to draft many good players, so 1964 was not a good year for us.

In 1965, the Bears had a great draft that included Dick Butkus and Gale Sayers in the first round. Dick had been a star middle linebacker at the University of Illinois, while Sayers was the real find out of the University of Kansas because no one knew his tremendous potential. That summer, Otto Graham was the coach of the College All-Stars, but he wouldn't play Sayers in that game. So, when the regular season started, since Halas was reluctant to start rookies, he didn't use Gale as a starter right away. Once Sayers, and then Butkus, began to start games, we took off. We had a record of 9-5 that year, and I think we were the best team in the NFL.

At the beginning of the 1965 season, we played our first two games on the West Coast and lost both games, and then came home to play the Packers in Green Bay. At the end of the first half, the Packers were leading 21-0, but we only lost the game 24-21. Halas decided to start Sayers in the second half and he scored three touchdowns. Rudy Bukich was our quarterback that year because Billy Wade had gotten hurt at the end of 1964. Rudy was the leading quarterback, by far, in the NFL. Halas decided to start Sayers in the second half, and he scored three touchdowns. Although we began with a 0-3 record, we won nine of the next 11 games and ended up with a 9-5 record for the year. In fact, we beat the Packers by 21 points when we played them in Chicago. But, we lost the last game of the season to the Vikings and didn't win the division.

In my years with the Bears, we won in 1963, challenged in 1965, and again in 1968. In 1968, we wouldn't have won the division because Green Bay had it locked up. However, a new playoff structure was introduced, so we had the chance to qualify for the playoffs even with a 7-7 record. We played the Packers in the final game of the '68 season, and if we had won, we would have been a playoff team. When Bart Starr got hurt and Don Horn, their backup quarterback, came into the game, he scored 21 points in the first half. We came out in the second half and went to our running game with Brian Piccolo and Ronnie Bull as the Bears' running backs. We had injuries to three offensive linemen, but we scored three touchdowns in the second half, and were moving downfield near the end of the game. But our quarterback, Jack Concannon, was intercepted by Ray Nitschke and Green Bay ended up winning the game by one point. Because of our injuries, that was the most inspirational game I ever played in as a Bear.

My last year with the Bears was in 1969 during which I lost my starting job for the first time in nine years. Jim Ringo was the offensive line coach for the Bears, and he just didn't like me, probably because I knew our offensive plan in detail, and he didn't. Although Jim knew how to coach, I was just trying to help and he couldn't really handle me giving advice. I started all but two games that year, but, late in the season with my ankle hurting, Ringo started another player. As it turned out, the '69 season was the worst won-loss record the Bears ever had with only one win and 13 losses.

Don Chandler of Giants kicks 13-yard field goal during NFL Title Game Against Bears.
As published in the *Chicago Sun-Times*.
Photographer: John Arabinko.
Copyright, 1963, by the *Chicago Sun-Times*, Inc.
Reprinted with permission.

Gale Sayers

I was drafted by the Bears out of the University of Kansas in 1965, the same time that the Kansas City Chiefs of the American Football League also drafted me. I thought that being on the Chiefs might be a good idea since I had gone to college at Kansas and knew Lamar Hunt, the team owner, and a lot of other people on the Chiefs. But, instead, I decided to sign a four-year contract with the Bears for $25,000 a year. The Chiefs were in a new league, and I thought they would offer me a little bit more money. They did, but only $2,500 more than the Bears, and since the best football was being played in the NFL, I rejected the Chiefs' offer.

That summer, I played in the College All-Star Game, and when I arrived at the Bears camp, all I wanted to do was make the ball club. The Bears already had several running backs, including Ronnie Bull, Andy Livingston, Joe Marconi, and Jon Arnett. But, I felt that, given the opportunity, I could play for the Bears. I didn't know how well I would play in the NFL during my first year, but was certain that I could make the Bears since I felt that I was quicker and faster and could recognize holes better than the other backs. It was common knowledge that George Halas never played rookies, but I felt that I could play in the NFL, even if not immediately as a starter.

During exhibition season, we played the L.A. Rams in Nashville, and I remember that I had a 65-yard punt return and a 93-yard kickoff return and threw a 25-yard pass to Dick Gordon. I considered that to be a decent exhibition season. Then, when we began the season, we played our first two ballgames against the San Francisco 49ers and the Los Angeles Rams, and Halas started Jon Arnett as the running back. I was biding my time, and in the 49er, game I scored one touchdown even though we lost to San Francisco by a score of 52-24, and then lost to the Rams, 30-28.

After that, we played the Green Bay Packers in Green Bay. George Halas had a style of not letting his players know who was going to start until right before the game. We were practicing and then came back into the locker room. Coach Halas began listing who was going to play offense and defense, and when he got to the halfbacks, he said, "Gale Sayers is going to start." That was a surprise to me and the other starting back, Jon Arnett. I started the ballgame, and although Green Bay ended up winning 23-14, I scored both touchdowns, including a 65-yard pass play from Rudy Bukich and a 10-yard run.

My first reaction to playing in Wrigley Field was quite simple: it didn't matter to me where I played, including the field or the fans since every football field is 50 yards wide and 100 yards long. I wasn't distracted by the fans yelling and screaming since I was just out there trying to do my job, make the team and win ballgames for the Bears. I had no concept about how old Wrigley Field was or that we were playing football on a baseball field. It was a nice field, and the fans were close to us and we had home field advantage. But, things like that didn't enter my mind and

I didn't play any differently there. When we defeated the Rams in Chicago by a score of 31-6, I scored a touchdown, and, even though we had lost our first three games, the Bears ended up with a winning season record of 9-5. We lost our last game of the season, 24-17, to the Minnesota Vikings and came in second to the Packers who won the division title with a 10-4 record.

It was a great rookie year for me. In the 49er game, I set an NFL record by scoring six touchdowns, and, then, in our first game against the Vikings, I scored four touchdowns in Minnesota. My teammates really supported me, and they knew that all they had to do was make a block for me and I could break into the open. It was a good season, and I was selected Rookie of the Year. My teammate, Dick Butkus, was second in the voting. I also went to the Pro Bowl, but Vince Lombardi, the Pro Bowl coach that year decided not to play me too much. We wanted to win every game we played, and although the Packers beat us in the first game, when they came to Wrigley Field in late October, we "killed" our main division rivals by a score of 31-10. It seemed that during my football career, the Packers would always beat us in Green Bay while we would beat them in Chicago.

At the end of February of 1966, I started working out in order to get ready for the 1966 training camp in Rensselaer, Indiana. I knew that although I had a solid rookie year, I had to improve since the opposition would be keying on me. I had caught them by surprise in my first year, but I wasn't sure it would happen in my second year. I did improve, led the league in rushing in 1966, went to the Pro Bowl, and was selected as Most Valuable Player in the Pro Bowl. In 1966, our record was 5-7-2, losing both games played with the Packers, even though we thought we had a very good team. Many of my teammates were in their 30s and might have been past their prime and thinking about retiring. However, we did have some very good young players, including Mike Ditka, Dick Butkus, Dick Gordon, Jimmy Jones, Ronnie Bull, and Ralph Kurek. But, we didn't have too many choices in the annual NFL draft, and I think that was why we didn't do well for the next several years. It was too bad since we had some players who would eventually go into the NFL Hall of Fame.

I was good friends with George Halas, and he was a person whom I probably would run through a wall for because I respected him that much. When I came to the Bears, he was 69 years old and still a head coach, and it was hard for me to believe that he was still

coaching football. Amazingly, he was out there every day, no matter how hot or cold the weather, while the team had 19 to 23 year-old kids who would say, "I have a cold, and I can't practice today." Halas was there all the time, and I really enjoyed him. He was a good man and clearly in charge of the Bears as owner and head coach.

In 1967, we were 7-6-1 and I ran for 880 yards. Then, in 1968, we had a chance to be in contention before I badly injured my knee against the 49ers in the ninth game of the season. Green Bay beat us late in the year by one point, 28-27 and knocked us out of the playoffs. My backups at running back were Ronnie Bull, Brian Piccolo, and Ralph Kurek. Our quarterbacks were Virgil Carter and Jack Concannon, but it seemed like we were changing quarterbacks every two games. Successful teams have consistency at quarterback, but the Bears didn't have it then. When I played, our focus was running and defense, and when I came back from my knee injury in 1969, we picked up Bobby Douglas out of Kansas, a left-handed quarterback who could throw the ball through the wall. That year, the Bears were 1-13 under Jim Dooley after Halas had retired, and I was the only person in the NFL to gain 1,000 yards for the season. I made All-Pro and was selected as the MVP again of the Pro Bowl.

In 1970, we were 8-8 under Abe Gibron, who had been selected as the head coach. Abe was head coach for a couple of years, and I decided to retire after the 1971 season. Although my first knee injury was very bad, when I came back in 1969, the injury never bothered me and I didn't even wear a brace. Then, in 1970, I was returning a kick-off and I got hit and I stretched a ligament. They operated on it and tightened the ligament back up. I was out for that season and came back to play in 1971. But, it never felt good again, and with the introduction of Astroturf, it was tougher when you fell on it. So, after the 1971 exhibition season, I decided to retire.

I was very surprised to make the NFL Hall of Fame since I had only played in 68 games over 4 1/2 years in my career in the NFL, and most people who are in the Hall of Fame had careers that lasted 10 to 12 years. I had no idea that I would be considered for the Hall of Fame or be in it. But, in 1977, I got the call and they said that I would be inducted. I believe what got me in the Hall of Fame was being the first NFL running back to return kick-offs and punts, run from the line of scrimmage, and catch passes.

Kenny Holtzman

When I was drafted by the Cubs in 1965, I immediately signed and went to the minor leagues in Idaho with one of the Cub rookie league teams. I was there for about three weeks or a month, before going to one of their Class A teams in Washington State where I stayed for about three weeks. In quick fashion, I went right to the Major Leagues at the end of August. My first reaction to Wrigley Field was one of sheer excitement. Buck O'Neil of the Cubs, who had signed Ernie Banks, met me at the airport, and drove me to Wrigley Field. It was the first time I had ever seen the park, but when I arrived, I was ready to go.

They had told me to be there at 9:00 am since they had a game that afternoon. Leo Durocher wasn't the manager until 1966, so the team was managed by the "College of Coaches," a rotating group of coaches. The coach at that time was Lou Klein, my first major league manager/coach.

Late in the '65 season, I pitched in three games, all in relief. I was probably the youngest guy on the team, and the pitching staff was primarily major league veterans, almost 10 years older than me. So, I sat in the bullpen because Klein had told me, "For the last month of the season, I will probably use you sparingly in relief in a game that probably doesn't mean anything." I didn't understand that because the Cubs were in eighth place, but I only pitched an inning here and there when the game didn't mean anything, and that was my first exposure to the major leagues.

Born and raised in St. Louis, I was a Cardinals fan. It is difficult to live in that part of the country without favoring the Cardinals. However, as I grew up and was lucky enough to become a major league pitcher, that loyalty became secondary. So being with the Cubs was very exciting, and I was also introduced to their rich history. It was great, and probably because Wrigley Field was so unique. Even back then, it was an old ballpark, but so special because of the coziness, the small dimensions, the ivy, and the fans. I still think that Wrigley Field is one of the toughest parks to pitch in, although some offensive players argue that when the wind blows in it is tough to hit a home run. Of course, when there wasn't any wind, or it was blowing out, it was challenging to pitch there. I learned to concentrate on the fundamentals of pitching, including moving the ball around and keeping it down in order to survive in the majors. If I lost my focus, I was likely to give up a home run at a very inopportune time, even if I have been pitching a very good game.

I didn't throw a sinkerball, which is a special type of pitch designed to sink at a less than optimum speed. Instead, I threw a fastball that I aimed low. When I first came up to the major leagues, I was considered to be a power pitcher because I threw the ball hard and got my share of strikeouts. However, I learned very quickly that my pitching style was fine except if I lost control, even momentarily, and surrendered a wind blown, fly ball home run. As a result of pitching at Wrigley Field, I learned how to be a pitcher rather than just a thrower, and those skills helped me later in my career when I was traded to Oakland and New York and pitched in more spacious parks.

In 1966, the Cubs decided to try having spring training in Long Beach, California because they expected the weather to be perfect. We stayed on the campus of Long Beach State University, and the weather turned out to be rainy much of the time. During the winter of 1965-1966, Leo Durocher had been hired as Cubs manager and he was going to come on board in for the 1966 season. Since we had a lot of aging veterans, Leo wanted to rebuild the team with young players like Don Kessinger and Glenn Beckert. Ferguson Jenkins, who had been in the Philadelphia system, was traded to the Cubs early in 1966 in a multi-player trade. That was also when we got Bill Hands and Randy Hundley from the Giants, and they became Cub fixtures for many years. Even though we didn't do so well that year, finishing last, it was the first exposure for all of us to what it took to get it done in the Major Leagues.

Leo Durocher was a mythical figure to me because he had started playing in the 1920s and had a link with Babe Ruth. When he was hired as the manager of the Cubs, everybody was a little bit in awe of him because he was very famous, married to an actress (Lorraine Day), familiar with all the Hollywood stars, and had been a coach with the Dodgers and the manager of the Giants in the World Series in 1951. The first time I met Leo that spring, he said to me, "I'm going to give you every chance in the world to make the team. I don't really care what your age is because, if you can do it, I'm keeping you." I thought that was great. He obviously made quite a positive first impression on me despite the fact that we disagreed on some issues over the five years he was my manager. I think that it was worth it to play for him because he knew a lot about how to play the game and had been in the Major Leagues so long that I couldn't help but learn from him.

In 1967, I first went into the regular Army and did my basic training at Fort Polk, Louisiana before being assigned to a National Guard unit in my home state. During my years in the Guard, I was activated two or three times to do federal riot duty in Chicago. Sometimes, during the late '60s, I missed several weeks of baseball because I had to report to a unit that had been activated. I wasn't sent overseas, but I was part of a unit that had to sit in an Armory in Chicago for a week or two. The next year, I was part of the National Guard at the 1968 Democratic National Convention, but I wasn't physically on the sidewalk in front of the Hilton. I was in a medical unit, so we were involved in medical-related issues, and although that was about it, I did miss some significant chunks of time away from baseball.

By 1967, most of the younger Cub players had at least a year of experience, and we started to play quite well. Amazingly, although I was absent at times for Guard duty, I wound up pitching in 12 games and finished the season 9-0. That year, Ferguson Jenkins, Bill Hands, Rich Nye, and Joe Niekro started to mature and, combined with the performances of our three great players—Ernie Banks, Billy Williams, and Ron Santo—the club started to be competitive. That year, we challenged the Cardinals for the lead in the National League well into the season although they went on to win the World Series. Other teams in our league began to take us seriously, and when the season ended, we had an 87-74 record, which meant that we were over .500 for the first time in many years.

I threw my first no-hitter on August 19, 1969 which we won 3-0 against the Atlanta Braves. That year became the culmination of the previous three years. All the players who had been brought up and traded for, young players who were the nucleus of the team, were with the Cubs by then and we felt that we had a legitimate chance to win the pennant. It was the first year of the divisional races, and there were six teams in each of the east and west divisions of the American and National Leagues. We were in the same division with the Cardinals, Mets, Expos, Phillies, and Pirates, and, in April 1969, we started the season like a "house on fire." Right away, we had an amazing won-loss record in the first month and we shot into first place. Little by little, over the first three or four months of the season, support grew in Chicago so that it seemed like there were 40,000 people at Wrigley Field each game. In addition, there were crowds of fans before and after the games to get players' autographs. It was just very, very exciting, but, unfortunately it didn't turn out the way we wanted.

The Mets were similar to us in many ways. They had invested in a lot of time and money in the development of their young players in the mid-1960s, including Nolan Ryan, Tom Seaver, Jerry Koosman, Tug McGraw, Tommie Agee, Cleon Jones, and Rusty Staub. They did what we did by bringing to the majors a bunch of young players, who also matured, and by 1969, they had two or three years of experience. By late August, they had passed us in the standings and won the pennant going away. Everybody said that the Cubs folded at the end of the season, but I don't agree. I would argue that the Mets were quite probably a deeper 25-man team and, over the course of the full six-month season, outlasted us.

The '69 Mets were an excellent team, and like the Cubs, built that team over four or five years, and were able to keep the component parts together even into the early '70s.

The Cubs also had winning records in 1970 and 1971 and challenged for the pennants from 1967 to 1972. Although I pitched my second no-hitter against Cincinnati on June 3, 1971, at the end of that season, I was traded by the Cubs to the Oakland Athletics for Rick Monday. I wasn't really surprised by it because I had discussed my feelings about the Cubs with John Holland, the general manager. I felt that the Cubs were not doing enough in order to stay competitive. When I saw what some of the better teams were doing by spending their resources to purchase new players, I didn't think that the Cubs had that kind of commitment. He obviously disagreed with me, so I said to him, "Do you think that there is a chance I might be traded?" He said, "Sure. You know that we don't want any unhappy players here." I remember that I came back to my home in St. Louis since we all had jobs in the wintertime to supplement our salaries. One day I received a call from John Holland and he said, "We've decided to trade you to the Oakland Athletics."

Quite frankly, even though I had expected something, it was still shocking to leave the team with whom I had started my career. In reality, the phone call was kind of jarring, but I was only shocked for about 10 seconds. Then, I thought, "The Oakland A's. Hmmm! They had a great season last year, and even though they are in the American League and I don't know anybody there, it's a wonderful challenge." I joined Oakland in 1972, had my greatest years there, and was lucky to play with one of the greatest teams to ever play baseball. We won three World Series in a row in '72, '73, and '74, and won the Western Division titles for years after that. Then, the owner of the A's, Charles Finley, decided to break up the A's and he got rid of Reggie Jackson, Catfish Hunter, Joe Rudi, Rollie Fingers, Sal Bando, and me. He just traded all of us, and I wound up with the New York Yankees and won two more World Series.

I spent 15 seasons in the Major Leagues, won 174 games, played on two of the greatest teams that ever played (the Oakland Athletics and New York Yankees), and have been lucky enough to be in five World Series and win five rings. But, the 1969 season was still my ultimate thrill. To this day, I can remember a lot of things about '69 and we talk about it whenever the players get together at Old Timers' games. So, 1969 made a very big impression on me, and as I have gotten older, I still regret that I never really experienced the thrill of winning a pennant in Chicago. I think that Chicago would have been the ultimate town to have that experience. The 1969 Cubs are still a favorite team of many Cubs' fans, and I receive mail regularly from fans who loved our team.

Kenny Holtzman of Cubs while pitching.
As published in the *Chicago Sun-Times.*
Photographer: Bob Langer.
Copyright, 1967, by the *Chicago Sun-Times,* Inc..
Reprinted with permission.

following page
Play at the plate on throw from left fielder, Billy Williams, to catcher Randy Hundley of Cubs, the umpire, Harvey, and Lee May, sliding Cincinnati Reds player.
As published in the *Chicago Sun-Times.* Photographer: Unknown. Copyright, 1969 by the *Chicago Sun-Times,* Inc.
Reprinted with permission.

125   Kenny Holtzman

Kenny Holtzman

Carmen Salvino

It all began in 1945 when, at the age of 12, I went to work setting pins in a local bowling center (there were no automatic pinsetters then) to help my family and that started my career in bowling. By the age of 17, I had become an accomplished bowler and was the youngest bowler to ever compete in the then famous "Chicago Classic League" and was tagged with the nickname "Chicago's Boy Wonder." Bowling started to become very popular, and it was an era of famous bowling teams in cities like Chicago, Detroit, St. Louis, and Minneapolis, and the competition between these teams was fierce.

However, being very young and bowling against men, some twice my age, they would use a lot of psychology on me and would give me a rough time. It made me very angry and bitter, and I started to view my opponents as enemies and felt they were very jealous. This unfortunately carried over to other people outside my bowling life, and it took me a while to learn how to control my emotions and to trust other people.

In 1954, Matt Niesen, a Chicago bowling proprietor, put together a bowling show for a local television station and called it "Championship Bowling." The format was two bowlers who would bowl each other for three games, and the winner of the match would come back the following week. I was 19 then, stayed on the show for eight consecutive weeks, and it caused me to become better known. The show helped put bowling in Chicago on the map, and new bowling centers were popping up everywhere. Bowling was a sport where everyone could participate, young children and adults alike. At that time we had 100 million people throughout the world bowling.

During the '60s, the sport of bowling was very popular and I continued to bowl in the classic league until the Professional Bowlers Association was formed in 1958 by its founder, Eddie Elias, a lawyer from Akron, Ohio. I was one of the seven original chartered members. Our PBA tour consisted of 35 tournaments, the show was televised on ABC every Saturday afternoon, and bowling became even more popular.

The sport attracted many people who were not directly associated with bowling, including Lamar Hunt in Dallas, plus other wealthy businessmen. They decided to form the National Bowling League, which had a format like professional baseball, whereby teams were developed in major cities, including Detroit, St. Louis, Dallas, New York, and Los Angeles, and these teams would travel to bowl against each other. Statistics were also kept, including wins and losses, and team and individual averages.

I felt this was a great opportunity to get in on the ground floor of a new venture as well as being paid a guaranteed salary for six months. I was offered a contract by Dallas and, in 1961, moved my family there. I had the best of both worlds at that time, with a guaranteed salary of $20,000, a lot of money in those days, plus the chance to bowl on the regular PBA tour whenever time allowed. But, I missed being in Chicago and when we would travel around the country, if time allowed us to stop in Chicago, I would visit the city to see other family and friends.

I won 10 PBA titles in the '60s and because the finals of each tournament were televised, I became well known with bowling aficionados as well as bowling ball manufacturers. I was offered contracts from several of those manufacturers, which also included traveling around the world to conduct bowling clinics for those companies. It was a great experience for me since I visited such countries as Japan (13 times), Mexico, Venezuela, Korea, and Germany. I was only 29 years old, so the trips served as an education for me and I was exposed to various customs, new types of food, and interesting people. We were treated like royalty when we visited Japan, and I had the chance to see 17 Japanese islands. I came to appreciate their beautiful gardens and palaces. Since I was 6'2", it was rare for the Japanese to see someone so tall, and I looked like a giant to them. On one trip with Don Carter, we were greeted by 1,000 kids at the airport and had a chauffeur to drive us to the bowling centers. We thoroughly enjoyed their hospitality.

With the exposure that the professional bowlers were receiving, we were treated like rock stars in the United States and around the world. The situation became so extreme that I could be driving down a highway and people would recognize me, blow their car horns, and wave hello. Bowlers were so recognizable in those days, as compared with other sports, because the television networks would use close up shots in their coverage of our various tournaments. Viewers really felt that they knew us personally.

Since the prize money on the PBA tour was not great at that time, I designed my game to not only win tournaments, but to at least be in the final group of bowlers. I wanted to make certain that I earned a paycheck, and I ended up the greatest cash winner in the history of the tour.

Although I was successful in the '50s and '60s, my game was starting to slip. I decided to work with Hank Lahr, a friend of mine, who was not only an engineer, but also a very good bowler himself. He opened up a new world for me because he taught me to approach bowling from the perspective of an engineer and I began to view the sport from an entirely different perspective. I reevaluated my game, learned about friction, translational motion, and rotational vectors. As a result, my career took off again. In the late '60s, Lahr changed my bowling style. At that time, I was holding the bowling ball high, and my friend said, "We are going to change your style so that it is like the 'no windup' used by baseball pitchers." I began to hold the ball about knee high, and suddenly my bowling started to improve. In fact, I broke the record for average in a single tournament. Hank passed away many years ago, but I will forever be grateful to him because he opened up my mind, changed my whole outlook on life, and bowling for the better.

I realized that through my early years in bowling I had been angry at everybody, and although I was a popular bowler, I did not have a very nice personality. I had developed a reputation as a cocky punk and realized I had lost the friendships of some very nice people. In my opinion, when you are involved in sports, you have to balance compassion for people while not losing your "killer instinct" toward your opponents. The '60s were years of great success for me in bowling. However, it wasn't until the 1970s that I really began to grow up as a man, thanks to my travels around the country and world, meeting a number of nice people, developing many great friendships, and having the support of my family. I look back and treasure all of the years and memories in bowling, as well as the fact that I have developed another career in the research and development of new bowling materials.

Photograph of Carmen Salvino
jumping in air while bowling a strike.
(Courtesy of Carmen Salvino)

Johnny "Red" Kerr

I grew up on the South Side of Chicago in Ogden Park in the '30s and '40s. As a matter of fact, everything that I learned to do in sports I learned at Ogden Park. I lived at 64th and May Street, and that was right behind Racine. Ogden Park was right there from 64th Street to 67th Street. I grew pretty quickly, and I used to play soccer at Ogden Park most of the time, as well as baseball. We would play basketball at the gym, but not really too much of it. I was one of the tallest kids around, and I grew up with a lot of kids who went to St. Brendan's, a Catholic school.

At that time, I was a Protestant. They wanted me to play with them in the CYO, but I said to them that I wasn't Catholic. I said, "Well, I have a cousin who is Catholic." They said, "Will you play under his name?" I played under my cousin's name of Eddie Benson. So, in 1944 or 1945, we ended up winning the CYO championship in Chicago. Some years later, when I did turn Catholic, Bill Gleason, the sports writer, gave me a medal for winning CYO basketball.

I grew to 6'1" in grade school, and then up to 6'8 1/2" when I went to Tilden, so that I was one of the tallest kids in the city. When I ended up playing basketball, there was a headline in one of the papers that read, "They found him on a soccer field!" Nick Kladis was a senior when I first came on the Tilden team, and he and the other starters were terrific players. I didn't think that I had any of the skills to play on that level. But, during my senior year, I was walking around the halls of Tilden, and the basketball coach saw me and said, "What year are you in, kid?" I answered, "I am just going in my senior year." He responded, "You've got to come out for basketball." I said, "No, I'll be embarrassed. I've seen those guys play." He said, "Hey, c'mon, you come out." So, he took me in the locker room, and he said, "Kerr, I'm going to give you a uniform, and you're going to come back here some day and thank me for it." In 1949, we won the city championship, I was selected All-City, went downstate, won our first game, but lost our next game to Johnny Biever's great Aurora West team by one point. We had a lead with about ten seconds to go, and we had the ball out of bounds. One of our guards threw it right into Biever's hands, he intercepted the pass, and went in for a lay up and they won the game.

I graduated from Tilden in January 1950 because I had been double-promoted when I was in grade school. I had off the summer of 1949 and came back and played with the team until I graduated high school in January 1950. Then, I went downstate to the University of Illinois. In those years, you couldn't start on a university basketball team as a freshman. When I went downstate, Harry Combs, the basketball coach, and Howie Braun, the assistant coach, decided not to use me that year because they didn't want to lose me in the middle of my senior year at the University of Illinois. In affect, I was downstate a year and a half as a freshman, so I went to college for four and one-half years.

I started playing center for Illinois as a sophomore in 1952. They already had a center named Bob Peterson, so I didn't start until my senior year at Illinois. I led the team in scoring all three years, but I didn't start until my last year when I was selected to the All-American team.

n my sophomore year, we won the Big Ten championship and we played two games in the Chicago Stadium during the NCAA Tournament. We beat Dayton and Duquesne, and, as a matter of fact, John Paxson's dad was on the Dayton team. Then, we went out to Seattle, and it was the first year that the NCAA had the Final Four. We won our first game, but lost to St. John's. However, we defeated Santa Clara for third place in the tournament. As a matter of fact, as big as the tournament is now, I didn't know until years later that I had been selected to the All-Tournament team as a sophomore, coming off the bench. Today, you would get a ring and probably drafted into the NBA as a sophomore.

I graduated from the University of Illinois in 1954 and was drafted by the Syracuse Nationals. At that time, there were eight teams in the NBA, with the four teams in the East being New York, Boston, Philadelphia, and Syracuse. I stayed with Syracuse for nine years until they moved to Philadelphia. The Warriors moved to the West Coast and became Golden State, and we moved to Philadelphia. Wilt Chamberlain was with the Philadelphia Warriors when they moved out, but, a year later, they traded for him and he became a member of the 76ers. I played against Wilt for seven or eight years and then played with him for about a year. When Wilt came to the team, I knew that I wasn't going to be playing much, even though I had worked for the owner of the team, Irv Kozloff, in his paper business. I said to him, "You know, Koz, this isn't going to go work out since Wilt is used to playing an entire game, and I would like to play." I had played in a continuous streak of 844 games. "I'd like to play one more year. Why don't you see if you can do something to trade me to another NBA team?" It wasn't a demand, but I wanted to play. I was traded to Baltimore for Wally Jones, a guard, and I finished my career at Baltimore after one more year. I was going to play maybe one additional year, but the expansion job of head coach opened in Chicago.

The Chicago Bulls were initially owned by Dick Klein, and he hired me in 1966. Chicago had several professional basketball teams before the Bulls, including the Gears, the Stags, the Zephyrs, and the Packers. Then, the Bulls came in, and we were playing at the Amphitheater before moving our games to the Chicago Stadium. The Amphitheater was just about the right size stadium for a team that was trying to make it back in Chicago. Then, in 1967, there was a fire at McCormick Place, and Mayor Richard J. Daley wanted everyone out of the Amphitheater because the city needed the facility for trade shows. So, we moved to the Chicago Stadium, which was just a high rent arena for us compared to the Amphitheater. At the Stadium, we didn't draw too many fans and

there was almost no media coverage of the team. In fact, after the games, I would walk around with about $5 in change in my pockets so that I could call the media and tell them about the results of the games.

I would call a newspaper and say, "This is Johnny Kerr, coach of the Bulls, and I'm just calling to give you the score of the game." They would say, "What happened? Who was the leading scorer?" And, I would usually say, "That was Bob Boozer." They would often say, "How do you spell that?" Then I would call the other papers, radio, and television stations.

It was great to be with this new team, and, at that time, Jerry Colangelo worked in the Bulls' front office. The players on the team during the first year included: Guy Rodgers, a flashy guard from Villanova who had played with Wilt on the Warriors and set a record that first year for us with 21 assists in a game; Bob Boozer, who was from Kansas, was the captain of our team, and one of the top scorers; and, Jerry Sloan, whom I wanted the Bulls to draft. Although I wasn't a player/coach with the Bulls, I had to be in the expansion pool. It was great going from a player to a coach because I missed the camaraderie and everything else. And, I could still do all the things I still liked to do in basketball. I was selected as Coach of the Year in our first year, and the team won 33 games as an expansion team. No other expansion team has ever come close to that victory total. We also made the playoffs, which no other first year team has done. In fact, when they asked Richie Guerin of the St. Louis Hawks, "How do you think the Bulls will do?" He responded, "They'll be lucky if they win 12 games." But, we went out and won 33 games, and I ended up coaching the Bulls for two years. In our second year, we won 29 games and one game in the playoffs.

After I was a coach, I left Chicago and went to Phoenix where Jerry Colangelo was the new general manager of the team. I was head coach there for two years. In fact, I think that I am the only expansion coach that ever won his first two games with two differ-ent expansion teams. My roommate for many years at Syracuse was Al Bianchi, and we were always very close friends. When I came to Chicago, I chose Al as my assistant coach with the Bulls. He left, got the job in Seattle, and coached there for a couple of years before he went to the Virginia Squires in the ABA (American Basketball Association). He called me when he got to Virginia and he said, "Johnny, I need a guy who can come out here and help me run the front office of the franchise." As a matter of fact, one of my claims to fame was that I signed Julius Irving and George Gervin to contracts in the ABA.

Jim Washington of Bulls doesn't give Art Williams of Rockets a chance to grab rebound." As published in the *Chicago Sun-Times*. Photographer: Mel Larson. Copyright, 1967 by the *Chicago Sun-Times*, Inc. Reprinted with permission.

Nick Kladis

When I was born, we lived at 42nd and Cottage Grove next to the first Walgreens built in Chicago. I later attended Tilden High School, and when I was a senior in the '40s, Johnny "Red" Kerr was a freshman at the high school and Bill Postl was our coach. Our team played basketball games against teams from such schools as DuSable, Dunbar, Englewood, and Hirsch. During those years, I was living on the South Side of Chicago at 79th and Dorchester in South Shore, and we built a small grocery store in 1948 at 43rd and Ellis, later moving to a new store at 43rd and Lake Park. It was an African American neighborhood known as Oakland-Kenwood.

I attended Loyola University where I played on their basketball team. During my last year at Loyola, "Red" Kerr was starring at Illinois and we played against each other. In 1951, in a very close game, he was guarding me and I scored 31 points against Illinois. I played forward and center at Loyola, and I was 6'3", which was considered tall in those years. I was at Loyola from the middle of 1947 to 1952 and played for three different basketball coaches, including Tom Haggerty in my sophomore year, Johnny Jordan in my junior year, and George Ireland in my senior year, when I was captain of the team. I scored over 1,000 points for the team from 1949 to 1952 and received All-American honors in my senior season. I was greatly honored when Loyola retired my number 3, the first time that a basketball number had been retired by the university. It was a big thrill for me. Looking back on my playing days, I remember that I was better at rebounding and scoring than defense, but I always played hard at both ends of the court.

In 1952, after graduation, I traveled with the College All-Stars against the Harlem Globetrotters and we had a great series that was originated by my close friend, Bill Veeck. We played about 20 games in 20 different cities, and it was just a big show. When I was selected by the Philadelphia Warriors in the third round of the NBA draft, I think that they offered me $3,000 to play for their team. However, since the Korean War was happening at the time, I went into the Army for two years, spending one year at Ft. Riley, Kansas and one year in Chicago at Fifth Army Headquarters. I passed up my basketball career at that point and went into the grocery business with my family before I got married.

One of the biggest thrills of my life happened in 1963 when Loyola won the NCAA Championship. At that time, I was a volunteer assistant coach for George Ireland and I still wear the championship ring. One of the star players for Loyola, Jerry Harkness, the famous All-American, had a job in my store, and I was very close to all the kids on that team, including Jack Egan, Les Hunter, Ronnie Miller, and Vic Rouse. After the '63 season, I remained in the supermarket business.

During the '60s, I followed the White Sox very closely, and I remember their great 1964 team that just lost the pennant by one game to the Yankees. I was very close with Bill Veeck, and, in 1975, I joined him when he bought the White Sox for the second time and was honored to be on his board of directors. From 1975 to 1980, I had a part ownership of the White Sox, and in 1996, I became a part owner of the St. Louis Cardinals. Sports have been a big part of my life, from high school to today. I played on some really good high school teams at Tilden, and we won the City Championship in 1946 and the last Stagg Tournament ever held in 1947 where we beat Tuley, and I was the MVP of the tournament.

Lee Stern

When I returned in February 1947 after serving with the U.S. Air Force in Germany, I went to work for the Cubs in the front office for a few months. They told me they had to make an opening for Vern Olson, a sore-armed pitcher, so I was the last guy in and the first guy out. Then, I went back to school, not at the University of Illinois where I had been prior to service, but at Roosevelt College, which was just opening on Congress and Michigan. As a GI, I could have gone anyplace for college, but chose to remain in Chicago because my father was recovering from a heart attack. When I started at Roosevelt College, I already knew about the Chicago Board of Trade. The employment bureau and student lounge were both on the second floor of Roosevelt, so I took my classes in the afternoon because I wanted to enjoy my new found freedom since I was just out of the service and 20 years old.

By chance, I saw a sign at Roosevelt that the Board of Trade was looking for runners from 9:15-1:30. It fit in with my program schedule, and since I knew about the Board, I got a job as a runner with Merrill Lynch. Ironically, if the employment agency had been located on the top floor and not next to the student lounge, then I probably wouldn't be talking about my career at the Board of Trade where I have been a member for 56 years.

I met my wife, Norma, at Roosevelt in 1949. We were married in 1951 and had four children in six years. Our first apartment was at the Bryn Mawr Hotel, and then we moved to the Sovereign Hotel located at 6200 N. Kenmore in Edgewater. It was a very popular first class hotel with a swimming pool and a great restaurant, the Stuart Room that was later called Frank and Marie's. Our first real apartment was at 6050 N. Fairfield Avenue, on the third floor of a new courtyard building. Then, I bought a piece of property in Glencoe, had a house built, and we moved there on February 14, 1955. At the time, we had two children, Jeffrey and Danny, and after we moved, we had Kenny and Jan. We began looking for a larger house, but in 1960, you could not find a five-bedroom house in Glencoe. I ended up buying a house in Highland Park in 1961 after I learned a friend and his wife had bought it and decided to live elsewhere.

My full time business was at the Board of Trade, and those were the good days when people understood the trading business. Unlike today, money was not the dominant topic of conversation. During my early days at the Board of Trade, trading closed at 1:15 p.m. So, in the afternoon, if you were interested in being a professional and learning the business, you would talk to other people and check with your senior people to find out what was going on. In those days, I would get home by 4:00 pm, and that gave me time to be with the kids.

In the '50s and '60s, my interest in sports was focused on playing golf at Green Acres Country Club in Northbrook, just west of the Edens Expressway on Dundee Road. In the 1960's, the club hired a pro named Jack Fleck. Jack had beaten Ben Hogan in a playoff for the championship at the U.S. Open. I had just started to play golf, and with Fleck's help, I went from a 23 to a 14 handicap. That was a disaster, because with a 14 handicap I was losing all the time.

I had been a hockey fan since the 1940's, and in the '50s and early to mid-'60s, there were only six teams in the NHL. I knew every player on every team, including their jersey numbers. I used to go to the Chicago Stadium back in the '40s when they had sellouts, and the Blackhawks stars included the Bentley brothers and Mosienko. A new highway was being built, and it was called the Northwest (later named to Kennedy) Expressway. I knew somebody who was with the electrical company doing work on the highway and he told me, "If you want to see something exciting, drive down the Expressway because they are almost finished." I used to drive down the highway while they were still working on it. It was so strange because you were looking at the city from an angle you had never seen before. When they finally opened it up, we could make a quick trip down to the Stadium from Glencoe and Highland Park. We decided to buy some season tickets for the Blackhawks games and were able to select our seats anyplace in the Stadium. I got seats in a corner of the mezzanine, not directly behind the goal, and went to the games with a group of my friends who worked at the Board of Trade. The great thing was that they changed the starting time for the games from 8:00 to 7:30 pm. because the Northwest Expressway had opened.

My best story about being a hockey fan happened at a game when the Blackhawks were playing the Montreal Canadiens in the Stanley Cup finals. I had an extra ticket, and my friends suggested I stand outside the Stadium and sell the ticket. I didn't want to do that and get in trouble, so I said, "Let's put our coats on the seat," so that is what we did. For some odd reason, I had brought a pair of binoculars to the Stadium for the game even though I didn't really need them. I had left the binoculars in the car, so, at the end of the first period, I wanted to go and get them. But, the Andy Frain usher wouldn't let me leave the Stadium. He was quite nasty and said to me "You can't go out!" I said to him, "What do you mean I can't go out?" He responded, "If you go out, you cannot come in again." I emphasized to him that I just wanted to go to my car. But, he refused and said, "You go out, you are not coming back in!" I said, "I will tell you what I will do. I don't know how much money I have in my pocket or how much you have in your pocket. But, I am going to take a chance that maybe I have a little bit more since you are working as an usher and I'm working in a business. I don't mean to be rude, but, whatever money I have in my pocket

I'm going to bet you that not only will I get back in, but you will let me back in." I went outside to my car and came back into the Stadium to his spot. I reached into my pocket and took out the unused ticket. He looked at the ticket, then looked at it again, tore the stub off, handed it to me and walked away.

In 1959, it was Bobby Hull's first year with the Blackhawks, and we bought the season tickets during his second year in 1960. We went to every game that year, and we loved it. The team included Hull, Mikita, Pierre Pilote, Bill "Red" Hay, Glenn Hall, and Eric Nesterenko. Those were exciting times. Hull was a great player, and I was there when they won the Stanley Cup in the spring of 1961. The 60's were a great decade for the Blackhawks, and Chicago Stadium was full of excitement and cigarette smoke.

In the winter of 1963, the Bears won the NFL championship beating the New York Giants at blustery Wrigley Field. The score escapes me, but I was in Miami vacationing with my family and was surrounded by Giants fans. They all wanted to bet me, so I obliged them and the end result was that they paid for the next three days of my vacation.

I remember as a kid I was always a Cubs fan, but being a Cubs fan when I grew up was not like being a Cubs fan today. We were more concerned about the team than the park, and I went to the ballgames because I lived on the North Side. The Cubs weren't very good in the 1960's, and the White Sox were the dominant team. As a schoolboy, I used to get in line at Le Moyne playground, near the ballpark, during the summertime, and they would give us free passes to Wrigley Field. I used to mooch passes because there were always extra passes for the game. They used to give us different tickets each time for seats in the upper deck; everyday there was a different color ticket. As a result, I had collected a variety of color ticket stubs, so I would find out what color was used that day. Then, I would go to the upper deck and show the usher the ticket stub and he would let me sit in the grandstands and box seats. During grammar school, I sat next to a woman in the box seats, and her name was Mrs. Reed, from Reed Candies. She had two seats located next to Pat Pieper, the Cubs field announcer, who worked near the screen behind home plate. I used to sit there with her when her son wasn't there. I also got to know a lot of players since I was sitting so close to the field.

We never called them Cubbies because for us they were always the Cubs. In 1969, when the Cubs looked like they were headed for the pennant, I was involved in the Better Boys Foundation and I remember that Ron Santo, Glenn Beckert, Jim Hickman, and Kenny Holtzman all played golf at Green Acres Country Club during the season. I really thought they were going to win the pennant because they were loaded with quality players. I remained a Cubs fan until the late '70s. In 1975, I had just started the Chicago Sting soccer team; Bill Veeck needed additional investors in order to keep the White Sox in Chicago. I put together a group of Board of Trade members, and we purchased about 20% ownership of the White Sox. I served on the team's executive committee. My wife couldn't understand what I was doing, "If you are putting all your efforts into the Sting, why are you getting involved in the White Sox?" I said to her, "I'm getting involved for only one reason. Hopefully, it will give me credibility with the sports media."

The 60's were a strange decade when 70 million children from the postwar "Baby Boom" became teenagers and young adults. There was the horrendous assassination of John F. Kennedy in 1963. I will always remember being on the trading floor when the news came over the wires and after the market closed, I went over to the teletype machine and pulled the news report off of the wire. I still have it to this day. Of course later were the assassinations of Martin Luther King and Robert Kennedy. I remember taking my family to Washington where Dr. King made his "I Have a Dream" speech. It was just by coincidence we had selected that weekend to visit D.C., and it was a moment I will never forget. The late 60's, of course, was the time of Vietnam. While those of us who served in World War II and Korea supported the war, the younger generation was certainly against it. My son Jeffrey, who graduated from Highland Park High School in 1969, was convinced our leaders were going in the wrong direction with the Vietnam conflict. He and the young people like him proved to be right, and those of us who supported Vietnam were wrong.

We were all misled by our patriotism that dominated our thinking when in fact Vietnam proved to be our undoing for many years to come. Our country is still suffering from the tragedies of the assassinations and the Vietnam syndrome. I am hopeful that the 60's created the ability for people to think for themselves rather than have someone think for them.

Northwest Highway at Lawrence, 1963
(Courtesy of CTA)

Politics of 1960s: Loc

and Nation

the
al, State
al

Adamowski for Mayor sign, 1963. (Courtesy, Bob Adamowski)

Newton and Jo Baskin Minow

Newt: In 1960, we were in Chicago, and I was practicing law with Adlai Stevenson. I was very enthusiastic about Jack Kennedy. In 1956, I tried to persuade Stevenson to choose Kennedy as his vice presidential running mate. Everything changed for us on the Saturday night before the election of 1960. We went to the Torchlight Parade that Mayor Daley had for Kennedy and were on a bus with an old friend, Bill Haddad. He asked me, "Are you going to go to Washington if Jack wins?" I said, "No." Bill said, "You're crazy. It's an opportunity of a lifetime." I looked at Jo, and she looked at me, and we said to ourselves that if Jack won, and if it was an interesting job, we would think about it.

Kennedy was elected in November 1960. The day after the election, Sarge Shriver called me and said, "The President-elect has made me his talent scout, and we would like you to come to Washington and be in our new government." I said, "Sarge, we just can't do it. I've got three small children, a wife, and a law practice in Chicago. I can't even think about it." So, he said, "Will you help me find people?" I said, "Yes." Bob Kennedy knew that there was only one thing I was interested in, and that was television. When they asked me to be chairman of the Federal Communications Commission, I went in to see my senior partner, Adlai Stevenson, and told him I wanted to do it. He responded, "They didn't offer you chairman of the FCC. That's impossible. Besides, I want you to stay here and keep the law practice going so when I leave the government as Kennedy's Ambassador to the United Nations, I can come back." But, we ended up going to Washington after I was offered the Chairmanship around Christmas of 1960, and it was Kennedy's first regulatory agency appointment.

Jo: It was Bob's idea for Newt to head the FCC because they were roommates during the '56 campaign and traveled together. He was aware of Newt's keen interest in the potential, as well as the dangers of television.

Newt: I left Glencoe for Washington in the winter of 1961, and the kids stayed in school until the semester was out. Then, the whole family moved to Washington in the summer of '61. We had been living in a house in Glencoe and sold the house. I had told the Kennedys that I really couldn't afford to stay more than a couple of years, and they agreed. We were away from Chicago from '61 to '63. Before I had left Chicago, I had been offered the job of general counsel of the Encyclopedia Britannica, and that is the position I took after we decided to move back to Glencoe.

Jo: I found it very difficult to leave Washington, just as, little more than two years before I had found it hard to leave Chicago. I had become very attached to my friends, my activities, and our lifestyle and we felt as if we were in the epicenter of the world in Washington. When, indeed, I knew that Newt's resignation was to be announced, I turned on the radio in the car, and listened. In less than five minutes, as I entered the house, the phone was ringing. It was a neighbor I knew slightly. She said she wanted to buy our home, which she did without ever seeing the inside.

We returned to Glencoe in September, once our new home became available and the kids returned to South School, and we resumed life pretty much as it had been before our departures. Newt spent a couple of years at Britannica and decided that he really preferred independent law practice. In 1965, he accepted a partnership in Leibman, Williams, Bennett, Baird, and Minow, which later merged with Sidley and Austin.

On that terrible day in November 1963, when the world stopped with the news of JFK's assassination, I heard about it on the radio at a Scholarship and Guidance holiday bazaar where I had volunteered.

At once, I called Newt's office, and he took the first train home. Then I rushed to South School to tell the kids before they heard the tragic news from someone else. Only six months before, they had joined Newt and me in the Oval Office to say goodbye to the President. They considered him their friend. It was on May 29th, his last birthday and our 14th anniversary. They each had made birthday gifts to present to him.

The 1960s ended up being a decade of a series of cataclysmic deaths of major figures in the country: first, JFK, then, Martin Luther King, followed by RFK's murder. As a result, we saw the city changing dramatically, and the riots that followed Martin Luther King's death led to seething anger in the city. We were very blessed in those years, but we never took our life for granted. Although I volunteered for a variety of organizations outside our home, I felt very strongly about being home to see the kids at lunchtime and after school, and it made a difference to them.

Newt: When we came home from D.C., Mayor Richard J. Daley called and invited me to lunch. It was just the two of us. He took me to the Empire Room of the Palmer House, and we had a good talk about the Kennedys and about the government. Then, he said, "Are you interested in running for office?" I said, "No, Mayor, I have no interest in that." He said, "Are you sure? Isn't there any public office you would like to hold?" I said, "No, Mayor." He said, "Are you positive?" I said, "Mayor, there is only one political office that I would like to have and that is a delegate to the Democratic National Convention." At that time, the delegates were picked in the "back room." The mayor groaned and said, "Ah! Everybody wants to be a delegate to the Democratic National Convention. Are you sure you don't want to run for governor or senator?" I said,

"No, Mayor, I really would like to just be a delegate." A year later, I was picked as an alternate delegate because I don't think that he quite trusted me to be a regular delegate. I was an alternate delegate in 1964 and 1968, and when the rules changed, I had to run for delegate and was elected in 1972 and 1976.

We were opposed to the Vietnam War, and in early '68, I had been in favor of Bob Kennedy's candidacy. After Bob was killed in June 1968, Senator Stevenson asked me to organize the Illinois Campaign for Hubert Humphrey, which we did, and I became state chairman of the Humphrey campaign. We gave a big party on the eve of the convention at the new Mid-America Club, and a lot of our friends from around the country were there. We had no idea then what was going to erupt in the parks and outside the Hilton. I blame a lot of people for what happened. Both the protesters and the city officials all share a lot of the blame. I remember that after the convention, my friend, Frank Stanton, who was the head of CBS, called me. He said, "A friend of mine who works for NBC got into trouble with the law during the convention. She needs a lawyer." Her name was Aline Saarinen, the widow of the architect, and she was a reporter for NBC television news. I said to Frank, "I'm not a criminal lawyer." But, he said, "Please take care of this." NBC had been accused of eavesdropping on a caucus, which was true, so they were going to arrest all of them, but we got her out of it.

Jack Kennedy had told me something very interesting when my partner, Bill Blair, and I picked him up at O'Hare on May 29, 1960. We drove him out to Adlai Stevenson's farm because we were trying to get Adlai to endorse Kennedy. It was JFK's birthday, and on the way out, I said, "Jack, if you don't get the nomination, then who do you think should be nominated?" He said, "Lyndon!" I couldn't believe it, so I said, "Lyndon?" He said, "He's a tough politician, but he's got talent." So, I was not surprised when Jack picked Johnson to be his vice president.

In 1968, the Democratic National Convention in Chicago was an absolute disaster. My old friend, Angelo Geocaris, and I organized a luncheon for Humphrey the week before the convention in Chicago at the Blackstone Hotel. When the lunch finished, Humphrey said to me, "Are you busy now?" I said, "No." He said, "Can you come up to the room now? I want to talk to you." So, we went up to his hotel room. He took off his shoes, loosened his tie, and lay down on his bed. He was exhausted.

He had two guys with him: his doctor, Edgar Berman and his campaign manager, Bill Conell. Humphrey looked at me and said, "You've been around a long time. What do you think?" And, I said, "Hubert. Next week is your bar mitzvah. Do you know what a bar mitzvah is?" He said, "Do I know what a bar mitzvah is? I've been to more bar mitzvahs in my life than you have." I said, "Next week, you have to convince the country that you are no longer LBJ's boy and that you are your own man. You've got to walk away from him, in public, on the war. And, the time to do that is in your acceptance speech." Dr. Berman was on one side of the bed, and he said, "Good, good!" The other guy was looking like he was going to kill me. I could see that Humphrey was getting contradictory advice.

Hubert said, "Would you do a draft speech?" I took him very seriously, and I wrote what I considered to be a great beginning of a speech. It started off—"Eight years ago, I ran for the Democratic nomination for President against Jack Kennedy. Jack Kennedy defeated me and later won against Richard Nixon. Well, Jack Kennedy is no longer here, but Richard Nixon is still here. I'm not going to see the man who Jack Kennedy defeated eight years ago become President of the United States...and neither are you! I am now the Vice President, and, as such, I owe an obligation of loyalty to my chief and I have honored it, seven days a week, 24 hours a day. But, at this moment, my situation changes because I accept your nomination for President. You've got a right to know what I would do if I were the President, and I've got an obligation to tell you what I would do if I were the President," and then I spelled out how he would walk away from Johnson's policy on the Vietnam War. I still think that if he would have done it, Hubert would have been elected President.

I don't think the country wanted to elect Nixon, but they were so disgusted with the Democrats that Nixon got in.

Jo and I became involved more and more in the affairs of the city. I became the chairman of WTTW, and Jo was head of "Know Your Chicago," a University of Chicago Adult Education program. When I served on the board of Northwestern, I was asked to give the Commencement speech at Northwestern. I told the graduates, "I met my wife at Northwestern. When we went there, we each had a very interesting roommate. My wife's roommate was the Oscar-winning actress, Cloris Leachman, and mine was NBC White House correspondent, Sandy Vanocur. It is obvious that both of us went to school much too early, because if we went to Northwestern today, my roommate would be Cloris Leachman." Cloris sent me a letter in which she said, "That is the most disgusting, filthiest insult of my life. Everybody knows that if I went to Northwestern University now, my roommate would be Sandy Vanocur."

Looking at the '60s in the city, country, and world, I've often reflected on the impact of the deaths of four people of significance: Jack Kennedy, and how his death robbed the promise of the future for an entire generation; Martin Luther King, and how his death impacted the future of the civil rights movement; Pope John, and how his death set back the process of reforming the Catholic Church; and, Bob Kennedy, and how his death impacted the '68 election. Those four people died untimely deaths, and all the progress and all the promise of the future evaporated. They were heroes for the young people, and when they died, many hopes for the future died with them.

Minow family with JFK in Oval Office,
Washington, DC, c. 1962
(Courtesy of Minows)

following page
Poem written by Martha Minow,
November 22, 1963

Seated beneath a huge picture of the late
President Kennedy, Mayor Daley prays.
As published in the *Chicago Sun-Times*.
Photographer: Jack Lenahan.
Copyright 1963 by *Chicago Sun-Times*, Inc.
Reprinted with permission.

Martha Minow
Nov. 22, 1963

To Mrs. John F. Kennedy
　　　Slowly but surely,
A Willow branch fell down,
　　While rain spread 'round the town.
A sad day it was for me
　For the Willow it my favorite tree.

　　　It was not just a sad day
　　　　　　for me......
　　　　Not just sad for myself,
　　I t was sad for everyone
　　Worse than a bad elf.

　　But if I take the branch right in
　The roots might then begin.
　　By spring I will know,
Whether it will grow.

　　　My little tree will grow again,
　I guess that's the same way with
　　　　　　　　　　rain.

Art Berman

In the '60s, my wife and I moved to an apartment on Ridge just south of Touhy. We lived there for a couple of years before buying a home at 2701 W. Sherwin Avenue, across from Rogers Elementary School, and lived there for almost 25 years. We had two children, loved the neighborhood, its people, and the fact that the elementary school and park were right across the street from our house. It was always a wonderful neighborhood to raise a family. The 1960s was not a decade of change for me. It was a very hectic and demanding but satisfying life. My law offices were downtown, and every morning I would drive to the office early and come back in the middle of the afternoon or late in the evening. I will always view the area as a great neighborhood, and it remained that way for many years.

Our neighborhood was a very safe and wonderful place to raise a family during the 1960s. Schools, parks, and overall conditions were good, and there was little, if any, crime. We had good retail shopping in the neighborhood as well as a large number of religious institutions available to community residents. Interestingly, from the age of two, in the 1930s through today, I have lived on the north side of Chicago within a one mile radius circle of my whole life. The farthest west I lived was on Mozart Street, the farthest east was Sheridan Road, the farthest south was 5800 Sheridan Road, and the farthest north was 7300 North. So, I am just a boy of the neighborhood.

In 1960, I was a practicing attorney and had become very active in the 50th Ward Democratic Organization and local Young Democrats. In 1964, there was an election for the legislature that was based on a new voting format where legislators were elected at-large. In 1966, we returned to the previous system of multi-member House districts. In that voting structure, there were three state representatives per district. Every voter had three votes to cast, but under each name there were three buttons: you could give one candidate all three votes, also known as bullet votes; you could give two candidates one and a half votes each; or you could give three candidates one vote each. This allowed the voters to participate on a bipartisan basis, if they so desired, by giving votes to candidates from the two major political parties. In my opinion, it was a great system because of the process and the minority parties would campaign on a bullet vote approach, asking supporters to give them three votes so that they could overcome their political minority status.

My district, which was on the far north side of Chicago, included the 47th, 48th, 49th and 50th Wards. In 1966, it was a big Republican year, with two Republicans elected from our legislative district, including Mike Zlatnick and Ed Copeland, and one

Democrat, Paul Elward. As we approached the 1968 election, I was chosen to run for the second Democratic seat in my district. The 1968 election was very interesting because Ed Copeland and Mike Zlatnick were the two Republicans, while Paul Elward and I were the two Democrats. When the election results were announced, Elward and I won, as well as Ed Copeland. That was my first election and the start of a political career that lasted 31 years in the Illinois General Assembly, including eight years in the Illinois House and 23 years in the Illinois Senate. I won a seat in the Illinois Senate race eight years later in 1976, and I remember it as a very tough race.

The unrest that occurred in the late '60s had no impact on local politics. I was involved in the 1968 Convention, and, as a member of the Young Democrats, I was an usher at the Democratic National Convention. During that time, one of my other brothers was in the Illinois National Guard protecting the convention from demonstrators, while my youngest brother was protesting the war and was a dissenter. So, the three Bermans represented different perspectives of those events, but 1968 didn't have a direct affect on me either as a lawyer or a resident of West Rogers Park.

What was interesting about the '68 election was that everything in my district was within the boundaries of Chicago with Howard Street as my north boundary. Every 10 years we redistricted the legislative districts, so, following the 1970 census, in 1971, a new map was drawn for the 1972 election. The redistricting ended with the Andersonville neighborhood, the 47th Ward, and a good part of the 50th Ward removed from my district. So, I had half of the 48th Ward, all of the 49th Ward, a part of the 50th Ward and about 2/3 of Evanston. That was what gave rise to the "heated" primary election of 1972. That year, Paul Elward was appointed to a judgeship while a young man by the name of Danny O'Brien was the other Democrat with me in the '72 election.

The primary candidates included me, as the incumbent, O'Brien, the incumbent, and Joe Lundy, the challenger who lived in Evanston. Lundy defeated O'Brien, and Joe Lundy and I were the winners in March and in the November elections. We served for four years together.

My interaction with Mayor Richard J. Daley was minimal, but positive. In my role as a member of the House Education Committee, I was the sponsor of legislation to increase school funding. I was just a young state representative at that time, and he was very supportive of my candidacy in the 1976 elections when I ran for the Illinois Senate. I was a loyal Democrat, and we had strong Democratic organizations in the three wards of the far north side. I can remember that there was a restaurant called the Walnut Room on the second floor of the old Bismarck Hotel at LaSalle and Randolph. Every work day, at lunch, you could walk in there and write a book about the politics that was being discussed by all the politicians in the restaurant. There were specific tables reserved for certain politicians, and it was a fascinating process just to observe and see who was there, who came up and shook hands, and who was chatting with each other.

As far as the Loop is concerned, it is a better place to visit today than it was the 1960s, but, even then, it was a great place. Loop shopping was only beginning to shift to North Michigan Avenue by the late '60s. There was more racial intermixing in the Loop during the '60s, as Chicago neighborhoods reflected the racial changes that were happening in numerous sections of the city. However, on the north side of Chicago, there were only some slow racial changes that had occurred in places like East Rogers Park, but none had really occurred in my West Rogers Park neighborhood.

Bob Adamowski

I was born in August 1940 and lived at 1647 N. Nagle Avenue in the Galewood neighborhood in northwest Chicago near Narragansett for the next 25 years. Our neighborhood, like so many in Chicago, was a mixture of people of diverse ethnic origins, including Scandinavian, German, Greek and Italian. In my grammar school, there were but one or two other kids of Polish extraction, so it was definitely not a Polish neighborhood, but since my mother was a second generation American with German antecedents, that was of no particular consequence.

My father, born in Chicago of immigrants of Polish origin was always identified as a Polish-American. Our home was less than a block from Oak Park; so much of our focus for shopping, entertainment, and religious activities was really Oak Park. I went to Lovett Elementary School at Narragansett and Bloomingdale, and then to Steinmetz High School at 3030 N. Mobile Avenue from 1954 to 1958.

In 1956, my father, Ben Adamowski, was elected as Cook County State's Attorney as a Republican. In 1958, based on the recommendation of a family friend, my father interviewed and, because he was such a bright young guy, hired James R. Thompson as a summer intern. The following year, he hired Thompson right out of Northwestern University Law School as an Assistant State's Attorney. As an intern, Jim had worked on an appellate brief to the Illinois Supreme Court. That case was then scheduled for oral argument before Jim's class of new attorneys were to be admitted to the Bar so Dad arranged to have Jim sworn in early so he could argue the case before the state's highest court, a very rare opportunity for a fledgling lawyer.

My grandfather had been alderman of a ward that included the Bucktown/Logan Square area. After my grandfather Max died in 1929, Dad was approached to run for the state legislature. At that time, Dad was 23 years old and the youngest member ever elected to the Illinois legislature. He represented his legislative district for the next 10 years. In those years, he was a Democrat and served as the House Minority Leader. In fact, he used to joke about making Richard J. Daley a Democrat. Daley was elected to fill a vacancy that belonged to a Republican, so at the opening day of his first session, he took that member's seat. Dad then made the motion to have him change sides of the aisle and sit with the Democrats. Abraham Marovitz, as well as Daley, served with Dad, and the three of them were close friends; my father often remarked about the fact that he felt they were all men with similar value systems.

In 1953, Dad ran for mayor in the Democratic primary against Richard J. Daley and the then current mayor, Martin Kennelly. Daley won the primary and then the general election. In 1956, the Republican Party approached my father about becoming their candidate for Cook County State's Attorney, and that was when he switched political parties. Dad was always viewed as something of a maverick and not a mainstream Democrat by the Democratic Party stalwarts.

When I first began practicing law, a judge I appeared before recognized my last name and said to me, "The problem with your Dad was he was just too honest." I went back to the office, and told him the story, and recall asking, "Dad, how can you be too honest?" My father was direct and candid but most of all could not tolerate, much less engage in, any practices that required a flexible conscience or worse.

As the Republican State's Attorney, he did not make the mayor very happy because he knew where "all the bodies were buried" because he had been inside the "political game" so long. One of the principal things he tried to do was to clean up government. I know that when he became State's Attorney in 1956, he discovered that there were outstanding warrants for the arrest of many of the reputed mobsters. So, dad asked his Assistant State's Attorneys, "What do we have on these people? Use these warrants and let's go arrest them and prosecute them." He was told that the warrants really were years old without substantive charges behind them and were just used for shakedowns and payoffs. So, he moved to quash the warrants, which led to charges by the opposition and the press that he was favoring the Mob.

When dad was running for re-election as State's Attorney in 1960, a reporter was at the precinct where Tony Accardo, the reputed leader of the Chicago mafia, voted in River Forest. Accardo sat down next to the reporter who said to him, "I'll bet I know who you are going to vote against." And Accardo said, "You do?" The reporter said, "Yeah, you're going to vote against Adamowski." According to the story, Accardo said, "Absolutely not. We need more honest men in government." Dad always said that organized crime would accept and respect you for standing up to them and trying to enforce the law, it was those who became their partners, took their payoffs, and then crossed them that wound up in trouble.

Mayor Daley wasn't pleased that Dad uncovered and aggressively investigated Democratic scandals, including missing bail bond funds and the "burglars in blue" of the Summerdale Police District. Dad also went after the Mob and broke up one of their biggest floating crap games. His plan was to prosecute the patrons as well as the operators as some of Chicago's well-known and respected citizenry frequented the game. But, in 1960, my father lost his reelection. The theory was that Nixon lost Illinois because Daley had stolen votes for Kennedy. However, others have argued that it was Dad's race that caused Nixon to lose Illinois because Daley was far more interested in beating my father than he was in getting Kennedy elected. Dad actually filed a challenge to the election and got funding for some of it, but the judge ruled that the recount couldn't be done based on selective precinct verification, but had to include all of the precincts and the entire cost of the recount had to be paid in advance. At the same time, Dad got a letter from Nixon saying that it wouldn't be good for the country to continue to challenge the results of the election. I believe if he had gone ahead with his own challenge, it would have resulted in his reelection and also shown enough discrepancies in the Nixon election results to have given him Illinois.

After the election, Dad took a position with Trilla Steel Drum Company, a cooperage house that reconditioned steel drums. They set up a line to manufacture new steel drums, and Dad was responsible for that business. He stayed with Trilla from 1960 until 1965, and while there, waged a mayoral campaign as the Republican candidate against Richard J. Daley in 1963. That race was one of Daley's closest, and he won by only a 137,000 vote margin of victory. In fact, Dad won a majority of the 50 wards and, as was common in Chicago elections of that era there were charges and evidence of vote fraud, election irregularities, and ballot miscounts. In 1970, Dad ran his last campaign seeking the office of Cook County Assessor, losing to the long entrenched "Machine" candidate, "Parky" Cullerton.

Meanwhile, I graduated from Cornell University in Ithaca, NY and then in 1965 from the University of Michigan Law School in Ann Arbor. During the early 1960s, although I was away at school, I was in Chicago every summer working a variety of jobs, most of them in construction. Construction jobs not only paid better, but the physical labor was a good break from schoolwork. And, since I was rowing on the Cornell crew, it helped me stay in shape. After my freshman year in law school, I worked in the preliminary title section of Chicago Title and Trust which was at 111 West Washington. The next summer, I was a summer intern at Raymond, Mayer, Jenner and Block (now Jenner and Block), which was then located in the Field Building at 135 S. LaSalle. I was fortunate that my Dad had so many acquaintances and friends that he could contact to help me get those summer positions.

When I received my law degree in 1965, I went to work with my father and his two law partners, Paul Newey, who had been his chief investigator in the State's Attorney's Office, and Frank Riley, who had been the Assistant State's Attorney and who headed the appellate division. We had our office on LaSalle Street, so I was downtown every day during a period when the central city was undergoing one of its greatest building booms and the face of the city was being transformed. This reformation and construction fervor fostered decades of subsequent growth and architectural experimentation resulting in the dramatic skyline and singularly unique buildings, many of which are hallmarks of today's downtown Chicago.

In the early '60s, Wells Street in Old Town was just coming into its heyday, and I along with friends would go down to visit the attractions. I remember enjoying the Pickle Barrel, which was my first experience being served buckets of peanuts with shells the patrons could throw on the floor. Major events like the Auto Show, the circus, every spring, the livestock show each November, and various conventions, and special concerts, and attractions were held in the International Amphitheater. The Hilton hotel had the Boulevard Room, which offered an ice show performed in a cabaret setting for the dinning patrons. The Sherman Hotel had the Well of the Sea and the Sirloin Room and the Stockyard Inn allowed diners to brand their own steaks. Kungsholm on Ontario served an extravagant smorgasbord in an old mansion before the guests went to the theater next door to enjoy a puppet opera. There was also the Blackhawk on Wabash with its "spinning salad bowl."

I finished law school just before all of the upheaval began to occur in Chicago, throughout the country and particularly on college campuses. The big changes came after I graduated, and they really accelerated in 1967 and 1968. By that time, I was married, our first child was born, we were living in an apartment in suburban Palatine, and I was commuting on the Northwestern Railroad each day to the Loop. Surprisingly, the major events that disrupted Chicago did not impact the day-to-day workday for those in the Loop. There were some demonstrations in the Loop, but generally the commerce of the city continued without disruption, which is contrary to what many imagine to have

occurred. What did bring the activity and routine of the city to an absolute halt was the blizzard of 1967 when 23 inches of snow fell in a 24-hour period. Even though I had a long commute, I could walk to the train in Palatine and from the Northwestern Station to our office on LaSalle Street, so I was one of the very few who went to work that day. Downtown was virtually deserted.

I was draft eligible in 1966, and I received a notice to report for a physical exam, a precursor to being drafted. When I took the physical, I remember being amused by the hearing test as they were only checking every third person. I guess the assumption was that if one out of three tested "OK," then everyone was fine. Before I was called for service, I enrolled at John Marshall Law School and started taking additional legal courses in order to get a Master of Law degree, which provided a deferment from the draft. In the spring of 1967, our son was born and once you had a dependent, you were given a permanent draft deferment.

In the 60's, Palatine was a small suburban community and had not yet experienced the growth that would happen later. Most of the growth was still within the town itself, and when you went outside Palatine into the country, you were surrounded by farmland and fields. There was so little development that a fire in a stable in Kildeer could be seen from Palatine which was some seven miles away. The Northwest suburbs were very rural in those days, and each community had distinct boundaries with the spaces between marked by open land and farming. With the completion of the Northwest Tollway the space between communities began to develop, and by the beginning of the 70's there was very little open land remaining between Palatine, Arlington Heights, and Mt. Prospect

Overall, the 1960s was a "bridge" decade that witnessed and fostered both social modification and cultural change. Everything seemed to accelerate. There was more mobility, the outlying suburbs began to come into their own, and to accommodate the commuter and the construction boom in the downtown core, new parking structures were built by the city on the perimeter of the Loop.

Benjamin Adamowski, James R. Thompson, and Al Ganz at Cook County State's Attorneys Office, October 16, 1959. (Courtesy, Bob Adamowski)

VP Nixon, Governor Stratton, and Benjamin Adamowski on Dick Nixon Campaign Special Train, 1960. (Courtesy, Bob Adamowski)

Senator Everett Dirksen, Benjamin Adamowski, c. 1960 (Courtesy, Bob Adamowski)

Leon Despres

I was first elected to the City Council in 1955 as alderman of the 5th Ward representing Hyde Park and Woodlawn. The local Democratic Organization was completely dependent on patronage, and, in 1955, Richard J. Daley was elected mayor.

Under Daley's administration as mayor and as party chairman, they boosted the number of patronage workers to as high as 45,000 who were not all city employees. They kept a vast card catalogue file in their central headquarters and depended on that to win elections. It was very costly to the public, because those patronage employees would do what their patronage bosses told them to do. They didn't pay much attention to their superiors in the line of work to which they were assigned because that wasn't what got them their job or kept them on the job. The city was really in bad shape.

Then, in the 1970s, the change came with the Supreme Court opinions, known as the Shakman decrees, that partisan political patronage was not proper. Although Mayor Daley did not believe that he would have to give up patronage, he did know that he had to abide by the Supreme Court. So, he signed a series of judgments and agreed to give up patronage. That is the root of the present situation. In my first two elections in 1955 and 1959 as alderman, the patronage employees were directed to defeat me at all costs. We had to mount a counter force to overcome them. We couldn't use public employees, so we had to use volunteers, people who were active and energetic and who believed in what we were fighting for. I was nearly knocked out of the box in my first and second elections, but, after that, the Machine gave up and decided to leave me alone. I was an alderman for five four-year terms from 1955 to 1975.

I got along well on a personal basis with Mayor Richard J. Daley, and he was a very courteous person. He lost his temper at me only once in 20 years when he called me a liar, and I think that speaks pretty well for him. Otherwise, he was courteous although he didn't spend time with me personally and didn't invite me to attend any of his events. For eight years, I was the only independent alderman in the City Council before others were elected, including some African American aldermen (Bill Cousins, Sammy A.A. Rayner), and then Dick Simpson and Bill Singer. We had a small group that could function as opposition to City Hall but never had much power or ability to block legislation.

Life in Hyde Park and Woodlawn went through some dramatic changes from 1955 through the 1960s. The big change in Hyde Park during that time period was an urban renewal plan that was laid out by planners who had been engaged by the University of Chicago and approved by the city. The city government proceeded to put it into effect and that included taking over buildings, tearing them down, creating parks and parking areas, and doing all the other things that led to a major change in Hyde Park.

In Woodlawn, which I also represented, there was no such activity. And, Woodlawn, which became more and more deteriorated in the '60s, was a totally African American community. Before 1948, Hyde Park was regulated by racial restrictive covenants which excluded blacks from owning in the neighborhood. When the Supreme Court outlawed such covenants, the community decided to welcome blacks into Hyde Park and make it into an interracial community with high standards. The high standards included being tough on crime, enforcing strong building codes, blocking the appearance of slums, and greatly reducing the number of taverns in the neighborhood. You have to make your community an attractive place to live, and we certainly succeeded in doing that. Not everything that was done was perfect, but, on the whole, it was a remarkable achievement, and, during the '60s there were very positive changes in Hyde Park as African Americans moved in and whites remained in the neighborhood.

Woodlawn, on the other hand, was in terrible shape during those years. When Dr. Martin Luther King came to Chicago, his visit did not have an immediate impact on my ward. He was a religious inspiration, but he did not have any great effect on social conditions since our communities were not his direct targets. By the mid-'60s, the Vietnam War was very unpopular in Hyde Park. We had a lot of people who took part in the demonstrations at the 1968 Democratic National Convention. In general, our community was predominantly opposed to the war, but it wasn't unanimous on the issue.

The '60s were a tremendous turning point for Hyde Park and by the end of the decade Hyde Park was a changed community, while Woodlawn remained neglected. Later on, the city, the University of Chicago, and the communities turned their attention to Woodlawn and it also improved.

Jackson Beach, 1967.
(Courtesy of Chicago Park District)

31st Street Beach, 1967.
(Courtesy of Chicago Park District)

Jackson Park Sand Modeling, 1960.
(Courtesy of Chicago Park District)

Ray Simon

I was born in the "Back of the Yards" and lived at 31st and Lowe until I got married. Then, we lived in a small apartment and eventually, we had children and built a house on Hood Street in St. Gertrude's Parish in the 49th Ward. During the 1950s, I was in law school at Loyola. I went to work for the city in 1955 after Richard J. Daley was elected mayor and was hired as a law clerk for the Corporation Counsel, John C. Melaniphy. When I graduated from law school and passed the Bar in 1956, I was hired as an Assistant Corporation Counsel and worked there in the Appeals Division for a couple of years before becoming an administrative assistant to the mayor. I performed that job for several years and then served as Deputy Mayor of Chicago before becoming Corporation Counsel in the 1960s.

Mayor Daley was a marvelous person to work for, and as a young lawyer, I would sometimes travel with him. I remember that when we would check into a hotel, he would say to me, "Ray, see what time the Masses are and where the closest church is located." He served as a marvelous example and was a mentor to all of the young people who worked for him. Although he could be a tough taskmaster, the mayor provided a very wholesome environment for a young person to work. Daley knew everything that was going on in the city because he was a detail guy and kept in constant communication with all of his department directors. As for Chicago's businessmen, Daley felt strongly that the more he encouraged the private sector, the better the city was going to operate. Among many of his accomplishments were introducing the street lighting program and the construction of O'Hare Airport, McCormick Place, and the University of Illinois at Chicago. McCormick Place was a State of Illinois program, while the building of O'Hare was unique because it was the first time that a revenue bond issue was used to develop a major public facility. It meant that the city got an airport from a $120 million bond issue, without using taxpayer money.

The mayor's most controversial project was the construction of the four-year campus for the University of Illinois-Chicago because it involved a lot of land clearance on the Near West Side. Under the law, we were required to pay the fair cash market value of the property, but we couldn't say, "Oh, this is a shame. Let's give them twice the fair market value." So, we'd have appraisers go out and look at a two-story building that had been cut into half to make into four apartments with the owner living in the first floor flat and rent the other three apartments. The appraisers would come in and tell us that a building was worth $21,000 or $27,000, and we'd send out an offer to acquire it. Daley told us, "We're not trying to take their property without fair compensation. We're trying to build a university here, and they're suffering because of it. So, give them as much money as the appraisers can justify giving them."

Well, they would come back and say, "With approximately $20,000, if they invest it, they might get $2,000 in a year. I'm getting $350 a month rent from three apartments, and I am also living there. And, my expenses aren't much because the taxes are only a couple hundred dollars a year. How can you do that to me? I can't survive if you do that to me." There was that terrible dichotomy with what we were trying to do and the impact that it was having on a lot of the individuals. That led to the neighborhood residents really getting up in arms, including leadership by Florence Scala from Taylor Street.

I liked Florence and understood what she and her group were protesting. But, they would come down to City Hall to meet with the mayor and often start shouting at him to stop because they didn't want it to happen and it was unfair to them. They would say, "Unless you stop it, we're not going to permit it to happen." It was just emotional opposition to a public works program. So, the mayor would try his best to explain what we were trying to do, and conclude the meeting. But, they wouldn't leave City Hall. Their alderman, John D'Arco, said to the mayor, "Dick, do you know what you are doing to my people? They're all telling me that you've got to stop it. And, you act like that's an unreasonable thing to do to stop the building of a great university. But, these are my people." I don't know that it was the only area where they considered building UIC, but the city felt that it had the advantage of the confluence of the transportation system and was close to downtown so the students could get part-time jobs in the department stores and the law offices.

The mayor was also every enthusiastic about the establishment of some of the new federal programs introduced during the '60s, including the War on Poverty and the creation of the Committee on Economic Opportunity. As a matter of fact, Daley was a lead witness before Congress to create the Committee on Economic Opportunity. I went to Washington with him and Earl Bush, who was his speechwriter and press secretary, and I worked with Earl to write Daley's testimony. We landed in Washington, D.C. and Jack Valenti, who worked for President Johnson, met us. He said, "Dick, the President would like you to stay at the White House." The mayor said, "Jack, that's very thoughtful of him, and I appreciate it very much. But, he's a busy man and we don't want to impose on him." Valenti said, "Well, he sent me out here to pick you up, and he'll be disappointed if I come back without you." The mayor said, "Well, Jack, we have reservations at the Statler Hotel, and I don't want to impose on the president at all." So, Valenti looked over at me in the back seat of the president's car and said, "Mr. Simon, what do you think?" And, I looked at the mayor and replied, "Mr. Mayor, I can get to the Statler on my own." He laughed, and said, "That's true Jack. That would be a nice experience for Ray. So, sure, we'll stay at the White House." We met with President Johnson and discussed numerous topics of mutual interest with Johnson.

In 1968, when I was still Corporation Counsel, I had a lot of people out there on the streets. One of the things that happened during that period was a scandal in the police department's Summerdale District. As a consequence, Tim O'Connor, who was the chief of police, was removed and O.W. Wilson was brought in as superintendent. He was a great superintendent and worked hard to get the police what they needed.

When O.W. came in, we were having demonstrations against Dr. Benjamin Willis, Chicago's Superintendent of Schools. Willis was very unpopular at the time because he was viewed by some, including those in the African American community, as outspoken, insensitive, and authoritarian. It was just the wrong time to have that kind of a person there, and that led to a lot of demonstrations against Willis. They would march in the Loop and disrupt traffic, and there would be arrests. All the cases were being dismissed because there was no one who could clearly identify the demonstrators. O.W. Wilson came in and said, "We've got to control this. So, the corporation counsel's office needs to have its lawyers on the scene since policemen are not lawyers. Policemen do a good job but they don't collect evidence the way you need it if you are going to prosecute somebody. So, we've got to work together and develop a program for this."

As a result, Dick Elrod, Deputy Corporation Counsel, had a program where he and his staff of assistant corporation counsels would go out on the streets with the police. When there was a demonstration in the Loop, and people were lying down in the middle of the street, Elrod's group of attorneys would take a photograph and note on a tape recorder the details of what had happened. Once the demonstrators had been there long enough, we indicated to them that if they didn't remove themselves from the street, they would be arrested and charged. When they were arrested, they were usually fined anywhere from $25 to $100, and the record of the arrest was reported. The rule was that when people wanted to demonstrate, they must walk on the sidewalk, and not on the street, and they had to form a rank so that other people could use the sidewalk. The idea was that demonstrators could not take over the city because they were protesting an issue.

When Dr. King was assassinated in April, 1968, people were so torn up emotionally that they vented their feelings by looting and burning, which I could understand because the assassination was such a terrible, terrible thing. We had police on the streets in 12-hour shifts, and then we asked Governor Kerner to send the Illinois National Guard. Eventually, we asked the president to send in federal troops from Ft. Hood in Texas. I remember being in a helicopter flying over the city and seeing the West Side in flames along Western or Crawford. It was something you thought that you would never see in Chicago, and it was like a scene from a war movie. The mayor's reaction was that it was as if they had tried to burn down his house, and it became a very personal thing to him.

In the summer of 1968, the Democratic National Convention presented us with an entirely different challenge. The purpose of the demonstrations at the convention was an organized effort to cause disruptions in Chicago by radicalizing the public against the war in Vietnam. I remember presenting our argument to a federal judge that, while we respected their right to communicate ideas, they could have such a forum in Grant Park, as well as Washington Park, Garfield Park, and Lincoln Park. However, if they wanted to demonstrate at the Amphitheater where the convention was being held, we couldn't allow that to happen.

I believe, in retrospect, that the city's decision to not let the pro- testers camp out overnight at Lincoln Park was wrong because it played into their hands. But, the concern at the time was that if people were hurt in the park, then people would say, "What's the matter with this administration that we are intimidated to the point of not enforcing the laws that we enforce on our own citizens in Chicago?" Of course, what happened is history, and they won that skirmish in terms of much of the public opinion because the police were perceived as acting brutally.

I believe that the police let the city down, especially the mayor. O.W. Wilson had trained the police in the use of the baton, in particular never to raise it above the head. If a person needed to be subdued, then the policeman should hit them in the back of the leg. But, when people at the Hilton or in the parks were hit above the shoulders or on the shoulders or the head, it looked brutal, and was counter productive. On too many occasions that week, the policemen didn't follow those guidelines and were banging kids, and the media, around.

Everyone has their own theory of what happened at the Hilton. The police said that they were called "pigs," feces were thrown at them, and balls with nails stuck out of them were tossed onto roadways. The police were being restrained because they had to let people demonstrate since it was their right and they had to protect them. By doing that, it helped prevent a conflagration that might lead to riots in the city, which would have been tough for the police to control. So you have to be under tight control, and the police understood that. However, when the demonstrations broke out at the Hilton Hotel, the police unfortunately released some of that pent up anxiety. The leaders of the Yippies like Jerry Rubin, Abbie Hoffman, David Dellinger, and others had no intention of being present at the site of the conflict, so they stayed away from the Hilton. They wanted the media to be there to record and broadcast the events.

It was during the 1969 "Days of Rage" that Assistant Corporation Counsel Dick Elrod had his neck broken. The Weathermen Underground were marching during that event, and they were violent marches. They would come along and throw rocks through big windows in the apartment buildings on the Near North Side, trying to create as much chaos as they could. Those were of a different intensity, but of the same genre as all of the other demonstrations. We tried to keep them under control, and when they violated the law, arrests were made.

Marchers on State Street as they march along.
As published in the *Chicago Sun-Times*.
Photographer: Howard Lyon. Copyright, 1965 by
Chicago Sun-Times, Inc.
Reprinted with permission.

following page
Fire destroys McCormick Place.
As published in the *Chicago Sun-Times*.
Photographer: Jack Lenahan.
Copyright, 1967 by *Chicago Sun-Times*, Inc.
Reprinted with permission.

James J. McDonough

I worked for Richard J. Daley before he was elected mayor, when he was the Clerk of the Circuit Courts and I was at St. Ignatius High School. In my senior year, I ended up in the Marriage License Bureau signing licenses for Daley. I remember him calling me into his office and saying, "Where are you going to college?" I said that I was going to John Carroll College in Cleveland Ohio. He said, "When you finish college, you come and see me." So, I went to college, and my major was transportation. When I graduated in 1955, I went into the Service and was in the military for two years in Korea. In late 1957, I came back to Chicago and my dad said to me, "I saw the mayor, and he would like to talk to you." I ended up becoming a supervisor on the Chicago Skyway and, then, in 1961, I was made the manager of the Skyway, which was built in 1958.

I got married in 1961, and Jacque and I lived at 117th and Campbell at St. Walter's Parish. Actually, we lived for about a year at 107th and Artesian in an apartment with a kitchen that was probably as big as a washroom. Then, we had our first child and moved to 117th Street and Artesian. I had grown up on the Southwest Side at 82nd and Marshall and had attended St. Ignatius High School.

After being manager of the Skyway for a few years, the mayor called me to his office one day. He made me First Deputy Commissioner of Streets and Sanitation, which was the largest department in city government. That was in 1964, and then I was made Commissioner in 1968, and I served there until 1974. A lot of interesting things happened in the '50s and '60s for me. One of the great things about working for Richard J. Daley was that he was very involved with the department heads and he always knew what was going on. I would see him sometimes, as much as four times a day, and sometimes I wouldn't see him for two or three days. But, that was unusual, because if I didn't see him for a week, I thought that he had gone somewhere.

On Monday mornings, he would have a big piece of paper in his hands after he had traveled all over the city. Thus, the mayor kept up with every detail, and I used to dread Monday mornings and his list of things to be done. Lloyd Johnson had been commissioner for many years, even before Daley was mayor. He decided to retire and Jim Fitzpatrick, who was Commissioner, was appointed to replace Johnson and I stayed as Deputy Commissioner a short time. After the infamous snowstorm of 1967, I was appointed commissioner when Fitzpatrick went into the private sector. I always had strong support of the mayor, even though I wasn't born in his neighborhood of Bridgeport. My parents did live there for several years before I was born.

The snowstorm of 1967 was one of the most challenging assignments in my city career. Jim Fitzpatrick went in the field to inspect conditions, and I was stationed at our central office in the First Ward. I became the contact with the mayor throughout the day and night. He would call every 10 minutes to check on conditions, and as the storm intensified, he asked if we should bring out the National Guard. I told him, "No, not yet." The storm itself was a total surprise to all of us, but on that Thursday, I was driving to work and I thought that the snow looked heavier than expected. I thought that we better check our forecast again, and the weathermen had moved it up from 3" to 6" to 9", and we ended up having 23" of snow. The next day, Daley said to me, "I want you to get in a helicopter and go see what the city looks like from the air." They got me a helicopter, but I don't know how we were able to get up in the air.

We were flying low along the lakeshore, and I could just barely see the cars because they were buried in the snow. The snow plows were actually hitting the cars because they couldn't even see them. Each little incident was being compounded, and when we came back downtown, we had to land in the middle of Michigan Avenue because it was the only place we could find that was somewhat clear on the ground. I went back to City Hall, and I told the mayor, "It's worse than I expected!" We didn't have the right equipment at that time, and much of it was out of date. For example, we didn't have any "V" plows, and we only had one phone in each ward office. It was unbelievable, and it is beyond my comprehension how we ever got by with the good press support that we actually received that weekend. Daley did a good job, and he was a great spokesman for the city and he asked all Chicagoans to pitch in to help shovel out the snow. It became sort of a party atmosphere, as bad as it was.

Then, we got help from the state with their big plows. The value of the '67 storm, as opposed to the snowstorm of '79, was that it got a little warmer for a while and we didn't get a second snowstorm. After the storm, we began to meet on Monday mornings with the mayor to develop a plan to deal with major snowstorms and snow removal in the future. That was when we came up with the snow command center, the big plows, and the new communication systems. We didn't clear the side streets during the snowstorms at that time because we didn't have the plows. And, the plows we did have would just push the snow over the cars and people couldn't get out of their parking spaces. We did some of the intersections after the '67 storm, but that was about all we could do.

As for the '68 Convention, I was Commissioner of Streets and Sanitation by then, and I sat in at all the briefings on how to deal with terrorism and the protesters. The mayor called me in to meet with the representatives of all of the big television networks. They wanted to know where they could put their cameras for the convention. Daley said, pointing to me, "Well, this man right here is going to let you know. He has full control, and wherever he tells you that's where you can put your cameras." I went back, and I thought to myself that I didn't want the network cameras next to City Hall, the sidewalk was very narrow, and it would be a mess. I finally said to the networks, "the Conrad Hilton has a wider sidewalk, and that would be the best place to put your cameras." I had not realized that the Park District had also given the protesters a permit to be in Grant Park. That was why the cameras were there when the protests happened in August, and that was the only place I allowed the television networks to be. I remember being in front of the Hilton with Jim Rochford, the Superintendent of Police, on the night that the riots began. I saw one protester go after Jim Rochford with a ball filled with spikes, but another policeman tackled the guy and broke his arm. Despite all the bad publicity, I think that the convention came off pretty well.

During the convention, I went back and forth between the Amphitheater and the Conrad Hilton Hotel. Most of the time, I was out with the delegates to make certain that things were going smoothly for them. Obviously, the national view of the convention was not good because it did show the protesters and the police.

Of course, when you sat in the meetings, like I did, and you heard from police officers that the convention could become a very dangerous situation and that the city could be in peril, it made me nervous and I think that it's what led to the city's reaction to the events. Overall, I think that the police did a good job despite media portrayals, although, by any stretch of the imagination, it was never good for the city's image.

Despite some negative perceptions, Richard J. Daley was a great administrator and very calm in a crisis situation. I remember the first time we ever had a strike of the garbage truck workers, and it was over a stupid thing. The Teamsters said, "The cleanup around the garage and trucks is our job." And the other labor union said it was theirs. So, the workers said they were going on strike, while the Teamsters said they would stay on and even man the trucks. I went up to the City Council, and Daley was in the middle of the meeting. I said, "Mr. Mayor, I've got some bad news. We're going to have a garbage strike." He looked at me, and he said, "Settle it!" The strike lasted about a day, and I told the union guys, "We're going to put the Teamsters out there, and they are willing to go out on the line." The strike was settled.

The mayor was not pleased when I first talked to him about leaving the job of commissioner. Some time passed before I spoke to him again about my leaving and he said, "What do you mean you're leaving?" I said I was going to work for a Chicago engineering firm as its president. His response was, "Well, why don't you leave today!" I was really upset, but about an hour later he called me back to his office, and he said to me, I'm sorry." I had never heard him say that before, but then he said to me, "They're going to get you to make their firm successful, and then they're going to sell it on you. Do you have a contract?" I said, "No, I never thought about that." He said, "Well, you get one, and make sure that they can't sell the company without your approval." As it turned out, he was right.

Several months after I had left my job with the city, the mayor called me back to his office. I was sitting there talking to him, and I said, "Mr. Mayor, what can I do for you?" He said, "Oh, how have you been?" I said, "Fine, Mayor." He said, "We're going to have a little press conference today. "I said, "You and I? Why would I be going to a press conference with you?" He answered, "You're going to be the new chairman of the CTA." I said, "Oh, my God, no. I can't do that. I just left the city. Don't make me do this. I'll work day and night and be a member of the board, but I can't be the chairman, that's a full-time job." He said to me, "Oh, you can be that for a few years." I said, "I can't, I really can't. I beg you not to do this." So, he cancelled the press conference and he wasn't too happy about my reaction. However, as a measure of his power, not only in the city but also in the state legislature, about six months later, he changed the law in Springfield. He went down there, and Mike Madigan introduced a bill called the "McDonough Bill." The bill made the chairmanship of the CTA a part-time job, and I ended up becoming the chairman.

Residents of the street one block south of
Addison just off Lake Shore Drive posted this at
the entrance to their street. As published in the
Chicago Sun-Times. Photographer: Gene Pesek.
Copyright, 1967 by *Chicago Sun-Times,* Inc.
Reprinted with permission.

The city is entering phase three of its fight to clear
streets of snow." As published in the
Chicago Sun-Times. Photographer: Bob Kotalik.
Copyright, 1967 by Chicago Sun-Times, Inc.
Reprinted with permission.

U.S. District Judge Marvin Aspen

In 1958, I graduated from Northwestern Law School, went into military service for six months of active duty in the Illinois National Guard, and was discharged in July 1960. My wife and I had an apartment at 4950 North Marine Drive, and I have vivid memories of the big snowstorm of January 1967 and trudging through two feet of snow on the Outer Drive while viewing all the abandoned cars. Most businesses were closed for days. I remember walking to the nearby grocery store to get some food, but other shoppers had already started to empty the shelves. On Friday night, we hiked through the snow to see a movie at the Riviera Theater. There were only about 15 people in the audience. A double feature had been scheduled, but only one film had been delivered due to the snow storm.

In 1960, I tried to get a job in the U.S. Attorney's Office. I had a letter of recommendation from my law school professor, and I went to see the U.S. Attorney who sent me to be interviewed by his first assistant. Although politics was not expressly mentioned, they asked me about my letter of "recommendation." In my naiveté, of course, I referred to my law professor's letter. At that time, the U.S. Attorney was a Republican-run office, and since I didn't have a Republican letter, I didn't get the job.

I had been working part-time on a Bar Association committee to revise the Illinois Criminal Code, and a member of the committee was head of the Cook County State's Attorney's Appeals Division. He said to me, "Why don't you apply for a position in the State's Attorney's Office?" I was a bit reluctant because I knew I didn't have any Republican letters of sponsorship. But I went anyway. Before I saw Benjamin Adamowski, Republican Cook County State's Attorney, I met with his first assistant, Elroy Sandquist. I had gone to high school with his sister, and he apparently had said some good things about me to Adamowski. Adamowski hired me even though he knew I was a registered Democrat. Jim Thompson, a neighbor and law school friend, had begun working there a couple of months earlier. He and I shared an office, and between us handled the bulk of the criminal appeals for the office, many of which we argued before the Illinois Supreme Court.

I was in Adamowski's office when he lost the 1960 election for State's Attorney to Dan Ward. Ed Egan was chosen by Ward as his first assistant. I knew Egan and had handled a grand jury investigation against Egan's client. I recall one time we were arguing a grand jury matter before the Chief Judge of the Criminal Courts, Dick Austin. Egan didn't know that Austin and I had worked closely together on the Bar Association's Criminal Code Committee and had become good friends. I, in turn, didn't know that Austin was a golfing buddy of Egan's. So, when we appeared before him, each of us had an undeserved confidence about how our relationship with Austin might help our respective positions. Both of us argued heatedly, and I won. I remember that when we left the courtroom, Egan had a few harsh words for me, which I thought nothing of at the time.

But shortly thereafter, when I learned that Egan would be Ward's first assistant, I assumed that because of our earlier encounter my career in the State's Attorney's Office would be ending soon. When Egan called me into his office, shortly after he was appointed, I figured that I was going to be fired, but, to his credit, he said, "You're one of the lawyers we want to retain in this office. So, just keep up the kind of work you are doing." I remained in the State's Attorneys Office until 1963, when I moved to the Corporation Counsel's Office.

I had received a phone call from Melaniphy, and he asked if I would come over to City Hall and talk with him.

I did, and he said, "I remember the work you did in the City Council television case against me, and it was very professional. We have a fellow who is head of the appeals division of the City of Chicago law department. That division not only handles appeals, but it also handles all of the city's important federal litigation as well. I would like you to work for me and then take over as head of that division when the other fellow retires." I declined the offer and said, "I don't have a political sponsor, so I just don't think it would work." But John said, "Well, just think about it." A few weeks later, he called me and said, "The mayor wants to talk to you."

That was my first meeting with Mayor Daley. Daley said, "John says that you are a very good lawyer and that he wants you with him in his office." I said, "Thank you Mr. Mayor. I'm very flattered. But, I have explained my situation to Mr. Melaniphy." The mayor said, "Yes, I know. Don't worry about the sponsorship stuff. Different folks serve in different ways. If anybody asks you, you tell them that I am your sponsor." So, I joined the Corporation Counsel's Office, eventually became head of the Appeals Division, and served in that office until 1970.

Daley was very impressive in other ways. He had an encyclopedic (and sometimes purposely selective) memory. He would sit at his desk, with no papers on it, and be able to discuss every issue intelligently. Because of his unpolished speech mannerisms, I think a lot of people assumed a lack of intelligence, and that was a fatal mistake. Richard J. Daley was extremely intelligent, not only in terms of "street smarts," but with a broad-based knowledge of many subjects. He disarmed people with his use of words like "dese" and "dose," but he was nobody's fool. In my view, nothing happened in Chicago in the political, business, labor, or education community without the mayor knowing about it and either expressly or implicitly approving it.

In the late '60s, my law school classmate, and fellow city lawyer, Dick Elrod, was involved with a lot of law enforcement cases and events related to what was happening on the streets. Elrod was the one in charge of representing the Corporation Counsel's Office at the law enforcement activities before and after the Democratic Convention. I remember one Friday night in 1969, just before he was injured, when both of us were working late and decided to have a quick dinner. We had a good conversation, and he told me of his political aspirations. After he broke his neck in a scuffle with a member of the Weathermen, I visited him at the rehab center. The Democrats had slated him to run for Cook County Sheriff, and Dick asked me if I would help him with his campaign. I ended up playing a significant role in his election campaign.

Earlier, when Edward Hanrahan was running for Cook County State's Attorney, he asked me to help him with some position papers for use in his campaign. After he was elected, he called and asked me to take a high position in his new administration, but I told him that I wanted to think about it. I decided to seek the mayor's advice on Hanrahan's offer, and Daley said to me, "Absolutely not. That's not something you should do." It was good advice.

I left the Corporation Counsel's Office in 1970 when I went into the private practice of law, but not for long. Illinois had enacted a new constitution in 1970, and, under that constitution, for the very first time, the Illinois Supreme Court could fill judicial vacancies. I had argued many cases before the Court, and knew Chief Justice Walter Schaefer very well. Early one morning, I received a call from him at home. He told me that he was going to make the first appointment under the new constitution, and he wanted to appoint me to the Circuit Court of the State of Illinois. I had recently purchased new furniture for my law office, and I was doing pretty well and making some real money in the private sector. So, I asked him if I could think about the offer. He replied, "Yes, but you can only think about it until noon because I am announcing my appointment this afternoon."

I first talked with my wife, and she thought it was a good opportunity. Immediately, I called the mayor's secretary, Kay Spear, at City Hall and said to her, "Kay, I've got to see the mayor. It is a matter that is very important to me, and I need to talk to him this morning. Can you get me in?" She said, "Okay, I'll get you an appointment." I had a very good working relationship with the mayor and think that he respected me professionally. But, I knew how things worked politically and that my appointment was only until the next General Election. I was not going to give up my law practice unless I had some kind of assurance that the Democratic Party would slate me at the next election, which would be a contested election. Without the endorsement of the Democratic Party, there was absolutely no chance of being victorious.

I went to City Hall, met with the mayor and said to him, "Mr. Mayor, I have been very honored by the Chief Justice of the Illinois Supreme Court who has told me that he wants to appoint me to the bench. But, I know that I have to be elected in another year and a half, and I certainly wouldn't want to take the position and then have to run in a contested election unless I have the support of the Democratic Party." He smiled at me because he knew exactly why I was coming to meet with him. He also probably knew about the offer from Justice Schaefer before I did. Daley gave me his "blessings," and I walked downstairs in City Hall and called Justice Schafer from one of the public phones. I said, "Mr. Justice Schaefer, I would be honored to accept the appointment." That's how I became a state judge where I served until 1979, when I became a United States District Court Judge, appointed by President Jimmy Carter at the recommendation of Senator Adlai Stevenson.

Charles "Arch" Pounian

When I was born in the mid-1920s, my folks lived at Grand and Racine in an Italian neighborhood. My parents were Armenian immigrants, and the apartment building we lived in had several Armenian families. When I was about three years old, my father bought a store in Rogers Park near Mundelein College and we moved north. We lived in a building on the 6200 block on Broadway with a streetcar in front and the "L" in the back. My dad's store was in a building that was called the Spanish Manor. A few years later, we moved into the Spanish Manor and had an apartment where the store was located. One of my fondest memories of growing up was the Devon Avenue beach a block away. I went to Swift Elementary School at 5900 N. Winthrop and then, Senn High School, and just generally had a great childhood. The gravel playground and field house at Swift was an important part of my life. We played ball there, and ping pong and volleyball.

After graduating from Senn in June 1944, I went directly into the Armed Forces since it was World War II. I enlisted in the Army, was put in the Army Specialized Training Program, sent to Ripon College, Wisconsin for sixth months and then to Ft. Hood, Texas for 15 weeks of infantry basic training. After that, I was sent to Ohio State University for another six months of college in electrical engineering, and by that time, the war was over. Next, I was assigned to the Second Infantry Division, which had just come back from Europe, and went down to Texas to spend some time there. Finally, I was shipped to Ft. Lewis, Washington and spent a delightful summer in 1946 under the view of Mt. Rainier. The toughest part of that assignment was trying to decide what lake to visit on the weekends. I was discharged in September 1946 and came back home to Chicago.

I wanted to get back to college as soon as possible, but the only place I could get into quickly was the University of Illinois at Navy Pier because of the late start of the semester. They were actually building the college around us as we attended class. There were carpenters in the classroom who were hammering while we were trying to learn French. My classes were located all over Navy Pier and we got a lot of good exercise racing from one class to the next. It was a great place just to go outside and read and gaze at the lake, but I was only there for one year. I followed some friends of mine to Lake Forest College and spent two years completing my undergraduate degree. I began graduate school at the Illinois Institute of Technology with a major in psychology and received my M.A. in 1951, started working for the city of Chicago in 1953, and eventually got my Ph.D. at IIT in 1960.

I was married in 1950, and my wife worked in the music library at NBC. She was the main financial support for both of us, although, during that time, I taught at a private trade school on the South Side called the Allied School of Mechanical Trades. They were training people to be tool and die workers, and, while there, I taught algebra, trigonometry, and electricity to students who had been recruited mostly from Appalachia and other places out of Chicago. These students were veterans who were going to school on the GI Bill. I taught from 7:00 am to 9:00 pm, two days a week, and then, I would have five days completely free to be a student. My wife became pregnant in 1953, and I started looking for a regular, full-time job.

When I first heard about working for the City of Chicago developing civil service examinations, I rejected it and started looking in other directions. I was faced with the decision about whether I wanted to work for an Insurance company or a flnancial company.

All of a sudden, the city job started looking a lot better. I planned to work for the city for 18 months to two years to get something on my resume. I took the job at the Chicago Civil Service Commission, headed by Stephen Hurley, who was determined to bring all of the jobs in the city under Civil Service. When Richard J. Daley was elected mayor in 1955, I figured that I might have to seek other employment because it was a new administration. Although I was still a student, trying hard to finish my Ph.D., I didn't really have enough time to devote to my degree. However, I made the decision to stay on my city job and still try to finish at IIT. I then began to get promoted, since the Civil Service Commission thought that I was doing a good job and I quickly became Director of Examinations.

In January 1960, I finished my Ph.D. in Industrial Psychology at IIT and was ready to move on to something else. Two weeks before I graduated, the director of personnel for the Civil Service Commission resigned and much to my surprise, Dolores Sheehan, then president of the commission, asked if I would accept an appointment as director of personnel, and I accepted. She introduced me to the mayor, and he put his blessing on the promotion. He was always persuasive, you really felt his presence, and he was an amazing leader. Richard J. Daley knew much more than you expected him to know including even the smallest details, and had an amazing ability to understand city administration. One of the things that he did, and one of the hallmarks of who he was and how he ran city government, was that he had very good people in every department of government. That was true whether or not it was the commissioner, the number two person, or the number three person. There was always somebody there to make sure that everything was running okay, and, if things got out of order, the mayor received information about it quickly and pulled in the reins as needed.

The Civil Service Commission continued to function through the 1960s, and it was clear to me that a large part of what was wrong with the personnel system in the city was the old civil service system established in 1895. The old ways of doing business created the general feeling of the central personnel agency versus the departments, including the sense that you're the people who are trying to screw it up and we're the people who know what is right and good for you. That was not my style and not what I accepted. We tried to make the Civil Service Commission as customer-oriented as possible, not only to the departments, but also to the people who were seeking employment. We sought different options in terms of what we could do in spite of the fact that any changes in the state law regulating an administrative civil service commission were controlled by the state legislature.

There were certain jobs that were covered under civil service as opposed to patronage jobs. Technically, they all should have been covered under civil service, except for the department heads. The way the law was set up, the mayor could only appoint about 50 people, including department heads and private secretaries. That made it very difficult to run things because there were some positions for which it was difficult to develop and administer examinations, like laborers and jobs like that. We had an understanding of which jobs were going to be covered under civil service and which ones weren't. All the police and fire jobs were civil service, as well as the bulk of professional and clerical jobs. While we didn't examine any of the blue collar jobs and the very top jobs, like deputy and assistant commissioners and confidential secretaries, the mayor's office and the department heads made those kinds of appointments.

During all the Daley years, I never was sent a referral from the mayor's office for anybody to work in the Civil Service Commission. In terms of the professional and clerical staff, there was not one case in which the word came from the mayor's office to hire a person. There was also never an expectation of people who held civil service jobs that they would help out during election campaigns. You would find some of that in other departments, but you would never find that in the Civil Service Commission. It was clear that the mayor wanted me to run the commission honestly, in a non-political manner, to the best of my ability. As for racial hiring, I was in the middle of those issues, and quotas were imposed by the courts. I spent a lot of time in federal court and in meetings with the U.S. Attorney's Office in trying to develop new kinds of selection procedures that would be acceptable to the federal government, the new standards that were being set up, and the new guidelines that were being developed.

I was appointed director of personnel in 1960, and the commission went out of existence in 1976. All during that time I kept the same position. I was encouraged by Daley to participate in a study funded by the Ford Foundation early in the '60s called the Municipal Manpower Commission Report. The thrust of the report that came out of the study was that civil service commissions were out-of-date and not responsive to the needs of cities and that they needed to create executive departments of personnel with strong merit systems. In 1972, with the passage of the new Illinois state constitution, the city of Chicago was given greater home rule powers which allowed it to create a Department of Personnel replacing the Civil Service Commission. I played a major role in creating it.

The Chang
Downtown
North and

State and Van Buren, 1967 (Courtesy of CTA)

Lois Wille

I grew up in Arlington Heights, and my husband Wayne grew up in Des Plaines. After graduating from Northwestern University, Wayne and I moved to Rogers Park in the fall of 1955 and lived about a block from the lake, at 1407 W. Jarvis. There were many small six-flats and three- or four-story apartment units built around courtyards in the area, priced low enough to attract a lot of young people new to the city. A number of our friends from Northwestern were living close by. But the neighborhood was already beginning to change; the nice old red or brick apartment buildings were being torn down and replaced with nursing homes or ugly "four-plus-ones" — cheaply constructed low-rise apartments that looked like big cardboard boxes with holes punched in for windows.

East Rogers Park had two distinct groups of residents: young people like us who were settling into their first homes, and much older people who were born there or had lived there for decades. Many of them were Jewish refugees who had come to the U.S. after World War II. The area was an ideal introduction to city life; the Sheridan Road buses and the Howard Street "L" line to the Loop were just a few minutes' walk, and so were the Lake Michigan beaches. And, it was just a short "L" ride to Evanston and Northwestern University or to Loyola University south of us. There was an old movie theater on Sheridan Road, the 400 Theater, that always had something worth seeing. Between our building and the Jarvis "L" stop was a small shopping strip with a grocery store and meat market, Fisher's Cleaners, Hartmann's Delicatessen — run by an elderly Jewish couple who were refugees from Germany — and Noskin's drug store. The "L" stop itself, in addition to a newsstand, had a little gift shop that sold greeting cards. The shopping area around the "L" was wonderfully compact and convenient, and we could walk north to Howard Street where Northwestern University students went because Evanston was "dry."

I started working for the *Chicago Daily News* in the so-called "women's section" at the end of 1956 as the assistant to Peg Zwecker, the fashion editor. In those days, there was only one woman at a time as general assignment reporter in the newsroom. Luckily for me, the lone woman quit to join the Marines in 1957 and I moved into her job. At the beginning, it consisted mainly of writing little feature stories, covering small conventions and doing stunts — like flying with the Navy's Blue Angels. But I had a city editor who allowed me to develop some of my own ideas, and I was able to shift the focus of my reporting on urban problems. I targeted issues involving children and poverty and the failures of institutions such as Cook County Juvenile Court, Cook County Hospital, and the public aid system. I began writing about racial issues in the city in the late '50s and early '60s, and these became major topics for an urban newspaper like the *Daily News*. The city had never stopped going through racial changes, from the first moves to Bronzeville from the 1920s through the 1940s, to the late-1950s when the big stories involving race included urban renewal, land clearance, and the building of the high-rise public housing developments.

Rogers Park seemed to be a transitional stop for a lot of young people. A lot of our friends from Northwestern and other young couples we knew moved out after three or four years there, often to Evanston. Some of them had children and wanted a bigger place, or something newer. We began looking around, too. We always knew that we weren't going to stay in Rogers Park. We had just three small rooms, and although it was a great place to start out and very convenient, people moved in and out too quickly to establish strong friendships. While we were looking around, an increasing number of new high-rises were going up along Sheridan Road, south of Rogers Park. We looked at some of them because we still wanted to rent, but Edgewater, especially along Sheridan Road, was too congested. We wanted a place where we could park without having to drive blocks looking for a space. Parking had been a real problem in East Rogers Park. We wanted something with public transportation as good as we had in Rogers Park, but we also wanted to live closer to downtown because my working hours were irregular. I wanted to be able to take a cab home at 2:00 am without spending $25 or $30 a ride. We also wanted a racially integrated neighborhood—that was important to us. This really limited our choices. We looked at several buildings in Hyde Park, which we liked and which fit many of our categories, but that neighborhood was a little too far from downtown.

In 1962, we decided to move to the new Lake Meadows develop-ment on the Near South Side. We were able to get a roomy two-bedroom, two-bath apartment with a big balcony overlooking the lake in a beautiful building designed by Skidmore Owings Merrill. Lake Meadows and its sibling to the north, Prairie Shores, were built on the site of a former all-black neighborhood that had deteri-orated into crowded slums during the 1940s, when blacks moving to Chicago had virtually no other choice of where to live. It was the first major federally-funded land clearance project in Chicago. Ferd Kramer, who later became my valued friend and teacher, developed and built the two projects with the goal of creating an interracial neighborhood of well-built, moderately priced rental units. Together, the two had 11 high-rise buildings that stretched from 29th Street to 35th Street and from King Drive to Lake Shore Drive. Lake Meadows opened first. It was probably about 80 per-cent black when we moved there, and could easily have become

all-black because there was such a severe shortage of decent housing for blacks in Chicago. After the first buildings filled up with black applicants, Ferd resorted to a quota system to achieve his goal of an integrated neighborhood. We jumped to the top of the waiting list because we were white. By the time Prairie Shores opened, more whites were applying and Ferd was able to achieve his goal of an overall 50-50 racial breakdown. Prairie Shores attracted a lot of employees from the nearby Michael Reese and Mercy medical centers.

The two developments were controversial because the city had made no attempt to relocate the low-income people who were forced out of their homes when the slums were cleared. They had to crowd into already deteriorating buildings to the south in Woodlawn and on the West Side, and probably were worse off than they had been.

During the early 1980s, federal housing authorities ordered Kramer to abandon the quota system he had used to keep Lake Meadows integrated, and because of the continued shortage of decent, moderately priced housing for African Americans, it soon became all black.

We lived in Lake Meadows until 1978, when we decided it was time to buy something. We moved to a townhouse on the Near West Side, on Laflin near Taylor Street. The 16 years we lived in Lake Meadows were a period of great racial turmoil in the city and some of the suburbs, but in our interracial community, everything was perfect. We had no problems. It was proof that integrated living can work beautifully in an urban setting. But there was one big caveat: Lake Meadows and Prairie Shores were racially mixed, but not economically mixed. It was definitely a middle class community. There were no poor people in Lake Meadows or Prairie Shores. Economic integration still hadn't happened in the Near South Side and in other city neighborhoods as well. That was something that has bothered me a lot. One other thing about the physical plan of Lake Meadows was that it was designed to be what the French architect and urban planner Le Corbusier called "towers in the park," with high-rise towers and lots of green space in between.

Over the years, it turned out that this gave people a feeling of isolation, and that certainly was true of Lake Meadows. It wasn't a neighborhood in the traditional sense. We knew and loved the people in our building, but when we walked to the bus, we would pass through big, empty expanses with just a few isolated high-rises and no shops nearby. In the 1990s, Ferd Kramer recognized this and added some well-placed, attractive townhouses to the Lake Meadows complex. It was his last project before his death at the age of 101.

As for the Loop, south of the river, it underwent enormous change after the violence that followed Dr. Martin Luther King's murder in 1968. The number of whites who went there for shopping and entertainment on weekends dropped drastically. Suburban families turned instead to the big new shopping malls, and in the city, the shopping and entertainment scene shifted north of the river. The huge public housing projects that the city was building on the South and West sides and the spread of housing abandonment and demolition surrounding them, scared away neighborhood groceries and theaters. Young African Americans had to go to the Loop for movies and snacks, and the theater owners responded by switching to the new black exploitation films. When black kids came downtown to State Street in the early evening, dressed up in the fancy, colorful clothes popular in those years, the whites fled. In the Loop, south of the river, by 6:00 pm, you rarely saw white people any more. That's what prompted the north Loop redevelopment effort to save and restore the Chicago Theater and the Oriental Theater, two of the survivors.

The big Loop department stores began to falter and lost a lot of their business. A number of them closed. The only two real survivors are Marshall Field's and Carson's, and they've had to struggle under continual changes in ownership. The North Loop redevelopment effort leveled several blocks where surviving small businesses once stood, and then came to an abrupt halt when the severe inflation of the early 1980s scared away investors and made new construction unaffordable. The Loop is only now starting to revive, thanks largely to the phenomenal growth of a new residential community immediately south of the Loop. It began in the late 1970s with the development of Dearborn Park on old railroad tracks, and then spread north of Polk Street with the Printers Row loft housing and south of 15th Street with new townhouses and condos. Now, some of the old underused Loop buildings on State Street are converting into housing, and new luxury high-rise condos are going up where the old Loop stores and restaurants stood. But so far, the grand old State Street shopping area has not revived, and probably never will. There are a number of new shops, but mostly of the budget variety, and some of them lean toward the garish. Various city administrations beginning with Jane Byrne in 1979 have tried to lure a major retail chain and other businesses into Block 37 without success; whether the current plan will be successful is still questionable.

When we lived in Rogers Park and then Lake Meadows, there were a number of nice places to eat in the Loop, south of the river. There was a wonderful little French bistro at State and Madison on the lower level. Berghoff's was still there, in two locations. Don Roth's Blackhawk Restaurant on Wabash was popular, and so was Stouffer's Restaurant on the corner of Wabash and Randolph. Stop and Shop had a wonderful gourmet grocery store on Washington Street just west of State, and is sorely missed. One by one the restaurants closed, moved north of the river, or opened in the suburbs. It was all part of the same phenomenon that occurred when the movie theaters began switching over and people were afraid to come downtown. I know it's irrational, but I resent this shift, this elitist snub of south-of-the-river. I was angry when Nordstrom's turned down a site in Block 37 and went north instead. The focus of fashionable shopping and elegant dining, entertainment, and pleasant strolling shifted north of the river, to North Michigan Avenue and the Near North Side. And that made me even more loyal to the Near South Side.

Prairie Shores, 1961 (Courtesy of CTA)

Jimmy Rittenberg

I was born in 1943 and grew up on the West Side near Jackson and Keeler. I attended St. Mel's for grammar school and high school, and then went to DePaul University on an Illinois State scholarship. However, I lost the scholarship in my sophomore year, but replaced it with a track scholarship for a semester. It was the hardest work I ever did in my life. I was so thrilled because I was a walk-on. The track coach had seen me playing intramural basketball and asked me to come out for track. The best I ever did in competition was to come in third in one race. I ran the 100-yard dash because I wanted to, but the 220 was my event, and I wasn't good at that either. In order to make money for college in the early '60s, I got a job working at night for the Rock Island Railroad. I was a switchman from 11:00 pm until 7:00 am before going to class, and while it was fine to do that work in the summer, in the winter it was the most dangerous thing I ever have done in my life as I would jump on and off moving trains.

When my West Side neighborhood began to go through racial change in the early '60s, we moved from Jackson and Keeler to Congress and Lavergne. Then, when my mother was mugged, my dad said, "That's it!" and we moved out to Cicero. When I went to DePaul, I lived at home for two semesters before moving to the area around DePaul. I have lived on the Near North Side ever since. During the Vietnam War, my friends and I did everything we could to maintain our educational deferments. When I graduated from DePaul, I took a teaching position at a Catholic inner city school in my old West Side neighborhood. All of my buddies were teaching at Loyola Academy in Wilmette and they were making fun of me since I was on the West Side. But, when the draft began to expand to the point where they were taking teachers, my school wrote a letter to the draft board and told them that since I was the athletic director, teaching and operating their community center, it would be a hardship if they were to lose me to military service. As a result, the draft board gave me another deferment for being in a critical occupation. On the other hand, my friends who were teaching at all-white schools got drafted.

I was teaching 7th and 8th grade at the Cabrini School, even during the Martin Luther King riots in 1968. When the riots began, my high school students came back and grabbed me, put me in the back seat of my car, and drove me on the expressway out of the city because they were afraid what might happen to me. As a result of the riots, the West Side was pretty much wiped out and those who were left living there had no shopping that remained available to neighborhood residents. During the summer, I worked for the Cicero Park District, took care of the playgrounds, and made sure all the attendants were on the playground and at the swimming pool. Ironically, I was working in a racist community during the summer and in the inner city during the school year.

During the mid '60s, Rush Street and Old Town became the center of my activities. We would have a couple of beers at Kelly's, stop at the old River Shannon, go either to Old Town or Butch McGuires, and then walk around the corner to Rush Street. The place where I used to work was originally The Gate of Horn, and that was where Lenny Bruce got removed from the stage by the police and the club was shut down. When it got closed, three young guys bought it and transformed it into The Store, a post-college bar. By that time, State and Division had become the location of several college bars, whereas Rush Street still remained the place for the "Boys," including entertainment, the Whiskey A-Go-Go, the Candy Store, the strip joints, and the "dress up" joints. So, the city's Near North Side was like three different cultures: Old Town, Rush Street, and State and Division. I worked in Old Town and tended bar at Chances R, and I was very fortunate because I had the opportunity to hear Steve Goodman, Bonnie Koloc, Johnny Prine, and many others.

I went to the college bars on a regular basis in the '60s and later became a mainstay at Mr. Kelly's, so I became known to performers like Jackie Mason, Shelley Berman, Joel Grey, Chad Mitchell, Bill Cosby, and Tom Jones. London House didn't have the big acts in the late '60s, but the Happy Medium, Mister Kelly's, and the Empire Room all had major entertainers during those years. The clubs began to lose their clientele because of television and the fact that you could see the comedy acts on television every night. Then, the bands started hitting big, and they couldn't fit into the little clubs.

During those years, I hung out with guys who were 20-25 years older than me, including Ben Stein, Harry Caray, Jack Schatz, Don Roth, Gene Sage, and many others. The stories I heard were phenomenal, and, for a young kid who was on Rush Street, I would sit and listen to these guys talk and I appreciated the history of the street. I would learn about who got killed at which joint and other interesting stories. Rush Street was heavily mob-oriented in those days, and you didn't open a place on that street unless you had the right connections, used the right insurance company, and did business with the right linen company. In fact, the only reason we were allowed to operate Faces was because my partner, Jay, had grown up on the Near North Side and knew everybody. The Mob said to us, "You guys are good guys, so you can come on Rush Street. You will use this guy for your linen company, and this guy for your cigarette machines, and that insurance company, and you'll get this guy a job. Then, you're all set. As long as you don't do any drugs, prostitution, or gaming, then nobody's going to bother you." We just said, "Okay, thank you." And, those were the rules of the game.

Faces became a hub for nightlife, and all the famous people came to the club. My good friend, Harry Caray, would be there all the time, and in the early '70s when he started announcing for the White Sox, he called me up and said, "Jimmy, I'm getting a commission from Bill Veeck on all the season tickets that I sell. I want the places on 'Restaurant Row" to help me out." I talked to friends I knew at the Rush Street clubs and restaurateurs like Jimmy Gallios from Millers Pub, Fletcher Ritchie from Adolph's, Vic Giannatis from Giannati's, and all of his cronies to help Harry sell his tickets. I said to Harry, "I've had four tickets behind first base at Comiskey Park for years, and now you want me to give them up and move my tickets to the upper deck." He said, "Yeah, that's the story." So, Harry sold 60 tickets in the upper deck and may have made $80–$100 a ticket. That was some nice change for him since he wasn't making a large salary from his broadcasting job at that time. The big money for him came later with the Cubs.

On Opening Day, we were in our new seats, and Harry used his microphone to announce that all of his restaurant buddies were there and he gave all of the Rush Street restaurants a plug. On the second day of the season, we arrived at Comiskey Park on a freezing day in April, walked to the Upper Deck, and discovered that the door was locked. The only tickets they sold for the season in the Upper Deck were ours. They forgot to unlock the door. I went downstairs to call Harry, and he said, "Stay right there!" About 15 minutes later, Bill Veeck was walking upstairs with a big, fat usher. Bill took out his keys, opened the doors to the Upper Deck, wiped off our seats, and said to the usher, "You stay here and if these guys want anything like hot dogs or beer or drinks, you get it for them." Every time the Upper Deck was closed, our usher's job was to open up the place and be our waiter to bring us food and drinks. They had a bar on the first base side that was the only place where the public could get a drink, and half-way through the season, we learned that our personal usher was going to the Press Box at the Purple Poodle to get us our drinks. We were paying him, and he was getting the drinks for nothing.

The two major events I recall from the '60s were the Martin Luther King riots and the Old Town murders. Old Town was the hub of activities for the people who liked folk music, including the college crowd and the tourists. You couldn't walk, or even drive down Wells Street on a Saturday evening in those years because it was the place to be. The most popular places there included Paul Bunyan's, the Fickle Pickle, the Plugged Nickel, the Earl of Old Town, the Old Town Gate, and the Old Town Pub. Then, in 1968, a suburban couple was killed while walking back to their car they had parked west of Wells Street. The next weekend, Old Town business was cut in half. Soon after, there was another murder, and, as I recall it, every single joint in Old Town closed. Since no women felt safe going to Old Town, that ended the night life there. It wasn't about entertainment, good drinks, or the pretty décor. The issue was that without women frequenting the places there, guys had no reason to visit Wells Street.

Race was an issue in those years because African Americans weren't welcome on the Near North Side. The bouncers at the various establishments would harass any blacks who tried to frequent the clubs, and once in a while, there were conflicts. The black guys hung out at the Playboy Club at Michigan and Walton, or there was a place called Dingbats on Columbus where Mr. T. worked the door as a bouncer. Then, there was a murder in the basement of the Playboy Club around '68 or '69, and that kind of wiped out what had become an integrated cocktail hour. Blacks simply didn't come down to where they weren't welcome. Thus, the '60s led to a variety of changes at the entertainment venues on the city's Near North Side.

Michigan Avenue night scene with
Water Tower, John Hancock Building and Palmolive
Building in background. *Chicago Sun-Times*,
February 10, 1968. Photograph by Jack Lenahan.
Copyright, 1968 by *Chicago Sun-Times*, Inc.
Reprinted with permission.

Michigan and Superior, 1961
(Courtesy of CTA)

following page
State Street, Looking South from Lake Street, 1960.
(Photograph courtesy of *Chicago Sun-Times*)
Copyright, 1960 by *Chicago Sun-Times*, Inc.
Reprinted with permission.

Tom Dreesen

I was born in the 1940s in Harvey, Illinois, a city located directly south of Chicago. It was a thriving little metropolis that could be considered a microcosm of Chicago. It had steel mills and factories all around the city, and the men and women who worked in those plants lived, shopped, and banked in Harvey, so the city's tax base was good. Harvey had Polish, Irish, Italian, and African American neighborhoods, so it really was a microcosm of the mix of people who lived in Chicago.

Harvey had Thornton High School, which was noted for its native son, Lou Boudreau. During Lou's sophomore, junior, and senior years, he led the high school's basketball team to the state tournament where they won one year and finished second the other two years. Boudreau was All-State and went from there to the University of Illinois where he was captain of the basketball team. At the age of 24, he played for the Cleveland Indians and was both the shortstop and the manager. In 1948, Lou led the Indians to a pennant and a World Series, and in celebration, there was a special parade in Harvey.

I was a little boy selling newspapers in the late '40s. I had eight brothers and sisters, and our family lived in a shack in Harvey, with five of us sleeping in one bed. We were raggedy-ass poor, so at the age of 6, I was out shining shoes in taverns. By age 12, I was setting pins in bowling alleys, caddying in the summertime, and delivering newspapers like the *Tribune, Herald American,* and *Sun-Times.* I was still quite young at the time when Harvey had its parade for Boudreau, so when I heard all the horns blowing and saw the cars, I got excited. I said to someone, "What's going on?" The answer was "It is Lou Boudreau day." I knew Lou had come from Harvey, so I sold all my newspapers and went to see the parade. Lou Boudreau came out of the Elks Club, spoke a few words to the crowd, got in a car with Bob Feller and Bob Lemon, and they all drove down to Thornton High School field while the big parade followed them there.

That day, going home, I said "Wow, they had a parade for someone from my home town!" I was so excited and thought to myself that maybe one day they'd have a parade for me. I started envisioning the parade with me riding on a horse down Harvey's main street, and I thought that would be the coolest thing. Well, in 1992, I went back to Harvey and they not only had a parade for me, but the city named 155th Street in my honor, the street where I had stood watching the Lou Boudreau parade in 1948. The guy who introduced me to the crowd was Lou Boudreau.

I started grammar school in the late '40s and then attended Thornton High School in Harvey at 152nd and Broadway in the 1950s. For me, high school was very difficult because with eight brothers and sisters, I was still setting pins in bowling alleys that had bowling leagues which began at 6:00 pm and 9:00 pm. Harvey had 36 taverns, and as a little boy, I shined shoes in a lot of them. Almost all those taverns had bowling teams. After the 9:00 pm league, around midnight, I would set pins at a "pot game" so I could get extra money when some of the bowlers would stick around and gamble. I wouldn't get home until 1:00 or 2:00 in the morning, and I would have to get up at 6:00 or 7:00 am to go to school. Since we had no bathtub or shower, I was going to school pretty raggedy and would fall asleep in study hall. It was difficult to get through high school, and in those days, Thornton High School, in my mind, had a clear grouping of kids: the cashmeres; the fur-blends; and the Orlons. I added one group that included me: the gunny sacks. By the time I was a sophomore, I decided to drop out of high school.

When I shined shoes in all the bars with my older brother, Glenn, we would bring home money to feed my brothers and sisters. My mother would take a nickel out and keep it in a little cracked cup, and when she had enough money, she would give money to my brother so we could take the I.C. from Harvey and go downtown to the Loop. We would go to the Randolph Street station, play video games, and then make certain to walk to the Blackhawk Restaurant on Wabash. Never having eaten a steak, we would look through the window at them being grilled in the restaurant. We would also walk to State Street, take the "L" to Wrigley Field, and sit in the bleachers for only $.50. I became a Cubs fan because when I was a little boy, my father used to listen to the Cubs on the radio behind our shack. Also, I had an uncle who was a Cubs fan and he had the games on the radio in his bar where I used to shine shoes.

After dropping out of high school in 1958, I joined the Navy and received a high school diploma through the military. I spent four years in the Navy, and when I finished my tour of duty, went to Thornton Junior College at nights after returning to Chicago. I played 16-inch softball from the moment I came out of the service in the '60s all the way up until I went to the West Coast in 1975. The thing that I missed the most, besides my family, was that I was going to leave behind my chance to play 16-inch softball three or four days a week.

By the time I went into the Navy, I still had never eaten a steak. One time, my buddies took me to a steakhouse in New York City, and said to me, "What kind of a steak do you like?" I responded, "I don't know, I've never had one." They started laughing because they thought I was joking. Finally, when I convinced them that I really had never eaten a steak, they said to me, "How do you like your steak cooked?" I also had no answer for that question.

After returning to Harvey from service in the Navy, I became aware that the city was starting to experience racial change. Real estate agents from Chicago began to "panic peddle" Harvey, meaning that they would tell people, "Blacks are moving in. Everything you

worked for and saved for all your life is going to be gone."
In those days, people's savings had been invested in their homes. So, they panicked and began to sell their homes. Then, the City Council approved some high-rise buildings, and the next thing you knew, gangs began moving from Chicago's South Side to the high-rises and getting active. In addition, the factories began to close down. I decided to join the Junior Chamber of Commerce (Jaycees) in order to try to help Harvey deal with these changes.

My early career included a wide variety of jobs. I first worked construction with concrete companies that would build sidewalks and basements. I helped my brother who had gone into the photography business. I tended bar and did a lot of odd jobs, including cleaning sewers on the Dan Ryan Expressway. I was also a private detective for the Polizzi Detective Agency. If you worked construction, that was seasonal work, so I needed to have other jobs. Then, I ended up selling life insurance for Columbus Mutual Life Insurance, and the first year that I sold life insurance, I was in the Million Dollar Roundtable. However, during the second year of my life insurance career, I quit and went into show business. The president of the insurance company flew into Chicago and told me that he couldn't believe I was quitting since I had been so successful. But, I had the bug for show business.

It all happened after I had written a drug education program to use humor to teach grade school children the ills of drug abuse. One of the big problems plaguing our community in those days, like today, was teenage crime and drug use. Because I had come from a poor background, I wanted to help those kids, black and white, who came from the same kind of poverty. I realized that 77% of all crimes by teenagers were drug and alcohol related. I decided to write a drug education program and proposed it as a Junior Chamber of Commerce (Jaycees) project. At that meeting, an African American guy named Tim Reid came up to me and offered to help with the program. I told Tim that I had already made arrangements to develop it with a friend. However, as it turned out, my friend called me the next day and said that he would have to drop out of the project. I called Tim and told him that I wanted to take up his offer to work with me on creating the program. So, Tim and I went into the classrooms and began teaching drug education with humor. I would do comedy by playing off of him, and we did things to get the kids' attention. Once we got their attention, then we began to get across the messages about drugs and alcohol. One day after a session, a girl walked up to us and said, "You guys are so funny, you ought to become a comedy team." We laughed about the idea, but a couple of days later we decided to create America's first black and white comedy team.

I had no intention of ever going into show business, nor did Tim. We wrote what we thought was funny material for about four months. And then, one day, Tim's wife Rita said, "You can't come over here anymore. You've got to go somewhere and do your act." So, we went on stage at a little club on the South Side of Chicago called The Party Mart Supper Club. And, we bombed. When we went up to the stage, all we wanted to do was just to remember our material, so we went through our routine at 150 miles an hour. Afterwards, we talked to the owner and asked him how we had done. He said to us, "Slow down. Come back tomorrow, but slow it down a bit." So, we came back the next night, got some laughs, and I realized that this was what I wanted to do more than anything else. I couldn't sleep all night, and the next morning went to the Ascension Church in Harvey where I had once been an altar boy. I prayed there and said, "God, if you let me make my living as a comedian, I'll never, ever ask for anything else, and I promise that I'll do charity work throughout my life." The thought of making a living as a comedian overwhelmed me.

Tim and I struggled for years with our act, and when the team broke up, I ended up sleeping in an abandoned car in Hollywood. Tim also struggled for awhile, but got his break with the series,

"WKRP in Cincinnati." I got my big break with my first appearance with Johnny Carson on The Tonight Show. Ironically, Tim and I were not only the first black and white comedy team. We were the last black and white comedy team. You have to remember that in the late '60s, the Vietnam War was raging, there were riots everywhere, and here were Tim and I going across the country trying to make people laugh. In fact, the fourth time that we appeared on stage, it was in Chicago Heights and a guy put out his cigarette on Tim's face. I went after the guy, who was a former professional football player. When I threw a punch at him, he pulled me towards him and tried to crush my chest. It was a real donnybrook. A year later, at the University of Illinois, a guy hit me in the face with an ice ball. An interesting thing about racism in those days was if a guy was a black racist he wasn't mad at me, he was mad at Tim for working with me. On the other hand, if he was a white racist, he wasn't mad at Tim, he was mad at me for working with Tim.

It is important to note that Tim and I toured for six years with great success. Then, after we split up our comedy team, our careers continued to blossom. No matter where I have appeared throughout my years in the entertainment business, I have always mentioned Chicago and the fact that I came from a great city.

Tom Dreesen's first Tonight Show
appearance with Johnny Carson
(Dreesen was bumped five times and publicity
created lots of interest back in Chicago), 1975.
(Courtesy of Tom Dreesen)

Tim and Tom at Mr. Kelly's on Rush Street
(now Gibson's Steakhouse), 1972.
(Courtesy of Tom Dreesen)

Tom and Freddie Prinze, new comedians at
LePub Restaurant, first comedy club in Chicago, c. 1974.
(Courtesy of Tom Dreesen)

Shelley Berman

In the 1960s, after my acting and comedy career had already begun in Chicago, even though I wasn't living in Chicago during the decade, I still was able to get back to Rush Street as often as I could. The Marienthal brothers were happy to have me, and I was still performing at Mr. Kelly's most of the time. Then, later on in the '60s, I tried performing at the Palmer House in the Empire Room, and although it was okay, I wasn't as happy with that as I was performing on Rush Street.

I never was asked to perform at the Chez Paree, and although it was a very nice nightclub, I guess that I wasn't the kind of comedian, like a Danny Thomas, who they felt was right for their club.

Each time I had the chance to return to Chicago in the '60s, I made certain to visit my old West Side neighborhood. But, the old neighborhood, which had mostly Jewish residents when I lived there, was fast becoming a black neighborhood. African Americans seemed to adapt nicely to their new surroundings, but I noticed a significant change at all of the former synagogues on the West Side. Although the Stars of David on the fronts of the synagogues were chipped off and crosses were put in their place, they still kept the stained glass windows that were there. The neighborhood looked good, and I would visit because I felt good walking around my old stomping ground. When I was growing up I would go down to Maxwell Street all the time, and when you needed a suit that was where you went. These guys would pull up your jacket and your pants as if they were doing something special, so you still left there with a wrinkled jacket. Happily, Maxwell Street remained in operation for many years after I had moved away.

I was hot in the '60s, and my career was going pretty well. In Los Angeles, I would play the Crescendo on Sunset Boulevard. This was after I had played the Interlude, upstairs of the Crescendo,

A view of the new Mr. Kelly's bandstand.
As published in the *Chicago Sun-Times*.
Photographer: Mickey Rito.
Copyright, 1967 by *Chicago Sun-Times*, Inc.
Reprinted with permission.

and then "graduated" downstairs. That was wonderful for me. It was a "hot" club, and Sunset Boulevard was a great place.

I still loved going to the Hungry i in San Francisco where my friend Mort Sahl was a big success. In the '50s, I was still a "punk improvisationist" with a group called the Compass Players, and not doing too much with my life. In 1957, at Mr. Kelly's in Chicago, I saw Mort Sahl for the first time. "My God," I thought, "the audience loves this guy though he's not telling jokes, only giving political and social commentary." With the Compass Players, I had developed some solo phone conversations—funny, but also no jokes. Seeing Mort killing the audience without telling jokes, I wondered if my phone calls might work as well. I wangled an audition at Kelly's and, of all things, I got hired.

I was beginning a career as a comedian. Later, it was Mort who convinced me I should make a comedy album. That album became one of the biggest selling comedy albums ever and won me the first Grammy for a non-musical record. I wound up making six such albums, the last one with Jerry Stiller and Anne Meara.

I didn't notice the changes in Chicago in the 1960s, although they surely had happened. I remember the Goodman Theater had moved from being in back of the Art Institute, and when I saw that, I was dismayed and unhappy with the change.

I watched it happen, but the change startled me, and although I had to accept it, I was not thrilled with their move. The Art Institute didn't change; it just kept being wonderful, and I visit it every time I get to Chicago. I also enjoyed walking down Michigan Avenue (the Miracle Mile), during the 1960s, and stopping and shopping at the many stores located there.

I did perform at Playboy Clubs, including the one on Walton, and I used to go to the Playboy Mansion on State Street. I watched Second City change over the years, and it used to be that the actors put scenes together and did dramatic scenes onstage and improvise those wonderful dramatic things, sometimes funny and sometimes serious. I watched Second City gradually metamorphose into the emphasis on games shared with the audience. What was happening there was that somebody would start talking about a topic, and the next guy would tell the big joke. He would get all the attention for telling the joke, but the thing had started to build so this guy could tell the big joke.

Recently I had a very successful run of "I'm Not Rappaport" in Chicago. I didn't do it on Broadway, but you don't have to do it on Broadway if you can do it in Chicago. As for Rush Street, a lot of people don't know that pizza was born in that area of Chicago at Uno's and Due's. If you want good pizza, wherever you live, go to Chicago, don't go to Rome.

Joe Levinson

I returned to the music scene in Chicago in 1963 after nearly four years in New York City, and I was happy to be back in my home town. I played bass and electric bass regularly with a variety of Chicago band leaders, working at weddings, country clubs, corporation parties, and political events. Several years later, in 1968, I was asked to join the instrumental quartet that would back up a play that was going to open in a few weeks at the Happy Medium Theater on Rush Street.

The play was "Jacques Brel is Alive and Well and Living in Paris." It was created in New York in 1967-68 by Mort Shuman, Eric Blau, and Jacques Brel and staged off- Broadway at the Village Gate on Bleeker Street in Greenwich Village. The play ran there for 4 1/2 years, and, soon after it opened, there were spin-offs run in several U.S. cities, the first one being Chicago, and then in London. It was made into a film, shot in Paris in 1974, and released in the United States in 1975. It starred Jacques Brel himself, most of the New York cast, and one member of the Chicago cast. Columbia Records issued a two-disc LP album of the original cast.

Four musicians were signed to back the singers: Hans Wurman, piano, celesta, and conductor; Jack Ceccini, guitar (doubling on banjo and mandolin); Hal Russell, percussion (marimba, orchestra bells, drum set, triangle, and other noisemakers); and me on bass violin (doubling on electric bass). Midway through the run of the show, Hal Russell left and was replaced by Shelly Elias. The show was comprised of 26 songs that were written by Jacques Brel, the Belgian-born singer-songwriter. The songs were a compendium of his compositions dealing with a wide range of human emotions reflecting the angst of the times, especially post-World War II remembrances and emotions related to the on-going Vietnam War.

Jacques Brel, who was born in 1929 in Belgium, became famous in Europe as a composer and singer and performed his songs in numerous French films and on nightclub stages around the world. Ironically, Brel had claimed that he never wrote a love song, but his works exhibited a wide range of joyful celebrations of wine, women, and song. He captured the strong feelings of people caught in war and fearful of old age, as well as cynical observations of drunks and people in bars, thoughts of religion, and of lust, false celebrity, rejection in love, and fears of obscurity, deception, and death. He was a heavy smoker and died of lung cancer in 1978 on Hiva Oa Island in the Marquesas, French Polynesia. Brel was buried next to the great French artist, Paul Gauguin.

We four musicians, while rehearsing "Brel," were playing music quite different from what many Americans were accustomed to hearing. Hans Wurman and Jack Ceccini were well trained in European classical music, and their training proved extremely valuable as we rehearsed the material. In addition, Hans Wurman was a gifted organist and concert pianist. The cast of the show included four singers, two men and two women. Some of the action on the stage used spoken dialogue as well as dancing and mime, and they performed nine times a week.

I remember that during rehearsals at Mister Kelly's, the famous nightclub across the street from the Happy Medium, several of us felt that the show wouldn't last very long because we concluded that the critics would find it politically questionable. For years, Chicago critics had bad reputations with performers from across the country, and in those days, there were some artists who absolutely refused to perform in Chicago because of the city's newspaper critics.

After rehearsing without the cast at Mister Kelly's, we then rehearsed at the Happy Medium for a week with the entire cast and stage crew. Several preview performances came next, and they seemed to go well, but there was still some final fine turning necessary to prepare for opening night. We played the music while on stage with the cast during each performance, and although we could see the stage action, the audience was unable to see us, as we were behind a scrim.

Finally, it was opening night, Thursday, September 12, 1968. I still thought that it was going to be a short run, and I was curious about the audience's reaction to Brel's musical genre. However, to my surprise, the first show was rewarded by the audience with tumultuous applause, and that was followed the next day by rave reviews from Chicago's major critics, notably a glowing review from Sidney J. Harris of the *Chicago Daily News*.

We immediately sold out for many months, and all of us in the orchestra were told to get alternate musicians in case we might be unable to play for any reason. I arranged to work one week on and one week off, alternating with an excellent bassist, Bob Surga. This allowed both of us to keep our connections alive in the city's busy freelance music scene.

That move also allowed me to retain my sanity because it soon became obvious to me that I'd wake up in the middle of the night hearing one or another of Brel's 26 songs and then try to get back to sleep. The ability to play a variety of other composers' music during the long run of "Brel" saved my sanity, although after the show finally closed, it took nearly a year for me to completely erase Jacques Brel's music from my brain.

"Jacques Brel" was so popular that people came to see it again and again. I remember leaving the stage one night, carrying my bass case, when someone from the audience spotted me in the lobby and told me how much he loved the show. "I've seen it 11 times," he said, "and I have tickets for several more performances." This happened many times over the show's run, and women would exit performances with mascara and tears running down their cheeks after the final, powerful song, "If We Only Have Love." It was a powerful, emotional experience for many people, and, for me, each show was so physically demanding that I would leave the stage drenched in sweat.

In the end, I performed in 422 shows at the Happy Medium and double that for the total number of performances. Its long run in Chicago finally came to an end, although it did return for a few short weeks several years later in a different theater.

View of North Rush Street from
East Oak Street, 1967. Photograph by
(Courtesy of Chicago Historical Society, ICHi)

John Hancock Center. Work on John Hancock
Building is held up because striking truckers
aren't delivering steel. As published in the
Chicago Sun-Times. Photographer: Bob Langer.
Copyright, 1967 by *Chicago Sun-Times*, Inc.
Reprinted with permission.

The Blair Building, Northeast Corner of
North Michigan Avenue and East Ontario Street, 1964.
Photograph by Sigmund J. Osty.
(Courtesy of Chicago Historical Society,
ICHi 31637.)

Mid City Aerial Views from John Hancock Center,
Looking South Towards Lake Shore Drive.
(Courtesy of Chicago Historical Society,
ICHi 05782.)

Hugh Hefner

The '50s were an important time for me because that was when I first published *Playboy* Magazine and in the 60s I continued the process of reinventing myself. However, my decision to create a new lifestyle had really begun when I was at Steinmetz High School in Chicago and had lost out to another guy for a girl on whom I had a big crush. I changed my wardrobe and started picking out clothes that had not been chosen by my parents (wearing saddle shoes and yellow cords). It was the first time in my life I began referring to myself as Hef and actually did a column for the high school paper called "Platter Patter" and signed it "Hef." Looking back on those years, I still have wonderful memories about growing up in Chicago and going to Sayre Elementary School and Steinmetz High School.

During the '50s, I would work afternoons and evenings, and then, around midnight, I would go out on the town and hang out with friends, including Mort Sahl and Lenny Bruce. By the late '50s, in a very real sense and although I wasn't conscious of it at the time, I continued the reinvention of my life. I had been separated from my first wife since the mid '50s, but, in 1959, she met somebody and made plans to remarry. The divorce became final in 1959, and that set me free in a certain psychological sense. Also, in the space of the next few months, we celebrated the 5th Anniversary of *Playboy* with the Jazz Festival at the Chicago Stadium in August 1959.

I started hosting a television show called "Playboy's Penthouse" in October 1959, but it didn't start airing until January 1960. We recorded the show at Red Quinlan's studios at WBKB-TV in Chicago and were on the air for two seasons. In the second season, we taped six shows at CBS. Thus, 1959 was a key year in my life as I started hosting the television show, and, in December that year, I purchased the Playboy Mansion at 1340 N. State Parkway. Before that, I had purchased some property on the Near North Side of Chicago on Bellevue Place where I was planning to build a townhouse, but instead, I decided to buy the Mansion. I started moving in there piecemeal in 1960, and when we would complete taping of the television show, the whole cast would go to the Mansion and party there, even before it was furnished. The ballroom had nothing in it but a couch and a couple of chairs, and it took a year or so to get a permit from the city to build the swimming pool. The city gave us some problems, as often happened in Chicago, because of the connections between the Archdiocese and the mayor. However, after going to court we obtained the required permit to construct the pool.

When I moved into the Mansion, it had a dramatic influence on my life because I decided to spend so much time there rather than at my office. By the early '60s, I was literally working full-time at the Mansion. Throughout the decade, I lived, worked and played there and weeks and months would go by without me even leaving the Mansion. My life had changed dramatically and forever, and I started living the life I was describing in the magazine and became "Mr. Playboy."

Those years were among the most invigorating of my life. Thus, within the space of a year, I was hosting the television show, had bought the Mansion, and opened the first Playboy Club. Our plan for opening a series of Playboy Clubs was for them to represent the life described in the magazine. Indeed, initially, at a subconscious level, I wanted to have my own bar/café like the one Humphrey Bogart owned in the movie *Casablanca*.

In the middle '60s, we took a long-term lease on the Palmolive Building instead of buying it, and changed the name to the Playboy Building. The Playboy Clubs were successful beyond words, and immediately, the most successful became the one in Chicago. We opened the first Playboy Club on Walton Street, right off Michigan Avenue, on February 29, 1960. It was across the street from the Palmolive Building, which later became the Playboy Building, as well as being within walking distance of the Mansion. The original notion was not to have a string of clubs, but to open up a club where you could hang out. The Gaslight Club was the model for the club and had been very popular in Chicago. My major reservation was that since the magazine created a kind of fantasy world, could we live up to it with the Playboy Clubs. Instead, I discovered that the Key Holders brought the fantasy with them. The Chicago Playboy Club was hugely popular as the magazine had become by then, and Playboy was the hottest magazine in America in the 1960s. We also opened a Playboy Club in New York, and it was successful despite the fact that the city of New York wouldn't give us an entertainment license. Despite the fact that the showrooms had no shows being presented in them, they still were packed because of the mystique of Playboy and the Bunnies.

Chicago didn't change very much during the '50s and the '60s, and the city of that time period and when I grew up on the Northwest Side were essentially the same. However, it was the period after Mayor Richard J. Daley had died in 1976 when Chicago became a different city. Chicago has always been, in my mind and in my own experience, the "city that worked." It is a curious phenomenon because despite the dynamics that were related to Machine politics,

the Mob, and the Catholic Church, the city was operated efficiently and it was a wonderful city in which to work and live. I think it would have been very difficult to successfully start *Playboy* somewhere else.

In the early 1960s, the magazine experienced its greatest success when circulation climbed from 1 million copies a month at the beginning of the decade to 7 million by the early part of the 1970s. That growth was unprecedented for a magazine of such limited scope and high price. In 1962, I began writing the *Playboy* Philosophy and we started printing a monthly *Playboy* Interview in the magazine, as well as other non-fiction. In the '50s, the magazine had essentially been a lifestyle magazine but in the '60s, we added the other half of who I was, and that was really the non-fiction, the interviews, and a variety of concerns such as Civil Rights, changing the sex laws, gun control, capital punishment, and then, opposition to the Vietnam War. In 1965, I formed the Playboy Foundation to help support these causes and "put my money where my mouth was." In the late '60s and early '70s, we spent several million dollars on those issues, including the fact that we were the major source of funding for the Masters and Johnson sex research, for the Kinsey Institute, for the changing of sex laws, censorship, birth control, and abortion, and a number of other things that were not getting funding from other major foundations.

When I went to the London Playboy Club in the summer of 1966, I saw the dramatic social and cultural changes taking place, including the introduction of the miniskirt and legalized gambling. The London Playboy Club included a casino and became the most successful place to gamble in all of England. I had been working on the Playboy Philosophy and came to the realization that what I had been writing about in my editorial series, including seeing the need for a sexual revolution, had come to pass. I didn't want to miss being a part of it. I returned to Chicago, and in the space of the next few weeks and months, I stopped writing the Philosophy, started taking better care of myself, gained some weight, selected a new wardrobe, ordered the Playboy jet, and started making plans to do the television show.

In August 1968, the city hosted the Democratic National Convention, and it seemed that Mayor Daley's greatest concern was a city able to control violent demonstrations during that event. However, young people from the anti-War movement were gathering in the city for the convention, and it led to a violent confrontation between the police and the protesters. The Playboy Mansion was a gathering place during that week for celebrities and the political people in town for the Convention, and we had parties every night. On the Sunday before the Convention, the word was out about an impending confrontation between police and demonstrators in Lincoln Park located about three blocks from the Mansion. I decided to join some friends, including Jules Pfeiffer and Max Lerner, in a walk to the park to see what was happening. When we arrived at the park nobody was around. We decided to wander west to Wells Street and then south on that street. Ahead of us, we saw the police and the crowds from Lincoln Park, and we decided to turn around, walk down Goethe Street, and head back to the Mansion. It became apparent that the demonstrators and police were getting pretty close, and very quickly, the cops were coming at us raising their Billy clubs. About a block from the Mansion, a police car pulled up, the cops got out with their guns drawn, and one of the policemen whacked me on my backside with his club, having no notion about our identity. That day, the cops were taking their badges off so that they couldn't be identified, and some of the events occurring that night led to the beating of numerous media people covering the demonstrations.

I had just returned to Chicago in August 1968 after taping the very first week of my new television program, "Playboy After Dark" at CBS in Los Angeles. In the summer of 1968, I was considering the idea of splitting some of my time between Chicago and L.A. We had already opened a Playboy Club in Los Angeles in 1965 in the Playboy Building on Sunset Boulevard, and I had an apartment on the top of the building, requiring me to be in California several times a year. When I began filming "Playboy After Dark" in 1968, I was splitting my time between Chicago and L.A., and during the second week of taping the show, I met Barbi Benton. It was a relationship that became central to my life and supplied my motivation to spend more time in California. I made a variety of important changes to my live in the '70s, including buying the Playboy jet, purchasing the Playboy Mansion-West in 1971, and deciding to move to Los Angeles, permanently, in 1975. But, as I look back, everything seemed to happen for me in the '60s when I truly reinvented myself and my image.

The Playboy Mansion. Hugh M. Hefner editing transparencies while sitting cross-legged on his circular bed. January, 1966. (Courtesy of Playboy)

The Playboy Club with Hugh M. Hefner
surrounded by one dozen
Playboy Club Bunny girls. August, 1960.
(Courtesy of Playboy Enterprises)

Exterior of the Chicago Mansion on
State Street with limousine in driveway. 1998.
(Courtesy of Playboy Enterprises)

Hugh M. Hefner at his typewriter. 1998.
(Courtesy of Playboy Enterprises)

The Playboy Club, exterior of the first
of the International Playboy Clubs. 1960.
(Courtesy of Playboy Enterprises)

Hugh Hefner with Bunnies outside the
Chicago Mansion. 1960.
(Courtesy of Playboy Enterprises)

The Growi
Rights Mo

ng Civil
vement

Reverend Jesse Jackson

I first came to Chicago in 1955, when I was 14, to visit my aunt and uncle. I came by train from my home in Greenville, South Carolina, through Atlanta and up to Chicago. It was amazing to see the huge buildings in Chicago and the throngs of people. The city was a powerful contrast to my life in the South and its rigid system of segregation. My aunt lived on Chicago's South Side and during my visit she took me to the Southtown Theater in Englewood. At that time it was the largest theater in the world. I also went to the Regal and Tivoli Theaters to see many fine artists in person. I remember seeing them walking down the street and eating in the Walgreens across the street from the Tivoli. In South Carolina, we couldn't eat at the lunch counters in the Walgreens. When I came to Chicago, I could go to Brookfield Zoo and Riverview Amusement Park where there were both whites and blacks enjoying themselves. In Greenville, blacks couldn't go to the zoo because it was for whites only. In those days, Greenville was extremely segregated. Race defined everything.

I remember one time riding the bus in Greenville. I sat toward the front. There were three white kids sitting across from me just laughing and making a lot of noise. The driver stopped the bus and announced to all the passengers, "I'm not moving until we get some order in this bus." He said it loud enough for the adults to hear his comments clearly in the back of the bus. I was certain that he wasn't talking about me because I was sitting quietly and the white kids were playing around, but he did mean me. There was a sign above the driver's head that read "Coloreds sit in the rear, and whites sit in the front." Then the driver said "I'm not going to say it any more!" My mother came to take me to the back, but I responded "I don't want to go. Why do I have to move?" She pinched me, causing me to cry from the hurt and humiliation. One of my father's friends said, "Don't cry. She did it because she loves you. Besides it's safer in the back of the bus. You won't get hurt back here." That was my South at that time.

I observed all the humiliating, ridiculous codes that were enforced against African Americans in Greenville then. One thing the police did was to come through our neighborhoods and round up any black men who were standing around. The police would call them a mob and would force them to do work for the city. It was devastating to see these men, our neighbors and my classmates' fathers, in the jail uniforms working, while the women had to beg the "boss" if they could give their husband a cigarette or a sandwich. Usually the "man" would tell the women or children "No, only when I give them a break."

I played on the football team at Sterling High School in Greenville, and after graduating, I had the possibility of attending several black colleges in the South. Northern colleges and universities were also recruiting blacks who had graduated and could play football. Ironically, the coach at Furman University, a white Baptist college in the South, could not recruit me because blacks could not attend there. However, he had been an assistant coach at the University of Illinois and suggested that I go there. In 1959, I was offered an athletic scholarship from Illinois. That football scholarship trumped all of the other offers because Illinois was a Big Ten school, and the scholarship was a breakthrough. In fact, even some coaches from other schools encouraged me to go there.

The University of Illinois was far from my home in South Carolina, but close to Chicago where several relatives lived. They were happy I was going to be at Illinois, as were my mother and my father. However, I quickly became disillusioned with the racial conditions in Champaign-Urbana in 1959. I soon realized that attitudes towards African Americans were much like those in Greenville. I realized that there wasn't a single black professor or coach at the University, and there were only a few black students at that time.

Social life was such a strain for me, and not all of the university facilities were open to blacks. I remember one time when I was walking on campus and heard music coming from Huff Gym. I looked in, and there was the Count Basie Orchestra practicing for a concert. The Pan-Hellenic Council was having their big annual dance that night, and the Orchestra was going to play. However, the black fraternities and sororities could not join the council, so blacks weren't invited to the dance. I was so fascinated to see the Basie band. I got into the gym by bringing some of the band guys their instruments in order to be there during practice. I had to hide behind a curtain to watch Count Basie play.

When I returned to Champaign after the winter break, I just couldn't adjust to the conditions that had been created for African American students. Also, on my way back to Illinois, I had seen friends who were attending a southern university and who were happy with their lives there. So, there I was with the prestige of going to the University of Illinois and no joy. I made the decision to transfer to North Carolina A&T University, which had also offered me a scholarship in the first place. The next year I switched schools, played football for A&T, and ended up graduating from there in 1964.

After graduation, I thought about going to law school, but the dean at Chicago Theological Seminary, with the help of Dr. Samuel Proctor and Rev. A. K. Stanley, recruited me to come to Chicago on a full scholarship. I was attracted because I considered Chicago to be a dynamic and exciting city.

When I began graduate school, I had met Reverend Martin Luther King only once. It happened when I was an officer in my fraternity at North Carolina A&T and had gone to Atlanta to give a speech at a district meeting. I met Dr. King coming to the airport. I had been involved in a protest in Greensboro in 1963, was jailed, and had been on television. Dr. King had seen the coverage so when I met him in the airport, he recognized me and we seemed to connect.

On November 22, 1963, I was walking on the campus at A&T when I learned that President Kennedy had been assassinated. When I heard the news, I stopped in my tracks, then walked another four or five steps, and pondered why they had killed the President. His death let all the air out of the balloon for our generation. It was such a sad event. There was great cynicism about Johnson, the Texan, and his motives. In my opinion, however, Lyndon Johnson turned out to be the most productive president since Abraham Lincoln. I believe that Lincoln and Johnson occupy the "tallest trees" in the American presidential forest, and that Lyndon was the greatest American president of the twentieth century.

While at Chicago Theological Seminary (CTS), I needed a summer job. I called North Carolina Governor Terry Sanford, for whom I had done some work when I was active in the Young Democrats. At his recommendation, a meeting was scheduled at Chicago City Hall with, among others, Mayor Daley and Marshal Korshak. I was the only black man in the room. The mayor said, "I think that we can do something for you. Why don't you set up a meeting with Mr. Korshak?" As a result, I went to Korshak's Hyde Park office, and he sent me down to one of the city offices on 63rd Street. I was offered a job as a toll collector, but that wasn't what I wanted to do.

In those days, I was attending a South Side church where the mother of John Johnson, the owner of *Ebony* and *Jet* magazines, was a member. I asked her if she could get me an appointment to see him and she said, with a smile, "I think so." She took me to see him. I told Mr. Johnson that I wanted to get a summer job and would be glad to load trucks or do any other work he might have available for me. He said, "No, you are a good communicator and shouldn't be loading magazines on our trucks." He gave me a company car so that I could sell the company's magazines to newsstands around the city. That contrast in perceptions about my skills always struck me: toll collector vs. communicator. It made me realize, more and more, who I was and who I could be.

In 1965, I saw the TV coverage about the beatings of marchers in Selma, Alabama, on "Bloody Sunday." The next morning, I gathered other students at the seminary, and about a dozen of us decided to miss our classes and drive to Selma to be part of the events there. Dr. Howard Schomer, the president of Chicago Theological Seminary, told us not to leave school to go to Selma. However, he was an activist and ended up going to Selma himself. It was in Selma that I renewed my connection with Dr. King.

When Dr. King came to Chicago in 1966, I was working to help create a situation where he would be invited to speak in black churches. Most of Chicago's black ministers would not invite him to speak. Mayor Daley's political "Machine" was fearful of Dr. King's impact on Chicago; they used intimidation to keep him from speaking in black churches by suggesting that the churches would be visited by building inspectors. Reverend Clay Evans and a few other ministers who supported Dr. King invited him to speak at their churches anyway. Dr. King was also trying to get financial support for the Civil Rights Movement, but was having difficulty getting money from Chicago banks and black civic leaders. Chauncey Eskridge, Dr. King's lawyer in Chicago, and I arranged for a meeting with several business leaders from the city's African American community. A group of them, led by John Johnson, gave Dr. King $55,000 in support of SCLC and the Movement, and their generosity and support amazed him.

I always believed that if we kept moving on the economic front, things would improve for African Americans in Chicago. We began to build our reputation when we launched Operation Breadbasket in Chicago in 1966, and soon, we had momentum going in our favor. By April 1968, my role in the Civil Rights Movement was growing. The week before he was killed, Dr. King had marched in Memphis with striking garbage workers despite the fact that paid provocateurs had tried to disrupt the march. Then, he called us together for a staff meeting in Atlanta that Saturday and told us that he had experienced migraine headaches all week. He was focusing on the future and told us that he was contemplating quitting as the central person in the Civil Rights Movement to become a college president. He told us that he thought our movement was fractured and that if he left it things would get better. Andrew Young said, "Doc, don't worry. Things will get better."

This was early on Saturday morning, and that meeting was very important because we didn't exactly know where things were going from that point. We were working on the Poor People's Campaign, and Dr. King had promised to return to Memphis. So, we returned to Memphis. There was a lot of tension because some black leaders had turned against Dr. King, as had the governor, and the FBI was continuing its opposition. In Memphis, Dr. King gave his last speech to a church congregation and referred to me in it. The next day we were with him at the Lorraine Motel. He was standing on the balcony above us talking to me and Ben Branch down in the parking lot, when all of a sudden there was the sound of a gunshot. Dr. King raised his arm, and we realized that he had been shot. Before the assassination, I didn't have a strong sense that he was in particular danger in Memphis. Afterwards, my mind always went back to the night he got into town and some television reporters provided his exact room number at the motel. Immediately after the shooting, I called Mrs. King to tell her what had happened to her husband. But how do you tell a friend that her husband has been shot?

Later that evening, the SCLC staff met to discuss our response to the tragedy. We were angry and hurt, but out of the assassination came our determination to carry out the Poor People's Campaign. In Illinois, our work also resulted in open housing legislation.We continued to build a base for civil rights and economic opportunity in Chicago and around the country.

U.S. Representative Danny Davis

I was born on September 6, 1941, and came north in 1961 during the last big wave of black migration from the South. The pattern was that as children grew up and became adults (in some cases after going to college), they left home. In some instances, whole families would leave, but my family left Arkansas one by one. There was usually somebody from my hometown who had already moved to Chicago, had housing and a job, and had a place for us to live in the city until such time as we could find our own housing.

I came to Chicago soon after receiving my B.A. degree, although I stayed home for a couple of months to help my father harvest his crops because we were sharecroppers. Once we finished with the harvest in July 1961, I left Arkansas and traveled north to Chicago where I had two sisters living in the North Lawndale community. By that time, North Lawndale was considered a big "problem area" in the city. It was 5 1/2 square miles wide with a population of 125,000 squeezed into a very small land area, so it was too many people living in too little space. There was no place to move in the city since, to the west of us, Cicero was forbidden territory for African Americans. Instead, we went further north of our neighborhood, but even that was limited in terms of housing available for African Americans.

My first job in Chicago was at the post office, and, soon after, I became a teacher at Magellan School at 3600 W. Ogden. The student body was all African American, and the school was for over-aged, underachieving kids who were between 15 and 17 years old with a reading score of 4.0. Our kids had been to correctional schools like Logan or Montefiore, or they came straight from co-ed facilities at St. Charles or Geneva. A few of them were girls who had become pregnant the year before. So, Magellan School was a repository for kids with troubled pasts. When we opened, the kids were given the opportunity to name the school. They suggested the name Magellan both in honor of Ferdinand Magellan, the famous explorer and as recognition that our school was a new exploration by the Chicago Public School system. Magellan worked quite well because it had small class sizes and dedicated teachers.

We were all new, young teachers in those years, full of hope, a belief in the Civil Rights Movement, how we could be a part of it, and a desire to make certain the kids learned. I liked it there so much that I used to arrive at school every morning before 8:00 am. The janitor and I became the best of friends because I would be waiting there for him to open the door. I taught for six years in the Chicago Public Schools system, and, when I left, I was so dedicated to my job that I had only taken two days off: one day to be examined for the Army, and another day because I was dating a young lady and she wanted to go to the zoo.

I decided to go to Chicago State for my master's degree because it was accessible and I could attend in the evenings after teaching. A bunch of us did the same thing, and by going a couple evenings a week, we were able to get six credits a semester and do it without any real disruption.

I actually had two jobs while I went to graduate school: teaching at Magellan and my part-time job at the post office. Then I added a third job by working at Sears, Roebuck.

I became involved in the Civil Rights Movement, and we just considered it a normal thing to do because we had started joining the protests when I was in college in Arkansas. Dr. Martin Luther King had come to speak to us, and we had demonstrations and protests against discrimination. The atmosphere of change was so great at that time, as well as the possibility of things being different. It led to programs resulting from the Civil Rights Movement, and my involvement in the Movement contributed to me becoming active in politics.

In addition to my regular teaching, I was also instructing GED students at night at a community agency called the Lawndale Urban Progress Center. I taught an elderly lady how to read, and she was so overjoyed that she said to me, "You've got to meet my goddaughter because both of you like to do things for people." So, I met Rose Marie Love who was working at the Urban Progress Center and who was a precinct captain. Rose was a real advocate for the neighborhood and the people, so we would talk every night after my class because she was the assistant director and responsible for closing up the Center at night. She was also on the board of the Greater Lawndale Conservation Commission and then chairman of the Commission's personnel committee. The executive director had just been fired, and Rose convinced me to apply for the job. I said, "Okay, it sounds like some interesting stuff," and took that job in 1969. Also, I was involved in the Lawndale community, going to meetings, and getting my "feet wet."

The Greater Lawndale Conservation Commission was the main neighborhood organization in North Lawndale at the time, although the Lawndale People's Planning and Action Conference was emerging. These two groups had a big split, and they became involved in a community organization dispute. Warner Saunders was a key player in the other group. The people who remained were more closely aligned with City Hall. The split between the two Lawndale organizations was based on opposing views about how to redevelop the neighborhood as well as their relationship with City Hall. One group figured that it was better to do whatever City Hall said, while the other group had some younger and more action-oriented people who opposed that approach.

Even though I was with the Greater Lawndale Conservation Commission when the split came, I was more philosophically aligned with the other group and didn't view them as the enemy. I didn't last too long with the Conservation Commission and quit to become part of a new community health center known as the Martin Luther King, Jr. Health Center. I had the position of director of training, and that's how I developed my interest in health care. Then, I decided to get a Ph.D., with a focus on health, and became involved nationally when we organized the National Association of Community Health Centers and locally, the West Side Association for Community Action in the late '60s.

In the '60s, my congressman was white, and, even after the area changed, the last congressman elected was a white man. When Ronetta Howe Barrett ran for Congress, her white opponent had died the Friday before the election. The dead congressman still got elected, and that became an incentive for us to change the political environment in the neighborhood. As I became involved in politics, I learned that practically everybody was part of the Democratic "Machine." You would be dealing with somebody and think that because the person was a civic leader or had a political job that they were free to do what they wanted to do. Then, you would discover that the arms of the "machine" were long and wide. Although you may not have had to deal with City Hall on all of these issues, people felt like they were required to do it. City Hall was perceived to be all-encompassing and all-empowering by a vast majority of the people.

Toward the end of the 1960s, one of the most important issues was to expose the great disparities that existed between African Americans and whites. That was the big revolution in the minds of black people, and when poor blacks arrived from the south in search of the "promised land," they discovered that they had moved north just to live in another kind of slavery on Chicago's West and South Sides. That "slavery" meant living in overcrowded, rat- and roach-infested tenements. Many of these people had never seen rats and roaches because they lived out in the country where they had plenty of space. Although they had lived in shacks and shanties in the south, those structures could be kept clean. Even though some African Americans thought about moving back south, they knew that the only jobs were share cropping and picking cotton for $.30 an hour. The only real option for African Americans in Chicago was to improve their own living conditions rather than returning to the south. Of course, African Americans loved going back south for visits, especially if they had a car and could show off in their hometowns and appear to have new found wealth. In truth, they had just enough money to buy gas to get back to Chicago.

By the mid-'60s, Dr. Martin Luther King, Jr. had become such an icon for African Americans that those of us caught up in the notion of change worshipped him and the positions he took on the issues. You could walk down the streets of Chicago's West Side and listen to his speeches playing on music store public address systems. We all tried to emulate talking like King, and you could listen to him and feel chills and shudders running through your body. When he was assassinated, of course, there was no way that we could contain our reactions to his death. Some thought that there may be a way to curtail some of the violence and initially, we were out on the streets trying to protect our children and help control of the situation. However, we immediately discovered that it was impossible.

Sadly, the resulting rioting and looting led to great destruction of the West Side. During the weekend following his assassination, I was in a car with a friend of mine who was very middle class. As a matter of fact, the school and the town where he grew up were named after his father, so it was not like he didn't have certain values. We were in the car, and all of a sudden he began to drive crazily. I said to him, "Man, you're running the lights. Why are you doing that?" His response was, "Everybody's running the lights." I said, "But, just because everybody's running the lights doesn't mean we have to do the same thing since the police could arrest you." He said, "Today, we are the police!" He drove his car right through the glass window of a supermarket and just jumped out and began gathering up cartons of cigarettes and whiskey and putting them into the car.

My reaction was to get out of his car. I was a young school teacher, and I didn't want to be arrested. He said, "Aw, c'mon man, what are you waiting on? Everybody's doing it." But, I ignored his comments and just got out of the car. In my mind, it didn't change him or make him a bad person. Like so many other people, he was simply caught up in the emotions of the moment and expressing uncontrollable rage about what had happened to Dr. King. People in the neighborhood who were breaking the law by looting saw all of this simply as acts of civil disobedience. But, I had grown up in an environment of order and respect for the law, and my mother used to tell us to do what is right and that wrong is wrong and right is right. So, all of those events after the assassination were different experiences for me.

Although some wealthier African Americans did move to suburban communities, they got out of the city because they didn't feel that they should subject their children to life in the ghetto. While I have always stayed, I could understand why some of the people decided they had to go. It is unfortunate that we have not done enough to help people from our community with their upward mobility, but the '60s got us to start thinking how to make that happen. When you think of the impact that John F. Kennedy and Martin Luther King had on us, the federal and local government and the Civil Rights and anti-war movements, they were an important way to get people involved in their communities. As a result, I would maintain that the 1960s was one of the most important decades in contemporary American life.

Warner Saunders

I was born in 1935 in Chicago and lived at 432 E. 47th Street on the city's South Side. In 1953, after going to grammar and high school in Chicago, I decided to attend Xavier College in New Orleans. I received several athletic scholarship offers to white colleges, but I turned them all down. Xavier was a wonderful college, I made many friendships, and we had the chance to explore New Orleans. I was a physical education major and, after graduation, I came back and began teaching school at Hess Upper Grade School on Chicago's West Side at Douglas and St. Louis. The school was located in the old Jewish Peoples' Institute (JPI), but by that time, North Lawndale was 99.9% black.

Once back in Chicago, I joined the northern portion of the Civil Rights Movement. I also went south for a number of events, including voter registration, and continued my avocation of civil rights through involvement in several organizations. I was drafted into the Army in 1957 and served in the military for almost a year. In the late '50s, you could get out of the Service after one year if you were a teacher in what was considered a "culturally deprived" area in need of teachers. I applied for it and went back to teaching school at Hess. After that, I became very involved with street kids who included gang members belonging to the Vice Lords and the Cobras. I knew all those kids because I had taught them.

It felt good to be back in Chicago after spending my college days in legally segregated New Orleans and my year in the Army as a cryptographer at Ft. Benning, in the Ku Klux Klan-infested state of Georgia. The de facto segregation of Chicago was not as constricting as the "in-your-face, 24-hours-a-day assault" I had known in the South. After all, Chicago was my home and I reasoned that the "devil I knew" was better than the "devil I didn't know." However, I was still a second-class citizen, albeit, Northern-style. I started doing unofficial street work in 1963 and left teaching to become the Executive Director of the Better Boys Organization. That was where I really began much of my militant activity, including close interactions with the Black Panthers, such as Fred Hampton and Bobby Rush, who had become good friends. The Black Panthers had breakfast programs for the community, and I found myself in the middle of the civil rights ferment and it gave a lot of focus to my anger.

One of our targets in the '60s was Dr. Benjamin Willis, the superintendent of Chicago Public Schools and a staunch supporter of racially-segregated schools. In those days, all-white Chicago schools were led by white principals, as were most, if not all, black schools. Dr. Willis created what became known as "Willis Wagons," temporary buildings constructed in the playgrounds of overcrowded black schools. Often, those schools were located on one side of a street, with underused white schools on the other side. Willis decided to build those temporary structures rather than send the black kids to the white schools. By 1965, Dr. Willis had become a symbol of Northern school segregation and the target of Chicago civil rights activists and protest marches.

In 1965, the West Side was beginning to show some positive signs of change, but there was an event at a West Side fire station that affected the African American community. Apparently, somebody pulled a false alarm, and a hook and ladder fire truck pulled out of the station without somebody on the ladder portion of the truck. The ladder swung around and hit a woman standing at the corner and killed her. The fire commissioner at that time was Commissioner Quinn, and he appeared to respond in a cavalier manner at the woman's death. That was the start of probably the first riot in Chicago on the West Side, and, because of it, the city asked for and the state brought in the Illinois National Guard.

During the mid 1960s, we had a burgeoning black community. Lawndale had quickly changed its racial makeup during the 1950s and 1960s when thousands of African Americans moved to Chicago from the South, primarily for economic reasons. Jobs were becoming very scarce in the South because new and modern machinery was replacing the picking of cotton by hand. There was also an enormous amount of competition between poor, Southern, rural blacks and poor, Southern, rural whites. That was perfect fodder for the Ku Klux Klan, and, during the '60s, there was an upsurge in beatings and lynchings of African Americans in the South, which contributed to the expansion of the Civil Rights Movement. As a result, Southern blacks were moving to Northern cities in great numbers to seek jobs and housing. It meant that there was a rapidly growing black community on the South Side of Chicago with few places to live and work.

Blacks began moving to the West Side while Jewish families and businesses moved out and started selling two- and three-flat apartment buildings to middle class blacks who were moving away from poor urban blacks. That has always been the pattern in urban areas when the middle class of any ethnic or racial group separates itself from the lower economic class. It was not a new pattern of change, and by the early '60s, the communities that surrounded the South Side had border skirmishes with working class, ethnic whites who felt that they had no place to move.

Since I was an African American living on the black, South Side of Chicago, it would have been difficult if not impossible to move to white neighborhoods without serious, and often violent,

repercussions. We were also very aware that although there were no "for-whites-only" signs at Near North Side bars and clubs along Rush and Division Streets, those places were clearly hostile to black revelers. Black males, especially, were turned away from the doors by burly, and determined, bouncers. Few black businesses and professional people could rent Loop office space, and local beaches were segregated so that on hot summer days, the cooling waters of Lake Michigan flowed only at 31st and 63rd Street beaches for blacks.

During those years, the Black Muslims led by Elijah Muhammad and Malcolm X grew into a very strong influence in the black community. Elijah was unquestionably "the man," and I remember being at a Black Muslim meeting at McCormick Place where Malcolm was speaking. In the middle of his speech, Elijah Muhammad walked on stage, and it was clear that "the man" was there. Elijah Muhammad was not as articulate as Malcolm, but he had a power that was so incredible that it stirred your vitals. He was a charismatic man with a very simple and appealing message that rejected the concept of integration with whites.

The message was, "Okay, you don't want to integrate. Then we will separate." I use that all the time to make a distinction between segregation and separation. You hear the two terms used interchangeably, but you can't use those two concepts in the same way. Segregation is when a greater power decides where a lesser power will live, work, and operate. Separation is when two equals decide they don't want to associate with one other. What was beginning to happen in the black community was the promotion of the concept of separation led by the Black Muslims. "You don't want us! Well, let me tell you something, buddy. We don't want you! Not only are you not superior to us, you are the devil!" That view had an amazing appeal for a very frustrated black community that had, for all those years during the King movement, attempted to say that we were going to send you the best and brightest that we have but it was rejected.

In 1966, Dr. Martin Luther King brought the Civil Rights Movement to Chicago. After an open-housing march through the white Southwest Side of Chicago, Dr. King said that he had never seen so much hate displayed—not even in the heart of Mississippi.

With the King Movement, I had found a place to channel my frustrations and energy, and had become a community activist. I participated in numerous marches and protests against the war in Vietnam and in favor of civil rights for African Americans in Chicago. It was an exhilarating time, and I felt that I was an active part of it.

The war in Vietnam and the reaction to it was a major component in the changes of the 1960s, both in Chicago and across the nation. When Dr. King took a stand against the war, he brought the issue home to blacks despite the fact that many African Americans had wanted Dr. King to concentrate only on being a civil rights leader rather than focusing his attention on the war. Black civil rights leaders were concerned with King's change of focus, and it is important to understand that, in the North, Dr. King was not immediately accepted with open arms by the black community. There was a feeling that he was too radical, and when he first arrived in Chicago, a majority of black ministers (the group that he got the strength from in SCLC) turned their backs on Dr. King. I believe that it was not to their economic advantage to support him because they appeared to be strongly influenced by the Democratic organization. Jobs had been meted out to them, they had their own little fiefdoms, and Mayor Daley had "taken care" of them through their black aldermen and Congressmen. So they weren't about to deal with this "trouble maker."

When Dr. King moved to the West Side, we were very hard pressed to find many ministers who would visit him and support what he wanted to accomplish in Chicago. He marched in Cicero in 1965, and later, in Marquette Park. To this day, I am grateful to Reverend Clay Evans and Reverend Shelvin Hall because they ignored other ministers, which was not easy to do, and invited Dr. King to speak from their pulpits. There was a strong negative reaction at that time because Dr. King was considered to be an outside agitator in the eyes of the Democratic organization ("Machine").

His opponents felt he had come to Chicago to put new and dangerous ideas in the heads of the "happy black people." In those years, it was not a "happy" black community because it was bursting at the seams and in need of new housing. That led to the border skirmishes and the resistance between blacks and whites. The politicians did not want anyone to stir up anything, and all they wanted was peace and quiet.

I had always lived on the South Side, and in those years, I was at an apartment in Prairie Shores. Then, on April 4, 1968, Dr. King was assassinated in Memphis, and that violent act altered the course of the non-violent movement in America and changed the direction of my life. His assassination split the city and led to riots and looting in many black neighborhoods. As the West Side of Chicago burned in the wake of Dr. King's murder, I was asked by the respected black disk jockey, Holmes "Daddy-O" Daylie, to accompany him to the local ABC television station to talk about "what could be done to stop the Negroes from rioting." As a result of that appearance, a weekly, public affairs half-hour show, aptly named "For Blacks Only" was created with "Daddy-O" and me as co-hosts.

During the 1968 Democratic National Convention, I was a marcher with Dick Gregory. My job was to recruit high school kids from the West Side to march against the war in Vietnam and in favor of the Civil Rights Movement. I wasn't arrested and didn't want to let that happen, so I made certain that I wasn't in Grant Park when most of the protesters fought with the police. Instead, I remained south of the Conrad Hilton that August night and was excited and exhilarated by what was happening in Chicago. The combination of Vietnam, the Civil Rights Movement, and the fact that the black community was beginning to show signs of standing up on its own two feet were so important that it didn't occur to me that anybody was going to get killed or that it was a riot, since I just considered it a logical protest.

Freedom Rally, Soldier Field, 1966
(Courtesy of Chicago Park District)

Jacky Grimshaw

I grew up in the 1940s and 1950s on 45th and Prairie in a community that is now known as Grand Boulevard. I went to school at Corpus Christi Elementary School at 49th and South Parkway (now King Drive). Then, I went to Loretto Academy High School that was located in Woodlawn at 1445 East 65th Street. Growing up in Grand Boulevard was a wonderful experience because, for me, it was a neighborhood with everything you wanted right there, including grocery and clothes shopping and entertainment. You really never had to leave the neighborhood, except that my mother loved shopping on State Street. So, unfortunately, on too many Saturdays, especially around the holidays and special events, including Easter, Christmas and birthdays, we would go downtown whenever I needed something special.

We would board the "L" at either the 43rd or 47th Street stations, and get off downtown. It was nice and easy and convenient. Then, we would walk up and down State Street. I didn't have any favorite stores downtown because I disliked shopping. But, for my mother, she would start at either the south or the north end of State Street and shop in the stores up and down the street.

As a kid, my two favorite things to do on Saturdays, when my mother wasn't taking me shopping, were Girl Scouts meetings that were at Corpus Christi and visiting my godmother who was head of the labs at Provident Hospital. When we went to the hospital, my godmother would take me up to her laboratory. It gave me an opportunity to discover the whole lab experience, and I think that I got my love of science from that experience of being with her in the lab.

One year, my godmother asked my sister and me what we wanted for our birthdays: a present or if we wanted to go somewhere. My sister chose a present, and it turned out to be a Cinderella watch. I was so envious because I had chosen to go somewhere and I began wondering if it would be as "cool" as a Cinderella watch. My mother dressed me up in my "Sunday-go-to-meeting" clothes, with my patent leather shoes and white anklets, gloves, purse and hat. To my surprise, my godmother took me for my first visit to the Lyric Opera House and we heard the magnificent Marian Anderson. It was so amazing to hear her sing, to see her composure, and it was like "Wow!" It is still something I have never forgotten. Just walking into the Lyric Opera House and seeing the grandeur of the place was eye-opening. So, I have a special place in my heart for my godmother and Marian Anderson and that experience.

While I was growing up in Chicago, I was not aware of race as an issue. My experience with race came when my mother would send my sister and me to visit my grandmother in Macon, Georgia by ourselves during the summer. The first time my mother took us down there, we were on the Georgian train that left from the Dearborn Station. When we arrived on the border between north and south, the configuration of the train changed. It would often happen in the middle of the night. When we awoke up in the morning, I noticed that the race of the people in the cars had changed so that what had been a combination of blacks and whites became all black people. By the time we got to Atlanta, there were new rules about being able to go to the food car. At first, I didn't quite know what to make of it.

When we got to Georgia, you would see the water fountains in the train stations that were marked "Colored" and "White," and I asked my mother what it was all about. By the time I was a little bit older and running around with my friends in Macon, we would go to the shopping mall. My grandmother would always say to me, "Jacky, you are not in Chicago. You have to act different." She knew that I was kind of headstrong and would do what I wanted to do. My friend and I were at the shopping center one day, and I needed to go to the bathroom. We looked around, and there was no bathroom. So, we went into the drugstore and I asked the woman at the counter if there was a restroom. She said, "No!" Then, I saw the restroom that said "Employees Only." I knew that I had to go to the bathroom, so I went in there.

They didn't really do anything or say anything, but when I got back home, my friend told my grandmother what I had done. My grandmother got all concerned, and she called up and apologized to the people at the drugstore. She said to them, "You know, my granddaughter is from Chicago. She doesn't understand, and didn't really mean to do anything wrong." I kept saying, "No, you don't have to apologize. I just had to go to the bathroom." But, she just felt the need to do that. I really got the realization about the differences in the races in the South. I don't think that I realized the meaning of the term "discrimination." It was just that there were some things you couldn't do in the South. When we first started going to Macon, I saw "Colored Only" signs, but, when my grandmother wasn't with us, my sister and I didn't pay attention to those signs. But, no one would ever say anything, and maybe it just was that the white people in the community heard us talk and figured we were "dumb" northerners.

I never experienced any of that type of discrimination in Chicago, not even downtown. Maybe my mother just protected me from it, but, I never felt there was anywhere I couldn't go when I was going downtown or had anybody saying anything to me. My range of free travel was also in the neighborhood. We would ride our bikes to Washington Park and ride around in the park. When I attended Loretto it was an integrated, all-girls high school and I didn't feel any discrimination there. In fact, the nuns were very encouraging in terms of helping me to figure out what I wanted to do with my own life. My only quarrel with the nuns was that they wanted me to go to a woman's college, and I absolutely rebelled. But, other than that, I had a great classical education there, including four years of Latin, science, English, and math. So, it was a terrific education, and they were really nurturing and guiding me in terms of my education.

I graduated from high school in 1960 and went to Marquette University in Milwaukee. Marquette was a compromise because my first choice was the University of Michigan where I had been accepted. But, the nuns told my parents that if I went there, I would be an atheist and a communist. That scared my poor parents to death because they didn't know anything about the University of Michigan. So, the nuns were pushing me to go to Our Lady of Notre Dame or Our Lady of the Woods. But, I said, "No, no, no!" So, Marquette became the compromise choice. I had a strong desire to go to a coed school because I had enough of an all-girls education. I was at Marquette for four years and graduated from there.

Marquette was probably the first time that I felt like a minority. At Loretto, the classes were pretty balanced in terms of blacks and whites, but Marquette was a white school. At the time I went there the school still had football, so it seemed that black students were football and basketball players. But, other than the athletes, I think that the students at Marquette who were black were very few in number. As for housing, I lived in the dorms off Wisconsin Avenue, including the Highlands during my junior and senior years.

The Highlands was an old mansion community with single family residences converted into dorm living space. I never had a black roommate at Marquette, but I didn't feel any discrimination and even joined a white sorority. One of my roommates was someone also named Jackie, and she had been raised in Brazil because her father worked for the oil companies. So, although she was a white American, she really was raised with Brazilians and spoke Portugese. My major in college was biology, and when I graduated in 1964, I returned to Chicago.

I first became aware of the whole scope of a political convention in 1956 during a trip to Georgia. In the car going to my grandmother's house, the talk on the radio was about the Vice Presidential candidate, and the question was whether or not this Catholic, John Kennedy, would be put on the ticket. That discussion got me interested in politics. When I got to the house, I turned on the radio to hear about the convention, but my great grandmother said to me, "Turn that off!" I learned that she was a Republican because of Abraham Lincoln, and it was a shock to me because my parents were Democrats. One day my father, who was at Hart, Schaffner and Marx, came home and he was talking about all of the tuxedos they were making. He said, "Whenever those Republicans get in office, the only thing we do is make tuxedos." I was trying to make the connection between Republicans and tuxedos.

The 1960 election of John F. Kennedy for president was galvanizing for me. Actually, in some ways, I felt more discriminated against as a Catholic than as a black in terms of my community and growing up. I was very aware of the various things happening with civil rights and Martin Luther King pushing, then Jack Kennedy's assassination, and Johnson pushing through Congress legislation on Civil Rights. These events helped interest me in the political arena and wanting to change the "Jim Crow" laws that established all the things I couldn't do when I went to Macon, Georgia in the summertime. However, in Chicago, I didn't feel any discrimination when I went downtown to the movies or when I went to black theaters or to the black Catholic Church in the neighborhood. It was, in some ways, a contained kind of experience, but I was a rebel when I grew up, always testing the limits of behavior.

I have strong memories of the mid- to late-'60s, and even at Marquette there was a recruitment for people to go south on the Freedom Rides. There were a bunch of things that kept me in the north. In 1963, there was a March on Washington, and that was where Dr. Martin Luther King gave his famous speech. When that was going on, my great grandfather became sick at that time, so I was more focused on going to Georgia and visiting him. I was on a plane to Georgia in '63 when the March happened, although I saw the King speech on television.

By 1964, my parents had moved out of Bronzeville into Hyde Park. In addition to my father's job as a tailor at Hart, Schaffner and Marx on Jackson Boulevard, he was also a waiter. So, he would work in the evenings at various hotels like the Palmer House, the Stevens, the Parkway Ballroom, and other hotels. I first saw politicians at the Parkway Ballroom, like Ralph Metcalfe, Harold Washington, and John Stroger. I got married in 1964, and we lived on the University of Chicago campus in Hyde Park, but I didn't experience racial issues in that neighborhood.

I became interested in politics in Chicago because of the Civil Rights Movement. Everything from the integration of the schools in the south and seeing those federal troops helping the kids enter the schools was like an emotional event for me. I never directly experienced discrimination in Chicago, but where I felt it personally was in the South where discrimination was the rule. My grandparents' neighbors were white, and my grandmother's best friend was white. When my sister and I got older and would go down to Georgia on the train by ourselves, sometimes my grandmother's friend, Mrs. Pearson, would pick us up at the train station. There were the rules of behavior, but there was probably more segregation in Chicago than it was in Macon, Georgia. It's really odd when I think about those kinds of things.

Freedom Rally, Soldier Field, 1966
(Courtesy of Chicago Park District)

Joe Levinson

In 1963, I joined the public relations department of Western Electric's Hawthorne Works in Cicero, Illinois. In those years, that monster plant and its nearby satellite plants had 24,500 employees working to make vital equipment for the Bell Telephone Companies across the nation. Western Electric was the single largest element of the entire Bell System, both in physical size and in number of employees, and the Hawthorne Works was the largest of its factories in the nation. I was a columnist for the plant's employee newspaper, writing press releases for its products and its people. I made many friends there, and several remain to this day.

Things were going well in the first years I was at Hawthorne, until our department chief brought us together and announced that the Student Non-Violent Coordinating Committee (SNCC) and CORE were planning a march through Cicero on September 4, 1966. That information hit us like a bomb. We'd long been aware of Dr. Martin Luther King's great efforts and through the media we had witnessed his quest for racial equality and justice. But, a SNCC march through Cicero? That was another matter entirely. The focus of this march was to protest the serious lack of open housing in Cicero and many other places in the nation.

At that time, Cicero was a blue-collar town, primarily Republican, with long historical connections to Al Capone during the Prohibition era. It was considered a "tough town," and in 1963, no blacks, Asians, or Hispanics lived there. If you mentioned Cicero to anyone in Chicago or anywhere in the nation, you would get a raised eyebrow and a knowing look. "Cicero? Ah, yes! Wasn't that the headquarters for the Capone Mob?"

It was true that Cicero played a major role in the Capone saga, but his "headquarters" actually were in Chicago, on the South Side in the Hotel Metropole. But, just the same, a march of black students through Cicero did more than raise eyebrows for me. It suggested big trouble and possibly, violence.

Western Electric's giant campus ranged from Cicero Avenue and 22nd Street (Cermak Road) south to 31st Street, and was bounded on the east by the Belt Line Railroad tracks and the huge Hawthorne rod and wire mill. The gigantic property covered hundreds of acres, with a large outdoor park near the main buildings at the northern end of the plant. Shortly before the day of the march, the authorities decided to permit the Illinois National Guard the use of Hawthorne's vast property to hold jeeps, trucks, and troops. It was the perfect place, near the line of the march along Cicero Avenue. SNCC members would be approaching the Hawthorne Works from the north, along Cicero Avenue.

The National Guard was certainly necessary, and previous King and SNCC marches through difficult places in the U.S. had proven that. But, why Cicero? Well, Cicero was an entirely different matter. It was "the devil's mouth" that SNCC was marching into, a town of tough guys, questionable bars and private sleazy clubs, prostitutes, gamblers, and tough, working people, and it was a white suburb.

News of the planned march traveled quickly, and photographers, reporters, and TV crews worldwide made plans to cover this historic and possibly dangerous event. The Hawthorne Work's main employment building was at 24th and Cicero Avenue from Gate One to the Works. The location housed our public relations department and became the place to house the press corps. We provided teletype machines, desk space, hot coffee, banks of telephones, Coke machines, pencils, paper, and rest rooms, and all of us in the public relations department helped the media with whatever they needed.

On the morning of the march, reporters and photographers from every major newspaper chain, TV network, weekly news magazine, and radio station descended on our newsroom at Hawthorne. I remember seeing one photographer from *Time,* who had four cameras slung across his body, and when I asked him about the large amount of film he was going to shoot, he said, "Back in New York, we have a sign over the darkroom that reads "Time is Short and Film is Cheap!" I gave him an ashtray and some hot coffee and left him alone.

The march south along Cicero Avenue was scheduled to reach 22nd Street about 10:00 am. Cicero Avenue had been completely blocked off by the Chicago and Cicero Police Departments. There was no traffic moving on the street, and all cross streets were blocked to traffic. Usually, the noise on Cicero Avenue during any weekday morning at 10:00 am had a high decibel level from the thousands of cars and trucks that drove along it. That historic morning, in the hour before the marchers arrived, it was deadly silent and felt quite eerie. I remember taking a few minutes to leave the press room, walk the few feet to Gate One, and go out onto Cicero Avenue. I heard a helicopter overhead circling the area, flying very low in order to check rooftops. I looked up at the three-story buildings across from Gate One that housed stores and taverns at street level and apartments on the upper two or three floors. There were men and women leaning from the window, peering north just looking for the marchers who were coming down the street. Also, there were soldiers with rifles stationed on the roofs of the Hawthorne Works.

Looking north on Cicero Avenue, I saw a group of men and women slowly coming toward the intersection of Cermak Road and Cicero Avenue. Along the sidewalks, on each side of the marchers, there were jeeps loaded with Illinois National Guardsmen with bayonets affixed to their rifles.

I stood in the middle of Cicero Avenue and began to hear the noise of the people above me who were in the windows on the West Side of Cicero, shouting obscenities at the approaching marchers. As the marchers came ever closer from the north, the level of noise increased until it reached a cacophony, aided no less by the sounds of the helicopters and the motors of the jeeps riding on the sidewalk. Each jeep had a machine gun mounted in the back. I actually couldn't move because I was frozen there just looking directly at the marchers coming toward me into that angry, white, tough town of Cicero, Illinois.

To this day, I cannot remember ever hearing more foul and violent words from the mouths of women who were screaming curses at the marchers. Somehow, I made my feet move and ran back to the comparative safety behind the Hawthorne Works iron entrance gates. There, gripping the bars of the fence, I looked at the marchers moving south past me. I saw and heard cherry bombs being tossed down and exploding among them, but somehow, they remained determined to continue marching south.

There actually weren't many marchers, and historical records indicate a group of no more than 200 people. Among them were a number of young women between the ages of 18 and 20, and I remember admiring their courage and sheer guts to parade into a den of very angry people. All the while, the marchers walked past, obviously hearing the screams and curses coming from Cicero residents looking out from the building windows above the street. They finally disappeared south down Cicero Avenue and out of my sight. Afterwards, I heard about the violent confrontations that had taken place between the people of Cicero and the marchers, and learned that the SNCC marchers had been forced to discontinue the parade and leave under the protection of the National Guard.

Thousands of photographs were taken that day, and hundreds of stories were flashed to newsrooms in countries around the world. When it was over, exhausted reporters and photographers sat in our press room, drinking coffee and preparing stories. One photograph taken that morning conveyed more than any words could: It showed a young soldier, a bayonet affixed to his rifle, facing a muscular, white Cicero youth wearing a sleeveless T-shirt. The bayonet tip was literally an inch away from that tough kid's chest as they stared intently at each other. It was a picture that, in an instant, summed up the passions of the people on that day in September, 1966 in Cicero, Illinois

Comes the
Revolutio
National D
Conventio
Politics an

: The
emocratic
,
d War

Norman Mark

I decided to go to Northwestern University because the girls were prettier there than at the University of Chicago, where I feared they could grow mustaches. By the time I graduated NU in 1961, I had been thrown off WNUR, the campus radio station, four times, which remains a modern-day record. I was associate editor of the humor magazine, *The Profile,* when it was thrown off campus, never to return. And, I created the entertainment page for the campus newspaper, the *Daily Northwestern.* I had a scholarship from the School of Journalism despite being a speech major. It was a strange and fascinating college career that included meeting my wife to be, covering a panty raid (what ever happened to them?), and writing clues for a network television quiz show. After graduation, being eligible for the military draft made me nearly unemployable. After working for TV College at WTTW, I was hired at WHAP, the "happy voice of Hopewell, Virginia, broadcasting on the tidewaters of the James River." That was when the dance with the draft board began.

I got a notice to appear for my physical examination in Chicago, but I was in Virginia. The next notice told me to appear in Richmond, Virginia, but by that time, I was on WHLT in Huntington, Indiana. The next notice asked me to come to Chicago (couldn't, I'm working in Indiana). Then, I was ordered to take a physical on the Jewish High Holidays (couldn't, I'm religious exemption). There were three or four months between notices, but, finally, the draft board in effect said, "Come to your physical in Chicago, or we will come and get you!" That same night, I took another physical for the Illinois National Guard and was sworn in. When I was in Basic Training, I received my draft notice. I couldn't accept that because I was already in the Army.

After basic training (and some unemployment), I became a reporter at the City News Bureau in Chicago, that legendary training ground for the best newspaper people in the business. After a couple of years, I became the City Hall correspondent with a salary of $125 a week. At that time, I was the highest paid City News Bureau reporter. I remember covering the old Mayor Daley when he said that Martin Luther King was a communist. Month after month we asked him for proof of that accusation. Finally, he said, "I'll show you your proof"—he threw a *Chicago American* at us that had that phony story.

In private, we could understand everything Mayor Daley said. But, he mumbled a lot during press conferences, and he rarely spoke in complete sentences. I began bringing a tape recorder to sessions with him. So did the other City Hall reporters. One time, there was some important question that we were asking him, and he gave us his response. Afterwards, all of the City Hall reporters played back their tape recordings and agreed on what the quote would be. The next day, City News and every paper in town had the same quote, which was pure Daley. It was also completely senseless, with wandering subjects and predicates, nouns all over the place, and verbs tossed about. It didn't make any sense at all. The next day, the mayor's press secretary, Earl Bush, came storming into the newsroom shouting, **"Quote what he meant, not what he said!"**

By the time of the riots in the late '60s, I was working at the *Chicago Daily News* and serving in the National Guard. Of course, I was avoiding Vietnam, but I ended up with lots of active duty time, including call ups for the riots in '65, '66, '67, and '68, floods in '67, the Cicero march in '67, the riots after the King Assassination, the riots that didn't happen after the Robert F. Kennedy assassination in '68, and the Democratic National Convention. Instead of going to Vietnam, I had the opportunity of being threatened by my own neighbors at home and having a chest full of medals.

In the late '60s, after the Michigan National Guard shot up parts of Detroit, President Johnson ordered extra training for the National Guard on how to deal with riots.

The only training film they had available showed us how to respond to a Hungarian food riot after World War II. There were dozens of rather overweight women storming a meat market. When dealing with rioters, the military was supposed to form a V-wedge, march into the rioters, split them into smaller groups and disperse the mob. During one training exercise in Southern Illinois, we were divided into shirtless "rioters," uniformed military, and observers. The Guard started going forward with their rifles and fixed bayonets. The "rioters" were screaming, yelling, throwing rocks, and doing everything they could to disturb the Guardsmen. That was when one of our gung-ho lieutenants, who wanted a promotion, threw a smoke grenade and yelled, "Tear gas!"

Doing what they were trained to do, the Guardsmen put their rifles between their knees in preparation for putting on their gas masks. The "rioters" immediately grabbed the rifles and began bayoneting and dispersing the "good guys." That day, the "rioters" won. The officers were all set to run another training exercise, when I asked, "What should we do if the rioters have tear gas?" No one knew so the exercises were called off that entire weekend, which was the real purpose of my question. Later, we heard that the Pentagon had to "war game" the question to come up with an answer.

In April 1968, when the West Side burned after the King assassination, the warrant officer who led my information unit decided to send us out on patrol so we could provide protection for *Sun-Times* columnist Irv Kupcinet. About 60 of us in a dozen jeeps and trucks (Kup and the general required a lot of protecting) were driving north on a side street when two drunks came out of a tavern. They were talking loudly to each other, but making no sense. The general in charge of the National Guard, affectionately known as "Killer" Kane, ordered the convoy to stop to investigate this disturbance. Everybody but my buddy Gary and I got out of our jeeps to accompany Kup and "Killer" when they walked across the street. At that moment, another convoy led by a truck with a machine gun stopped. Two foot patrols on each side of the street also converged on the area. The drunks had disappeared into the crowd, but now the street was completely blocked. I looked up and saw people in every window of the three- and four-story tenements. Then, Gary started to get out of the jeep, but I warned him, "Look up. We're the cowboys in the valley, and the Indians have the heights. I say we stick with the jeep so, if something bad happens, we can escape and tell the world the story of our brave but silly troops."

Whenever a riot or a problem occurred, our Headquarters Company was always the last to go home. One day, we were sitting in the Armory east of Michigan on Chicago Avenue, when peace demonstrators decided to picket us. We went on high alert and treated the demonstrators as if they were beginning an invasion. We had .50 caliber machine guns on the roof with fully armed Guardsmen standing at the door ready to repel the protesters and their dangerous pamphlets.

They were marching back and forth in front of the Armory, when the same lieutenant who wanted a promotion decided, on his own, to throw an actual tear gas grenade at the peaceful protesters. The Guardsmen weren't prepared and so, when the wind shifted, our guys were gassed. Then, another wind shifted and the cloud of tear gas also blew into nearby Northwestern Memorial Hospital. That lieutenant ended up gassing the patients in the hospital.

According to the after-action reports, the Illinois National Guard nearly killed Senator Hubert Humphrey, the Democratic nominee for President and the man we were assigned to protect. The general in charge of the 33rd Brigade, which was on the Lake Michigan side of the Gregory march, ordered his helicopter into air space reserved for the Secret Service. A fixed-wing Secret Service plane had taken off from Meigs Field to make sure the air space was safe when Humphrey flew to the convention to accept the nomination. The general's helicopter came within 50 feet of the fixed-wing Secret Service plane. There was almost a collision, and both craft had to take desperate evasive measures. Humphrey was grounded for fear that the 10,500 men of the Illinois National Guard might accidentally kill him if he took to the air.

By 1965, I was working for Dick Christiansen in the Panorama section of the *Daily News*. He was a great editor. Panorama would cover everything about entertainment, and Dick would give his staff a variety of great writing assignments. I did regular stuff like interviewing celebrities, but I would always be working on a major piece for *Panorama*. Among my many assignments were following street performers through the West Side for a couple of days and hanging out with singing groups like the Beatles, the Monkees, or The Who when they came to Chicago. In less than three days, Dick and his talented staff came up with an in-depth, devastating critique of the city's official inventory of our cultural resources. Then, I became the TV columnist, covering how TV covered the first landing on the moon, battling to change the management of WTTW, getting the Surgeon General to reverse early coverage of his report on TV violence and its effect on children, and championing *Sesame Street*.

The 1960s were significant because of the sudden discovery of the power of young people and the political protests that changed the country and got us out of a war we never should have gotten in to in the first place (the echoes of which we should be hearing today). In addition, there was the awareness that we didn't have to wear the clothes—or have the attitudes—that our parents had. The music and our generation's outlook on life were changing as we had moved out of the Eisenhower era and the "button-down" life of the '50s towards the first man to walk on the moon. The sexual revolution was about freedom and sex, with no hint that AIDS was in our future. OK, so the '60s were also a decade of bad hair and the miniskirt. But, the '60s offered the fabulous intellectual ferment, including terrific books by new voices, new hopes politically, and the feeling that our world could be better than our parents' world.

Joel Weisman

I went to the University of Illinois in 1960 and graduated in three and a half years, but not until later did I realize that those were the best years of my life. While I was in school, I was a writer and columnist for the *Daily Illini,* the school newspaper, and I worked with Roger Ebert and a number of really good writers. I also worked for the *Champaign News Gazette* while I was downstate.

When I came back to Chicago from the University of Illinois, I was living at home in West Rogers Park for a year, before getting married in 1965. When I got married, we lived on Ridge near Howard for two years in a third floor, walk-up apartment. One of my biggest breaks happened in January 1967 when Chicago's great snowstorm hit. We lived only a mile from the Howard Street "L," which was still running after 20+ inches of snow, so, I was able to get to the *Chicago American* newsroom. I could do all the snow-related stories, even with the paper being vastly understaffed during those days. However, I soon discovered that the farthest they could deliver the papers was North Avenue. But, I was able to show that I was capable and dedicated, and the paper started giving me some really good assignments. I had the opportunity to spend a lot of my time covering the "old school" politics that occurred in the late '60s.

I began my post-college journalism career at City News Bureau, then, briefly for the Associated Press. Next, I worked for the *Gary Post-Tribune* and became a stringer for the *Chicago Daily News* before getting hired by the *Chicago American.* I was going to Chicago-Kent Law School at the time, so, in a lot of my job interviews, the issue was whether or not I would be able to attend classes and work. There was a wonderful city editor at the *Chicago American* named Ernie Tucker who gave me time off whenever I had to study for my final examinations. I thought that I was using my vacation time, but he would come up to me and say, "Aren't you going to take vacation this year?" I said, "I already took the time to study." He answered, "No, no, take a vacation." By that time, the *Chicago Tribune* owned the *Chicago American,* and the *Chicago Sun-Times* owned the *Chicago Daily News.* So, the *American* became the Tribune's afternoon newspaper.

It was fascinating to watch the city evolving throughout the 1960s. I saw the downtown changing by the mid-'60s, and symbolic of that, there was an ad campaign by the Boulevard National Bank where they said it was located in the "new downtown," which really meant that State Street was for blacks and Michigan Avenue was for whites.

As the decade progressed, there was great division. You were either in favor of civil rights and against the war in Vietnam, or you were patriotic and for the war and against everything that the hippies and the Yippies stood for. That included "free love," dressing crazy, being against the establishment, or any demonstrations. They thought that the kids were terrible and didn't understand anything. I do remember the intense camaraderie among the journalists, and how we would go out to drink after work and have these raging debates about public issues at places like Riccardo's and Billy Goat's. It was a wonderful time to be working in journalism. I was also a stringer for several national magazines and wrote articles for some local publications too.

I was able to do a lot of work on the April 1968 riots that had occurred after the King Assassination because I was in the *Chicago American* newsroom doing rewrites from reporters rather than being on the street. In those days, many reporters didn't write their own stories, so I found myself doing a lot of writing for them. Then, in August, during the Democratic Convention, I basically stayed downtown most of the time. I covered the demonstrations at the Daley Center, Lincoln and Grant Parks, and the Hilton. I was an eyewitness to police beating the kids, and I remember that my first assignment at the convention was to write about all the security arrangements in place at the Amphitheater. We had just witnessed the King and the Kennedy assassinations, and the idea was to stakeout the Amphitheater with sharpshooters. I did a series of stories for the *Chicago American* at the time about that.

In addition, I was in charge of getting security clearances for most of the reporters at the paper and negotiating for space at the Amphitheater to cover the convention. Then, I was assigned to cover Humphrey at the convention, so I would go wherever he would go. He was utterly naïve. The kids were yelling and screaming as he'd go in the hotel lobby. They would say, "Dump the Hump! Dump the Hump!" and he would just be waving and saying, "Hi! Thank you!" He thought that they were kind of his fans. But, he started getting smarter as the week wore on, and eventually, he changed his position on Vietnam. If I had one memory from the decade that will always stand out, it happened the night I was up in Hubert Humphrey's suite in the Conrad Hilton and they were rioting below on Michigan Avenue. His wife, Muriel, was at the Amphitheater at the Democratic National Convention.

I was the pool reporter for newspapers in that suite, and there was a separate pool reporter for magazines, as well as one for television, and one for radio. I'm not sure why I was selected, but I was given the opportunity to watch him watch himself be nominated as the world was coming to an end below the hotel on Michigan Avenue. He would peer over at the window and kept talking about how beautiful Muriel looked, and he was heard to mutter to someone, "Did I ever think that it was going to come to this?" This was the both the beginning and end of Humphrey's goal to be president, even though he came pretty close to winning the 1968 election. He hoped that Daley supported his candidacy because the mayor was a strong partisan at the time.

But, Humphrey wasn't fully trusting because there was some talk at the time about getting Ted Kennedy drafted, or someone else. So, there was not this full trust that you would see prior candidates give to the mayor when they felt they had his full support. Daley was still enamored with the Kennedys, and the mayor didn't think that, given all of the events, Humphrey would necessarily have the chance to win. But, Daley came through for Humphrey in the end. He gave him a great torchlight parade and the support of the Cook County Democratic Party. I think that, in the end, Daley and the Democrats thought that they would win, and Daley hated Nixon. Even though Humphrey's prior history had been as a liberal, he was really on Daley's side in terms of preserving order. Once the die had been cast at the convention, Daley was willing to work hard for him and defend him, while at the same time distancing himself from Humphrey. During that election, I think that Daley was more concerned with Daley and Chicago politics and defending the reputations of his police and the city.

As for the supporters of the mayor's position on the Convention and the subsequent Days of Rage, it is quite possible, from their perspective, that they thought that, no matter what had happened, they would be blamed. There is no question that the demonstrators were looking for a confrontation to dramatize their view, but the city was so dumb that its people played right into it. Daley was telling people that he had to take action because the Yippies or the Hippies were going to put LSD into the city's water supply, as impossible as that may have been. As for the demonstrations, there was a great pre-convention exaggeration about the vast number of protesters and what they were going to do.

Looking back, it is obvious that Chicago-style journalism was great in the '60s in the sense that it was so competitive among four daily newspapers. So, if you did an investigation, the other papers had to investigate and write about it. If your competitors dealt with it, then your paper couldn't ignore it or you would look like an idiot. So, if three papers were suddenly reporting it and one wasn't, then it would look like the fix must be in. There was this pack mentality, and people really read the papers in those days. There were also numerous editions of each paper, each day, and it was difficult to keep up with so many changing stories. I liked working for the *American* because it was an underdog paper and there were so many good journalists working there. Like many people, I thought that the '60s was the most remarkable decade ever, and I was in a very interesting position during those years because I had become a full-time journalist. I was a guy who caught a lot of good breaks early in my career, or maybe it was just a combination of luck and some skills too. It was a fascinating time to have been in the Fourth Estate.

Richard Lang

I was born on January 31, 1944 on Chicago's West Side. We lived close to Douglas Park in the 1400 block of South Millard Avenue, near Pulaski and Douglas Boulevards. My parents were upset when the neighborhood began to change from predominantly white to black. There was a black family in the apartment below us, and when another bought the building, my folks decided to move. We landed on the North Side in 1950, in a seven- room Morse Avenue apartment with large rooms, high ceilings, and a sun porch. The rent was only $95 per month even though it was a half block from the wonderful parks and beaches along Lake Michigan. I had an idyllic childhood there. Parents allowed children to meander through the neighborhood without supervision. Crime, drugs, and gangs were the features of a later time.

I was 16 years old in 1960 when John F. Kennedy was elected President at a time in American history when there were more students than farmers. Young people were excited about that election, seduced by the stylistic contrast between the boring, avuncular WWII-hero, General Eisenhower, and the youthful "New Frontiersman." Kennedy energized feelings of enthusiasm and optimism, but the decade went through a kind of national mood swing. The early 1960s witnessed a palpable optimism about the present and the future and ended in a type of collective societal depression after the assassination of the Kennedys and several Civil Rights leaders, especially Dr. Martin Luther King.

I was a student at the University of Illinois in Champaign having lunch in a school cafeteria on November 22, 1963. Suddenly, a voice over the loud speaker informed us that the President had been shot and within half an hour, it was announced that he was dead. People were shocked, confused, contrite, and almost speechless. They hardly knew how to react. For many, the political and cultural balloon was pierced and noxious air was escaping.

The assassination politicized me a bit, but my radical days were still to come. I didn't care much about what was going on initially, and Lyndon Johnson didn't capture my interest. Yet a single conversation before the 1964 election permanently altered my relationship to politics. I was trounced in a friendly debate with a high school friend, Steve Chernof, who was majoring in political science at the University of Wisconsin. While 20-year-olds couldn't vote, and even though my knowledge of politics was superficial and my attention minimal, I had somehow decided that Barry Goldwater was the right man for the presidency. He appeared to me to be a "straight-shooter," confident and direct, while Johnson was too wishy-washy. Barely conversant with political issues and realities, I was persuaded by cursory images. I was no match for Steve's knowledge, and this embarrassing defeat led me to begin to study the contemporary and historical aspects of the American political situation. My defeat was not ideological; I simply had no clue about the nuts and bolts of American politics.
Yet, as I looked more deeply into the origins and evolution of the political culture in the United States, I quickly acquired the views of a mainstream liberal.

I earned a bachelor's degree from the University of Illinois in 1965 and a master's degree the next year. In the mid-Sixties, many were affected by a heightened media attention to civil rights matters and the continuing war in Vietnam. With my new wife, we often traveled to Washington, D.C. for weekend marches, protests, and demonstrations. We were accompanied and supported by a growing youth culture that was simultaneously idealistic, frustrated, as well as politically involved, but skeptical about the ideological propaganda emanating from the establishment. At the same time that I was in earnest pursuit of what I thought this country's proper course should be, I began to wonder if there were any real solutions to America's ongoing problems within the existing political system.

Told that there was "light at the end of the tunnel" in Vietnam, the war dragged on and on. Told that we lived in a democratic society, we wondered which segment of "government by the people" sent us to war and kept it going. This government's hypocrisy peaked with assurances about the equal treatment of its citizens. The administration said that it was exporting American democracy overseas while we watched televised reports of blacks being hosed down by the authorities when they marched in favor of the Voting Rights Act and the Civil Rights Acts of '64 and '65. Beyond obvious injustices like those, it was clear that there were inequitable divisions in this society, differential privileges based on race, class, and gender.

In 1965, when I was at the University of Illinois, I traveled to Selma, Alabama to be part of a nationally organized civil rights protest. One of our professors had made the arrangements for a group to ride there in two carloads. We drove straight through to a rendezvous point where we were to meet with others. However, as soon as we arrived in Selma, we were stopped by the police. There were peace symbols and civil rights decals all over the cars, so the police identified us easily. We were jailed immediately and charged with loitering and being outside agitators. After spending the night in crowded and filthy jail cells, we were escorted out of town the next day without having participated in any of the activities. Freedom of speech in democratic America? Freedom of assembly? My cynicism was growing rapidly.

With a focus on national politics, I became a dedicated activist. Yet, I needed to have an income and made the mistake of entering the business world at the Allstate Insurance Company. Political on my own time, I worked for a conservative corporation that reminded me of William Whyte's "Organization Man" and the conformity studies of David Riesman. We were uniformed in ties and white shirts and allowed to have only minimal facial hair. The best programmer in our group was fired when he refused to shave a barely noticeable thin blond mustache that had appeared during his two-week vacation. There were no blacks or women in my large department and few anywhere else in the organization with substantial work duties. I looked like a stereotypical corporate employee, but was uncomfortable being away from the political and social events of the day. My head and heart were elsewhere; I felt trapped in the business environment.

My first step toward a personal answer to the dilemma came in 1967 when I was hired as an instructor at the new William Rainey Harper Community College in suburban Palatine. I also joined Students for a Democratic Society (SDS) at that time. My wife and I lived on Juneway Terrace, near Sheridan Road in Rogers Park. There were student sit-ins during those days, and I was an outside agitator at Northwestern University and at the University of Chicago where they had a big sit-in and an overnight protest in the Administration Building. I looked for trouble everywhere, always interested in stirring the political pot. I went to countless SDS strategy meetings and was a spokesman and pamphleteer for a local Rogers Park antiwar and civil rights group. No longer a liberal, I had become aligned with the New Left.

By 1968, I had become more active in SDS and attended many strategy meetings prior to the Democratic National Convention. My draft status reflected the privileges and protections of the middle class. I received various education, teaching, and marriage deferments while working class and minority youngsters went to war. Woody Allen captured my feeling about the war when he said, "In the event of war, I am a hostage." In April of 1968, one of my older students at Harper walked into my evening class and announced that Dr. Martin Luther King, Jr. had been assassinated.

Students in this conservative suburb expressed the sentiment that my hero "got what he deserved." I called off class on the spot. Later in '68, I began teaching at Wilson Junior College in Chicago, later called Kennedy-King, and I was much more comfortable there.

Like many antiwar activists, I experienced an ebb and flow of optimism as we considered Eugene McCarthy and Robert Kennedy as possible replacements for Lyndon Johnson. The first task was to end the war, even if it meant working within the existing system, and after that, we would endeavor to bring about radical, comprehensive change in America's political culture. When we learned that Johnson had lied about the Gulf of Tonkin in order to accelerate the hostilities, it was obvious to me that the Democrats were no better than the Republicans. In protest against the hypocrisy of the Democratic National Convention, SDS made assignments for its members. We had squads that were assigned to different locations, and with angry, violent police everywhere, we knew that our task was difficult. I wasn't at the notorious Lincoln Park demonstration earlier that August week, but was at Grant Park during the tumultuous events on Wednesday and Thursday nights at the Hilton. I also spoke out against the war at Bughouse Square at Clark and Oak Streets while standing on an overturned garbage can and at a few high school rallies. When I was at the Hilton and bending over on my knees to help a kid by giving him first aid, a cop came by on a horse and smashed me on the head with his Billy club. It was a scary thing to have happened here in the "free" world. I thought about the American democratic experiment as I was getting my scalp stitched.

I look back on that era with mixed feelings. I was a true believer and was sure at the time that we were really going to change the world, stop the war, and be the agents for eventual realization of worldwide peace and justice. In retrospect, my naiveté is upsetting and I was angry then and now about the inability to end war, democratize the government and extend human rights to blacks, women, and all members of society. And yet, there was never a more interesting time for me and others like me who spoke of participatory democracy and institutional change. Apart from politics, cultural changes and experiments in the arts were provocative and exciting. Unlike any decade since, the 1960's asked significant questions and posed major challenges to all social institutions. Rather than passively accepting timeworn values and practices in political, educational, familial, and economic institutions, '60s people were analytical and reformist, sometimes radical and revolutionary. I was influenced by many. Some were well known scholars (Herbert Marcuse, Michael Harrington, C. Wright Mills, Howard Zinn, William Appleman Williams, Noam Chomsky, Angela Davis, Staughton Lynd, Richard Flacks, etc.), while others were anonymous devoted activists. My radicalization was complete when I arrived at the position that internal (liberal) reform was futile in the face of militarily entrenched powers so that sweeping systemic change was necessary.

During my time in SDS, I was not persuaded by the approach of the Weathermen Underground; my fealty to Dr. King was steadfast. The hopeful idealism and unwavering commitment to democracy of early SDS was most appealing to me. I met and conferred with many of the primary SDS leaders who came to town, including Jerry Rubin, Mark Rudd, Todd Gitlin, David Dellinger, and Tom Hayden. I was a propagandist for democracy and active and involved in several groups and subgroups. I spoke frequently to labor unions and students and have retained to this day the progressive values that crystallized for me in the '60s. Egalitarian notions of peace and justice, developed then, have endured in my thinking. Contradicting the old saw that we become more conservative with age, I still argue today for democratic socialism.

Grant Park Protest Rally, 1968
(Courtesy of Chicago Park District)

Grant Park Protest Rally, 1968
(Courtesy of Chicago Park District)

Marilyn Katz

I was born in 1945 and grew up at Wellington and Sheridan. I was a normal kid, went to Nettlehorst Elementary School and Lake View High School, and lived in a middle class Jewish community. I went to college, first at Tulane in New Orleans, and then to Northwestern University. Many of my friends were getting married, and I came back from New Orleans with the same goal, but decided that marriage would be a fate worse than death. I was a sorority kid, but the Civil Rights Movement was growing and Martin Luther King and SNCC were becoming more active in the South – there were the beginnings of anti-war movement. And, it appeared to me that everything that I had been taught in life compelled me to be involved in these actions that were premised on the notion that U.S. should live up to its democratic promise. So, in the early '60s, I decided to do three things: break my engagement; go to my first SDS meeting; and, quit my sorority.

I was an unlikely radical, but was more than ready to join Students for a Democratic Society. To me, it was very clear that the kids who went off to the Army were kids with no other choices. They were not like those of us who had college as an option and who had our pathways set forth. That made me more sympathetic to them because they were just working-class kids whose life experiences had led them in another direction. At that time, I hadn't had any direct experience with African Americans, and remembered that in New Orleans, blacks couldn't go to the bars. Growing up in the '60s meant that you had certain expectations, still accepted the mythology of World War II, were a champion of democracy, and believed that America was a land of opportunity. So, it was shocking when I learned that all those preconceptions were not necessarily true.

When John F. Kennedy ran for president in 1960, I was in high school and it was really exciting because it was politics that was new and seemed to be outside the normal. His election seemed to be part of a great endeavor, and we were proud the country elected an innovative thinker with a great vision for the country. I was going to school at Tulane when he was assassinated, and that was a real shock. In addition, the good old boys in the South were happy with his assassination because of his support for civil rights.

Negative things were beginning to happen in Vietnam, SNCC and SCLC were growing in the South, and Selma occurred in 1965. I decided that I wanted to make history and not just write about it, so when I heard about an SDS meeting at Northwestern, I went to it. I looked very different than the rest of the people there, and it wasn't my crowd at all.

In 1965, I participated in anti-war demonstrations and noticed that SDS was particularly weak because the group was afraid to challenge the university. My attitude was that I was going to show the world that you could look cool and still have politics, and I was absorbing everything that I learned. When someone came to the university to talk about the Freedom Riders, I became involved in that.

Soon after, leaders from the Joint Community Union came to Northwestern to recruit for that group, which was a community-based SDS project in Uptown. I was immediately intrigued by the project and viewed it as my chance to take some concrete actions. I went to Uptown and lived there for the summer. I never received my degree from Northwestern because I left there as a senior in the spring of 1968. For a while, I was living in two worlds that included the Northwestern University campus and the Uptown neighborhood of Chicago in the SDS-based community action project. The name of the group was Jobs Or Income Now (JOIN), and it was focused on the poor.

In the black community, the most active groups included SNCC, SCLC, Leon Finney and The Woodlawn Organization, all in existence before the Black Panthers. Our Uptown group worked very closely with African Americans on Chicago's South Side for a long time. When Martin Luther King marched in Chicago, blacks were pleased that there were a bunch of white kids and southern whites at the Marquette Park march whom they saw as a critical ally. There was a loose coalition of all of these groups among blacks, whites, southern whites, and Puerto Ricans, as well as welfare workers, women's groups, young intellectuals, union members, and university students. Civil rights was the predominant issue in the black community, but when King opposed the war, then Vietnam also became a focal point for many blacks. In the white community and among white activists, the war and civil rights were always linked. There was also an incipient youth movement that was forming, so we began to organize working class high school kids and there was a growing worldwide youth movement.

In the spring of 1968, there was increasing tension that included the riots that followed the King assassination. In addition, there was a strong reaction to the assassinations of Bobby Kennedy and Malcolm X. However, there was a lot of nervousness among those of us working in the city when Tom Hayden, Jerry Rubin, and Abbie Hoffman suggested that they were coming to Chicago to hold demonstrations at the convention and use their "theater politics," which we felt could be very injurious to our activities. There was a group of us, including me, Don Rose, John Froines, David Dellinger, and Rennie Davis, who were working out of SDS. We had a growing youth base, but although there was a kind of coalescing of all the forces, we were still small in our overall membership and it looked like it was going to just be Yippies in Chicago in August with their few hundred participants.

During the weekend before the convention, we were in charge of security in Lincoln Park. It was a bit ridiculous because we only knew how to do "snake dances." But, somehow we prepared for it and separated ourselves from the larger groups of kids who were coming with party delegations to support candidates for president. The first days in the park were very mellow, and there was a "love-in." There were about 2,000-3,000 people who were just smoking dope and listening to music. Then the city decided to clear the park because they wouldn't give us a permit to stay there past the 11:00 pm curfew. Huge fire engines with lights and tear gas came to the park along with the police, so it scared the kids and quickly turned into a disaster. There was very little damage on Wells Street when the kids who had been in Lincoln Park were forced into that neighborhood. Whatever damage occurred was mostly done by a bunch of white kids who had never been attacked before by the police, but who got scared, then angry.

On Monday night, the prospect of a good fight began to draw lots of kids from the neighborhoods. All of the people who lived around Lincoln Park, a bastion of anti-Machine politics, began to come out, see what was going on, and become involved in the fray. There was the police attention and the news cameras, and it was pretty much drawing on the frustration of kids from the neighborhoods. Thousands of kids from throughout the city and the suburbs were drawn to the park like a magnet, and it became a protest against authoritarianism.

By the time we got downtown on Wednesday, they had called in the National Guard. It became a mixture of doped-out hippies, politicos, and North Side gangs, but the group was almost exclusively white people, except for some of the speakers and the Black Panthers. No one there had ever had real experience with any kind of violence until Wednesday and Thursday nights, when there was the confrontation with the police after the big rally in Grant Park. Daley, himself, became emblematic of political repression and dissent.

Soon, there were almost 20,000 to 30,000 protesters gathered in Grant Park around Michigan and Balbo. The National Guardsmen and police decided to draw a "line," just like in the park, and they made it clear they weren't going to let us go beyond the line. The police were pushing the crowds, the crowds were pushing back, and there was a lot of chanting, yelling, and singing. There was also political debate going on within the crowd. We were aching for a fight, but not prepared for the police and National Guard reaction that happened. There were a lot of injuries by the time of the actual confrontation, although, luckily, no one was killed.

Under the cover of dark, the kids decided to fight back, and we outnumbered the police and the Guard. It is true that the National Guard had rifles, but none of us thought they would fire on us. The cops picked the fight, and they wanted it even more than we did, and were better prepared with Billy clubs. I thought that there were two fights of significance: Wednesday night at the Hilton; and, Thursday, on the east side of Grant Park near Balbo. The confrontation on Thursday was a really nasty one because it happened in the middle of the day and there was no curfew or speakers. The cops decided that they were going to clear the park again, after the kids had climbed the statue on Wednesday night. But protesters broke up into little bands, and some began to march to the Amphitheater where the convention was going on. In the end, hundreds of people were arrested, and I would place all the blame on the cops.

After the convention, it was a great opportunity to organize youth because we had defined what was possible. That is exactly what we did by beginning youth organizations that capitalized on the activity, and all the kids who had become involved over the spring and summer in anti-war activities began to join the movement. I became more active with the leadership of SDS, and in the fall of 1968, Slim Coleman and Cathy Archibald arrived from SNCC and began to establish an office, organizing around the trial of the "Conspiracy Seven."

At the same time, Fred Hampton and the Black Panthers were growing in size and strength and had provided a clear alternative to the gangs around the city. By the spring of '69, it was a challenging time for us. There was an alliance between the Black Panthers, who had grown in membership in the city and the suburbs, those of us in SDS, and the Young Lords. It was pretty impressive. In the spring of '69, before the SDS convention, we had marches down Chicago Avenue that involved a few thousand folks. The Weathermen hadn't emerged yet, and we were a unified group. So, SDS decided to ally ourselves with the Black Panthers and the black working class and work against racism. We had tremendous mutual respect and a great working relationship with the Black Panthers because each group had its own base.

During the spring of '69, things intensified both in organizing the city and conducting a lot of rallies. We had become the poster children for revolutionary change that included hillbillies in the Uptown neighborhood, blacks on the South Side, women's groups that were made of working class women, and young gang girls. Then, at the SDS Convention in Chicago in June 1969, things blew up. There was a split between those of us who had been together for a year and a half in the Revolutionary Youth Movement (RYM) and the Weathermen Underground. The SDS split into the Weathermen and RYMII and expelled the Progressive Labor Party from SDS. We were at the apex, and hundreds of thousands of people across the nation began protesting the war.

We maintained dual organizations at the same time, but the Weathermen took control of the SDS office. In October 1969, we had two different sets of demonstrations: one organized by SDS and the official office run by the Weathermen; and one organized by us. The one organized by them met in Lincoln Park, and that led to them running down the Near North Side, which was the excuse for them to go underground. We were at 26th and California, but I don't think that we had any battles with the police. The Black Panthers were with our faction, and even though the Weathermen made a huge showing, they quickly disappeared from the scene, and by December 1969, Fred Hampton was killed.

Most of us didn't start out as revolutionaries. Rather, we were kids looking to fulfill the promise of America. It was only when this view was increasingly and intensely rejected by all the nation's institutions that we looked for other support and deeper answers to why our nation would deny peace and racial justice. That was why we became Marxists.

Police and demonstrators in front of
Hilton Hotel, August, 1968.
(Courtesy of Chicago Park District)

Steve Zucker

In 1966, after graduating from DePaul Law School, I wanted to get a job in the Cook County State's Attorney's Office because I thought that it would provide me with experience in criminal law. But instead, my committeeman, Robert Cherry, was able to get me a job in the Corporation Counsel's Office. I fell into the most unbelievable situation I could have imagined. I was sworn into the new job in the Corporation Counsel's Office in August 1967, and my first assignment was Traffic Court. I was there during the last three months of 1967, and in 1968, I moved into the Ordinance Enforcement Division with Dick Elrod as my boss. Our group of lawyers from the office would go out to the protests and riots and advise the police about the proper charges to place against the demonstrators. We would then follow the cases through the court system, and as a result, I had the opportunity to prosecute many high profile cases.

In April, 1968, as a result of the assassination of Martin Luther King, many people were arrested for rioting and looting. We were at 11th and State assigning charges against defendants, and I remember looking out the window from the top floor of police headquarters and seeing the red and orange glow of the fires that were burning on the city's West Side. Those racially-motivated riots were different than the politically-motivated riots that would occur during the summer of 1968. I could never understand why people were burning down their own neighborhoods. But I did not have to live there.

That year, there were also numerous peace demonstrations protesting the Vietnam War going on all over the city almost every day. According to the law, the demonstrators didn't need a permit to march as long as they left half the sidewalks open, stopped for the traffic lights, didn't impede traffic, and didn't block ingress and egress from the buildings.

In August, the assignments came out for the Democratic Convention. All of the assistants, except me, were sent to the Amphitheater. I was assigned to Lincoln Park. I was so angry about that assignment because I thought that I was being left out of the action, but, as it turned out, everything happened in Lincoln Park, and then in Grant Park. All the action happened on the streets and not at the Convention, and I was happy to be in the middle of it. Since I was assigned to Lincoln Park, I was there on the Sunday before the Convention watching all the demonstrations.

The week before the convention, the Yippies staged a Festival of Life. Young people practiced snake dancing, held a beauty contest (there was no winner), listened to antiwar speeches and music, and for the most part, were orderly. At one point, Abbie Hoffman and Jerry Rubin brought a pink pig into the park, claimed its name was "Pigasus," and announced that he was their candidate for President of the United States. A policeman asked me what he should do about it and I said, "Arrest the pig," which he did. All during the week before the Convention, everybody would leave the park in the evening around 11:00 pm when Lincoln Park was officially closed. That first Sunday, it was just "fun and games." However, on Monday night, the demonstrators decided to try to stay in Lincoln Park overnight. The demonstrators set up a barricade, but since it was pitch black, the lawyers stayed in back of the police especially when they shot off the tear gas to get the demonstrators out of the park. But, the police forgot to gauge which way the wind was blowing, and we really got gassed that night.

I thought that a group of demonstrators tried to agitate the others in order to get them to confront the police. They were erecting barricades and setting fire to things, and it didn't take many of them to cause the confrontations. The crowd grew "ugly," and it wasn't fun anymore.

On Tuesday night, the police allegedly went after the press and chased them into the Old Town neighborhood. The demonstrators were seeking to get as much press coverage as possible. We were all shocked the next day when we learned about all the members of the press getting hurt. Then, on Wednesday, the demonstrators climbed on Logan's Statue in Grant Park and one put up the North Vietnamese flag. The cops said to me, "What should we do?" I said, "Get him off of there, and take down that flag." They forced him off the statue, and he broke his leg when he fell from the statue. The picture was in every paper across the country and around the world.

Wednesday was the day of maximum activity. At about 1:30 pm, I was in Grant Park and the demonstration had moved from Lincoln Park to Grant Park across from the Conrad Hilton Hotel on south Michigan Avenue. The city had a plan to lift the bridges across the Chicago River and halt the demonstrators, but they didn't do it. Thus, the demonstrators were able to come from Lincoln Park on the city's North Side to Grant Park in downtown Chicago, cross the Michigan Avenue Bridge, and descend on Grant Park. The police chased the demonstrators from Grant Park east to Lake Shore Drive, then other cops came to get them off the Drive to keep it from being blocked. The demonstrators had no choice but to go to Jackson and Balbo while moving back west in front of the Hilton Hotel. As the demonstrators were coming, the police were in back of them, and by then, it was early evening. Finally, everything was going crazy, and the entire corner of Balbo and Michigan was surrounded by the demonstrators and police lines that had been set up. What everybody didn't see was the police group was leading a large group of policemen on Wabash coming east as the demonstrators were being forced into the police lines. The police west of Michigan Avenue thought that they were being attacked and that contributed to the confrontation.

Separately, Reverend Ralph Abernathy, who was leading the Poor People's Wagon Train, came to talk to Elrod, Jim Rochford, the Superintendent of Police, and me, and he told us that he wanted to get through the crowd at Michigan and Balbo. His group just

wanted to make their statement about poor people. In order to accomplish this, the police had to push the demonstrators apart to get the mule train through.

Those events made some of the police think that they were being attacked because the demonstrators were being pushed from east to west. All of a sudden, all hell broke loose. I remember the glass breaking in the Haymarket Lounge at the Hilton Hotel, demonstrators went in there, and plain clothes cops went in there after them. The police had been pelted by all kinds of stuff including packets of urine and feces, so they finally reacted to the situation. Although there were a lot of people hurt during the riot, no one was killed. The National Guard was finally called out around 2:00 or 3:00 am, and then everything calmed down.

The following year, they conducted the "Chicago Seven" trial (originally there were eight but the Bobby Seales case was separated) with U.S. District Court Judge Julius Hoffman in charge of the trial. Judge Hoffman was the perfect judge for the defendants to have. He was dogmatic, mean, and one-sided and, as a result, the findings of guilty against the defendants were reversed by the Appellate Court. That trial made Chicago the focus again of the anti-war movement. The seven or eight people who made up the "Chicago Eight" and who were prosecuted hardly knew each other. So, to call it a conspiracy was crazy since they all seemed to act individually.

One of the most notorious anti-war groups was the "Weathermen." I became aware of them the following year, in the fall of 1969, when there was another series of major protests in Chicago. From October 8 to October 12, the event known as the "Days of Rage" was planned by the Weather Underground in order to protest the trial. Everything that happened was confrontational. There was a protest that began in Lincoln Park, and the protesters left the park after being escorted out by the police around 11:00 pm. However, the Weathermen went crazy and they started breaking windows in buildings and cars up and down State Street in Chicago's Loop.

I was in a squad car with Sergeant Kevin O'Malley, who was assigned to me, and we trailed the demonstrators all the way. We were outnumbered, and although I wasn't a policeman, I was acting like one. The main police force hadn't come yet, so a few of us and our bodyguards were trying to stop this group at State and Division. They were coming at us, they were violent, and were wearing helmets because they were there to confront us.

On Saturday, October 11, 1969, the main demonstration took place. It started at the famous Haymarket Square at Randolph and the Kennedy Expressway where the Haymarket Riot statue had been located. The statue was dedicated to the policemen who died during the Haymarket riots in the late nineteenth century. In addition, it was Puerto Rican National Independence Day, and a big march was going to take place on the city's Northwest Side. The mayor sent all his police task force people, with their helmets, to monitor the Puerto Rican march. It meant that the policemen who were with us at Haymarket Square and in the Loop were badly outnumbered and they were only wearing soft police caps. At first, we were just standing there watching the demonstration, and then we began to follow along with the march. The demonstrators were in front of City Hall, when somebody yelled, "Off the pig!" They went wild, and this time, the demonstrators had chains and clubs and they started attacking the police officers. There was a long line of protesters with some police in front and some in back and very few on the side. Although we had received intelligence that something was going to happen, we didn't know what and we weren't fully prepared for it.

Thus, we found ourselves in an all-out battle with the Weathermen. The riot spread out all over the place, and as the demonstrators turned the corner of Washington and Dearborn,

I was standing out there on the street. They were coming at me while police were chasing them, and it was wild. Other people were attacking the police when I was told that someone yelled at me, "Steve, stop that guy!" I couldn't hear it at the time because of the total chaos. The person who they wanted me to stop was Brian Flanigan. Elrod heard the yell, and he tried to stop Flanigan, who, later, would be charged with attempted murder, aggravated battery, and mob action.

I believe that Dick broke his neck when he missed Flanigan and hit the corner of a building and he was lying there paralyzed. The photographs show me on my knee with a Billy club in my hand while Dick was all spread out on the sidewalk. It was like the end of the world because Dick was like a father to me and to see what had happened to him really affected me. Flanigan was found not guilty on all counts, and, if they hadn't overcharged him they could have nailed him on mob action. Right around this time, the Democrats were slating for county offices and Dick was supposed to be a state representative. However, Dick was in the hospital paralyzed from the accident, and the mayor called him up and told Dick that he was going to be slated for Cook County Sheriff in the spring of 1970. Elrod ended up running against Bernard Carey, the Republican candidate, and it was a hotly contested campaign which Dick won. He served as Sheriff of Cook County for 16 years.

Soldiers reading Chicago Daily News
with caption 'Reading All About It.'
As published in the *Chicago Daily News*.
Photographer: John Tweedle.
Copyright, 1968 by *Chicago Sun-Times*, Inc.
Reprinted with permission.

Rick Fizdale

In the late 1960s, my childhood friend, Steve Zucker, was an assistant corporation counsel for the city of Chicago. His responsibilities included riot control, a plum assignment in those days. I was an unemployed hippie opposed to the war in Vietnam. Chicago had been chosen to host the 1968 Democratic National Convention, and months before the convention, Steve and I discussed the certainty of massive protests and the likelihood that we would find ourselves on opposite sides of the battle line. In one of those conversations, Steve told me that the city had already decided not to let the demonstrators sleep in Lincoln Park. Why he told me this at a time when the city appeared to be negotiating in good faith with representatives of the far left was surprising, unless he expected me to spread the word, which is exactly what I did.

In March 1968, my brother, girlfriend, and I visited Arthur Naiman, a friend from Evanston, who had moved to New York City. During an all-night bull session, Arthur told us that he was coming to Chicago in August to participate in the protest. I asked if he needed a place to stay and he said, "No, I'm going to sleep in Lincoln Park with everybody else." When I relayed Steve's inside information, Arthur was stunned. He asked if I'd be willing to share what I heard with a friend of his. "Why not," I said, and we were off to see Abbie Hoffman at his apartment in the East Village. Except for Arthur, none of us knew the flamboyant Hoffman, although I had witnessed his failed attempt to levitate the Pentagon, one of many put-ons he devised that helped unite the drug culture and the antiwar movement.

Seated around a glass coffee table decorated with phallic-shaped candles were six celebrities of the counter culture. In addition to Hoffman, the group included: Timothy Leary, his dilated eyes suggesting that he was once again adrift in uncharted waters; Allen Ginsberg, the bearded poet and Tibetan Buddhist; Phil Ochs, the protest singer; Paul Krassner, the editor of the satirical journal, *The Realist;* and Jerry Rubin, political organizer and Hoffman's sidekick, who had once dressed as George Washington when forced to testify before the House Select Committee on Un-American Activities. When we barged in, the group was expressing their pleasure with the moniker they had picked for a bogus political party, the Youth International Party, or Yippie. The moment I heard the name, in part a play on the word hippie, in part a rallying cry to entice young people to Chicago, I decided to assume that identity when the time came. At a break in the conversation, Arthur told them I had news from Chicago. Intoxicated with self-importance, I gave my report. "You heard this from a pig!" shouted a dismissive Rubin. "And you believed it!"

A week before the Convention officially opened I was walking down Clark Street near North Avenue when I saw Rubin walking on the other side of the street. He was being followed by two plain clothes cops. Every time Rubin stopped, they stopped and pretended to read newspapers. Once, when Jerry glanced over his shoulder, they tried to hide behind a lamp post. I laughed, crossed the street, and reintroduced myself. Much to my delight, he remembered me. "You were right. The city's playing games with us." I smiled and whispered, "You're being followed."

"Everywhere I go," he said. "They've cut off the phone where I'm staying. I need to stay in touch." He didn't say with whom or over what. "At night, a dozen cop cars are parked outside." Trying to sound in the know, I said, "The Red Squad, probably. Where are you staying?" He gave me an address on Armitage around the corner from where I lived on Mohawk. I suggested he stay with me. "Why?" he asked. "They'll just stake out your place." With great bravado, I said, "Not if they don't know you're there."

That night, I waltzed past the cop cars on Armitage, rang the bell, and walked up to the third floor. Ed Sanders, a former football player and one of the founders of The Fugs, a proto-punk rock group, blocked the doorway. He held a baseball bat; his eyes focused on my forehead. Rubin's voice called out, "Easy Ed. He's okay."

I hung out for a while and listened to paranoid patter about Chicago's mayor. Then, I looked for a way to get up to the roof and found a trap door ceiling near the back stairs. A short rope dangled from it. I jumped to grab it. When I pulled on it, the trap door opened and a wooden ladder slid down from the roof. We climbed up. Crouching low in the style of Steve McQueen in "The Great Escape," we searched the perimeter looking for a way down. Two police cars were parked in the alley. We found a fire escape on the side of the building which wasn't visible from the alley or Armitage, and 10 minutes later we were safely inside the house I shared with two roommates, various guests, and assorted hangers-on.

Rubin couldn't relax. He tried the phone and discovered a comforting dial tone. He inspected every room. He searched the closets and the pantry, and even pulled back the shower curtain to see if anybody with a badge was hiding there. I introduced him to my friends. "Hey man, good to meet you." Adjusting to his new surroundings, he asked, "What am I going to do tomorrow? Abbie and I have a press conference. We're running a pig for president. I'll be spotted. They'll tail me here. We'll be surrounded, and your phone will be cut off."

I wondered out loud if it made sense for me to call Steve on Jerry's behalf. Maybe Steve had the authority to cut him some slack. Jerry resisted, "Negotiate with a pig, never." One of my roommates, a future psychiatrist, interrupted our conversation to challenge one of the Yippie's wilder threats, "You can't pour

LSD into Lake Michigan and expect it to enter the city's water s supply. The lake's too big." "I know that," admitted the architect of that nut-ball scheme. "But the mayor doesn't." Jerry looked at me and shrugged. "Go ahead, make the call."

I called Zucker, and fantasizing that I was about to step into the pages of history, I settled on what I thought was a dramatic opening. "Hey, Steve, I understand you guys lost Rubin." Steve seemed puzzled, "We did?" Without mentioning my role, I said that Rubin evaded his surveillance and hinted at the superior skills of left wing operatives. "I've been authorized to tell you his whereabouts on the condition that you won't cut off his phone." Steve promised to get back to me.

Not much time passed before Steve called to say that Rubin, wherever he was, would be allowed to use the phone. "Of course we'll be listening. Where is he?" I used a grand pause for effect—"My place!" Steve laughed. "I'll be darned." I'm not sure how the signal was conveyed, but within seconds, a convoy of vehicles, sirens blaring, swarmed on to Mohawk and stopped outside my house. Steve and I kept talking. I suggested that he meet Rubin to see if anything could be done to head off a bloody confrontation. Steve agreed and said, "Tomorrow morning in Lincoln Park near the entrance to the Zoo."

From the get-go, my peace initiative was doomed. Rubin refused to shake Steve's hand and screamed at him, "How can a Jew be a damned pig?" His spittle-laden abuse continued relentlessly; the English language reduced to a torrent of expletives and an occasional oink-oink. Steve left in disgust. That I hoped for better was a testament to my naiveté. I may have been calling myself a Yippie, but I hadn't internalized the raison d'etre of their street theater. Hoffman and Rubin invented outrageous claims: putting LSD in the water; painting cars like taxis to pick up delegates and drop them off in Wisconsin; releasing greased pigs in the Loop; and assigning super potent Yippie men to seduce the wives and daughters of delegates. They knew these madcap rants would entice the reporters and TV cameras assigned to the Convention into covering the protest instead. The comedic duo understood the sound bite before it had a name, but when the delegates assembled at the International Amphitheater, darker forces prevailed on the street.

On the evening of Monday, August 26, I was in Lincoln Park and witnessed the beginning of the violence. As predicted, permits allowing protesters to sleep in the park had been denied. Nevertheless, a few thousand of us gathered to see what would actually happen when push confronted shove. Most of us wore sandals, headbands, and beads. I saw the red flags of revolution and the black flags of anarchy. Somebody handed me a Viet Cong flag which I later passed on to a stoned hippie chick. Some demonstrators built barricades of trash cans and picnic tables. Since we had no command and control, this was an homage to the student movement of Paris which had battled their government to a standstill for two weeks in May. A few toughs wore football helmets and carried baseball bats, one of which had a spike driven through it. A trio of what looked like motorcycle gang members minus colors ominously brandished tire irons and chains. At 11:00 pm, the police enforced an obscure curfew that had gathered dust for decades. They drove us from the park with Billy clubs and tear gas, indiscriminately beating protesters, press, and passersby. The last I saw of my friend Marvin Garson, the editor of the *Berkeley Barb,* he was walking toward the police, a brick in his hand. Above the shouts and screams, I swear I heard the unmistakable, useless "om" of Allen Ginsberg. A wet rag over my mouth and nose to cut down the effects of the gas, I ran home. Rubin was eating potato chips, watching the massacre on TV.

Wednesday night was worse. The protest had moved to Grant Park and the Conrad Hilton Hotel, the Democratic Party headquarters. Protesters and authorities were twitchy with anger and exhaustion. All day long, skirmishes had broken out. A demonstrator climbed a statue waving the Viet Cong flag, while others hurled insults at the police. (It was said that they also threw balloons filled with excrement. Probably so, but I saw none of that).

The police beat their tormentors and threw them into the paddy wagons. As night fell, I positioned myself at Balbo and Michigan on the Hilton side of the street and waited for the arrival of Reverend Ralph Abernathy's covered wagon, part of his "Poor People's Campaign." "There it is!" someone shouted. I stood on my toes to see a rickety wooden wagon pulled by a team of mules, a dash of humility from the Civil Rights Movement sprinkled on an antiwar rally about to spin completely out of control.

To create a lane for the wagon, a cordon of police tried to move protesters who were standing on Michigan Avenue back to the curb. But the curb was occupied. We, the people, were densely packed as uranium atoms on the verge of explosion, all the way to Wabash where a phalanx of police was also stationed. As the group of protesters nearest to the wagon willingly stepped back, the next group (which included me) had no choice but to move backwards. The compression flowed like a wave toward Wabash until the good guys and bad guys collided, and a battle began which drove the entire crowd back toward Michigan Avenue where those police thought they were being attacked, and they retaliated with a level of brutality. I was trapped between a long haired hippie, two teenage sisters holding hands, and a businessman with a briefcase. We joined in a chant that had begun spontaneously. The whole world is watching. The whole world is watching. The whole world is watching. And it was. The TV cameras were soaking up horrific black and white images that resembled footage from the early days of Nazi Germany. In a matter of hours, those images circled the globe. On the night that Hubert Humphrey was nominated, blood in the streets sealed his fate: Richard Nixon would be the next president of the United States. Squeezed between contending forces of history, I somehow popped free and joined Rubin in front of my television.

Judge Dick Elrod

I graduated from Northwestern University in 1955 and Northwestern University Law School in 1958. I married my wife, Marilyn, in 1955 and we lived in West Rogers Park. Our son, Steven, was born in 1957, while our daughter, Audrey, was born in 1960. I was elected Chairman of the Young Democrats of Cook County in 1959, and during the 1960 Presidential election, was in charge of Young Persons' Activities. I helped organize the 50th Ward's involvement in the 1960 torchlight parade during the presidential campaign for John F. Kennedy. Each ward had to have 300 people participate in the event with the groups divided into thirds: 100 people to march in the parade; 100 to line Madison Street; and 100 to go into the Chicago Stadium. Since we were the 50th Ward, we were the last to leave the kickoff area and by the time we got to a block from the Stadium, the whole entourage of dignitaries was leaving since Kennedy has already been there, spoken to the crowd, and was on his way back to the airport.

In 1960, as a precinct captain in my neighborhood of West Rogers Park, I would visit constituents to discuss the coming election. During weekly visits, I would discuss the issues and give people pictures of Kennedy to place in their windows. I decided to skip those whom I knew to be Republicans, but one neighbor yelled to me, "Hey, Elrod, why are you skipping me?" I said, "I didn't think that you would want a picture of a Democrat in your window." His response was, "Kennedy is a good Irish Catholic, and I support him." Religion became an important factor in that election.

In 1960, I was in the Corporation Counsel's Office headed by John C. Melaniphy, the Corporation Counsel from 1955 to 1964. I had gone to work there in 1958, right out of law school, and was in the Housing/Building Court with my specialty being the prosecution of zoning law violations using information provided by the zoning inspectors. From that job, I moved into the General Counsel's Division, where I defended the constitutionality of city ordinances. Then, in 1965, the new Corporation Counsel, Ray Simon, appointed me head of Ordinance Enforcement.

Those were very troubled times in Chicago because so many people seemed to be protesting one issue or another, including the Vietnam War or Benjamin Willis, the Superintendent of the Chicago Board of Education and his so-called "Willis Wagons," the temporary school buildings he was opening in minority neighborhoods. There were also civil rights demonstrations from 1965 to 1969, and it seemed that I was on the street almost every day to provide advice and counsel to the police department about how to handle demonstrators who were exercising their first amendment rights. Often protesters would walk to the mayor's home in Bridgeport. Their goal was to arrive at Daley's house during dinner time between 5:00 and 7:00 pm and march around his neighborhood. Many neighbors became incensed when up to 100 demonstrators showed up each evening. In order to try and force them to leave, some Bridgeport residents turned on their lawn sprinklers and aimed them at the protesters.

One night, we almost had a riot against the demonstrators in Bridgeport. More and more police kept arriving to control the situation, but it wasn't helping. The person heading that particular demonstration was the comedian, Dick Gregory. I called Gregory and a couple of his group's leaders aside and said, "We can't protect you even though we're getting as many police reinforcements as we can. We are asking you to leave for your own safety." He said, "Well, we refuse to leave." I said to him, "Dick, if you refuse, you're going to be arrested." He said, "Fine." I asked him, "Can we do it peacefully?" He said, "Yeah." We pulled up a police squadrol and arrested about 10 of them. I prosecuted them, and they were found guilty in a jury trial, but the case was reversed by the United States Supreme Court.

Martin Luther King came to Chicago two or three different times between 1965 and 1967. On one of his visits, he moved into an apartment in Lawndale. He led demonstrations in Marquette Park, and it was very similar to the events in Bridgeport, except that his group had a parade permit and marched down the middle of the street. At another march, Rev. King got hit with a rock thrown by one of the neighborhood residents. There was also an incident that sparked a riot on the West Side when a Chicago fireman backed his truck out of the fire station and killed an African American girl. The neighbors tried to get him arrested, and that started the riot.

After a few years of protests and near riots, the city was "quiet." In 1967, we didn't have any riots, and as a result, Mayor Daley went to the Democratic National Committee (DNC) and said that since, unlike Detroit and Los Angeles, Chicago wasn't having any racial problems, the 1968 Democratic National Convention should be held in Chicago. He was successful in persuading the DNC to hold the convention here. In April, 1968, Martin Luther King was assassinated, and the reaction in several African American communities led to major riots, looting, and the burning of buildings across the West Side of Chicago. That was when the mayor announced his "shoot to kill" order against arsonists and "shoot to maim" order for looters. The police did not carry out these orders.

In August 1968, during the week before the Democratic National Convention, there were a series of protests. On the Saturday and Sunday nights before the convention, the protesters were gathering in Lincoln Park. The mayor decided to enforce the city's 11:00 pm curfew law. Personally, I don't think that we should have had a confrontation over whether they could stay past the curfew and sleep in the park. It was very difficult to enforce, but I had no choice. Those who disobeyed the police orders were arrested and taken to the 18th District Police Station, and I had to go there and prepare the cases for prosecution. On Monday night, the demonstrators went into Grant Park, across the street of the Hilton Hotel.

I didn't think that the country was coming apart as a result of these events since there was a great deal of exaggeration, including the claims that there were tens of thousands of demonstrators when there was probably just a few thousand. On Tuesday night, some of the police used excessive force on people in front of the Hilton. I was there and could see how the situation had escalated. Then, on Wednesday night, there was another protest outside of the Hilton. A contributing factor was Rev. Ralph Abernathy's "Poor People's" mule train pushing through the crowds. We decided to let them go through so we opened up a path for them in a diagonal route on Michigan Avenue in front of the Hilton. The demonstrators were also moving in that direction and people got pushed from one side of the street to the other. The demonstrators were moving

quickly because army troops used tear gas against them. First Deputy Police Superintendent James Rochford and I could not understand why such extreme action was necessary.

The next year, in October 1969, the Weathermen faction of the SDS came to Chicago with the express purpose of creating disturbances in the city. They weren't interested in civil disobedience. They came dressed in leather jackets and football helmets, and carried lead pipes and sticks, and were a different group of demonstrators than those who had been at the convention. Their thoughts were to cause harm and havoc, not to have peaceful demonstrations. On Wednesday night, October 8, about 300 of them met just north of North Avenue in Lincoln Park at Dearborn and decided to march to Judge Julius Hoffman's house in the 800 block of East Lake Shore Drive. Hoffman was the judge hearing the trial of the "Conspiracy Seven." By this time, the Chicago police were hesitant to use any force because of the criticism of their actions during the Democratic Convention. I was there in an unmarked squad car along with a member of the press and a police officer. When the Weathermen started walking and then running south on Dearborn, they were systematically breaking windows of the cars and buildings on Dearborn with rocks and lead pipes. They were focused on destroying property, and when two squad cars of policemen tried to stop them, they had a confrontation with the police. The Weathermen weren't going to allow themselves to be peaceably arrested since they wanted to fight the police. There was extensive property damage that day.

Then, on Friday, October 10, at a church in Evanston, the undercover police, who were with the Weathermen since Wednesday, made arrests. Early on Saturday morning, October 11, I got a call and had to go to Police Headquarters at 11th and State to make a determination, with the help of an assistant state's attorney, as to what charges to place on each person arrested. We charged some with felony mob action and some with disorderly conduct. Then, I hurried over to the 5th floor of City Hall to a meeting that Mayor Daley was having with his department heads. I told the Mayor about the arrests. We also discussed the parade permit for 10:30 am which had been issued to the Weathermen. The parade was to start at the Haymarket Statue at Randolph Street and the Kennedy Expressway, and some of the department heads wanted to stop the march. But I said, "Mr. Mayor, if you stop them, they'll go to Federal Court and the court will permit the march like the court did in Selma, Alabama." The mayor agreed to let them march. The Weathermen started down Randolph, went east and then south on LaSalle, and they were supposed to go east on Jackson into Grant Park. That was the route granted in their parade permit, but at Madison and LaSalle, they broke from the route and went east, breaking plate glass windows in stores and buildings on Madison.

I think that was their plan all along. The Chicago police were wearing soft hats and white gloves, not riot helmets. The rioters were breaking up everything they could in downtown Chicago. Somehow, I got to Madison and Dearborn near the First National Bank. The telephone in my car was not working, so I communicated with the mayor's office through a walkie-talkie. I was out on the street with Police Commander Jim Reardon and was being interviewed by a reporter from WBBM radio.

All of a sudden, I looked up and saw a protester, who turned out to be Brian Flanigan, running down the middle of the street with a policeman chasing him yelling, "Stop that man!" I asked the reporter to excuse me, put down the walkie-talkie, and tried to stop Flanigan by tackling him. He was wearing big construction boots, and I recollect that when I tackled him, he kicked me in the head, breaking my neck. He actually kicked me a couple of times trying to extricate himself. The police knew that I was seriously injured, and they wanted to get me to a hospital as quickly as pos-sible. Instead of waiting for an ambulance, they put me on the floor of a squadrol without putting me on a gurney or stabilizing my neck, and that decision was probably a contributing cause of my permanent partial paralysis. Flanigan was arrested and was charged with attempted murder. The trial took place in June, and Flanigan came to court all dressed up in a coat and tie. When I was going to testify, the judge wouldn't let me walk into the courtroom because he felt that seeing me walking with canes as a result of my partial paralysis would prejudice the jury. The prosecution was unable to prove the attempted murder charge, which I personally felt was an overcharge, and the jury found Flannigan not guilty. As he left the courtroom he said, "All power to the people. My regret is that I have only one neck to break for my country."

In November 1969, the Democratic Party slated me as the candidate for Sheriff of Cook County. I won the election and served as Sheriff for 16 years.

A mob of the radical Weatherman faction SDS. As published
in the *Chicago Daily News*. Photographer: Perry Riddle.
Copyright, 1969 by *Chicago Sun-Times*, Inc.
Reprinted with permission.

Detectives remove a demonstrator from the south end
of the Loop. As published in the *Chicago Sun-Times*. Copyright, 1969
by Chicago Sun-Times, Inc. Reprinted with permission.

Aftermath of melee...Jane Furness. As published in the
Chicago Sun-Times. Photographer: Bob Kotalik. Copyright, 1969
by *Chicago Sun-Times*, Inc. Reprinted with permission.

Entertainn
the 1960s:
Television
the Sixties
Regional 1

ent in
Radio and
Music of
Chicago
heater

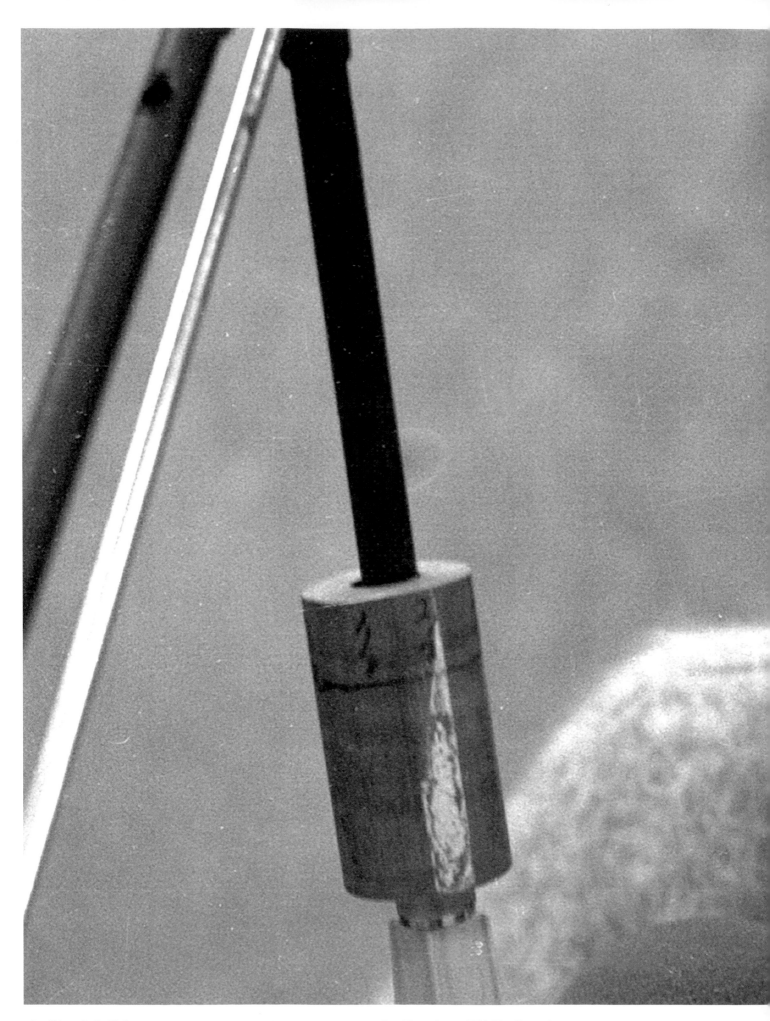

Sun-Times photo of Dick Biondi, c. 1967

Dick Biondi

I was born in 1937 and grew up in Endicott in upstate New York. The first time I was on the radio, I was eight years old and read a commercial on a station in Auburn, New York. I loved it so much that when I got back to Endicott, I started hanging around the local radio stations and worked at two different radio stations in my hometown while I was in high school. After high school, my first job was in Corning, New York for three months and then I got fired, which was the first of many times being fired in my radio career.

previous page
Candid Strip of Dick Biondi.
As published in the *Chicago Sun-Times*.
Photographer: Mickey Rito.
Copyright, 1967 by *Chicago Sun-Times,* Inc.
Reprinted with permission.

In Corning, I was a disc jockey, before going to Alexandria, Louisiana for four years doing play-by-play sports as well as being a disc jockey. In the late '40s and early '50s, the popular music included Perry Como, Patti Page, Frank Sinatra, and the Ames Brothers. I came back north to York, Pennsylvania to be a disc jockey, and after York, I went to Youngstown, Ohio where I really started going crazy as a disc jockey, playing rock and roll in late '54 when it had first been made popular by singers like Bill Haley and the Comets and Little Richard.

My work record on radio has been like a crazy quilt. In 1958, I went from Youngstown to Buffalo, New York for two years, and then to Chicago and WLS-AM in 1960. I got the nickname of "The Wild Itralian" from Buffalo radio deejay Russ Syracuse. As far as I am concerned, WLS was the highlight of my career, and when I began there in 1960, it was as if they had given me a free pass to Disneyland. My first impression about the city was the size of Chicago. I had just driven there from Buffalo, and when I entered the city from the South Side, I drove down State Street and was overwhelmed. After I got settled into my hotel, they brought me to the old WLS radio station on West Washington Boulevard in Skid Row. At that time, it was still the Prairie Farmer station with the National Barn Dance. In fact, because of the neighborhood, they gave us tear gas guns because the winos were always begging for money. On May 2, 1960, WLS-AM changed to a rock and roll station, and we moved the studios to the southwest corner of Michigan and Wacker above the London House.

In the early '60s, Chicago was a very important radio market because it was the second largest city in the country. It was wild when we made the change because we began receiving mail from across the country from people who wondered why we had changed our format. But, once we got started, the reaction was just magnificent and the kids loved us. WLS had the most loyal audience any disc jockey or any entertainer could ever want, and if I burped, somebody knew about it someplace. When we left the studios, teenagers would wait downstairs as late as midnight just to say hello.

We did a lot of record hops in those years, and I remember one time appearing at a Hobart, Indiana high school in 1961 or 1962 because I had been hired to be the deejay at a post prom dance. They said they wanted me to appear after the prom, play records, and do a record hop from midnight until 6:00 am in order to keep the kids off the streets. I arrived there with my secretary and driver, walked into the restaurant where we were scheduled to do the record hop, and said to the owner, "Hi. I'm Dick Biondi, and I'm here to do the post prom dance. Where can I get dressed?"

He said, "You can't get dressed in here." I said, "Excuse me?" He said, "We still have customers (it was around 11:00 pm). You can't do anything until we're closed." I said, "What am I going to do? I've got to get ready." His response was, "Go to the Clark Station across the street." I went to the men's room at the Clark Station, and while my secretary and driver waited outside, I began changing into my tuxedo. I put on my pants, my patent leather shoes, my tux shirt, and my cummerbund. I was starting to put on my bowtie when the door opened and a drunk staggered in and threw up all over my shoes and pants. I had to get my secretary and driver to help me wash off the stuff, and then I went on stage. Thank heaven nobody at the record hop knew what had happened.

WLS was a 24-hour station, and when I started there, it was just a wild and crazy place. It took us about six months until we realized what we were doing. I was just being crazy on my show, and if I tried to do it today, I would be fired in two weeks. We had one of the greatest program directors in the whole world at that time—Sam Holman. His philosophy was, "I hired all of you because you are good, and I like what you do. Get in the studio, entertain the people, and don't lose our license!" My first slot at WLS, right off the bat, was 9:00 pm to midnight. We would get mail from people all around the country, and even in Canada, and during the Cuban Missile Crisis in 1962, we were one of the only radio stations in the United States that Castro wasn't blocking. WLS was 50,000 watts, clear channel, and so powerful that when I got fired in 1963 and went to California, I drove up to Mt. Wilson, turned on the radio, and heard WLS just like I was in Chicago.

I was the first guy to "cluster" my commercials because I got so tired of having a commercial being played after each song. One night, I played 19 commercials in a row at the top of the hour, and just played music for the rest of the hour. That didn't make me too popular with the WLS sales people, which ultimately led to my demise there. We made appearances around the Midwest during about six or seven months a year. One time, the shoe company, U.S. Keds, put me in a helicopter and we went to several Chicago area shopping malls including Harlem-Irving, Randhurst, Scottsdale, and Hillside and began dropping tennis balls to the kids below. If anybody found a little slip inside the ball, they would get a free pair of U.S. Keds.

During my first year at WLS, the record industry realized that we were really popular across the entire country. At one point, the Chicago-based show was number seven in the listing of Top Ten radio stations in Pittsburgh at night from 9:00 pm to midnight.

I was so popular that to this day I receive emails from people who used to listen to me as teenagers and who are now in their 50s and 60s. We did lots of record hops with all the big recording stars in places like Crown Point and West Lafayette, Indiana for Catholic churches, and the McHenry Skating Rink, and, for three years, it was just like a wild rocket ride into outer space. We really didn't realize the influence we had on the kids. We answered the question about our impact on the kids when, one night, a Methodist Church in Anderson, Indiana burned down. Soon after that happened, I asked every kid who was listening to my show to send a dime to the church. They were able to build a whole wing, which they called the WLS Teenager Wing.

We were so popular that while we were on the air at night, you didn't even need to have a radio. In fact, you could walk down the street and just hear us from radios that were on in each neighborhood. After my first six months at WLS, I found out that my first name wasn't "Dick." Every parent in the Chicago area was yelling at their kid, "Turn that damn Dick Biondi off, and go to bed!" I was the number one disc jockey on WLS during those years, and in '61 and '62, I say this humbly and modestly, I was the number one pop music disc jockey in the United States with 57% of the national listening audience.

We met many rock and roll stars over those years, and among the many singers I met or worked with were Glen Campbell, whom I saw sitting with Nancy Sinatra at the London House having dinner. I also remember meeting Jackie DeShannon who had the hit song, "What the World Needs Now Is Love." When I had been in Chicago for three or four weeks and we hadn't made the shift to a rock and roll format, I was staying at the North Park Hotel on North Clark Street. Jackie and I got to know each other and got into trouble with her manager because we were having a pillow fight that caused us to go out into the hall, and we ended up keeping everyone awake. During my years in Chicago, I was living in Evanston, and Gene Taylor, who was on the air from 6:30 pm until 9:00 pm, when I went on the air, had found a place in Evanston and I moved in next door to him.

I left WLS because I was fired, but I was used to it. I just didn't want to put up with the crap, and I was pushed to the point of losing my cool when I had a conflict with some sales guy about the number of commercials being played on my shows. If I wasn't stopped by the engineers that night, I would have probably tried to beat his butt into the floor or been beaten myself. But when I got home and settled down, I realized that it just wasn't worth it so I decided that the heck with it and I never went back. I got fired on May 2, 1963, three years to the day that I was hired.

Following that, I went out to California for about five or six months, then came back in 1964 and worked at the Mutual Broadcasting System as the first rock and roll deejay show on a radio network for a year. Then, back to California until 1967, and back to Chicago. I did meet the Beatles during those years when I was California, and we introduced them at the Hollywood Bowl and at Dodger Stadium. As for Chicago, I wasn't here at the time when they performed in the city.

From 1967 until 1973, I was at WCFL-AM in Chicago, and it was wild at that station with people like Jerry G. Bishop, Jim Stagg, Joel Sebastian, Dick Williamson, Ron Britain, and Barney Pip. In those days, we were always fighting WLS for the top rating, so there was never a true number one station. We had a great program director named Ken Draper when I first got to WCFL. He believed in having strong personalities at the station and

referred to his disc jockeys as "my talent." I was there until 1973. When I first came back to Chicago, my time slot was the all-night show. Then, after I was there for a while, they put me on in the afternoons as the drive-man. WLS was so huge, but so was WCFL. I would say that WLS topped it because of the fact that it was so unusual and was the first station to play full-time rock and roll. The kids went nuts, but it was also great at WCFL.

After leaving WCFL, I went to Cincinnati for a year, and throughout my career, I haven't been able to hold a job for too long. After Cincinnati, I went to North Myrtle Beach, South Carolina where I was for 10 years until 1983. Next, I came back to Chicago again to B-96 where I worked for a year, got fired, and came to WJMK-FM in Chicago where I still am a deejay. Now, I am on the Internet and I can make the whole world nauseous.

The decibel rate rising from Comiskey Park during Beatles' concert. As published in the *Chicago Sun-Times*. Photographer: Gene Pesek. Copyright, 1965 by *Chicago Sun-Times,* Inc. Reprinted with permission.

Crowd of Beatle fans standing in line between the International Amphitheater and the Stockyard Inn, July 26, 1964. (Courtesy of Chicago Historical Society, DN- Alpha, October 18, 1964)

Beatle Car, 1964. Photographer: *Chicago Daily News.* (Courtesy of Chicago Historical Society, DN- Alpha, March 9, 1964)

Twisting at a teen club. As published in the *Chicago Sun-Times*. Photographer: Charles Gekler. Copyright, 1964 by *Chicago Sun-Times,* Inc. Reprinted with permission.

Clark Weber

I was born in November 1930 and grew up in Wauwatosa, Wisconsin. From the time I was 16 years old, I wanted to have a career in radio. I was in high school and a guest teen disc jockey at a radio station, and after being on the air for just a few minutes, I knew that broadcasting was what I wanted to do. I was at the University of Wisconsin-Milwaukee before I went in the Naval Reserve when the Korean War broke out. When I finished my military service, I decided not to go back to college because I felt I could get into broadcasting without a degree. I decided that I was going to "roll the dice," and it worked out. I got jobs at several Wisconsin radio stations in Waukesha, West Bend, and then Milwaukee where I worked at my first rock and roll station, WRIT-AM.

At the Milwaukee station, I worked with Sam Holman, who later came to Chicago and became the program director when the Prairie Farmer station was purchased by ABC and became WLS-AM. About a year later, he called me and said, "I want you as my all-night disc jockey." So, on September 13, 1961, I came to Chicago, got off the train, and walked down Wacker Drive toward 360 N. Michigan. My legs were like rubber, and I thought to myself, "Holy mackerel, I've hit the big time!"

I spent my first 18 months at WLS on the all-night show. I commuted to Chicago every day from Milwaukee because we had a brand new home in Brookfield, Wisconsin, outside Milwaukee, and we couldn't sell it. But, in 1962, we finally sold the house and moved to Evanston. Then, for a short time, I did the afternoon show before being assigned the morning show. For a little extra money, I also accepted the job of program director at WLS. After I would get off the air at 10:00 am, I would put on my program director hat, and I was responsible for deciding all of the music that the deejays played on the station. That required two or three days a week, meeting all of the record promoters, and then deciding what songs to place on our "Silver Dollar Survey." There wasn't a conflict between me being program director and doing my own show, and, as a matter of fact, it gave me an even better insight because I could actually hear the music. I was also getting feedback from the kids, so I knew what they were reacting to and what they wanted to hear. I was program director for almost three years, from 1964 until 1967, and then I told WLS, "I can't do this anymore because it is taking up so much of my time."

WLS was so popular because it typified kids' listening habits. At that time, demographically, kids from teenagers to 25-year-olds made up the largest part of the population in the 1960s. We were the number one radio station in Chicago, and that allowed us to be free-wheeling in those days. The only criterion presented to all of us was, "We hired you because you are the best. Do what you do!" And we all did—Dick Biondi, Art Roberts, and the rest of us. Ron Riley and I created a "feud" that was reminiscent of Jack Benny and Fred Allen in the '30s. Ron was on WLS between 9:00pm and midnight, and he would complain about me as program director. The "feud" worked, and the kids listened to him and then, they listened to me to see what I had to say about him. One of the reasons that WLS was so popular was because we were a 50,000-watt, clear channel station that could be heard across the country. In fact, we used to get fan mail from all over the world.

The station was phenomenally popular and at night, Dick Biondi had humongous Arbitron numbers that have never been equaled. But, Dick was fired from WLS in 1963 because he complained about his commercial load, not because he had told a dirty story on the air. That story remains an urban legend to this day. He had been complaining about his advertisement spot load for several weeks, and when they added one more spot to it, Biondi saw it on the log and he screamed at the sales manager. The two of them got into it, nose to nose, screaming at each other. Gene Taylor went in there and tried to calm him down, but Dick stormed out of the studio and refused to go back on the radio even though he was still on the air. He pulled out a cardboard box, threw all of his stuff into it, and walked off. The next morning, the station's general manager called Dick and Gene in and blamed Taylor for letting Biondi go. Biondi refused to apologize to the sales manager, and said, "I quit!" And he was let go.

During those years, there were a lot of rock stars, and we were doing many record hops around the Midwest. I had a plane that I used in order to get to those dances, so I flew all over the Midwest and did as many as two record hops a night. One night, in the early 1960s, I was doing an appearance in South Bend, Indiana in an armory, and Peter, Paul and Mary and Bobby Darin were on the bill with me. They were flying by charter from Chicago to South Bend, while I was flying my plane and following them. Darin wanted to talk to me from plane to plane and was apparently under the influence of alcohol. He was using profanity in our conversations and by the time we got into South Bend to perform, I thought that he wouldn't be capable of getting on stage. But at the last minute, he pulled it together and went out and did an amazing show.

Every generation of teenagers claims their own music and, while amazing to me, people recognize the "Clark Weber" voice and they almost become reverent towards me because I was a part of their youth. There was one guy who told me, "You were in the back seat of a '57 Chevy with me one night." I said to him, "I don't want to know about that." It is an interesting phenomenon in music that many rock and roll singers have been "one-hit" wonders, but that certainly didn't apply to singers like Diana Ross and Elvis Presley. I worked with Diana and the Supremes, but I never had a chance to work with Elvis because of an argument with Colonel Parker over Presley's appearance at the Amphitheater. They wanted WLS to sponsor it, but they wouldn't give us access to Elvis. So, our station manager, Gene Taylor, told the Colonel that it wasn't acceptable.

I had a lot of fun doing radio and working with all the singers because music was exciting in those years. I remember one time, a record producer brought in a song called "Gloria." In that song, there were very suggestive lyrics, and since it was the '60s, as a program director, I couldn't play the song. So, the producer said to me, "If those lyrics weren't in the song, could you play it at WLS?" I said, "Yeah." So, he gathered a group, and they went to the cafeteria of the Shore Microphone Company in Evanston, spent all night recording the revised song on an old Webcor Recorder, cut it into an acetate disc, and brought it to me the next morning at 10:00 am. The record producer said, "What do you think of this?" I said, "It's going on the air." That was "Gloria," sung by the Shadows of Night.

On another occasion, Herb Alpert, who was a record promoter in the early years of his career, came to see me. We went downstairs to the Brief Encounter restaurant and had breakfast after I got off the air. He said, "I have a record that hasn't been pressed, but I've got it on aluminum acetate. I want you to listen to it." I did, and I said, "Eh!" He said, "I'm looking for some backing. My partner and I need $3,000. We've got a recording machine and a little audio board in a garage in LA. I'm looking for a little backing—only $3,000." I said, "Boy, that's interesting." My wife, Joan, was coming downtown later that day, so I said to Herb, "Let me think about this." I told Joan about it, and she asked, "What do you think about the record?" I said, "Well, it's all right." She said, "You may have problems with ABC if you own a record." I took my contract out, and it prohibited me from making that investment because I was WLS program director and it was a record that I might have to promote. As it turned out, I couldn't own anything in the record business. I said "no" to Herb. How ironic that a $3,000 investment in the "Lonely Bull" would have given me a third of the ownership of A&M records.

There were two things that changed in popular music in the 1960s. First, the 11 to 13- year-old preteens of the late '50s who listened to rock and roll were predominantly girls who latched onto Elvis, the Platters, and other popular singers. But, they were becoming a little older, some of them were already in college, and the population demographics were beginning to change. The Beatles were so different from Presley and the rest of them, and that led to a revolution in popular music. By then, the Twist and Chubby Checker had faded, and music trends seemed to change every two or three years.

When the Beatles hit it big in the mid-'60s, they reminded me of four unpolished, middle-class kids who had a great manager who groomed them for the big time. I think that, as a musician, Ringo Starr was only mediocre, while George Harrison was a quiet, soft-spoken kid who let the fame pass him. On the other hand, John Lennon was crude, already into drugs, and I didn't care for him, while I liked Paul McCartney. He had the most positive image of all four Beatles.

In 1964, some of the popular songs were "You Can't Buy Me Love" by the Beatles as well as hits by The Four Seasons, Dusty Springfield, Bobby Goldsboro, Mary Wells, and the beginning of the Motown hits. Motown began to hit its stride in '64 and '65 and have a big impact on the record charts. Prior to that time, rhythm and blues music wasn't crossing over into white radio stations. A record promoter named Kent Beauchamp was representing that crossover at the time, and he also represented a guy named Neil Diamond who had recorded "Solitary Man." No one would play his record, but Kent got me to listen to it and I decided to play it on WLS. The rest is history.

The Beatles were still number one each time they released a new song, and by the mid-to late-1960s, the successful singers included the Zombies, Dionne Warwick, Sammy Davis, Jr., Smokey Robinson, Bobby Hatfield of the Temptations, and Sly and the Family Stone. By the late '60s, there was beginning to be a harder edge to the music, and it was definitely reflecting the times. Another generation had grown up by then, so that 48% of the population in 1965 was under the age of 25.

Larry Lujack, who had been at WCFL doing the all-night show, came to WLS in 1966, and was hired by Gene Taylor. Gene called me in and said, "The kid's got a horrible track record. He's been fired from practically every radio station he's ever been at." Ralph Bodine, the WLS general manager, said, "Be careful. If this kid gets out of line I will fire him fast!" Lujack came over, and soon after, alienated Sears Roebuck, one of our biggest advertisers. They were upset about the way he was doing the ads, so we went in to Gene Taylor and said, "We've got a problem here. This guy is not what the sponsors want." So, Gene talked to Lujack and toned him down a little bit. Larry was at WLS for about three or four years, and then he went over to WCFL before returning to WLS. During the '60s at WLS, there wasn't any clash among the various personalities. It was a perfect meshing of people, and there were no prima donnas. We all were experienced with a minimum of five years experience on the air, so we knew what we were doing. So, it just meshed very, very well, and I stayed at WLS until late 1969, at which time I went to WCFL for two years.

Diana Ross and the Supremes with Clark Weber, 1964.
(Courtesy of Clark Weber).

Sonny and Cher with Weber children, c. 1965
(Courtesy of Clark Weber).

following page
Beatles in concert at Comiskey Park, August 21, 1965.
(Courtesy of Clark Weber).

WLS
silver dollar survey

CHICAGO'S AUTHENTIC RADIO RECORD SURVEY

THIS WEEK	SEPTEMBER 16, 1961	WEEKS PLAYED
1.	MOUNTAIN HIGH .... Dick & Dee Dee — Liberty	7
2.	THIS TIME .... Troy Shondell — Goldcrest	6
3.	TAKE GOOD CARE OF MY BABY .... Bobby Vee — Liberty	6
4.	CHEWING GUM .... Lonnie Donegan — Dot	5
5.	MEXICO .... Bob Moore — Monument	6
6.	HEART AND SOUL .... Jan & Dean — Challenge	6
7.	LET ME BELONG TO YOU .... Brian Hyland — ABC Para	10
8.	PRETTY LITTLE ANGEL EYES .... Curtis Lee — Dunes	8
9.	STARBRIGHT .... Linda Scott — Cam Am	8
10.	MORE MONEY MEDLEY .... Four Preps — Capitol	4
11.	WITHOUT YOU .... Johnny Tillotson — Cadence	4
12.	MICHAEL .... Highwaymen — UA	12
13.	LOVERS ISLAND .... Bluejays — Milestone	9
14.	LET THE FOUR WINDS BLOW .... Fats Domino — Imperial	4
15.	ASTRONAUT #1 .... Jose Jimenez — Kapp	5
16.	THE WAY YOU LOOK TONIGHT .... Lettermen — Capitol	5
17.	WHO PUT THE BOMP .... Barry Mann — ABC Para	8
18.	AMOR .... Ben E King — Atco	6
19.	FOOTSTOMPING #1 .... Flares — Felstad	5
20.	A LITTLE BIT OF SOAP .... Jarmels — Laurie	6
21.	JOHNNY WILLOW .... Fred Darian — JAF	4
22.	MAGIC MOON .... Rays — XYZ	5
23.	KISSING ON THE PHONE .... Paul Anka — ABC Para	5
24.	MAGIC IS THE NIGHT .... Kathy Young — Indigo	5
25.	BAND OF GOLD .... Roomates — Valmor	4
26.	CANDY MAN/CRYING .... Roy Orbison — Monument	4
27.	LITTLE SISTER .... Elvis Presley — RCA	3
28.	BACK BEAT #1 .... Rondels — Amy	3
29.	I'M A TELLING YOU .... Jerry Butler — VeeJay	5
30.	AS IF I DIDN'T KNOW .... Adam Wade — CoEd	4
31.	BEAUTIFUL BABY .... Bobby Darin — Atco	2
32.	BLESS YOU .... Tony Orlando — Epic	3
33.	HIT THE ROAD JACK .... Ray Charles — ABC Para	2
34.	LOOK IN MY EYES .... Chantels — Carlton	2
35.	YOU'RE ON TOP .... Untouchables — Liberty	4
36.	I'M THANKFUL .... Steve Alaimo — Checker	4
37.	NAG .... Halos — 7 Arts	3
38.	MY TRUE STORY .... Jive Five — Beltone	3
39.	I REALLY LOVE YOU SO .... Sterios — Cub	3
40.	SAILOR MAN .... Bobby Bare — Fraternity	3

FEATURE ALBUM OF THE WEEK
COME SWING WITH ME — FRANK SINATRA — CAPITOL

Tune in Monday night Sept. 11 for
"EAST OF MIDNIGHT"
and meet personable
CLARK WEBER
Midnight to 5:00 A.M.—Monday thru Saturday

WLS · DIAL 890 · 24 HOURS-A-DAY
ABC RADIO IN CHICAGO

This survey is compiled each week by WLS Radio/Chicago from reports of all record sales gathered from leading record outlets in the Chicagoland area. Hear Gene Taylor play all the SILVER DOLLAR SURVEY hits daily from 3:00 to 6:30 P.M.

WLS
The bright sound of Chicago Radio
SILVER DOLLAR SURVEY

Chicago's Official Radio Record Survey

THIS WEEK	JANUARY 25, 1963	WEEKS PLAYED
1.	HEY PAULA .... Paul & Paula — Phillips	7
2.	WALK RIGHT IN .... Rooftop Singers — Vanguard	6
3.	GO AWAY LITTLE GIRL .... Steve Lawrence — Columbia	11
4.	THE NIGHT HAS A THOUSAND EYES .... Bobby Vee — Liberty	9
5.	CAST YOUR FATE TO THE WIND .... Vince Guaraldi Trio — Fantasy	9
6.	I SAW LINDA YESTERDAY .... Dickey Lee — Smash	9
7.	FROM A JACK TO A KING .... Ned Miller — Faber	9
8.	HE'S SURE THE BOY I LOVE .... The Crystals — Philles	5
9.	RUBY BABY .... Dion — Columbia	4
10.	MY DAD .... Paul Peterson — Colpix	4
11.	WALK LIKE A MAN .... Four Seasons — Vee Jay	3
12.	UP ON THE ROOF .... Drifters — Atlantic	10
13.	LOOP DE LOOP .... Johnny Thunder — Diamond	8
14.	WHAT TO DO WITH LAURIE .... Mike Clifford — UA	4
15.	THE 2,000 POUND BEE (Part 2) .... Ventures — Dolton	8
16.	LITTLE TOWN FLIRT .... Del Shannon — Big Top	5
17.	IT'S UP TO YOU .... Rick Nelson — Imperial	6
18.	PUDDIN N' TAIN .... Alley Cats — Philles	7
19.	BONNIE DO .... Johnny Cooper — Ermine	5
20.	CINNAMON CINDER .... Pastel Six — Zen	7
21.	PROUD .... Johnny Crawford — Del Fi	5
22.	THE BIRD .... The Dutones — Columbia	5
23.	I WANNA BE AROUND .... Tony Bennett — Columbia	5
24.	YOU'RE THE REASON I'M LIVING .... Bobby Darin — Capitol	3
25.	COME BACK LITTLE GIRL .... Ronnie Rice — IRC	4
26.	THE BALLAD OF JED CLAMPETT ... L. Flatt & E. Scruggs — Columbia	7
27.	TROUBLE IN MIND .... Aretha Franklin — Columbia	5
28.	GREENBACK DOLLAR .... Kingston Trio — Capitol	3
29.	WHAT WILL MARY SAY .... Johnny Mathis — Columbia	3
30.	THE POPEYE WADDLE .... Don Covay — Cameo	4
31.	BACHELOR MAN .... Johnny Cymbal — Kedlen	4
32.	STRANGE I KNOW .... Marvelettes — Tamla	8
33.	YOU'VE REALLY GOT A HOLD ON ME .... Miracles — Tamla	5
34.	RHYTHM OF THE RAIN .... Cascades — Valiant	3
35.	FLY ME TO THE MOON .... Joe Harnell — Kapp	2
36.	SEAGRAMS .... The Viceroys — Bethlehem	4
37.	LET ME GO THE RIGHT WAY .... Supremes — Motown	3
38.	JAVA .... Floyd Cramer — RCA	4
39.	WILD WEEKEND .... The Rebels — Swan	3
40.	WHO STOLE THE KEESHKA .... Matys Bros. — Select	2

FEATURED ALBUMS
SINATRA – BASIE – REPRISE
WALK RIGHT IN — THE ROOFTOP SINGERS — VANGUARD
OUR MAN AROUND THE WORLD — PAUL ANKA — RCA

Don't miss the fun with
Dick Biondi
9 to Midnight — Monday thru Sunday

WLS · DIAL 890 · 24 HOURS-A-DAY
ABC RADIO IN CHICAGO

This survey is compiled each week by WLS Radio/Chicago from reports of all record sales gathered from leading record outlets in the Chicagoland area. Hear Clark Weber play all the SILVER DOLLAR SURVEY hits daily from 3:00 to 6:30 P.M.

WLS
The bright sound of Chicago Radio
SILVER DOLLAR SURVEY

Chicago's Official Radio Record Survey

THIS WEEK	AUGUST 16, 1963	WEEKS PLAYED
* 1.	MY BOYFRIEND'S BACK .... Angels — Smash	5
* 2.	HELLO MUDDAH HELLO FADDAH .... Allen Sherman — WB	4
* 3.	WIPE OUT .... Surfaris — Dot	8
* 4.	CANDY GIRL .... Four Seasons — Vee Jay	7
* 5.	DETROIT CITY .... Bobby Bare — RCA	4
* 6.	IT'S JUDY'S TURN TO CRY .... Lesley Gore — Mercury	4
* 7.	I'M AFRAID TO GO HOME .... Brian Hyland — ABC Para	6
* 8.	SURF CITY .... Jan & Dean — Liberty	8
* 9.	BLOWIN' IN THE WIND .... Peter, Paul & Mary — WB	5
*10.	DENISE .... Randy & Rainbows — Rust	7
*11.	GREEN GREEN .... New Christy Minstrels — Columbia	4
*12.	FINGERTIPS (Part 2) .... Little Stevie Wonder — Tamla	8
*13.	TRUE LOVE NEVER RUNS SMOOTH .... Gene Pitney — Musicor	4
*14.	THE KIND OF BOY YOU CAN'T FORGET .... Raindrops — Jubilee	5
*15.	ABILENE .... George Hamilton IV—RCA	5
*16.	MORE .... Kai Winding — Verve	7
*17.	DANKE SCHOEN .... Wayne Newton — Capitol	4
*18.	WHAT MAKES LITTLE GIRLS CRY .... Victorians — Liberty	5
*19.	AT THE SHORE .... Johnny Caswell — Smash	7
*20.	BUST OUT .... The Busters — Arlen	4
*21.	YOU CAN NEVER STOP ME LOVING YOU .... Johnny Tillotson — Cadence	3
*22.	BREAKWATER .... Lawrence Welk — Dot	4
*23.	ANOTHER FOOL LIKE ME .... Ned Miller — Fabor	4
*24.	MONKEY TIME .... Major Lance — Okeh	5
*25.	DESERT PETE .... Kingston Trio — Capitol	4
*26.	IF I HAD A HAMMER .... Trini Lopez — Reprise	3
*27.	MOCKINGBIRD .... Inezz Foxx — Symbol	4
*28.	THIS IS ALL I ASK .... Tony Bennett — Columbia	4
*29.	PAINTED TAINTED ROSE .... Al Martino — Capitol	4
*30.	MARTIAN HOP .... The Ran-dells — Chairman	3
*31.	HEY GIRL .... Freddie Scott — Colpix	4
*32.	S P C L G .... Society Girls — Vee Jay	5
*33.	THEN HE KISSED ME .... Crystals — Philles	4
*34.	FRANKIE & JOHNNY .... Sam Cooke — RCA	2
35.	HEAT WAVE .... Martha & Vandellas — Gordy	2
*36.	MICKEY'S MONKEY .... Miracles — Tamla	1
37.	MAN'S TEMPTATION .... Gene Chandler — Vee Jay	2
*38.	CHINA NIGHTS .... Kyu Sakamoto — Capitol	1
*39.	MAKE THE WORLD GO AWAY .... Timi Yuro — Liberty	4
*40.	REV-UP .... Manuel & Renegades — Piper	3

FEATURED ALBUMS
MY SON THE NUT — ALLEN SHERMAN — WB
SUNNYSIDE — KINGSTON TRIO — CAPITOL

Swing Along with
Clark Weber
3:00 to 6:30 P.M.—Monday thru Friday
3 to 6 P.M. Saturday and Sunday

WLS · DIAL 890 · 24 HOURS-A-DAY
ABC RADIO IN CHICAGO

This survey is compiled each week by WLS Radio/Chicago from reports of all record sales gathered from leading record outlets in the Chicagoland area. Hear Bob Hale play all the SILVER DOLLAR SURVEY hits daily from 3:00 to 6:30 P.M. *Denotes record first heard in Chicago on WLS.

WLS
The bright sound of Chicago Radio

SILVER BEATLE SURVEY

Chicago's Official Radio Record Survey

THIS WEEK	FEBRUARY 21, 1964		WEEKS PLAYED

* 1. I Want To Hold Your Hand .... The Beatles — Capitol 7
* 2. She Loves Me .... The Beatles — Swan 5
* 3. Dawn Go Away .... Four Seasons — Philips 7
* 4. Penetration .... The Pyramids — Best 7
* 5. Out Of Limits .... The Marketts — WB 7
* 6. See The Funny Little Clown ...... Bobby Goldsboro — UA 9
* 7. Navy Blue .... Diane Renay — 20th Century 5
* 8. You Don't Own Me .... Lesley Gore — Mercury 10
* 9. A Letter From Sherry .... Dale Ward — Dot 8
*10. Hey Little Cobra .... The Ripchords — Columbia 10
11. For You .... Rick Nelson — Decca 4
*12. Hi Heel Sneakers .... Tommy Tucker — Checker 6
*13. A Fool Never Learns .... Andy Williams — Columbia 9
*14. Java .... Al Hirt — RCA 13
15. Fun Fun Fun .... The Beach Boys — Capitol 4
16. California Sun .... The Rivieras — Riviera 7
*17. Stop And Think It Over ... Dale & Grace — Montel 7
18. Please Please Me .... The Beatles — Vee Jay 2
*19. The Shelter Of Your Arms .. Sammy Davis Jr. — Reprise 7
*20. Abigail Beecher .... Freddie Cannon — WB 7
*21. I Love You More and More .... Al Martino — Capitol 7
*22. Um Um Um .... Major Lance — Okeh 7
*23. Rip Van Winkle .... The Devotions — Roulette 5
*24. Southtown U.S.A. .... The Dixiebelles — Sound Stage 7 7
25. True Love Goes On And On ...... Burl Ives — Decca 4
*26. Wow Wow Wee .... The Angels — Smash 7
*27. Glad All Over .... Dave Clark — Epic 6
*28. Bird Dance Beat .... The Trashmen — Garrett 4
*29. Bye Bye Barbara .... Johnny Mathis — Mercury 4
*30. I Saw Her Standing There ... The Beatles — Capitol 2
*31. It's All In The Game .... Cliff Richards — Epic 4
*32. Pink Dominoes .... The Crescents — Era 4
*33. Good News .... Sam Cooke — RCA 4
*34. Puppy Love .... Barbara Lewis — Atlantic 5
*35. Long Gone Lonesome Blues .. Hank Williams Jr. — MGM 4
*36. Think Nothing About It .. Gene Chandler — Constellation 4
*37. Vaya Con Dios .... The Drifters — Atlantic 4
*38. Little Boxes .... Pete Seeger — Columbia 3
*39. Shimmy Shimmy .... The Orlans — Cameo 3
*40. He Says The Same Things ..... Skeeter Davis — RCA 4

FEATURED ALBUMS
THE GREAT HITS OF FRANK SINATRA — FRANK SINATRA — CAPITOL
THE SERENDIPITY SINGERS — PHILIPS

LISTEN TO
THE NEW
WLS BEATLES

WLS · DIAL 890 · 24 HOURS-A-DAY
ABC RADIO IN CHICAGO

WLS
The bright sound of Chicago Radio

SILVER DOLLAR SURVEY

Chicago's Official Radio Record Survey

THIS WEEK	APRIL 17, 1964		WEEKS PLAYED

* 1. Crooked Little Man .... Serendipity Singers — Philips 8
* 2. Suspicion .... Terry Stafford — Crusader 9
* 3. Can't Buy Me Love/You Can't Do That ...... The Beatles — Capitol 7
* 4. White On White .... Danny Williams — UA 7
* 5. Glad All Over .... Dave Clark — Epic 14
* 6. Dead Man's Curve/New Girl In School ..... Jan & Dean — Liberty 4
* 7. Hello Dolly .... Louis Armstrong — Kapp 6
* 8. Thank You Girl/Do You Want To Know ... The Beatles — Vee Jay 6
* 9. My Heart Belongs To Only You .... Bobby Vinton — Epic 7
*10. Bits and Pieces .... Dave Clark — Epic 5
*11. Fun Fun Fun .... The Beach Boys — Capitol 12
*12. Twist And Shout .... The Beatles — Tollie 9
*13. Forever .... Peter Drake — Smash 9
*14. All My Lovin' .... Jimmy Griffin — Reprise 7
*15. That's The Way Boys Are .... Lesley Gore — Mercury 6
*16. Stay .... Four Seasons — Vee Jay 7
*17. Little Donna/Let's Have A Party ... The Rivieras — Riviera 4
*18. Understand Your Man ...... Johnny Cash — Columbia 8
*19. Ain't Gonna Tell Anybody .... Jimmy Gilmer — Dot 7
*20. She's A Bad Motorcycle ...... The Crestones — Markie 5
*21. Kiss Me Sailor ...... Diane Renay — 20th Century 5
*22. Romeo And Juliet .... The Reflections — GW 5
*23. Tall Cool One .... The Wailers — Golden Crest 5
*24. My Guy .... Mary Wells — Motown 5
*25. Ronnie .... The Four Seasons — Philips 4
*26. Yesterday's Gone ... Chad Stuart & Jeremy Clyde — UA 5
*27. Breakin' Up .... The Ronettes — Philles 5
*28. Beatle Time .... The Livers — Constellation 7
*29. Whenever He Holds You ..... Bobby Goldsboro — UA 4
*30. Make Me Forget .... Bobby Rydell — Cameo 4
*31. Spring Cleaning ...... Angello's Angels — Ermine 4
*32. Where Does Love Go ..... Freddie Scott — Colpix 3
*33. Not Fade Away .... The Rolling Stones — London 4
*34. Congratulations .... Rick Nelson — Imperial 4
*35. Invisible Tears .... Ned Miller — Fabor 6
*36. Hey Mr. Sax Man .... Boots Randolph — Monument 3
*37. Stay Awhile .... Dusty Springfield — Philips 3
*38. Red Ryder .... Murry Kellum — M.O.C. 3
*39. The Matador .... Major Lance — Okeh 4
*40. My Girl Sloopy .... The Vibrations — Atlantic 3

FEATURED ALBUMS
ALLAN IN WONDERLAND — ALLAN SHERMAN — WB
LET'S HAVE A PARTY — RIVIERAS — U.S.A.

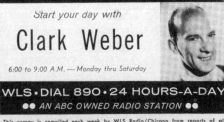

Start your day with
Clark Weber

6:00 to 9:00 A.M. — Monday thru Saturday

WLS · DIAL 890 · 24 HOURS-A-DAY
●● AN ABC OWNED RADIO STATION ●●

WLS RADIO 89 abc
HIT PARADE

THIS WEEK	MARCH 17, 1969		LAST WEEK

* 1. Dizzy .... Tommy Roe — ABC Paramount 1
* 2. Time Of The Season .... Zombies — Date 2
* 3. Traces .... Classics IV — Imperial 10
* 4. No, Not Much .... The Vogues — Reprise 7
* 5. Indian Giver .... 1910 Fruitgum Co. — Buddah 5
* 6. This Girl's In Love With You .. Dionne Warwick — Scepter 4
* 7. Hot Smoke & Sasafrass ... Bubble Puppy — Internat'l Artists 14
* 8. May I .... Bill Deal/Rhondells — Heritage 13
9. Proud Mary ..... Creedence Clearwater — Fantasy 3
*10. Long Green .... Fireballs — Atco 12
11. I've Gotta Be Me ...... Sammy Davis Jr. — Reprise 4
*12. Mendocino .... Sir Douglas Quintet — Smash 20
13. Baby, Baby Don't Cry .. Smokey Robinson/Miracles — Tamla 6
*14. Hair .... The Cowsills — MGM 37
15. My Whole World Ended ..... David Ruffin — Motown 16
*16. Only You .... Bobby Hatfield — Verve 21
*17. Rock Me .... Steppenwolf — Dunhill 23
18. Run Away Child, Running Wild .. Temptations — Gordy 22
19. Ramblin' Gamblin' Man .... Bob Seeger — Capitol 12
*20. Do Your Thing .... Watts 103rd Street Band — W.B. 27
*21. Mr. Sun, Mr. Moon .... Paul Revere/Raiders — Columbia 25
22. Everyday People .... Sly/Family Stone — Epic 9
23. Aquarius/Let The Sunshine In ...... 5th Dimension — Soul City 40
*24. It's Your Thing .... Isley Brothers — T. Neck 32
25. Twenty Five Miles .... Edwin Starr — Gordy 30
*26. Only The Strong Survive .. Jerry Butler — Mercury 28
*27. Brother Loves Traveling Salvation Show .. Neil Diamond — Uni 34
*28. You Gave Me A Mountain .. Frankie Lane — ABC Paramount 35
29. Galveston .... Glen Campbell — Capitol 36
*30. You've Made Me Very Happy .. Blood, Sweat & Tears — Columbia 38
31. In The Still Of The Night ..... Paul Anka — R.C.A. 31
32. The Letter .... The Arbors — Date 33
*33. Don't Give In To Him .. Gary Puckett/Union Gap — Columbia —
*34. I'll Try Something New ... Supremes & Temptations — Motown —
35. Johnny One Time .... Brenda Lee — Decca 39
36. You Showed Me ...... The Turtles — White Whale 17
37. I Can Hear Music .... Beach Boys — Capitol —
38. Gimme Gimme Good Lovin' ..... Crazy Elephant — Bell —
*39. Will You Be Staying After Sunday .. Peppermint Rainbow — Decca —
*40. Sweet Cherry Wine .. Tommy James/Shondells — Roulette —

WEBER   ROBERTS   LUJACK   BUELL   STEVENS   KAY

A tip O' the top to ALL

Harvey Wittenberg

We put WLS-FM on the air on July 16, 1965, and we did it because the FCC had decreed in 1964 that any FM station in markets having a population of 150,000 or more had to broadcast at least 50% different programming than its AM station. Up until that time, a lot of the AM/FM combinations just simulcast their AM signal. WLS-FM was originally WENR-FM, broadcasting the audio of Channel 7 on the FM band which was the same sound that viewers heard on television.

When the FCC said we had to do different programming, WENR-FM ran six hours of classical music from noon to 6:00 pm to maintain their license. They broadcast ABC Radio news without any live announcers and just did station breaks. When we took over WLS-FM, Ralph Beaudin was the general manager of WLS Radio and he asked me to put together a programming format for the FM station. At the time, FM radio only had about 10-15% car radio penetration and about 30-35% FM radio penetration in the Chicago radio market. We wanted to create something a little different, and in those days, there were really only two formats on FM: classical music and background music. I simply developed a new format in order to develop interest in our station.

Since we didn't have a lot of advertising promotion dollars, I wanted us to have a personality that was middle-of-the-road. My thought was that we would include sports coverage because that could get us the greatest attention in a short period of time. We kicked off in July, 1965 by carrying the National Clay Court Tennis Championships from River Forest, Illinois, and used a four-man engineering crew with shotgun mikes. Paul Harvey, the award-winning news commentator, and one of the few people who had stereo FM in his car, paid me the ultimate compliment when he reported that he could hear the tennis balls being hit from one side of his car to the other on his speakers.

We also broadcast Chicago Blackhawks hockey and Big Ten football and basketball. At that time, we had the opportunity to do Blackhawks hockey because they weren't doing any radio coverage. The Blackhawks had some games on Channel 9-TV with Lloyd Pettit doing the play-by-play. In 1965, the Blackhawks contracted with WGN to telecast all of the road games, but the team's management wouldn't allow us do the home games on radio because they felt that it was going to detract from attendance at the Stadium. However, we did carry pre-season games and the NHL All-Star game. As far as I know, it was the first time that the NHL All-Star game was ever carried on FM radio in the United States or Canada. I was doing the announcing of the Blackhawks road games on WLS-FM, but I also worked as the announcer at Chicago Stadium for Blackhawks home games. We also carried Big Ten football, which was kind of unique since we didn't originate any games, but picked up Big Ten networks for our coverage. At that time, Northwestern University had suburban stations like WEAW-AM and the University's station, WNUR-FM. They had no local major outlet because their football team was not doing too well. We also carried other Big Ten games, including Michigan, Ohio State, and Michigan State, and, at times, we broadcast two or three Big Ten games in one day: 11:00 am, 3:00 pm, and on Saturday night. We were providing sports programming to listeners who had FM radios and who wanted sports coverage.

For our middle-of-the-road format, we hired Mike Rapchak after he left WCFL-AM when they switched to a Top 40 format. Our announcers also included Steve Hodges, Ernie Simon, who was a personality at WGN-AM before he left the Chicago market, and Art Hellyer. Since WLS-AM had a Top 40 format, they decided not to continue broadcasting Don McNeil's "Breakfast Club," which was first broadcast from the old Sherman House before moving to the Allerton Hotel. Since it was an ABC-owned program, ABC decided to make WLS-FM the radio outlet for the program.

Until 1960, WLS-AM was owned and operated by the Prairie Farmer Publishing Company, the leading farm publication in the United States. They broadcast the old Barn Dance program that included such stars as Gene Autrey and George Gobel, as well as live music. After World War II, WENR-AM had to be split from the old NBC Red and Blue networks, and the FCC said that NBC had to sell off one of the radio networks, which became ABC Radio. When television became popular, WENR-AM (which became WLS TV, Channel 7 and was originally WBKB TV, Channel 4) didn't have morning or afternoon drive time slots. Instead, they had mid-day and night time, and WLS-AM had the morning and afternoon drive. As a result of television, radio took a big hit after World War II, and FM radio wasn't a factor at that point. WLS-AM and WENR AM both shared the 50,000 watt clear channel frequency, but with the popularity of TV after World War II, WENR-AM didn't have the better radio listening times of morning and afternoon drives. So, ABC merged with WLS-AM, but Prairie Farmer Publishing retained programming jurisdiction. In late 1959, ABC bought out Prairie Farmer Publishing Company, and in May, 1960, they introduced their new Top 40 format.

I started working as a news writer when I got to WLS on December 1, 1958, but I wasn't on the air at that time. It was still a Prairie Farmer station, but when it switched to rock and roll programming in May 1960, I was able to go on the air with stock reports and the high school sport reports. Because WLS became so popular with teenagers, we provided high school sports information, and during the annual state high school basketball tournament, I covered the events and called in reports to be broadcast on Dick Biondi's very popular nighttime rock and roll program.

In 1965, ABC owned and operated 14 stations, 7:00 am to 7:00 pm in major markets plus 5 TV stations in addition to the national TV and radio networks. Only two of the owned FM stations, WLS in Chicago and WABC in New York had separate staffs and totally separate programming. New York was classical music while WLS-FM in Chicago was personality, middle-of-the-road music plus play-by-play sports. The other ABC-owned FM stations aired 50% AM simulcasts and 50% separate FM formats to meet FCC rules while they transitioned into full time programming. Hal Neal

headed up the ABC-owned and operated radio stations, but was better known from his Detroit ABC days when he was the announcer on The Lone Ranger and Green Hornet radio programs. In late 1968, the former assistant program director at Chicago's WCFL radio, Allen Shaw, sold Neal the idea of turning all the ABC-owned FM stations into the growing sound of AOR (album oriented rock), now called classic rock.

At WLS-FM, we became the first Chicago station to play progressive rock music (now classic rock) at the urging of the record companies to provide them with an outlet. That was before Woodstock, featuring artists like The Doors, Cream, Vanilla Fudge, Jefferson Airplane, Jimi Hendrix, and Three Dog Night. That music didn't fit the Top 40 radio format at WLS-AM and WCFL, although their albums were becoming very popular with college students and older teens. Some called it "underground music." In 1969, Neal adopted Shaw's plan, and all the ABC-owned FM stations were to run the format which they named "Love" with Brother John. I resisted the idea because WLS-FM had become the first ABC-owned FM station to turn a profit, and the "Love" format was going to eliminate our local programming.

Since we weren't selling much of our nighttime radio because of the popularity of television, we put on a program called "Spoke" which we ran from 10:00 pm to 1:00 am, seven days a week, sponsored heavily by the record companies. We kept expanding the hours on our progressive rock show, and when I left WLS-FM in the fall of 1969 to go to FM-100, we were the number one FM station for adults, ages 18-49, during the daytime with our middle-of-the-road format (we had trimmed back on sports quite a bit by that time), and we were the number three station at night, behind WLS-AM and WCFL-AM, with teenagers.

As far as FM radio at the end of the '60s, everything was burgeoning, and it was starting to have a measurable impact on the overall music audience. Then, WBBM-FM became Chicago's first pure rock FM station and they called it the "young sound." That was the first full-time departure from a station doing easy listening or middle-of-the-road or classical music. In the 1960s, the FM stations included WFMT and WNIB, which presented classical music, WEFM, the Zenith station (which is now US-99), and WAIT, the leading easy listening music AM station which only broadcast during the day. When I left WLS-FM in 1969 to go to work for FM-100, the station's owners, Howard Grafman and his partner George Collins, had bought WFMF from Maury Rosenfield who thought that FM radio was never going to make it, but it did. Ten years later, Century Broadcasting (FM 100) bought WAIT-AM from Rosenfield. I was with WLS for 12 years (seven years with AM and five years with FM), and at FM 100 for 19 years, from November 1, 1969 to 1989.

Joel Daly interviewing Dr. Martin Luther King, c. 1966. (Courtesy of Joel Daly)

Joel Daly

I started out in broadcasting at the age of 17 at a little radio station in Coeur d'Alene, Idaho near where I had grown up in neighboring Spokane, Washington. Then, while in college at Yale University and on a scholarship, I did radio on campus and in New Haven. Frankly, I grew up with a generation that didn't watch television because we didn't have it in Spokane until later. I saw my first television program at my roommate's house in Bridgeport, Connecticut in the fall of 1952, and it was pretty exciting. So, it meant that radio was my focus while growing up.

Broadcasting was so exciting to me that I did just about everything, including news, music, and sports, in order to continue in it as a career. With a student deferment during the Korean War, I was sure about being drafted into the Armed Services after college graduation. After my enlistment, I was able to get an assignment working as a broadcaster in the Panama Canal Zone where they had both radio and television and broadcast music and news. At that time, we had Armed Forces Radio and Television, which was the only television station in all of Central America. Since it was a showcase, we had some good programs and equipment, but my first reaction to working on television was that the studio lights were very hot. Of course, being in Panama, it was hot anyway, but supposedly, the studio was air conditioned. We wore typical khaki uniforms, but were allowed to wear Bermuda shorts. I just loved it there.

After leaving the military in 1959, I got a job in radio in Cleveland, Ohio. Married by then, we had our first child, and about six months later, I moved over to a television station to become both a cameraman and a reporter. Ironically, we were on strike at the station in Cleveland on November 22, 1963, when President Kennedy was assassinated. I had only been there for about six weeks, but was doing picket duty in the alley behind the station. While talking to somebody, a woman came driving down the alley with her window open, and shouted at us, "I just heard on the radio that the president has been shot!" It was just devastating, and all of us offered to go back to work immediately. The station manager said, "No, you guys went on strike, so just stay out." The network was on that day almost 24 hours, so they didn't have much local programming anyway. Fortunately, we were able to watch all the events surrounding the assassination on television, including Ruby shooting Oswald, and then JFK's funeral. It was a very emotional time, but it was also frustrating since, as a newsman, I was not able to participate in the coverage.

I remember interviewing Dr. Martin Luther King, Jr. several times in the '60s and being very impressed by his eloquence when he spoke to the City Club of Cleveland. He was quoting Shakespeare, and he was very esoteric, as opposed to when he was "on the stump" talking to demonstrators and the civil rights workers. He just knew how to communicate. There was a very active civil rights movement in Cleveland during those years, and we had riots in 1965 in the black neighborhood of Hough. It was a similar situation to what would happen on Chicago's West Side in 1968 when that neighborhood was pretty much burned down.

We had a two-person show in Cleveland, which was one of the first of its kind in the country. My co-anchor and I did a 6:00 pm and an 11:00 pm news show, and we developed the format that eventually became a national benchmark. The show consisted of 12 minutes of news followed by a commercial, five minutes of the weather, another commercial, and then 10 minutes of sports. Afterward, we were able to integrate the program so that it was a consistent half hour with commercials within their segments, and we were able to add a personal relationship with the other members of the news team. The general manager at ABC-Chicago saw our show on tape, said that he wanted to use the same two-anchor format in Chicago, and asked us to come for an interview. My partner in Cleveland didn't want to come to Chicago, while I did. Ultimately, we worked out the contractual deals in order for me to leave for Chicago while he signed a long-term contract at the station in Cleveland. I came to Channel 7 as a solo anchor in 1967, but the station still wanted to try the two-person format. So, when Fahey Flynn decided to leave Channel 2, Channel 7 teamed up the two of us. Dick O'Leary, the general manager at Channel 7, took my wife and me out to dinner to make the announcement, and my wife made the only mistake of her life when she said, "An Irish father-son team will never work."

Ironically, I missed being in Chicago during the famous January '67 snowstorm, since we interviewed at Channel 7 one week after the storm. We were eating lunch at the Drake Hotel during my interview visit, and I remember sitting on the second floor of the hotel looking out over Michigan Avenue and the lake. The snow was piled so high that you could hardly see the girders of the John Hancock Building that was under construction at the time. That was a real introduction to Chicago. When I took the job in Chicago, I knew that I was coming to the big time because it was such a large city compared to Cleveland.

I recall the very first day I came to the station when the program director and some other people took me out to lunch at a famous corned beef place on Chicago Avenue. The assistant program director was walking in with me and several other people, and he said, "Joel, enjoy this day. This will be the only day you won't be recognized walking into the restaurant." I said, "That's kind of presumptuous, isn't it?" He said, "No. You'll see." As it turned out, he was right, and my experience has been that Chicagoans are really that way. If they like you, they love you. They're loyal, and as long as you give them back that loyalty and trust, they're very devoted. So, almost immediately, I became a recognizable figure.

When we first moved to Chicago, we lived in the southwest suburbs, first in LaGrange, and then in Countryside. We had lived in the suburbs in Cleveland, and, like Chicago, were used to green grass and hedges and trees, and with small children, it was our favored style of living. We have always been suburbanites in attitude and in residence. I made the decision to drive downtown rather than take the train because my schedule required it. While doing the 10:00 pm news, if I took the train back and forth, I wouldn't get home until after midnight. It was an easy driving commute because I would arrive at the station at mid-morning and leave around 10:45 pm, thus avoiding most of the rush hour traffic.

Fahey and I were the only news anchors at the station in the late '60s. We actually split up the weekend broadcasts for a year or two, and were on the air at 6:00 pm and 10:00 pm. Ironically, there were some media consultants who took credit for the two-anchor format concept and promoted it around the country. They cited the program in Cleveland, its immediate success, and the incredible success of the Flynn-Daly news program in Chicago as the best way to present the news. It has only been modified to create a male-female news team, often mixing people of different ethnic and racial groups. When we began the show, the number one news program in Chicago was at Channel 5 with Floyd Kalber, but we passed him in the ratings. The other members of our news team included the famous weatherman, John Coleman, who came over from Channel 2 the night we first went on the air on February 12, 1968, and the sports announcer, Bill Frink.

We celebrated being the number one news show in May 1968, although it wasn't really true. It was part of the *chutzpah* we used, and the very first promo the station made with Joe Sedelmeier was "Will Success Spoil Fahey Flynn and Joel Daly?" That was where the station used the unfortunate sobriquet "Happy Talk." I contend, to this day, that we did not do "happy talk" on the news, but that our commercials were funny. So, humor just became part of our reputation. Our weatherman, John Coleman, was a crazy man, but very bright, funny, and clever. He used what was, at that time, a rudimentary graphic system for the weather. But, those were good days because we did a lot of quality news stories. We were so low in the ratings when we first went on the air, even before Fahey came to the station, the general manager had no compunction about stripping an hour out of ABC's Saturday night schedule in order to put on a local news special.

And, we would do that maybe once a month since there was always something going on in Chicago. That is what I loved about broadcasting in this city because it has always been an interesting place.

When Martin Luther King was assassinated in April 1968, I was covering it by using the telephone to get reactions from many people, like the Archbishop, Chicago civil rights leaders, and the mayor. We had film then rather than video tape, so we were much more limited in the amount of material we could gather between programs. I remember that the assassination occurred during our 6:00 pm news broadcast at about 6:22 pm, and we had it on the air before we closed off at 6:30. It was stunning. We anticipated that the town was going to go nuts, but, at first, there was a quiet before the eruptions on the West and South sides.

The Democratic Convention in August 1968 is still probably the most incredible week I ever spent. I was doing the early news and personal commentary at 5:00 pm, and again during the 6:00 pm newscast. In between shows, I would run down to either the Amphitheater or Grant Park, wherever the action was going on, to report on the action. It was an exhausting, albeit, invigorating week, in terms of exposure to a huge news event. I was behind the cops during the night that the crowd tried to cross Michigan Avenue from Grant Park, and the cops blocked their movement. I reported that the police were being pelted with a variety of things and taking verbal abuse before their discipline broke down. I put that on the air, particularly in the form of a commentary. The networks were reporting just the opposite and stating that

this was another Prague with the theme of "The week the world was watching." As a result, the head of ABC News came to look at my copy in order to better understand what this local, young guy was reporting. By the end of that week, the city was so polarized you couldn't say anything without making half the people mad.

We had talked a lot about the "generation gap." As it turned out, the events surrounding the convention were the best examples because there was such a division between the younger and the older people. It is obvious that a bridge of understanding between the two age groups did not exist. I really thought that the country might come apart and believe that it nearly happened in Chicago.

In the fall of 1969, we covered the "Days of Rage" where Dick Elrod had his neck broken while chasing a Weathermen Underground protester. As I recall, there was extensive vandalism by the Weathermen, which I only witnessed after it had already happened. They were still running through the streets, the cops were chasing them and windows were broken. Although I didn't provide direct coverage of the "Conspiracy Seven" trial, I did offer a lot of personal commentary on our news programs. My view was that the young people were out of control at the Convention and during the "Days of Rage." However, I also felt that Hoffman, Rubin, Dellinger, and the other defendants were really bright, articulate and open to the media. It just didn't add up to a charge of conspiracy, and I thought that something was wrong there. I had a sense that conspiracy was not appropriate. So, my attitude started to change with respect to listening to the young people.

Joel Daly, Fahey Flynn, John Coleman, and Bill Frink, c.1967.
(Courtesy of Joel Daly).

Frank Mathie

I was born in Milwaukee in 1941, grew up on the East Side, and attended Marquette University. I always knew that I was going to Marquette because my dad and all of the kids in my family went there. The only one who didn't go there was my mom. She went to a state teacher's college that later became UW-Milwaukee. I was at the university from 1959 to 1963. I was going to be a teacher like so many in my family, but then during my sophomore year, one of my friends suggested that I try the radio and television curriculum. He told me it was fun, and that's exactly what I was looking for in college. So, I did it and I just really liked doing writing, producing shows, as well as the creativity, fun, and camaraderie of it. Our radio and television studios at Marquette were so primitive in those days that we only had a few crummy little cameras. It was strictly closed circuit from the studio to the control room, there was no taping capability, and it meant that our "program" wasn't even shown on campus.

I really, truly didn't know what I wanted to do in the television business. In those days, there was no such thing as a feature reporter in television, and news programs only had a single anchor. Usually, they would just sit before the camera and read, and sometimes, the station would roll some silent film. When the news was more complicated, they might include a sound bite, but that was pretty much it. After graduating from Marquette in 1963, I had to serve in the Army because military service was usually required after college, but I was lucky that Vietnam hadn't really started yet. In those days, the Army Reserve was recruiting and that's what I selected. So, I put in my six months in the Army, got out, and went to work in television.

My first television job was at WISN-Channel 12 in Milwaukee, the CBS affiliate. They weren't doing feature reporting, so my first job at WISN was in the shipping and film department at a salary of $60 a week. The films would come in, and I would have to screen them, add the commercials, and ship them out. The only reason I got into the newsroom was because they needed a booth announcer who could sit in a booth and read "WISN-TV, Milwaukee." They had a guy with a big, deep voice doing that, but he drank too much, and, one day showed up so drunk that he couldn't even read. An assistant to the general manager had heard me read in church, thought I had a good voice, and told the general manager, "I know that the Mathie kid can at least read. Right now, he's back in the film department." So, they decided to put me in the announcer's booth. A writer in the newsroom suggested I be moved into the newsroom because she knew I could put programs together and splice film. That's how I got into the newsroom and then just started developing my style of feature reporting.

I stayed at WISN until 1967 when I was offered a position at WLS-TV by news director Dick Goldberg. He called me in Milwaukee and said, "I've heard about you. Do you want to come down for an interview?" I said, "Sure. I'd like that." So, I came to Chicago, showed him some of my work, and he said, "When can you start?" I said, "When do you want me?" I started at WLS in April 1967, lucky enough to miss the big snowstorm of January 1967.

I was scared about doing the new job in Chicago since I was only 25 years old. I remember driving into Chicago, looking up at the Channel 7 antenna on top of Marina City, and thinking to myself, "What am I getting myself into?"

I was hired as a news writer and weekend reporter, and, in those days, you could do that because they allowed you to be a member of two unions (NABET writer and an AFTRA reporter) at the same time. I did that for about six months, and since I was single at that time, I lived on the Near North Side at State and Elm in a crummy studio apartment. Of course, it was unbelievably exciting for a young guy to live and work in Chicago in the '60s. Although Milwaukee was a great town, it didn't compare with Chicago where there were things to do all week long and I was having a ball.

At Channel 7, I started doing more of my features and I was a combination general assignment and features reporter. I worked five days or even six days a week as a full-time reporter because we didn't have too many reporters on staff. At that time, we were in last place in the ratings. I began working at the station just before Joel Daly, and then Fahey Flynn switched to Channel 7. I began to do more features, even though I was still doing general assignment pieces. In those days, I was required to do a lot of stories, and would be out on one, shoot the story, take the film to the lab, and then be sent out on another assignment. When they sent the film to the lab, I was always leaving instructions either on the film or writing up the text for the editors. One Saturday, I was covering so many stories that I probably set a record with five stories in one 15-minute news program. It wasn't that uncommon for me to have multiple stories on a newscast.

When I arrived in 1967, there were some "touchy" situations happening in Chicago that summer, although nothing big or compared to the events of 1968. When Martin Luther King was assassinated, it was scary and I was covering the situation on the West Side. The whole place was burning down, and it was really frightening and I still remember looters standing in line to go into some of these buildings. They were organized, and they would wait their turn to go in. The police were overwhelmed, and about a day or so later, Mayor Daley announced at his news conference that he was issuing a "shoot to kill" order to kill looters. All the reporters just sat there in stunned silence, before we began to come up with follow-up questions. I am just glad the mayor changed his mind and the police didn't shoot looters.

Those events were really frightening and very sad. We had verbal threats when we were out on the streets, but never threatened with a gun. The National Guard came in a few days after the riots had begun, and I don't think they even had bullets in their guns. So, they would just stay on guard, block off a street, and let the cops do the tough work I didn't enjoy covering it at all, but overall, it was a great learning experience for me. Reporters had to learn about staying behind the police lines and not going into the wrong area at the wrong times. In those days, we didn't have ABC trucks, so we got around in ABC cars. Since this was done on film, we had a four-man crew: a cameraman, a soundman, an electrician, and a reporter. We also drove around with an armed guard with us who was an off-duty Chicago policeman. So, you did learn a lot of things about how to be safer, and you became street-wise.

The mayor was very quotable and fun to cover. After McCormick Place had burned down in '67, and later rebuilt, he said, "We built McCormick Place...twice." It is hard to believe now, but I remember a couple of times when we would go into his office in City Hall, sit down in front of his desk with reporters from only one radio station, one or two newspapers, and one television station, and film his comments. Of course, as the mass media exploded in numbers, those smaller sessions ended, and they would have to set up the news conference room.

In August 1968, when the Democratic National Convention was in Chicago, I was out chasing the Yippies in Lincoln Park and enjoying the experience because it was so different, exciting, and invigorating. I did that all day long, and, amazingly, because John Coleman, our weatherman, was on vacation that week, I was the weatherman on Channel 7. I did the news stories during the day, and at night, I had to do the weather. At that time, it was just a bunch of boards and no electronic tools. We didn't even do visual things except draw on the board with a big magic marker, and it was a strange feeling mixing coverage of the serious events on the street and then coming to the studio to do the weather.

Since I was born during World War II, I grew up with a sense of patriotism and really believing in America. When Vietnam came along, I thought that we were doing the right thing because we had to stop the "domino effect" of Communism in Asia. When all the protesting began, I have to admit that I would cover it as objectively as I could. But, I was opposed to it. I just didn't believe in the protesters' philosophy, although, since they were mostly young kids, I didn't think that they were Communists. Slowly, it began to dawn on me that Vietnam was the wrong war in the wrong place at the wrong time.

In 1969, I also covered the "Days of Rage" and remember that Dick Elrod broke his neck in a freak accident. I don't think that there was any doubt that during the convention you soon realized that the police went too far in punishing the demonstrators. A lot of reporters got hit, beat up, and tear gassed during the convention, although I had been trained to stay up wind when tear gas was being used. The whole situation in '68 and '69 became organized chaos. From the time I came to Chicago, through the mid-'70s, I really saw the downtown area change. In 1967, much of the Near North Side, and even State Street had become more and more seedy. That all started to change in the '70s and has continued through to the present as downtown and the areas around the Loop have been rebuilt.

When I was leaving Milwaukee, I was still single, 25 years old and living at home. As I was walking out the door to drive to Chicago, my mother was all upset. She said to me, "You shouldn't be leaving home without being married. Now you'll probably meet one of those Chicago girls." When I met my wife, she was working at Channel 7. Although she worked in ABC national sales on the 10th floor, we didn't meet at the station. We met in the bar called Catfish Row on the Near North Side, and I admit that I fell for her right away and chased her for three years. Fortunately, my mother loved her, and it didn't hurt that my wife was "South Side Irish" and that her maiden name was Keegan. My mother's name was Keelan, so she started saying novenas. My wife is a real Chicago girl, having grown up at 85th and Stony Island in the Pill Hill area. I was still living near north when I got married in 1970. We lived on Mohawk, north of Armitage, in a little coach house, and our first baby was born at that time. We were in such a tiny place that we had to move to Evanston, and we lived there for several years at 1112 Oak Street just east of Ridge. We liked it in the suburbs and thought that we would buy a house in Evanston, but, as it turned out, we found a house in Wilmette on the border with Evanston on Isabella, west of Green Bay.

Frank Mathie as WLS-TV weatherman, August, 1968
(Courtesy of Frank Mathie)

Harry Volkman

I came to NBC-TV in Chicago from Oklahoma City in 1959, and the weatherman on Channel 5 at that time was Clint Youle. The station's ratings were declining steadily as a number of viewers were lost to Channel 2, CBS-TV because of the increasing popularity of Fahey Flynn and P.J. Hoff. Alex Drier had become the news anchor on Channel 5 after the station's general manager, Lloyd Yoder, had talked Alex into anchoring the 10:00 pm news with a salary of $2,000 a week, which was huge money at the time.

When the ratings at Channel 5 continued to decline, the station decided to make a change in its weatherman because they concluded that Youle's salary was not compatible with his ratings. They began looking for a less expensive weatherman who might prove more of an audience draw. I heard about the potential opportunity, and, as it turned out, the New York-based new head of NBC owned- and operated-stations had been my boss in Oklahoma City. He knew me and my work, so I called him about the weatherman's job in Chicago. I said to him, "I understand that NBC-Chicago is thinking of replacing Clint Youle, and I would like to apply for the job." He said to me, "Well, I'll tell you what you do. You call Lloyd Yoder, the general manager at Channel 5 in Chicago, tell him your interest in the job, and set up an interview."

In March 1959, I came to Chicago with a scrapbook full of my successes in Oklahoma, including testimonials from sponsors and viewers and the station bosses. Yoder didn't even look at it because he had already decided he wanted to audition me. That was scheduled for May 1959. When I returned to Chicago in May, I somehow thought that I might be the only person who had applied for the weatherman's job. To my surprise, when I walked into the studio, there were about 25 other people waiting to be interviewed. They said to us, "We're doing the auditions in color because we are the first, all-color television station." After the auditions at the Merchandise Mart were finished, we were told, "Something happened to the tape, so we want you to do it again." I was informed later that they really wanted me to do a second audition tape to make sure I was their choice. Despite that, we were told, "All of you should go back to your homes. We are going to look at all of the tapes because we can't make a decision right now. We'll call you if we are interested."

Almost three months went by, and I had given up on the chance that they were going to call me. But, in early August 1959, I got a call from the program director at Channel 5 and he said to me, "I was down in Oklahoma City and watched you on television from my hotel, and I liked your work. So, I wanted to know if you would be interested in coming to Chicago to work at Channel 5." I was both flattered and flabbergasted, but managed to say, "How soon do you want me there?" He said, "We want you there in two weeks." I went to my boss in Oklahoma City, and his response was, "Two weeks? You've got to give me at least four weeks since I can't find a replacement for you in that short of time, and you've got to help me find a replacement."

On August 27, 1959, my wife and kids and I said goodbye to Oklahoma City, got in our station wagon, and drove to Chicago. Two days later we arrived in Chicago, and amazingly, on Saturday, August 29, Channel 5 said that they wanted me to go on farm reporter Everett Mitchell's Saturday National Farm and Home Hour in order to be introduced to the audience as the new weatherman. I began my official on-air duties as regular weatherman the next Monday when I was on at noon with Len O'Connor and Dorsey Connors. When they finally asked me what kind of a contract I wanted, I said, "Well, I would like to have a year." The program director laughed and said, "A year! You'll be lucky to get 13 weeks with a four-week option, and if we like you, we will sign you for another 13 weeks. At the end of a year, if you are still here, we will probably want you to sign a seven-year contract." I thought, "My gosh! By then, I will be 41 years old and an old man." But, in the summer of 1960, I did sign a seven-year contract with NBC.

That summer, Alex Drier had gone on his late-summer vacation, and Floyd Kalber was brought in from Omaha, Nebraska as Drier's vacation relief. Floyd had been doing segments on the network for Chet Huntley and David Brinkley, and whenever they had Midwest-based stories from the Plains States, they would go to Kalber in Omaha. He filled in for Drier for a couple of weeks, and when Alex came home, one of the local newspapers printed a story suggesting that Kalber had become the anchor of the 10:00 pm news. Everything "hit the fan," and Alex was really "bent out of shape." He said, "Isn't it great that I have to read in the newspaper that I've been replaced!" Although he hadn't been replaced, he went to talk to Yoder who responded that Drier was making too much money and that the station couldn't afford his salary of $2,000 a week. After the meeting, Lloyd sent a note to Drier stating that he would have to sign a new contract with an immediate 40% reduction in pay, or $1,200 a week. Naturally, Alex blew his stack about that and said, "You didn't have the decency to call me in and have a face-to-face meeting. We used to be good friends, but not anymore."

Alex called a "grand press conference" with the media at the Merchandise Mart where he announced his immediate resignation. He changed stations and went to Channel 7, WBKB-TV where he took over the evening broadcasts. Drier wanted me to go with him, and said, "I'll pay you out of my own pocket. What are you making?" I said, "I'm making $400 a week." He said that he would pay me that amount, but my response was that I couldn't change stations because the Channel 7 weatherman, Warren Culbertson, was a good friend of mine, I was under contract to Channel 5, and I had a good job there. Also, my attorney told me that if I broke my contract, the station might serve me with an injunction.

I don't think that Alex ever forgave me for not going with him, and in retrospect, I might have been happier if I had gone to Channel 7 since Floyd Kalber and I didn't really "hit it off." But, in those days, none of us felt that ABC was going to amount to much in the news business. Leonard Goldenson, who was in charge of ABC in New York, along with some of the people in senior management, still hadn't gotten their act together to know how to really compete.

It seemed that their strategy was to go around and "steal" people from the other networks. So, I stayed at Channel 5 and worked with Floyd Kalber from 1960 until 1967. Floyd was rather officious and acted like a "king" anchor, and he remained as the station's sole anchor at Channel 5 from 1960 until 1974. His contract included the clause that he would not co-anchor with anyone else, and, in fact, Floyd would not even have station reporters show their faces on the air, although their voices could be heard.

Kalber concluded that I had too much time to present the weather, Len O'Connor had too much time for his commentary, and Johnny Morris had too much time to report on sports. We were taking away from the time Floyd felt should be devoted to the news. In those days, evening broadcasts were only 15 minutes long, and, based on tradition, I had a five-minute segment for the weather. The five-minute weather segment had sponsors, so the station made money off the 10-minute news and the five minutes of weather from 10:10 to 10:15 pm. In those days, I was also on the 6:00 pm news, and it was in my contract that talent would do anything that management dictated. For example, if they had a sponsor who said that he wanted Volkman to do the beer spot, then that is what I did.

During the time that I was at NBC until 1967, I had five minutes for the weather and as soon as I left in '67 to go to WGN Channel 9, Channel 5 changed all that and integrated the weather segment into the 15-minute news program. Local news changed in the early '60s when stations went to half-hour evening news programs. Channel 2 was the first to change 15 minutes to a half-hour, and when that happened, they lost their number one rating. Viewers were so used to having the weather by P.J. Hoff around 10:10 pm before they went to bed. They would turn on to see the early part of the newscast, then the weather, and then they'd go to bed. Viewers wouldn't stay up until 10:30, so when CBS switched the weather to 10:20, viewers decided they weren't going to stay up longer to see P.J. Hoff. So, if they could get the weather at Channel 5 at an earlier time, they would switch stations, and Channel 5 rose in the ratings. We became number one in 1964 after we also went to a half-hour broadcast, but kept the weather at 10:10 pm, ahead of P.J. Hoff, and we remained the most popular 10:00 pm news program until 1970. In the '60s, I also occasionally substituted for Jack Eigen on his late night radio program, broadcasting from the Merchandise Mart.

One of the biggest reasons I went to WGN was to join John Drury on the news program. When I saw that John had "flown the coop" from Channel 2, I thought that he was an anchorman whom I would love to work with, and I needed to be happy in my work. Money was not the only issue for me since I felt we could build up the ratings and I could make a decent living.

So, Drury went to WGN in the late spring of 1970, and I went there in August 1970. I worked with John and Wendell Smith, who covered sports, and we were a great team. We also had a great boss in Ward Quaal who was so good to all of us. He actually bought all of us big console color televisions and built our own offices, and for me, he also built a weather station on the roof of WGN.

When Drury decided to leave WGN, I decided not to stay there. Also, NBC was after me to come back there, and they kept saying, "We're not like NBC was in 1967, so please come back." Since I had another year on my contract, I said, "I'm interested in the offer, so please call me back next year." And, sure enough, they did. So, I went back there and worked with Kalber and was unhappy all over again. Kalber couldn't joke around, and he didn't believe in on-air conversations between the anchor and anybody else on the set. He thought all that stuff with ABC was strictly *schlock*. Channel 7 had told John Coleman, their weatherman, to copy me when he first went on the air because I had been successful in my audience ratings. But, Coleman said that there

was no point in trying to copy someone else since he wanted to have his own style. Besides, he was a comedian with a great voice, he was very creative and innovative, he was smart enough to have a good artist and, his maps looked terrific. So, Coleman's ratings went up and mine went down.

I went back to NBC for four years from 1970 until 1974, then back to WGN again from 1974 until 1978. So, it wasn't until 1978 that I decided that the team that was really coming along was Walter Jacobson and Bill Kurtis, and I knew that they had tried to get rid of John Coughlin a couple of times. They brought in Melody Rogers in 1973, and in 1976, they brought in Tom Alderman, a personal friend of Walter's. However, he didn't last long at the station. Coughlin didn't like it when I showed up because he thought that here was another guy coming to take my place. I told John, "I'm not coming here to take your place. I'm coming here to work with you. This is a great channel, and I want to be here with a winning team. I know that it's going to go places." So, I won him over and we became great friends and co-workers.

Harry Volkman at weather map, c. 1967.
(Courtesy of Harry Volkman).

Chicago's weather people, including,
(from l to r) Jerry Peterson, Joe Fulks,
John Coughlin, P.J. Hoff, Harry Volkman,
John Coleman, and Linda Alvarez.
(Courtesy of Harry Volkman).

Photo from WGN Brochure, c. 1968.
(Courtesy of Harry Volkman).

Al Hall

I joined WGN-TV on August 28, 1961. Two weeks later, on September 11, I directed the first Bozo Circus show. Ned Locke was a member of the two-man cast, and there was no Bozo on our first show. That was corrected for the second show when Bob Bell was added to the cast to play Bozo. Ned's role was that of the "Boss," the father figure who was trying to keep the clowns in line. He was the Ringmaster, the supervisor of the clowns and the authority figure. In the lead-in to each show he introduced himself with "...and Ringmaster Ned, that's me!" Initially, Ned's role was that of the live commercial announcer, and in the early days of the show we had a lot of them. As a matter of fact, we had so many live advertisements that in 1964, the third year we were on, the station gave us a third camera to handle the number of commercials.

Ned did such a good job on the live ads that we were the first television station that McDonald's used for its commercials. Ned went to Hamburger U. for a week to learn all about McDonald's and how they did their thing. On the days their promotional spots were going to be on the show, the McDonald's people would deliver to us a McDonald's product and Ned would ad lib a commercial about the product.

Another success we had with live promotions happened when, in February 1962, Ned did commercials for Sears. Sears had bought a series of spots to advertise a weekend sale of the X-15 shoes. The Saturday of the weekend, I happened to go to a Sears store and decided to check the shoe department and see how the sale was going. The salesman just shrugged his shoulders and said that they were all sold out of the shoes. After that, Sears started advertising a great deal on television, and they were very big in television in the '60s and '70s.

Ray Rayner and Don Sandburg joined the show on November 8, 1961. Don was assigned as the producer of the show and played Sandy the Tramp, a very popular mute clown. Ray had come to WGN-TV that fall to play Sgt. Pettybone on the Dick Tracy Show that ran in the evenings. On Bozo, Ray played "Oliver O. Oliver," a dumb hillbilly from Puff Bluff, Kentucky and he was a good foil for Bozo, playing the character very well. In 1963, Ray got an additional assignment: The Ray Rayner Show in the mornings. This was a very popular show. In fact, the load of this show grew so much that, in 1971, he had to leave the Bozo Show and devote his entire energy to his morning show.

As the producer of the Bozo Show, Don Sandburg created the format that proved to be very successful. His character of Sandy the Tramp was very warm and lovable. Then, in 1962, Marshall Brodien, who was a magician, made 22 appearances which were more than any other guest act. He showed himself to be very creative both in his performances and material. In 1968, he was given the name of Wizzo, a wizard from the mysterious land of Arobia, and he made intermittent appearances on the show. I had left the show in 1965 to handle other production and direction responsibilities at the station.

In 1973, when I returned to the show as the producer, it was suggested to me that we should have Wizzo on the show on a regular basis. I had seen Marshall's act in a nightclub, but not on the show as Wizzo. But, I went along with the suggestion. We put him on a couple of days a week as a tryout. Although Marshall wasn't a comedian, he was great comic relief and his magic gave us a new and broad set of materials. Marshall, as Wizzo, remained on the show until the late '90s.

One of the hardest things to do was to come up with a good format for a show that ran for an hour. We knew that we could run three cartoons that would take up about 12-13 minutes and then commercials for another 12 minutes. However, because we had to fill the rest of the time, we decided to get the kids involved with playing a game on the show. Sometime in the spring of '62, the actors and staff were sitting in the bleachers after we had done our 9:30 am read-through and were talking about what we could put in the show that would be something different. Bob Bell, who played the role of Bozo, said, "Why don't we get something simple like a game? Let's get some buckets and have kids throw a ball in a bucket." Don Sandburg thought about it a second, and the next day we had the Grand Prize Game.

If the child threw the ball in bucket number 6, the prize was 10 silver dollars. Every day that somebody didn't win, we would add a dollar. If there wasn't a winner, Ned Locke would have the kid take the silver dollar and drop it in bucket #6. We would add it to the silver dollars in the bucket. One time, we had two kids win on the same day by getting the ball in bucket #6, and each won $84. Somebody told me that, at one time, the dollar value rose to $110 in silver dollars, all of which we left in the bucket. In the middle '70s, the price of silver had a big increase in value when some investors tried to corner the silver market. One day, somebody stole all of our silver dollars and we never found out who did it. We just had to replace the silver dollars, and from then on, we locked up the bucket with the money after each show.

There was an apocryphal story about a kid getting upset when he didn't win the game and said, "F--- you clownie." But, I am certain that never happened. However, on one occasion, we did a show on Friday, finished it and everybody went home. We all returned on Monday morning, and when the musicians got there, they all came running over and said, "Why didn't you tell us about that kid!" I said, "What are you talking about?" They said, "The kid who said, 'F--- you Bozo.'" I didn't know what they were talking about. They said, "The kid who swore at Bozo during the Grand Prize Game! It's all over town. The kids are calling each other and talking about it." I asked Ned, "What are they talking about?" He said, "I don't know." I don't think that the event ever happened.

About 15 years later, Frazier Thomas was doing the Bozo Show when we received a frantic call from an engineer's wife in Master Control. "Did you hear that?" I asked, "Did I hear what?" They said, "Right before Bozo started to talk, somebody said, 'I'm already screwed up.'" Well, we never heard it. We listened to a device that recorded all the audio, and we heard something. It sounded like somebody was swearing, but we couldn't figure out where it came from or who did it. About two days later, Frazier Thomas figured it out. We had a little routine that we would do. The assistant director on the floor would yell, "Ten seconds!" to give everybody a warning, and Bob Bell, as Bozo, would yell, "Puff yourself up and blow the whistle, Frazier!" And, Frazier would say, "I'm already puffed up." That was what got on the air, and I think that was what happened with the kid who people thought had swore at Bozo.

It took about a year and half or two years after the show first was broadcast on WGN-TV before the ticket list for Bozo started growing. It really built, and by the '70s, they were running from five to seven years behind. In 1979, they stopped taking reservations because they just couldn't handle it anymore, and we ran out of those reservations in 1990. People were always begging for tickets, and whenever they put tickets up for raffle, they would get from $400 to $600 apiece for them. In 1990, when we had used up all of those ticket reservations, we created a phone reservation system and announced it on the St. Patrick's Day Parade. We said that you could call in during a time window from 1:00 pm to 5:00 pm, and, if you got in, you could reserve four tickets. Illinois Bell said that in that time period, when the phones were active, they had over 27 million phone calls in the state of Illinois with many, many more coming from outside the state.

Walter Jacobson

I was born on July 28, 1937, and I went to Swift Elementary School in the Edgewater neighborhood until 6th grade before my family moved to Glencoe. From the time I was growing up in the late '40s, I began taking the "L" by myself to go to Wrigley Field and sitting in the bleachers. I am not certain why I became a Cubs fan, but maybe it was the experience of standing next to my mother when she was ironing and listening to the games on the radio. At the age of 14, when I was a freshman at New Trier High School, I wrote a long letter to P.K. Wrigley, the owner of the Cubs. I described my love for the team and asked if there was any chance that I could possibly be a Cubs batboy.

Several months later, in late '51 or early '52, I was listening to Bert Wilson's Cubs show on WIND-AM. One evening, I thought I heard Wilson say, "Upson has been named the Chicago Cubs' batboy for the 1952 season." I was disappointed they hadn't chosen me, but our phone began to ring off the hook and people were calling to say that they had heard Wilson say "Walter Jacobson." The house went up for grabs. To my utter amazement, we received a call from Cliff Jaffe in the Cubs' public relations department, who talked to my parents and said, "Mr. Wrigley received Walter's long letter and would like him to come in for an interview." I did have the interview, but I'm still not sure why the Cubs would give a suburban kid the chance to be a bat boy with the Cubs. Soon after, before spring training, I was asked to come to Wrigley Field to be fitted for a uniform.

I had to rearrange my high school classes so that, once the season started, I could take the "L" to Wrigley Field. When the team was in town, during April and May, I would get to the ballpark by 11:00 am. Then, during summer vacation, I arrived at the ballpark by 8:00 am, often staying until 6:00 or 7:00 in the evening. In addition to my regular duties as batboy, I cleaned dirty jock straps and swept out lockers, for which I received the royal sum of $1.50 a day. I did that for one year, and I say, immodestly, that I was so good at it because I was determined and loved it so much. The next year, I wanted to be the batboy again, but the Cubs said that the rule was that you could only have that job for one year.

However, I had done such a good job as the batboy they allowed me be the visiting team batboy the next season. In 1953, I was in the other dugout, and that was when I got into all sorts of trouble for stealing signals and running back to the Cubs' locker room to tell them what I heard. I remember the time that Russ Meyer, the hot-headed Brooklyn Dodger, caught me doing that, swung a bat at me, smashed the bat into the dugout, broke it, and missed my head by a couple of inches.

After I graduated from high school in 1955, I went to Grinnell College, a small liberal arts college in Iowa. I decided to leave Grinnell during my junior year because it was just a little too rural for me, and I went to Columbia College in New York on my own. Since my dad didn't want me to leave Grinnell and go to Columbia, he wouldn't pay for it. But, I had saved some money from summer work, applied to Columbia on my own, and was accepted. I just packed up and went to New York, a place I had never been. I found my way up to Columbia, but, as it turned out, I thought that I had been accepted at the undergraduate school of Columbia University. But, instead, I had been accepted by the Columbia University School of General Studies which was an adult night school.

When I went there, I didn't know the difference and didn't know I was at another institution. When I filled out the registration forms, it dawned on me that those were evening classes and the other students were 40 years old and older.

I stayed just one year and then went back to Grinnell to graduate in 1959. In that one year, I probably did more personal and psychological development than in my whole time as a teenager. I just absolutely loved it in New York, and after I graduated from Grinnell, I returned to Columbia for graduate school, and received my M.A. degree in one year at the Columbia School of Journalism.

I returned to Chicago in September 1959 and got married. Before leaving for our honeymoon, I called the *Sun-Times* about a job, and Larry Fanning, the highly respected editor of the *Sun-Times,* said he would look over things I submitted from Europe and the Middle East—a dozen stories, of which one was printed. So began my journalism career. My wife and I drove our car to New York and ended up selling it there before going to Europe. We bought a used car in Paris, loaded it with camping equipment, andtook a six-month tour of Europe as well as Turkey, Syria, Jordan, and Israel.

When we returned to America, I tried getting a job in New York, and was offered one as a copyboy for the *New York Times.* But, I turned it down because I was also offered a writing job at the *Chicago American* and that was better than being a copyboy, although what I really wanted to do was be a foreign correspondent. Back in Chicago, my wife and I found an apartment near the corner of LaSalle Parkway and Clark Street, one block north of the Chicago Historical Society.

I worked for the *American* for several years as the Cook County beat reporter. *The Daily News* beat reporter at that time was Mike Royko, and we just tore up the town trying to scoop each other. Every time he would get a story through one of his contacts, I would get a scoop through people I had befriended. It meant that on days when Royko got a *Daily News* front page story, I would get one the next day in the *Chicago American* with an equal size headline. One day, I happened to be the only reporter in the press room when P. J. Cullerton, the Cook County Assessor, came in with some kind of a tax proposal. The press releases were dropped on the table in the middle of the press room to make sure everyone got them, but since I was the only one there at the time, I scooped them all up and ran back to the American. The next day, the headline in our paper was in huge type above a story about the Cook County tax issue. So, I got the pleasure of scooping Royko.

Interestingly, my nickname of "Skippy" came from mistaken identity by a guy who thought I was someone named Skippy Richeimer. I was a rookie reporter at *Chicago's American* and was walking on Clark Street near City Hall with the paper's ace political reporter, Sam Blair, when from across the street, a guy was running through traffic and yelling, "Hey, Skippy! Hey, Skippy!" Sam and I turned around to see whom he was referring to. Although it was a mistake, Blair made the name stick.

Several years later, I moved to Channel 2 news as a reporter because John Madigan, an assistant city editor at *Chicago American,* and whom I had known at the paper, had left to go into television. When he became news director at Channel 2, he phoned me and said, "Walter, why don't you come over to Channel 2 as a reporter/writer." I went to the editor of the *Chicago American* and said, "May I take a leave of absence just to try television?" His response was, "Heck no." If you want to go over to television, then just get out of here and go!" So, I went to CBS-TV, and that was the end of my print career.

My assignment at Channel 2 was writing and producing a Sunday noon news program that was anchored by Carter Davidson. Carter got sick one Sunday, and since I was the only one in the newsroom, I anchored the newscast. I lived in Hyde Park at the time and remember coming in on Sunday mornings, wearing shorts and sneakers because my role was to write and produce the show for Carter to read. Two years later, Carter died, and I became the anchor and had to come in on Sunday mornings to write, produce, and deliver 15 minutes of news. When Carter got sick, I had to stand on bricks behind the set to be at camera level. But, when I took over as anchor, I could sit down.

During the late '60s, I focused on reporting about the wide range of events in Chicago that included the 1968 Democratic National Convention and the killing of Fred Hampton of the Black Panthers. After the Black Panther shoot-out happened in 1969, I called State's Attorney Edward Hanrahan and asked him to come on my Sunday morning program to talk about what happened. They didn't have many live guests on the news in those days, but Hanrahan agreed to the interview. So, I made a pretty big splash, and not too long after that, CBS allowed me to expand the Sunday fifteen minutes into a half hour show with the second fifteen minutes used for live interviews.

However, due to my rambunctious attitude and my determination to reveal what was going on behind the scenes, I was unceremoniously let go by CBS. I had become too much of an irritant to City Hall. The political and governmental establishments weren't accustomed to being badgered, especially by some young, upstart reporter.

I began standing in front of the mayor's office to report what was going on in his news conferences. Daley would say something, and then I would report what I knew he meant. Trouble was I didn't have the gravitas to merit that kind of a reporting assignment, but I did it anyway. CBS wanted to change that situation, so I was fired. However, I was aware of what might happen to me so I prepared for the inevitable. At that time, Bob Lemon was the general manager at NBC-TV in Chicago. Lemon was a wonderful, bright guy who was commentator Len O'Connor's boss and supported the idea of commentary on the news program.

I contacted Mr. Lemon, and he told me that he liked my kind of commentary-news reporting and had appreciated the role of commentary on the news because Len O'Connor had been so successful at it. He hired me after I was bounced by CBS. And when I got to Channel 5, I was assigned to commentary on the weekends. Len's commentaries were during the week. Luckily, Len never complained to me about what I was doing, and I also started doing commentary during the week in the early broadcasts.

I was at Channel 5 for about three years before going back to CBS and being partnered with Bill Kurtis in the early '70s when CBS-Chicago was at the bottom of the heap in the news ratings, and really struggling. At that time, CBS-New York picked two very bright television guys to come to Chicago to change the situation: Bob Wussler, who became General Manager at Channel 2; and, Van Gordon Sauter. Wussler and Sauter were very creative and imaginative guys, and they decided that a new and fresh approach for Chicago television news would be to combine this rather stentorian personality, Bill Kurtis, and this pushy little Jewish guy. I think that really had something to do with it because we were so opposite and this town is so ethnic that I think Channel 2 saw some value in that mix. In addition, John Coughlin was doing the weather and Johnny Morris was doing the sports with us, and I went on the air with Bill in March 1973. Our news team became very popular in Chicago for several years.

1952 Chicago Cubs team photo,
Walter Jacobson can be seen as
bat boy, first row center,
(Courtesy of Walter Jacobson).

Walter Jacobson in news room, c. 1970
(Courtesy of Walter Jacobson).

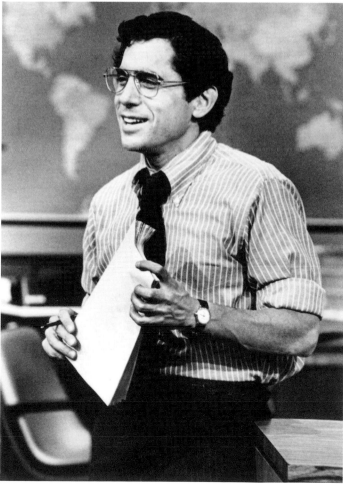

Bill Kurtis

I came to Chicago in 1966 after graduating from law school in Kansas. I had sent out tapes to several television stations and was lucky enough to get a job at WBBM-TV, Channel 2, as a street reporter/writer. As it turned out, my timing was right because I ended up being in Chicago to report on the events of 1968. The opportunity opened up in Chicago after Fahey Flynn left Channel 2 to go to Channel 7, and then John Drury left WBBM. I became the 10:00 pm news anchor and ended up covering the Democratic National Convention, although during that week, the CBS network took over our late evening air time. As a result, we didn't even have a 10:00 pm news program since Walter Cronkite and the national reporters were covering the convention. I said to my boss, "Since the network is at the convention, I'm going to go out on the streets!" As a reporter, I moved around with the demonstrators and the cops in the parks and at the Hilton during those four days. Then, each evening, I would return to the station to do a half hour news show that aired at 10:30 pm.

Those four days were probably among the most interesting and challenging times in Chicago history. The pre-convention activities began in Lincoln Park that Sunday night, August 25, 1968, and the police seemed to be spoiling for a fight. They were taking it out on the press, and on Sunday and Monday nights, some members of the press had their heads split open, but, luckily not me. In response to that situation, Chicago's superintendent of police told the cops to leave the press alone and to focus on events that were occurring in Lincoln Park, Grant Park, and at the Conrad Hilton.

More than 10,000 demonstrators gathered at the Grant Park band shell on Wednesday, August 28 to speak out against the war in Vietnam. It became a key date because, that evening, there was a confrontation between the police and the demonstrators in front of the Hilton Hotel. The demonstrators had not been given permission to hold the rally, and the police and Illinois National Guardsmen forced the demonstrators into the band shell area. There was give-and-take between the police and protesters who were being pushed out of Grant Park. The protesters moved down Columbus looking for a place to march over the IC tracks and get to Michigan Avenue. But, they could not go over the little bridges because the National Guard was there, had spread concertina wire across the bridges, and was using tear gas. Finally, down by the Art Institute, the protesters found a couple of open places to cross to Michigan Avenue.

The protesters then spilled onto Michigan Avenue, and it became an impromptu parade. Thousands of people were in the street and on the sidewalks at or around the intersection of Balbo and Michigan, and they just sat down there and blocked the street. That event became a formative experience for me because I was standing on top of a parked car on the west side of Michigan Avenue at Balbo. The police were literally right in front of me in a line across Michigan Avenue. It was dusk by then, and the demonstrators were sitting quietly for a while. As it got darker, Reverend Abernathy wanted to come through with his mule-drawn wagon from the "Poor People's March." The police decided to let the wagon and the mules through and allow it to head for the International Amphitheater where the convention was taking place. The crowd thought that the police were also permitting them to go through, so they tried to force their way against the police. The police closed ranks, and from my vantage point, it wasn't long before I saw the demonstrators push against that line. I thought that they were trying to move in the direction where the "Poor People's March" had gone. Then, somebody gave the cops the order to clear the intersection, and that's when we filmed the historic footage of the event. I remained on top of the car, and since I was wearing a suit, the police paid no attention to me.

Sam Iker was the correspondent for *Time* Magazine, and several months later, he told me that the events I witnessed didn't quite happen the way I thought I saw it.

He was on the second or third floor of the Hilton, but on the Balbo side. From his vantage point, he was looking down at the intersection at Balbo and saw about 200 police reinforcements come marching up Balbo toward the demonstrators who were sitting at the intersection. The demonstrators recoiled from that because it was scary and they thought the police were going to charge into them. In turn, the police pushed the kids against the police line across Michigan Avenue. Certainly, what I saw was truthful from my location, but it wasn't the complete story, and the key was where you were standing or sitting that evening during the chaos. I must emphasize that from my perspective I never saw cherry bombs, balls filled with nails, or feces thrown at the police. However, the testimony was offered at the 1969 trial of the "Conspiracy Seven" that described those materials and weapons. As far as I know, it developed into an urban myth.

We were shooting with 16 mm film that night, and I wanted to get it to the lab and then, get some more film. We had guys dressed up like cops riding motorcycles, and all they wanted to do was to get through the traffic. I think that one thing contributing to the atmosphere at the Hilton and the parks was that Mayor Daley cleared the streets of the television remote trucks, and there was a taxi strike. Our people took the film, threw it on the back of one of these motorcycles with a courier, and delivered the unedited reels directly to the International Amphitheater. Walter Cronkite was sitting in the CBS booth that night when the director said, "Walter, we just received some tape of the events going on downtown at Michigan Avenue. I think all hell is breaking loose, so why don't you look at it for the first time and give us a read." Well, to Walter and his staff, it looked like the end of the world, with batons flashing, police in blue helmets, and kids bleeding.

Walter saw the film and was startled. Suddenly, sweeping through the International Amphitheater, and, at the same going out on national television, was this unedited, unfiltered, raw tape that carried more of an impact because everybody was seeing it for the first time. They didn't know what had happened because they really didn't have any way to communicate directly with reporters. As a result, there was no live context and it looked like there was a revolution in the streets.

The year after the convention, I covered the "Conspiracy Seven" trial in 1969 and the "Days of Rage." In reaction to the Weathermen, the cops were lined up shoulder-to-shoulder in a long skirmish line. The Weathermen were trying to sleep in Lincoln Park and just smoke pot, but unlike 1968, I noticed that they were all dressed in black leather jackets and wearing motorcycle helmets. At one point, they reached down and picked up lead pipes, sticks, and baseball bats. I thought to myself, "These guys look like they mean business." Anybody could move along with the Weathermen, and since I had a cameraman with me, we ran alongside them. First, they raced down LaSalle, and then, they tried to go to Judge Hoffman's house on Astor Street. They swung over to Goethe Street, and then down State Parkway where there were a series of shops. One member of the Weathermen just ran from one plate glass window to another smashing each one with his baseball bat. Then, a group of probably 300 Weathermen somehow made it over to Lake Shore Drive.

The cops seemed to be caught "flat-footed" because they were all in Lincoln Park and didn't seem prepared for the Weathermen to start running through the town. The police didn't seem mobile enough to go running around to Michigan and Oak and stop them. These guys could have run right down Michigan Avenue and broken everything. I had stopped at Elm and Inner Lake Shore Drive, and I could see this group of protesters coming up the street, so we continued filming them. Sgt. Jim Clark of the 18th Precinct on Chicago Avenue had a small team of about six cops, and they were sitting in an unmarked Chicago police car at the scene. Another police car screeched to a halt in front of the mass of Weathermen and forced the group to split in two. That tactic seemed to diminish the group's effectiveness, and then, the six policemen got out and absolutely just started "kicking ass" with their night sticks. They were the only thing standing between Chicago and this mean group of Weathermen, and single handedly, they dispersed the group.

After that, I remember seeing a policeman chasing demonstrators and then pulling his gun and firing into the crowd. I saw it, but nobody appeared to be shot, so I don't know whether or not he was firing blanks. No one was killed that day, and I could not find information about any wounded people. My cameraman and I were only 10 feet away from the event when the cop said to a demonstrator whom he was chasing, "Please don't move, sir. Please don't move. Stay here and I'll be back." And, the kid stayed there, and the policeman went off to help beat the hell out of another kid. But, he didn't lay a hand on the kid who was waiting for him.

The next day, on Saturday morning, I didn't come into Channel 2, but was out on the streets. We were tired because we had been covering the trial and the protests, but I realized that the Weathermen were just going to run into the Loop again. Dick Elrod of the corporation counsel's office tried to tackle Brian Flanigan, one of the protesters, but Dick broke his neck as a result of the attempted tackle. I was not there and didn't see it, although we were all terribly angry at Flanigan. It seemed that when they were out there, the corporation counsel's office lawyers would pitch in and help the police to try to stop or apprehend the protesters. The Weathermen were different from the '68 demonstrators because the Weathermen were bent on destruction, and they would fight back using clubs, pipes, and other weapons. It was a "no-holds-barred" situation, and everybody was surprised. As a result of all those events and confrontations, I think that the late '60s were a raucous time. However, I would argue that the city wasn't actually coming apart but only on the ragged edge.

Ramsey Lewis

I went to the University of Illinois during the 1950s, but also studied music at Chicago Musical College where I took piano classes with Dorothy Mendelsohn, the piano teacher at both Chicago Musical College and, eventually, DePaul University. I had met Red Holt and Eldee Young, the drum and bass players, in the early '50s. Red had to go into the military during the Korean War, and while he was in the Army, we used a drummer named Butch McCann. However, when Red got out of the military, Eldee, Red, and I got together again in the mid-'50s. The famous recording company, Chess Records, produced our first records, and we were playing in a nightclub called the Lake Meadows Lounge on 35th and South Parkway, later King Drive.

We were pretty much part of the wallpaper there because when we played our music, people weren't as attentive as we wanted them to be. A few people came in just to hear us, and one of them was Holmes "Daddy-O" Daylie, a big-time disc jockey/jazz jockey in Chicago. Daddy-O was on WAIT-AM in those days and would come in there to hear us after we were playing at the Lounge for a year or more.

Daddy-O arranged for a meeting between the members of the trio and the owners of Chess. As a result, we got our first record deal and they recorded it under the Argo label. In those days, they recorded their blues under Chess and Checker and their jazz under Argo. They eventually had to give up that name because some other company was using the Argo name, so they changed their jazz label to Cadet. We continued to record with them until 1969 or 1970. Then, I signed with Columbia Records. In the late '50s, we went to New York to play Birdland for three weeks and we stayed about three months because we were asked to play at the Randall Island Jazz Festival, the Village Vanguard, the Village Gate, and a supper club up in Harlem called the Prelude. We came back to Chicago and felt pretty good about ourselves. Before going to New York, we played the SRO Room on the corner of Clark and Goethe for several months before being signed to play as the house band at the Cloister Inn in the Maryland Hotel at the corner of Rush and Delaware.

While we were at the Cloister Inn, Joe Glazer, from the Associated Booking Corporation, a huge jazz booking agency, became interested in us. In 1965, we recorded our 17th album. Then we thought we had the meat and potatoes and wanted something light and gay, so we decided to put a song called "The In Crowd" in the album and it caught on. After that, there were several other hits and Joe Glazer got involved and booked us all over the United States in the major concert halls and nightclubs.

At that time, Eldee, Red and I were still a trio. But, in January 1966, after we had become a huge hit in August of '65, and although we had been together from 1954 or 1955, we decided that we didn't want to continue working together any more. We were making lots of money and had great notoriety from our popular album sales and concerts. But we just decided to break up the group.

After Red, Eldee, and I broke up in January 1966, by that summer they had a minor hit called "Whack, Whack" and then, after that, they had a huge hit called "Soulful Strut." In fact, they appeared on the Fred Astaire Show on television, so they were really doing it. They called their new group, Young, Holt Unlimited. Then, they broke up and Red formed his own group and Eldee formed his own group, and they are still playing.

I formed a new trio with Maurice White, who later became the leader of Earth, Wind and Fire, and a bass player named Cleveland Eaton, who went on to play with the Count Basie Band for many, many years. My new trio played together for several years until the mid-'70s. I had already recorded our hit song, "Hang On Sloopy," with Eldee and Red before the group broke up, but it hadn't been released. When it was released, "Hang On Sloopy" became a very big hit. In late 1966 or early 1967, I went in the studio with Maurice White and Cleveland Eaton and we recorded an album called "Wade In The Water," and that became another huge hit. So, from the late '60s through the mid '70s, we sold a lot of single records and albums but had no huge hits until Maurice White had left to form his own group, Earth, Wind and Fire.

Maurice called me one day in '74 or '75. He was in New York, had already moved to L.A., and called me to say that he was finished recording and had a couple of songs left over because they were mostly instrumentals. He was recording a lot of vocals in those days, but he felt these were great instrumentals. He said, "You should really do one of them, because one of them is going to be bigger than "The In Crowd," bigger than "Sloopy," and bigger than anything you have ever recorded." So, I said, "Really?" And, he said, "In fact, if you want, three or four of us to stop in Chicago and meet you at the studio, show you the song, and maybe a couple of us will play with you. I'll help you produce it, and it will be your next hit record." We spent three days on this song, and finally we got it the way he thought it should be, and I said, "What's the name of it?" Maurice said, "The name of it is 'Hot Dawgit.'" Finally, he said, "Okay, well, we're going to leave, but, you know, there's this other little tune. It's just a nice melody, and you ought to hear it." So, they played it, it had a nice melody, and it was sort of a Brazilian jazz song. We finished that.

We had kept "Hot Dawgit" to three or four minutes length because he thought that was going to be a smash hit, and radio liked shorter songs. This other song we allowed to go six or seven minutes, and I took a long solo, the saxophone took a long solo, Maurice felt the spirit, and he went out and played some rhythm and percussion stuff in the background, and we were through with it. He said, "Now, you know, maybe voices should be added, but there are no words to it." So, he said, "Now we will just add some vowels and syllables to sort of give it a melody." We said, OK, and they left and went back to L.A. We put "Hot Dawgit" out and, I think we sold four copies. But, people were coming and asking for the album. In fact, the album started selling like a single record, and the song that became a hit was called "Sun Goddess." And, fortunately we had named the album the same. That became nearly a million-selling album. In those days, there were a lot of different kinds of music because you never knew what the big hit was going to be. People encouraged you to be yourself and to be an individual and to come up with what you thought was a reflection of your own musical personality. You just put your effort out there and left it to the public to determine what they liked.

In Chicago, unlike New York City, a jazz musician could allow himself to be influenced by a wide variety of music and play whatever appealed to him, including gospel music, which had always been important to me. So, growing up in that atmosphere and then, coming from a family that just encouraged me to be whoever I was, musically, I enjoyed that freedom as I still do. The environment in Chicago is still one of quite a bit of musical freedom. Although I didn't realize it until later, my classical and gospel background really influenced my music. We were playing a jazz festival in Hawaii, and I heard Dizzy Gillespie being interviewed. In the '70s, there was that term "fusion," and he didn't like that word. He said, "Jazz musicians have always drawn from the era they lived in and from other kinds of music. Look at Ramsey and his song "The In Crowd." What do you think that is? That's gospel and jazz all mixed together, and the classical music he plays." So, I said to myself, "Maybe that's my style."

Kent Beauchamp

I was born on April 10, 1934 and we lived in my grandparents' home in South Shore. Then, the family moved to Princeton, Illinois for a year before we returned to Chicago where I attended Dixon Elementary School. Then, I went to Myra Bradwell Elementary School at 77th and Burnham, attended South Shore High School from 1948 until 1952, and went to college in Champaign/Urbana at the University of Illinois from 1952 to 1956.

I graduated in three and a half years, and, in 1956, served in the Navy for two years until 1958. During the six months before I went into the Navy, I worked for Lenny Garmisa in his record distribution business. He had just opened an ABC-Paramount distributorship. My job was to take record orders and visit radio stations with Lenny. When it was time to leave for the Navy, he said to me, "If I am still in business and you want to do this work when you come back from the Service, I will have a job for you."

When I got out of the Navy, I had a degree in geology and wasn't really thinking about a career in the music business. However, jobs were difficult to find in the late '50s. For a period of time, I went to work for the O'Cedar Division of American Marietta, thinking that I was selling building materials, but I was really just selling sponge mops. After a year, I asked my friend Eddie Yalowitz if his uncle, Lenny Garmisa, had a job opening. Luckily, they created a position for me and I went into the record business on a full-time basis doing promotion and sales. I traveled throughout southern and central Illinois and got to know all the disc jockeys in Peoria and Davenport. I also worked in Chicago and met the people at all the local radio stations. I spent a lot of time promoting music to stations in the city's black neighborhoods because I loved jazz and blues music and felt comfortable being a white man in African American neighborhoods. I would sit with the famous disc jockey, Sid McCoy, while he did his all-night radio show. I was fairly street smart and knew my way around the city including where it was safe and unsafe for me to go. I was at the radio station where Al Benson worked on the West Side, and I hung out at the different blues and jazz clubs. I remember seeing Ramsey Lewis at the Cloister Inn off Rush Street and Ahmad Jamal at the Pershing Lounge.

My work in the music business was wonderful, and the most enjoyable part was the people I met and worked with, especially the deejays. Although I worked at both the white and black radio stations, I was the only one from Garmisa's company who visited the deejays at the black radio stations. I hung out with them, often having dinner with the black disc jockeys, and promoting records to them. I remember when Rodney Jones, the program director of WVON, had a nightclub that opened in the '60s. He invited me there, and I had an attractive woman with me.

There were only a few white people in the club that night, and as we were coming in, a black guy saw my date and said that he wanted to be with her. When it was time to go, I was nervous about leaving the club, so I talked to Rodney about the issue. He and his people walked us out, got us a cab, and we were able to leave the club without incident. In the early '60s, there were African Americans who opposed whites coming into their neighborhoods just like whites made it difficult for blacks to go to clubs on theNear North Side.

During those years, I got to know the Chess family so well that I was on a first name basis with Phil Chess. They were recording the top blues singers and performers at their studio on South Michigan Avenue where they made Chess, Checker, and Argo records. I met a lot of record artists, radio personalities, and national stars like Edie Gorme and Steve Lawrence, Ferrante and Teicher, and Martin and Lewis during the 1960s. I remember the time that Van Morrison, a very talented kid, came to Chicago and I had to drive him to the television and radio stations for interviews. I don't think that he said two or three words to me during the five or six hours we were traveling around town together. Ironically, his interviews were positive, and he was talkative with the deejays. Another guy who wasn't very talkative and sort of guarded was Neil Diamond, but it didn't matter since he became one of the greatest recording artists of all time. In those years, we also promoted the Righteous Brothers, the Four Seasons, and Nancy Sinatra.

During the early '60s, I was dealing with some of the best known black recording artists of the day, like Aretha Franklin, who was really down-to-earth in her behavior. She was recording for Atlantic Records, and we handled their other labels too. In the course of my promotion activities, I met Aretha on several occasions. I also worked with Dick Gregory, who was a very nice guy. As for the great Ramsey Lewis, I infrequently hung out with him at the Cloister Inn, but I promoted his records which were being recorded on Mercury Records, a Chicago-based label. Another popular local artist was Eddie Harris, and "Exodus to Jazz" was his top recording. In fact, it was Sid McCoy who gave that record its initial major push on the radio. When I was working with Garmisa, I was promoting rock and roll records and we would visit the big radio stations, like WIND and Howard Miller, and then WLS with Dick Biondi, Gene Taylor, and Clark Weber. I had known Clark since his early broadcasting days in Milwaukee, and, as it turned out, he introduced me to my wife.

I remember working with Sonny and Cher when they came to Chicago in the early '60s to publicize their big hit record, "I Got You Babe," during a national tour. They used the record to promote a movie they were trying to produce, and I remember Cher coming to town with 110 suitcases and trunks. I enjoyed my time with them when they spent two weeks in Chicago. Also, in the early '60s, a group called the Jackson Five came into our offices at 1209 S. Michigan Avenue, just south of Roosevelt Road. They wanted us to promote their songs, but, not having the foresight to see their great potential, we turned them down. I am certain that they wouldn't have remained as our clients, but we could have made some early money from the success of their records. Over those years, I promoted a variety of other great performers including Rod Stewart, who recorded for Mercury Records, the Bee Gees, with Barry Gibbs as the lead singer, and Buffalo Springfield, who had an enormous hit with her pop classic, "For What It's Worth." In addition, I promoted the Righteous Brothers, who recorded for Moonglow Records, Errol Garner, who was with ABC Paramount, and The Shadows of Knight, a local group from Arlington Heights.

When the Beatles signed with Capitol Records, they came out with their first big hit, "Please, Please Me." It was their first smash hit, and they performed it during their first tour of America in the mid-'60s. We promoted the heck out of it and sold an additional 25,000 copies. It went on to become a Billboard Top 20 hit song. Around that time, VeeJay Records had a popular blues singer named John Lee Hooker. He recorded a tune called "Boom! Boom! Boom!" Up to that time, neither WLS nor WCFL would play blues-oriented tunes because the music did not fit their play list format which was geared exclusively to the pop market. However, my good friend and program director at WLS, Clark Weber, sensed it "might" fit. He did me a huge favor and put it on their play list. It clicked and sold probably 25,000 copies locally and went on to become a national hit.

In the late '60s, I left Garmisa, and with my good friend, Ed Yalowitz, we opened our own company and became the first total (all labels) prerecorded tape distributor in the United States. I believe that we were the first ones to handle cassettes, which were only being sold in Europe then. Also, at that time, 8-track and 4-track car tapes were vying for the U.S. market, but neither made it because, in my opinion, they were inferior products.

Ewart Abner, president, Vee Jay Records,
Dick Gregory, Kent Beauchamp
(Courtesy of Kent Beauchamp).

Ray Charles, Eddie Yalowitz and
ABC Paramount distributors
(Courtesy of Kent Beauchamp).

Ronnie Rice

My parents were from Germany, and I was born in Haifa, Israel on March 30, 1944. They had left Germany and went to Israel because of the Nazis, and my family's real name is Schlotsover. When they came to America, there were people here by the name of Reiss and they were helping all of my family who came over from Europe. So, when my family came to the United States, they took the name of Rice. I was raised in Evanston from the time I was 13 years old, while, prior to that, I lived on the North Side in Lincoln Park and West Rogers Park. I went to Clinton Elementary School, and then I went to Nichols Junior High School.

In 1959, I started at Evanston High School, and it was actually okay. I didn't dread going to school, and for the most part, I enjoyed the kids there. I hung with a bunch of good people, but I couldn't make up my mind to be a "greaser" or a "dooper" so I was both. We used the term "dooper" for the collegiate kids. Actually, I didn't use grease on my hair, but used water to make my hair into a pompadour. I would also wear button-down shirts to look Ivy-league. I had friends in both groups, and that worked out well for me. In 1959, I met a local disc jockey named Bob Greenberg, and he was working on a radio station in Evanston, WEAW-AM. That was the first time I ever heard myself on the radio when he played a demo of mine that was just me singing and playing a guitar.

I met Dick Biondi when I was 16 years old. I knocked on his door one day when I found out that he lived in Evanston. I also brought that same demo to Biondi's house and knocked on his door because he was the hottest disc jockey on WLS in 1961. He was the guy who got me started and introduced me to his next door neighbor, Gene Taylor, the program director at WLS. Later, Gene introduced me to a guy named Pete Wright, who along with Howard Bedno, were two of the biggest record producers in the city of Chicago.

Wright and Bedno said to me, "Okay, bring a tune with you and come on into the studio." So, I brought these guys to back me up, and we recorded on a Chicago label called IRC (International Recording Company). Pete became my manager, and I decided to take the song "Runaway" with me. I went in there, listened to the playback, said, "No way! That isn't going to work." I wanted to do it again, but it was one of those things—don't call us, we'll call you. Then, after that, IRC gave me a little local record contract; I had my first record come out when I was only 16 years old. It was pretty thrilling. WLS would play the records I made for IRC, and because Pete Wright and Howard Bedno had connections with WLS, they were able to get my songs on the air. Pete and Howard owned Twilight/Twinight Record Company and were affiliated with Don Carone and his orchestra.

When I graduated from Evanston High School, I went to Columbia College for about 10 minutes, and I realized that I wasn't interested in college. For my whole life, the only thing I ever cared about was music, from the first day I listened to radio. When I was just a little kid and we went on vacation, we listened to a guy named Randy Blake who played country-type music. That was before I became interested in rock and roll. Later on, I would get into Top 40 music, and I think that it gave me an appreciation for a variety of music.

I am the type of person who kind of jumps around anyway, and it is difficult to keep my interest on any one thing. Around the age of 13, I asked for a guitar, but, before that, I wasn't either singing or playing a musical instrument. So, once I had the guitar, I took lessons for a year. My influences at the time were blues singer, Jimmy Reed, and I liked the honky-tonk, "Chuck Berry-feel" to my music. I also had a strong affinity for ballads.

As the years went by, I never had a big hit record nationally although I was getting plenty of air play in Chicago. Nothing happened to my career from my first recordings, so I graduated high school, went briefly to Columbia College, and got all of these other jobs, like working at Marshall Field's and Goldblatt's. I didn't have jobs for long periods of time because I was only interested in getting a record out.

At Columbia College, I met these guys who were in a band called The New Colony Six. They had never had a hit record, and all these kids had gone to St. Patrick's High School. They were familiar with me because they had heard my records on the radio. So, they asked me to join the band. Prior to that, I went to see them record a song called "I Confess," which was their first single in Chicago. The kids' fathers owned a record label called Centaur Records, and "I Confess" came out on that label. Because of Wright and Bedno, who had promoted the tune after I introduced them to The New Colony Six, the record became the number two song in Chicago. However, at that time, I had not been asked to join the band. I recorded my first single, "Over the Mountain," at Sound Studios in Chicago where The New Colony Six recorded their hit song. Later on, after "I Confess" came out, and they had established themselves by the next year, they released another song, "I Lie Awake." That was also a top ten song in Chicago, but didn't do anything nationally. Then, they asked me if I wanted to join their group because they wanted to get rid of their keyboard player.

So, although The New Colony Six came out in 1965, I didn't join them until late '66 or in 1967. I played on their record, "I Love You So Much," that came out in 1967. It was actually their third top ten recording in Chicago, but, once again, it wasn't a national hit. In 1967, I did one of the vocal parts for "I Love You So Much." Then, it just turned into a situation where I wound up singing whatever I wrote. I hooked up with Les Kummel, a friend of mine in Chicago, and, later, he joined The New Colony Six as a bassist. He wasn't yet part of the band, but he and I sat down one day and we both wrote "I'll Always Think About You" and "Things I Like to Say." So, now, at the age of 22 or 23, I was part of a successful recording group with hit records.

The New Colony Six was the first big rock and roll band out of Chicago. I wrote a song called "Treat Her Groovy," but it didn't do well. In the New Colony days, there was a guy named Ron Malo at the Chess recording studios, and he gave us the opportunity to record our songs there. He was great, and he had recorded all the top Chicago groups, including the Buckinghams and American Breed. The guy who did all the arrangements for our band and for American Breed ("Bend Me Shape Me" and "Kind of a Drag") was Eddie Higgins. Higgins used to play at the London House all the time. He did very, very good work, including "I Will Always Think About You," which I wrote with Les Kummel after "Treat Her Groovy." Wright and Bedno thought that would be a hit record. We recorded it, and a week later after it was released, one afternoon I heard it being played on WCFL (the big rival of WLS at the time). They were playing their top ten countdown every evening with new records that had just been premiered that day. I didn't hear the song and thought it had done nothing. As it turned out, it was the number one song requested that evening. A week later, it was number one in Louisville, Kentucky, and we realized the song was really hot and going to be our biggest record up to that time. It was a national Top 20 record for us and number one in Chicago. We were elated and excited.

Then, "Things I'd Like To Say", recorded on Mercury Records, came out in late 1968, originally as the "B" side. Larry Lujack pushed the record on WLS-AM, and although "People and Me" was the "A" side, Lujack felt that the "B" side was better, and he told Pete and Howard to promote "Things I'd Like To Say." He felt it was a hit record and he was right on. We traveled all over the country to promote our biggest hit, "Things I'd Like To Say." That song became a Top 5 in all the major markets, but not Top 10 in the country, only for one reason: it was not promoted everywhere at the same time.

The '60s were the height of my early career. I got started in 1961, met The New Colony Six in 1963 or 1964, and was invited to join The New Colony Six in 1965. I think that if it weren't for the right timing, me meeting Ray Graffia and New Colony Six, and being invited into the band and the fact that they were already established, who knows if I would ever have had a hit record in my life. So, the combination of the timing of my getting with those guys and them getting airplay in the mid- to late-'60s, if it wouldn't have happened for them, it wouldn't have happened for me. It was just pure luck.

Richard Christiansen

I held the title of critic-at-large and chief critic, but never had the title of the drama critic. I first started reviewing plays and theater in Chicago around the early '60s, but didn't take over the Panorama section in the *Chicago Daily News* until 1965. In the '50s and up until the early '60s, most of the theater in Chicago included shows that were brought in from New York with touring companies. The plays were seen downtown at theaters like the Shubert, Blackstone, Erlanger, Harris, and Selwyn. There was not much Chicago-based theater at the time, and, in the late '50s, things were in a rather sorry state among the touring companies. The great stars of the past were no longer touring since the lure of movies and television had taken the bloom off the desire of Broadway stars to travel around the country doing plays.

They wanted to perform in New York, and then go into movies and television and make some money right away. Chicago didn't get many first-run Broadway shows, and, instead, we would get sort of smudged carbon copies of the Broadway productions, with only a few exceptions. One example of a different approach was the pre-Broadway production of *Raisin In The Sun,* which played at the Blackstone on its way to New York. You would get things like that occasionally but, on the whole, the touring companies were not first quality.

The Chicago scene began to change when The Second City opened in December 1959. It was a very significant date because here was a home grown resident company made up of Chicago talent which caught on and was an immediate success. It justified the fact that you could put on a very good evening in the theater, albeit a cabaret theater, without the inclusion of former television or movie stars. Compass Players had been a predecessor to Second City, but I have to confess that I never saw the Compass Players when they performed in Chicago. They were a brilliant group, and included people like Shelley Berman, Mike Nichols, Elaine May, and Eugene Troobnick who were incredibly talented. Then, when Second City came along in '59, there had also been the Studebaker Theater Company in the old Studebaker Theater on South Michigan Avenue. It had been started by Bernie Sahlins in an effort have a resident theater company, but it only lasted two seasons during the mid '50s and closed because they had no real funding base. Despite those previous failures, Second City caught on. The cabaret format worked very well for it, the talent was there, and the time was right. People like Barbara Harris and Alan Arkin came in very early, and were supported by a great local cast of people who were incredibly brilliant doing political and social satire.

One of the great turning points in local theater came in 1963 when Hull House Theater opened in the old Jane Addams Center, at Belmont and Broadway, directed by Bob Sickinger. As far as I am concerned, it was Sickinger who really made an exclamation point statement that Chicago could produce good theater on its own. He used such great actors as Mike Nussbaum, who was working in the pest exterminator business when Sickinger came along, and was a part time actor. Mike became a stalwart of the Sickinger theater company when they performed at Hull House. Bob had an amazing work ethic, and he brought to Chicago plays by Pinter and Beckett and Albee for the first time. Hull House was a little theater that only had about 110 seats, but the impact was tremendous among people who went to the theater.

It was a revelation you could have casts with people whose names you had never heard of, and yet, they were quite wonderful. Sickinger did productions of *The Three Penny Opera,* the Chicago premiere of Albee's *Tiny Alice,* Kenneth Brown's *The Brig,* and a lot of off-Broadway and European avant-garde plays that were superbly done by this cast of primarily non-Equity actors. It expanded for a while up to the Hull House on Beacon Street on the North Side, and added musicals there. For about five or six years, Sickinger's flame was very, very bright in Chicago, and, then, Bob sort of burned out. He had a falling out with the trustees of the Hull House Theater and left town with some bitterness. But, he had absolutely made the point that you could produce very, very exciting and rewarding resident theater in Chicago.

In 1969, when the Sickinger explosion had taken place, at long last, John Reich, who was the head of the Goodman Theater at the time, was able to turn the Goodman from a student into a professional operation. It had been working since the Depression as a place where student plays were produced. Reich, with the aid of Danny Newman, the publicist and subscription maestro, brought in professional guest artists to work with the students. Then, by the '60s, the mood was right for it to become completely professional. In 1969, it became a professional resident company, still under the aegis of the Art Institute. But, it wasn't really until David Mamet came along in the mid-'70s that the Goodman acquired its luster. It had experienced successes as a professional theater, but Mamet and Greg Mosher, the director, gave it a kind of pizzazz and flash that it had not had before. Then, when Mosher took over as artistic director of the Goodman in 1978, it was right in tune with the march of resident theater in Chicago.

I think that it was a gradual dawning for New York to recognize that Chicago regional theater was important. Of course, it didn't hurt when we had a playwright in our midst named David Mamet. David had his first full-length play, *Sexual Perversity in Chicago,* produced by Organic Theater in 1974, and he was certainly recognized by 1975 when *American Buffalo* was written and produced, first at the Goodman Stage Two, and then transferred to David's own St. Nicholas Theater on Halsted Street. When that came along, and *A Life In The Theater* was produced, it was obvious that he was a playwright of great talent. He won the New York Drama Critics' Prize for the best new American play of the season in 1975-76.

At that time, there was a small theater movement beginning to form in Chicago. The Chicago City Players began in a little church on Wellington Avenue. Their plays were produced by June Pyskacek, who, in turn, founded the Kingston Mines Theater on Lincoln Avenue. The group did wonderful productions of the off-Broadway plays of the time, and launched the world premiere of a little show called *Grease* in 1971. That again was an important breakthrough because it showed that a Chicago show had potential to go beyond the borders of the city and to become an important

force in the theater business. Once *Grease* had left Chicago and was transplanted to the commercial marketplace of New York, for a while it was the longest running show in Broadway history, later eclipsed by other shows. That was important because it demonstrated the fact that you could produce something of local value with national importance. Every high school and church group in the United States, I suspect, has produced *Grease* at one time or another and it was the basis for a very popular movie.

I became aware of Gary Sinise and Steppenwolf when they started in 1975 at a church in Highland Park on Deerfield Road. That was another significant move forward for resident theater in Chicago because it was a phenomenal instance of a group of talent coming together in a really incredible way. You would go up there and see Terry Kinney, Gary Sinise, Joan Allen, Lorrie Metcalf, and John Malkovich performing together, and it was an exciting mix of talented actors. They did the kind of very intense productions that Gary would loosely call "rock and roll" theater. It was a physical and emotionally tight theater with brilliant ensemble work from those young people, many of whom had been students at Illinois State University.

The Body Politic, started by the Reverend Jim Shifflet at 2257 N. Lincoln Avenue, was truly a product of the youth movement of the late '60s and early '70s. When Jim opened that, he opened a theater as well as other branches of the visual and performing arts. One of his first residents in the Body Politic was Paul Sills' Story Theater, another groundbreaking theater. When Paul moved out, Stuart Gordon moved in with his Organic Theater, which had come to Chicago about a year or so earlier. It was there that they produced such terrific shows as *Warp,* the three-part, science fiction comic strip extravaganza.

Victory Gardens was in operation in 1974, and Billy Peterson got active as an actor in the '70s. He was a student of Dennis Zochek at Victory Gardens on Clark Street. He starred in a play called *Dillinger* there, and then, Billy and a group of other actors formed Remains Theater in the late '70s. Again, it was a group of incredibly talented people including Billy, Amy Morton, Gary Cole, and Donnie Moffett, and they had a real ensemble heat among them. They were up in a little pie-shaped space on north Clark Street and did amazing work there.

By the mid to late-'70s, the foundation of Chicago theater was established. This included "poor" theaters, not in terms of quality but in terms of financial strength, such as the storefront and second floor theaters, which included Victory Gardens, Body Politic, and Wisdom Bridge. Later on, the Evanston Theater Company was formed, and that evolved into the Northlight Theater Company.

Mike Nussbaum

I was born in 1923 in New York, but when I was one year old, we moved to Chicago and I was raised in Albany Park. I attended Hibbard Elementary School for the first four years, Peterson Elementary School through 8th grade, and Von Steuben High School. When I was about 9 or 10 years old, I discovered an interest in acting at summer camp at Camp Ojibwa in Eagle River, Wisconsin, and going to that camp was one of the more important events of my life. I had contacted rheumatic fever as a young boy and was unable to engage in a lot of activity. However, when I was cured of it, my parents sent me to camp and I suddenly discovered that I had athletic ability as well as the ability to act on stage. The clean, cold air of northern Wisconsin was good for me as well as the fact that it was a highly competitive environment and I discovered that I thrived under competition. One would have thought that was a bad thing, but, for me, it was good.

I began at Von Steuben High School in 1937. It was a wonderful school, but I really focused more on the social aspects of my life than on my academic studies. While in high school, I continued to develop my acting skills by participating in school plays like *Romeo and Juliet,* and I even used to do some stand-up impressions of famous actors of the time. In 1941, I graduated from Von Steuben and first attended the University of Wisconsin in Madison for a year and a half. Then, I was inducted into the Army in March 1943, assigned to the Signal Corps, and was shipped overseas to join the 3118 Signal Service Battalion that was assigned to Supreme Headquarters-Europe. I didn't see combat during my one and a half years overseas, so I had what I consider to be a very easy time during the war. We were first in England, then we moved to France, and then, eventually, to Germany. I was released from the Army in March 1946, came home to Chicago, and got married five weeks later to a high school friend because our romance had blossomed during the war.

My wife and I returned to the University of Wisconsin, but we couldn't find a place to live in Madison after the summer semester. I had to drop out of school and come back to Chicago where I applied to the Goodman Theater to join their theater program. The program was filled up, and I couldn't get in there either. They told me to wait for a year, and during that time, I found a job and we had our first child. I realized that I had to create a life for my family with some stability, as well as for myself. I wanted the American dream, including a home and family and some level of security. At that time, we were living in Rogers Park in a small, English-basement apartment at 6808 N. Wayne Avenue near Morse Avenue. The apartment had radiators on the ceiling, and when our son was born, we put his crib in a closet. But, in retrospect, it was a fun time for us. I decided to make some money, not to continue with acting at that time, and go into the exterminating business with my brother-in-law. Over the years, our business was very successful.

However, acting was in my blood, and during those years, as soon as I was able to have a little free time, I began acting in community theaters at places like Wilmette Little Theater and the North Shore Community Theater. During the 1950s and early '60s, the strongest memory I have, of course, is being with men and women of my age who had all experienced the war and the Depression and who were seriously trying to carve out a life for themselves and their families.

Our aspirations were in a sense purely middle-class because we wanted a home, a backyard, and a barbecue, and we wanted our kids to have good schools. We wanted the things that somehow certify that you are doing well. That led to our decision to move, first, to Budlong Woods, and then, to a small house in Highland Park in the '50s. It was just great and our kids grew up there, but living in the suburbs has its pluses and minuses. As far as we were concerned, Highland Park was just another bland suburb, and as soon as our youngest child graduated from high school, we moved right back to the city. My acting career was growing, and since I wanted to be located near the theaters, living in Chicago made much more sense. I also wanted the stimulation of life in the city, and didn't want to continue driving back and forth from the northern suburbs.

After I had become well-known in the theater community for work I was doing at Hull House, Sheldon Patinkin and Paul Sills asked me to join the Second City Repertory Company. They had a program on the South Side at the Harper Theater where they planned to produce three plays. But, they only did two because of low attendance, and then Bernie Sahlins withdrew as the producer. I was also in the original company of the Body Politic that Paul Sills started, but when they moved to LaSalle Street, I dropped out because it required more time than I was able to give to it.

In the early '60s, Bob Sickinger had begun Hull House in a little theater near Broadway and Belmont. Bob had operated a theater in Philadelphia and had somehow hooked up with Hull House run by Paul Jans, and that was the beginning of the Chicago theater renaissance. All of the 200 or so theaters that Chicago has today can trace their lineage back to Bob Sickinger and Hull House. He was doing plays by Pinter, Ionesco, Delber and Orton, and every one of the important playwrights of the period was first seen in Chicago at this theater. I think that I learned my craft at Hull House because Sickinger was such a fantastic director, the plays were so demanding and interesting, and the audiences were so exciting to work for. It became, for me, the real school that I had neglected in my earlier days.

Sickinger began to produce chamber theater readings of the hot new plays, like *Who's Afraid of Virginia Wolff?* in the homes of shakers and movers in Chicago. These were high income, high intellectual people, and they would invite their friends to these readings at which they would serve food and drink. The play would be followed by a question-and-answer discussion led by

some well-known psychiatrist or professor, and it became the thing to go to and see readings from the nascent Hull House that still hadn't done a play. It was from that beginning that he raised a lot of money, and, more importantly, he raised an audience and interest of influential people who controlled the cultural life of the city in a way that had never been done before.

Richard Christiansen would come to review the plays, and it was the first time that non-professional theater got reviews, and the audiences represented the kind of intellectual seekers who had not in the past gone to that kind of theater. It was just a remarkable upsurge. In the early days of Hull House, the future playwright, David Mamet, was a "gofer" working backstage as a 14 year-old kid while I was doing a play there. David and I have become great friends, and I remember the time we were acting in a play written by Dick Cusack. It was a terrible play, and David was a dreadful actor, and I used to tease him about it because he was so bad. One night, he gave me a copy of a play he had written called *The Duck Variations,* and I realized that David didn't have to act because he was a brilliant playwright. Subsequently, I did some Mamet plays including *American Buffalo, Life in the Theater* and *Glengarry Glen Ross.*

I was in a play at Hull House called *The Tempest and the Tiger* that co-starred Pat Terry, a wonderful actress. That was the beginning of the theater program, and St. Nicholas, the Organic Theater, and Steppenwolf grew out of that environment. I think that the 1960s was the growth period, not only for me because it began my career, but also for a burgeoning Chicago theater scene. The '60s was a growth period for Chicago "Off-Loop Theater" partly because it was a turbulent decade with the excitement of the period including the Vietnam War, the cultural protests, and the creation of the new "theater of the absurd." During those years, there was a wholly new and exciting intellectual attack on society as we knew it. I think that we were just primed and ready for a change, and Sickinger was at the forefront of that. My favorite play that I have ever done was a short, one-act play by Pirandello that I did at Hull House called *The Man with the Flower in his Mouth.* It was a stunning piece of work and I loved it.

In 1970, I sold my extermination business to my partner and went into acting on a full-time basis, and since then, I have acted in almost every theater in Chicago, as well as New York (Broadway and Off-Broadway), Los Angeles, San Francisco, Moscow, St. Petersburg, Tbilisi, Tokyo and Dublin.

Gary Sinise

I was born in 1955 and lived in Harvey until I was nine years old. I went to Bryant Elementary School, and then Sandburg Elementary, and one thing I remember about being at Sandburg is that in 1963, I was in third grade when Kennedy was assassinated. I have only a few early memories of downtown Chicago, including going to the Prudential Building with my parents when I was around five years old. We took the elevator to the top of the building where I stood in front of the large windows and looked across the city to the south towards Harvey. One of my favorite places to go was Marshall Field's on State and Randolph, and since my grandmother and my mother liked to go there, we would take the train into the city and walk over to the store. It was especially great at Christmas time.

When I was nine years old, we moved to Highland Park. I was in fourth grade by then, and I attended Indian Trail Elementary School before going to Elm Place School through mid-seventh grade. Highland Park was very different from what I was used to in Harvey. There was a large Jewish community there. On the South Side, I hadn't known any Jewish people. I became friends with many kids who were Jewish, and it seemed like every Saturday they couldn't play because they were going to temple. That was an unusual and different experience for me since I had only gone to Sunday school until I was five or six years old. My family stopped attending church, and that meant I wasn't really raised in a particular religious faith. I actually went to some of my friends' bar mitzvahs, and when I started my first band in fourth grade, we played at some of those events. I am still good friends with many of these Highland Parkers.

In mid-seventh grade, my family moved again, this time to Chicago's western suburb of Glen Ellyn. We lived there through 7th and 8th grades and my freshman year at Glenbard West High School before moving once again, back north again to Highwood, the suburb just north of Highland Park along the lake. My father, Robert Sinise, was a film editor, the first editor in the city to have his own company. There was a film company owned by Fred Niles, where dad had worked, doing television shows and cutting commercials. Later, he broke off from Fred Niles and formed his own company called Cam-Edit. In the late 60's and early 70's, he had another company called The Reel Thing, and I remember he had offices at 70 E. Walton and, then, at 520 N. Michigan. I actually did errands for him at his Michigan Avenue office when I was 19 years old. I would ride down to the office from Highland Park in the morning or sometimes take in the train.

I was playing guitar more, and I really began getting active with my music when I joined a band while we lived in Glen Ellyn. The move to Glen Ellyn was tough for me because I didn't know anybody in that suburb, and it's always hard when a young kid is new to a neighborhood. Luckily, I met somebody who also played guitar. He asked me to join their band, and we began playing at parties and doing various events. When I moved back to Highwood, I stayed in touch with the guys in Glen Ellyn and kept playing with the band. We even named the band after a street in Highwood, Half Day Road. In order to get out to Glen Ellyn, I would take the Chicago and Northwestern Railroad downtown, get on the western line, and head out to Glen Ellyn.

My band mates would pick me up at the train station, and the band would practice until it was time for me to head back to Highland Park. My musical influences in the late '60s were Jimmy Hendrix, The Who, and Led Zeppelin, and, a little bit later, the Allman Brothers and Grand Funk. In fact, Gary Sinise and the Lieutenant Dan Band that I have today play an eclectic mix of genres: country, blues, pop, rock, and classics by these same artists who influenced me early on.

During the late '60s, I had no direct involvement in the politics of the time, although I did go to a war protest when I was a freshman at Glenbard West High School. All of the students were going to walk out of class, so I joined them and wore an armband. I have to admit that I wasn't paying attention to the reason for the protest because I just wanted to get out of class. However, I was aware of the demonstrations happening at the Democratic National Convention in 1968, and there were riots at Grant Park during the Sly and the Family Stone concert. I remember I wanted to attend that concert, but my parents refused to let me go. I was out cutting the grass in my front yard when my dad called me into the house to see the riots that were being broadcast on television. He said, "See! I am not letting you go there to be a part of that situation."

I became a Cubs fan in the 1960s, and I remember watching the team on WGN on a regular basis. I don't have a lot of early memories of going to games, but I did develop into a "Die-Hard" Cubs fan, which I am still today, and there is nothing you can do about it once it is in your blood. Regardless of how the team is doing! Wrigley Field is such a great place, and every year I am invited to Chicago to sing "Take Me Out To The Ballgame" during the Cubs' seventh inning stretch.

My acting career began with a minor role in a play at Glenbard West during my freshman year. I think it was an original play that a student wrote called Who *Says There's a War On?* I really got involved in acting at Highland Park High School, as a sophomore when I was in the musical *West Side Story* in the early '70s. I was standing in the school hallway one day with members of my rock band and we looked pretty scruffy. The drama teacher was walking down the hall, and when she passed us she turned around, walked back and said, "I'm doing *West Side Story* and you guys would be great gang members for the play. So, come to the audition." We kind of laughed, but a few of us went and auditioned and two of us were cast. That was when I really started doing theater, and, after that, I just wanted to be selected for every play they were producing at the high school.

I graduated from Highland Park High School in 1974, but didn't go to college, and, instead, started Steppenwolf Theater. We began doing plays at a Unitarian church on Half Day Road in Deerfield near the 294 Toll Road. It was a beautiful building, and my parents knew the architect. I asked them if they thought the church would let us do a play there, and the church agreed to it. They gave us a key so we could go in there after school and rehearse our plays. That was when and where Steppenwolf was born which I started with my friends Terry Kinney, Jeff Perry and some others from Highland Park High School who were involved in those early days. We only did a few plays as Jeff and Terry were in college at that time. So, the three of us made a bond to get together when they completed college, start a theater company, and make a serious attempt to make it successful. We were watching Pacino, DeNiro, Brando, Robert Duvall, Gene Hackman, Dustin Hoffman, and guys like that in the early '70s. We were heavily influenced by them, Elia Kazan, and John Cassavettes.

So, in 1976, Terry, Jeff, and I got together with John Malkovich, Laurie Metcalf, my future wife, Moira Harris, and other actors and began working out of the basement of a catholic school on Deerfield Road in Highland Park where we had built an 88-seat theater. It was a talented group, and we remained in the basement until 1979 when we moved to the North Side of Chicago into the Jane Addams Center at Belmont and Broadway. We opened there in March of 1980 and were there for a couple of years until 1982. Then, we moved the company to 2851 N. Halsted into a building that was a former milk company garage. The St. Nicholas Theater with David Mamet and William H. Macy was started there in the early to mid 70's, but they went bankrupt about six years later, and the building sat empty. We were looking for a new space, so we took over that building in 1982 and were there until 1991 when we opened our new building at 1650 N. Halsted. Although I am still actively involved at Steppenwolf at the executive level and I raise money for the company, I haven't been in a play there recently because of my television series (CSI: New York). In fact, the last production in which I was involved at Steppenwolf was *One Flew Over The Cuckoo's Nest* in the spring of 2000. The production moved to Broadway the following year and won the Tony award for Best Revival of a Play.

No matter what I do or where I go, Chicago will always be in my blood. I am always proud to say that I am from Chicago. My kind of town.

William "Bill" Petersen

Born in 1953, I grew up in Evanston in a fairly idyllic life. I was a big sports fan, and my friends and I used to regularly sneak into the Northwestern University games at Dyche Stadium. We were teenagers and called it "rushing the gate," which meant getting in the stadium with a group of people who had tickets. We may have been stopped a couple of times, and when that happened, we would go to a fence on the North Side of the stadium where we could look through and watch the games. My memories of living in Evanston in those years also included going to the beach at Lake Michigan, skating in the parks that they would freeze over in the winter, and playing hockey on the ice with all the crevices and the bumps. I even remember kissing my first girlfriend at Lighthouse Beach and making out in the bushes.

My passion was baseball, and I was a Cubs fan from a young age. I recall going to my first Cubs game in 1960 when Jim Brewer threw a pitch that hit Billy Martin, and Martin responded by charging the mound and punching him so hard that he broke Brewer's jaw. Several years later, when I was in 8th grade at St. Athanasius Elementary School in Evanston, I convinced my 7th grade buddy to call in sick one day so that we could go to the Opening Day of the 1967 baseball season. We were walking around the ballpark on that April day, and it was freezing, but the ballpark was still packed with fans. As we walked near the box seats on the third base side, Don Kessinger, the Cubs shortstop, came to bat in the bottom of the first inning. He hit a foul ball toward the third base dugout and it was coming right for my friend's head. He was walking ahead of me and was not even looking, so I put my hand out in front of him and the ball hit me in the wrist. It bounced about 40 feet up in the air and into the grandstands. I turned around, although my wrist was really hurting, and the ball hit a steel frame and bounced right back into the aisle where I caught it. I had this ball, and I was so pumped about it, but of course, it was my luck that the entire event was captured on television. The result was that I got into trouble at school, and the nuns made me spend the whole last month of 8th grade helping the janitors after school.

When the Cubs got Lindy McDaniel, the great relief pitcher, in the '60s, somebody told me that he was living on Lincoln Street in Evanston. Everyday, I would come home from school, watch the end of the baseball game, and then ride my bike over to the house where he was supposed to be living. I would sit on my bike outside this guy's driveway because I figured that in a half hour he would be home from the game. I could only sit there until 5:30 pm because I had to go back home for dinner. Of course, he never showed up, and I not only didn't see him, I don't know if he was ever living there.

My father was a member of the North Shore Country Club and knew Jack Brickhouse, the Cubs announcer. Dad convinced Brickhouse to interview me for a job at WGN because all I ever wanted to do was to be a sports broadcaster. I had done some demo tapes, and my dad arranged for me to meet Brickhouse, but secretly told him to tell me that I should go to college. I went to WGN, entered Brickhouse's office, nervously sat there, and told him that I wanted to be a broadcaster, thinking that maybe I would get a job at the station. He said to me, "Well, son, if you want to be a broadcaster, you've got to go to college.

So, go to college, get a degree, and come back and see me in four years. Then, he handed me his book, signed it "To Bill, Good Luck, Jack Brickhouse," and then said, "I'll see you." I was so pissed because I knew that he was dismissing me. I couldn't believe that he had signed the book, because the last thing I wanted was his autograph or his book.

During the '60s, I just wanted to play basketball and football, but then Woodstock and the Vietnam War happened and I ended up going to all the protest rallies at the Daley Center. I was also at Grant Park in August 1968, but, ironically my friends and I left Grant Park the night of the confrontation with the police before things happened. We had become bored of just standing around, and, besides, we had gone to the park to listen to the bands that were playing near the hotel. But, instead of the bands, there were all these people making speeches from a stage in the park across from the Hilton. We were with our girlfriends and, after standing around for six hours, we decided that it sucked. So, around 5:00 pm, we left and walked back to State Street to get the "L."

We passed a building construction site, and since they had wooden fences along the sidewalk and the overhang, and cutout windows along the side of the construction, we looked in. Instead of construction materials, we saw hundreds of policemen wearing light blue shirts waiting there for the protesters. We thought, "Wow, what is that? The cops are hanging out at this building site." It was weird, and we wondered what was going on. But, rather than stay there and get ourselves in trouble, we walked over to the "L" and went back up north to Evanston. Some of us just partied by the lake and hung out there for the rest of the evening.

My parents were at home watching the events on television, and they thought I was still downtown, caught up in the riots. I came home around 11:00 pm that night, and my dad was out of his mind with worry. I said to him, "We weren't even down there and had left downtown by 5:00 pm." When I watched the news that night, I said, "Oh my God!" Conceivably we could have been caught up in the middle of those events, but since there were so many people downtown that night, it could have gone either way. It was during the next couple of years that I became much more vocal and active about the war. But, back then, it was, "What's going on? Hey, that sounds cool. Let's go down there." I also missed being in Chicago in 1969 during the Days of Rage.

However, I had gone downtown for a couple of the rallies at the Daley Center where they clogged up the Loop and REO Speedwagon had a concert at the Civic Center during an anti-Vietnam rally. We just sat on the Picasso statue and watched the concert.

Since I wasn't serious about my education, I goofed around a lot in high school and I got "booted" out of Loyola Academy. Next, I went to Evanston High School for a while, and I quit for a year and followed the rock festivals and the Cubs. I finally finished up high school in Idaho and had gone there because my brother lived out west. I stayed with him and went to high school. If I wasn't playing basketball and football, I wasn't really that interested because school didn't work for me. I went to Idaho State to play football and basketball, but I had such a bad grade point average that I had to get my grades up by taking classes in the drama department. I would get automatic Cs just for showing up in class and doing things like stage craft where we painted flats and lighting design, which meant setting up lamps for the shows. It was bonehead work, but I fell in love with the theater department and all the people who were in it.

In 1973, they gave me a scholarship at Idaho State and offered me a job as auditorium manager. The following year, instead of going back to Idaho State, I joined my friends who were going to Spain to be in a special study program. I also met a guy who was a theater teacher who was going there. I went to Spain and spent a year doing plays, including *Hamlet,* and directed a play in a little church. While in Spain, I got married and our daughter was born there. So, everything really changed for me in 1974.

When I returned to Idaho with my wife and child, I worked as a logger for a while as well as in a truck stop. We lived in a trailer park and oddly enough, while I was working nights at this truck stop and living in a trailer, there was a little black and white television in the truck stop booth. Sometimes I would sit in the booth for hours and watch television. One Saturday night, I saw *Howard Cosell Live,* a show that was only on for about two months during the same year that *Saturday Night Live* premiered. Howard Cosell had a group of people on his show called "The Prime Time Players." Then, *Saturday Night Live* came up with *Not Ready for Prime Time Players*. All of a sudden I saw an acquaintance from high school, Bill Murray, who was on Cosell's show. Murray was ahead of me at Loyola Academy when we both went there, and I had actually seen him at Second City during one summer the year before when I was in Chicago.

My dad knew about my interest in theater and was sending me some articles from the *Chicago Tribune* about the Organic Theater. Those guys were all going over to Europe and doing tours, and the off-Loop theater scene was starting to happen. I started reading these articles and then I saw Murray, and I thought to myself, "Why am I in Idaho sitting in a truck stop in a trailer park?" So, I got my wife and kid into our car and we came back to Chicago.

The first acting I did in Chicago was at the Jewish Community Center in Skokie. I read that they were having open auditions for a play called *Darkness At Noon* based on a book dealing with Russians captured by Germans in World War II and written in the 1950s by Arthur Koestler. The director wanted me to play the German prosecutor since there were all Jews there and I looked Aryan. It was a big thing even though it was only two weekends of performances. At that time, I was working for Nels Johnson Tree Experts in Evanston because I had worked as a logger and spoke Spanish. They hired me instantly, and I had some income, even if only a net salary of $85 a week. All the guys who were

working on the crews were Mexican, so my time in Spain gave me an advantage. We lived in an apartment in Rogers Park on Hermitage off of Pratt in an old brown building. It was a nice little apartment, and the rent was only $120 a month. After that, we lived in downtown Evanston in an apartment across from the Northwestern University Music Department, on Clark.

I started the Remains Theater Company in 1979 and acted at Remains Theater, Victory Gardens Theater, and Steppenwolf Theater during those years. For the next 15 years, that's pretty much where I worked. In addition, I did *The Belly of The Beast* at Wisdom Bridge, *Glengarry Glen Ross* at the Goodman Theater, and *Balm In Gilead* and *Fool For Love* at Steppenwolf. My group of acting friends during those years included Gary Sinise, John Malkovich, Joan Allen, Joe Mantegna, Denis Franz, Aidan Quinn, and John Mahoney. And, nobody had any thought that any of us would ever end up anyplace but Halsted Street. Now, every time I turn on television, it seems that a friend of mine is on a show.

Joe Mantegna

I was born in 1947 and grew up on the West Side, first on Polk Street, across from the old Sears, Roebuck on Homan and Arthington. My mother worked at that Sears, and we lived in an apartment nearby. One of my clearest memories of growing up in Chicago was the Sears, Roebuck building because we were right there, and through my bedroom window I could see that big tower with the green sign "Sears." I remember once when the "S" broke on the sign and it just said "ears." Later in life, I thought that my ears were on the larger side when I was smaller and that it was subconscious because I had to stare at that "ears" sign outside the window. We moved to a new building on Flournoy Street that was owned by my grandparents, and we lived upstairs from the time I was about four or five years old until I was 12. I remember when they built the Congress Expressway near us, with the "L" going through our alley.

I started grammar school at Gregory School in the Garfield Park neighborhood and went there from kindergarten to 5th grade, before changing, in 6th and 7th grades, to Mother Cabrini, across the street from Manley Technical High School. My bedroom window was located only about 200 feet from the "L" tracks, and when we moved to Cicero, it took me weeks to fall asleep at night because I was missing that sound. I remember when they opened the "L," and in the first week of operation, the CTA offered free fares. My friends and I decided to just ride the "L" all day from Logan Square out to Des Plaines on the other end.

We would play 16-inch softball underneath the "L" tracks, and since our alley was wider than most alleys, we were able to play a shrunken version of softball. I have memories of sometimes hitting the Clincher up on the tracks, climbing up the metal stanchions, and retrieving the ball by walking along the tracks. We were crazy taking that chance, and if the train hit the ball, it would grind it up and all of those little feathers would come floating down.

I remember racially-based "block-busting" and that we were literally the last white family to move off our block. There were signs in windows that said, "I'm not selling." I have to give my dad credit that race was never a factor in his life and he favored racial tolerance.

When I went to 8th grade, we moved to Cicero. My father worked for Metropolitan Life Insurance, but he was always sick since he had tuberculosis in his early twenties, and they took out one lung and part of the other. Dad had to pretty much quit working in the early '60s, and my mother had to take over supporting the family by working at Sears. My dad was permanently disabled and died at a young age in 1971 because all those illnesses finally caught up with him. My dad had a sister who lived in Cicero and had a store there, so we got an apartment in Cicero and moved into a completely different neighborhood, an all-white enclave located on the western border of Chicago. I went to Morton East High School and Morton Junior College. Cicero was fine, and although it has changed a lot, it still is the same in many ways.

I became a Cubs fan because my father was a Cubs fan, and it is a curse that your parents pass on to you. My next door neighbor and good friend, Ernie Majerus, was an incredible Sox fan so we would have endless arguments about which team was better.

I also became a Cleveland Indians fan because they were the White Sox' arch rival and I grew up with a real hatred of the White Sox and love of the Cubs. I have pictures of me at five years old in front of the television watching Hank Sauer and Ernie Banks, whom, to this day, is a god to me. Over the years, I have tempered my hatred for the White Sox, and now I embrace them since I am for any team from Chicago that does well. But, there are still some of my friends who have never changed their feelings. I would go to Sox games on the "L" just because I wanted to see other American League teams like the Boston Red Sox and New York Yankees. As for Wrigley Field, one year I clearly remember going 10 times to see the Cubs, and when they lost all 10 games I considered it my fault. That became the seed for the play *Bleacher Bums* that I conceived and co-wrote in 1977.

Before going to Morton East High School in Cicero, I had no more desire to be an actor than the "man in the moon." However, it was the play and film, *West Side Story,* which had a huge impact on my acting career that developed in high school. When the movie came out, they had auditions for the play that fall when I was a junior in high school. I didn't know it was a play, and, at that point, I had only seen two plays in my life because my family did not go to the theater. The high school drama teacher wanted to cast as many kids as possible because the teacher needed all these guys to play the gang members. They were making a concerted effort to recruit kids from the school who normally wouldn't try out for plays.

I was big into baseball at that time and played ball a lot, so one of the other guys who was a member of the Pony League team I was on dared me to try out for the play. We both went down there that night and had rehearsed a song from the record album. Going to the school at night was weird since I didn't even know that the school had a little theater located upstairs. I went there even though my friend, Glen Sowa, chickened out and wouldn't follow through at the audition. I figured that since I had learned a song and was already there and was intrigued by the theater, nighttime, and all these kids working on the play, I auditioned by singing the song "Maria." I used to sing around the house, and my parents and relatives told me that I was a hambone when I was a kid.

I was on the stage with the footlights in my eyes, and it was magical for me, like being in a fantasy world. I sang the song and heard applause in front of footlights, and, I swear at that instant I knew I wanted to become an actor.

When I walked off the stage, I felt like I was floating, and I heard people saying "Thank you, thank you very much, that was wonderful!" Maybe it was because I just had never gotten any real recognition for anything before. I went home that night, and all I could think about was that audition and how badly I wanted to be in the play. It was so strange for me because 24 hours earlier I didn't even know about the play. The next morning, I got to school early because I wanted to see if my name was on the cast list. I looked at the list, and I was devastated to find that I hadn't been selected for the cast.

At that moment, I became aware that my interest in the theater was real. In fact, I decided to talk to the head of the drama department because I heard that one of the kids in the show had been injured during rehearsals. I thought that I could get into the play that way. I talked to the teacher who was directing the play and who was the head of the department. He said, "No, the kid just sprained his ankle and he'll be fine. But, I remember you from the audition, and I really like your enthusiasm. Why don't you come into my advanced drama class?" I was amazed by his offer since I had never taken a drama class in my life. I said, "Okay." So, I juggled my schedule, and the next thing I know I was taking drama during my junior year at Morton East High School.

I graduated from Morton East and then went to Morton Junior College for two years, which was on the same campus. I couldn't afford to go anywhere else anyway. It worked out well for me because it was the same drama department for the high school and the college, and they combined students from the junior college and the high school for a lot of the productions, as well as students from Morton West High School in Berwyn. One of my friends, who was a year ahead of me at the junior college, had enrolled in the Goodman School of Drama in the Art Institute, and he suggested that it was a cool place to go. Again, I had no money and my parents had no money, so I couldn't go away to college. I applied for a government loan and used that money for the tuition that was around $800. Although auditions were not required to be admitted to Goodman, you did need letters of recommendation, and I had such letters from Morton Junior College. I was admitted to Goodman, lived off the student loan, and went there for two years from 1967 to 1969. In my second year, I received a scholarship that paid for some of the costs. But, I still needed another government loan to have money to live on because, by that time, I had moved out of my parents' house and was living with friends in an apartment in Old Town.

In the summer of 1969, they had tryouts for the play *Hair*. It was a summer-long process, but ultimately, I was cast in the play about a couple of weeks before school would have started. I had to make the decision whether to join the cast of *Hair* or go back to school for my third, and final year at the Goodman. I met with the dean, and he said, "Look, you've been here two years. You go to the school in order to become a professional actor. So, since somebody offered you a job, go do it." Thus, in the fall of 1969, in Chicago, I began my professional acting career.

I did *Hair* in Chicago for over a year and worked with my wife-to-be, Arlene Vrhel, whom I had known at Morton West High School. We had been in some plays together when I was in junior college, but, I hadn't seen her in a few years. We became a couple during that time, and we still are today. We did the show for over a year in Chicago at the Schubert Theater before they moved the play to the Blackstone where it lasted for a few more months. When the show closed in Chicago, Arlene and I were both asked to do the national tour. We felt good about the opportunity and went from Chicago to Cincinnati and Pittsburgh. It was while I was in

Pittsburgh that my father passed away, and a lot of things in my life seemed to culminate at that time. We came back to Pittsburgh after the funeral, and I realized that, for me, my stint in *Hair* had run its course. So, we both quit the show, rented an apartment on the North Side of Chicago, and I ended up spending the next 10 years in the city as an actor.

I didn't do much acting for about a year after *Hair*, so we lived off money we had made from that play, until I was chosen for *Godspell*, which I did for a year at the Studebaker Theater. When that closed, I segued into the Organic Theater. The Organic Theater had gone to New York with the play *Warp*, which had been running for about the whole year I was doing *Godspell*. When they got back from New York and *Warp* closed, they were basically regrouping and starting over with a new location and a new acting company on Beacon Street. That was when they held general auditions, and when I, Dennis Franz, and Meshach Taylor, among others, became the new incarnation of the Organic Theater. *The Wonderful Ice Cream Suit* was the first play we did together with that new group in 1973. Steppenwolf began in 1974.

View of entrance of Goodman Theater.
As published in the *Chicago Sun-Times*.
Photographer: Charles Gekler.
Copyright, 1960 by *Chicago Sun-Times,* Inc.
Reprinted with permission.

Sheldon Patinkin

When I was growing up in the '30s and '40s, we lived at 1248 W. 64th Street on the South Side. We were there until 1951, and then we lived at 87th Place and St. Lawrence in Chatham. My mother wanted a home, and since my father worked for his brother and cousin's junk business, he was able to provide enough funds to buy one. After a short time, my mother hated it because it was more work than she expected and, as on 64th Street, the neighborhood was starting to "change." So, we moved to an apartment in South Shore because we realized that we weren't "house people."

I went to high school at The University of Chicago Laboratory High School and then attended the University of Chicago. I became part of University Theater there when I was 16 years old because I wanted to become an actor. However, when I started working backstage at University Theater, I discovered I liked that a lot better. In 1953, during the end of my third year in college, we opened Playwrights Theater Club, which was created after we broke away from University Theater. We opened our own space in a converted Chinese restaurant at North and LaSalle on June 23, 1953, located upstairs of a drugstore and an all-night restaurant. Many of the actors at Playwrights had gone to the University of Chicago, including Ed Asner, Mike Nichols, Elaine May (sort of), and Joyce Piven, nee Hiller.

Playwrights existed for almost two years during which time we put on almost 30 plays. I was the box office manager, production manager, lighting designer, costume designer (once), and musical director and pianist, as well as assistant director, and an actor only when there were more roles than we had people to fill them. It was quite an exciting time. The plays were very successful, even though we only seated 100-125 at a performance. Compass Players, which opened in July 1956, was the next logical step and was totally improvisational. The shows included a living newspaper from that day's paper, a seven-scene scenario written by a member of the company and then fully improvised out, and a set of improvisations based on audience suggestions.

In 1958, Bernie Sahlins opened the Studebaker for a year to do repertory, but that didn't work out too well. As a result, Bernie, Paul Sills, and Howard Alk decided to open Second City, which was named after a series of articles in the New Yorker, by A. J. Liebling that was a snotty investigation of Chicago, calling it "the second city." The early days of Second City were very exciting because we had a built-in audience based on people's familiarity with Compass Players and were sold out every night. By that point, Old Town was exploding, and we originally opened on December 16, 1959, at the north end of Old Town at 1842 N. Wells that was then the last block of Wells. We built a summer beer garden on the vacant lot next door north. I started working at Second City a few months after it opened for business.

Within months of opening, *Time* Magazine had reviewed us and called us a "temple of satire." We then built a larger theater in half of the beer garden at 1846 N. Wells and called it Playwrights at Second City.

Business wasn't really all that great at Playwrights at Second City, so we moved it next door to the old Second City, which was smaller, and moved Second City to the larger theater. With the switch, Playwrights at Second City was in a 125-seat theater with an Equity cast, but, after a while, it couldn't support itself. The first time we had a show that didn't sell out for a long period of time (an original play by Bernie Sahlins called *The Puppet*), we closed it. We just couldn't afford to keep it going financially. At the same time, Hull House began with Bob Sickinger in charge, and they took over the kind of repertory we were doing at Playwrights. That was fine with us.

I was the assistant director and manager in the early years, Bernie Sahlins was the producer, and Paul Sills was the artistic director. Later, we hired Joyce Sloane to do group sales and fill up our previews when we opened at 1846 N. Wells with Jules Pfeiffer's review, *The Explainers*. We did two shows in that space as Playwrights at Second City. The Pfeiffer review did okay, but the next show, an original improvised scenario adaptation of "Three Penny Opera" called *Big Deal,* about Chicago ward politics with Alan Arkin, wasn't as successful. So, Bernie, Paul Sills, and I figured out that it would be better to put Second City in the bigger space and move Playwrights to the smaller space. That is what we did, which meant that Second City's second space was at 1846 N. Wells. The remainder of the beer garden was still open where we showed silent movies in the summer and had an ice cream stand. In fact, during one summer, the soda jerk was David Mamet, who was also taking improv classes at the time with Paul and me. In the winter, we showed silent movies in the bar downstairs at 1846, but it was a very difficult configuration because in order to get to the waiting room bar, you had to go through the lobby.

When Second City opened at 1846 N. Wells, we did very well and continued to sell out performances. We had more seats than we could sell for the 11:00 pm show since more people could get in for the 9:00 pm show. So, we eventually dropped the 11.00 pm show on Tuesday, Wednesday, Thursday, and Sunday, and just did one show along with a set of improvisations. Eventually, we also dropped the 1:00 am show on Saturday night, and just did ones at 9:00 pm and 11:00 pm as well as a set of improvisations after the 11:00 pm show. In the early days, the Second City cast that moved from 1842 N. Wells to 1846 N. Wells included Avery Schreiber, Hamilton Camp, Del Close, and Joan Rivers among others. Mike Nicols and Elaine May never did Second City, but they did Compass Players in the '50s before that moved to St. Louis, and they were already major entertainers by the time that Second City opened.

In 1963, I became the artistic director of Second City and stayed in that role until I left town in 1968. We moved to where we are now from 1846 N. Wells to Piper's Alley when it opened, and we were the first tenants. We brought back David Steinberg for the first show there, and the rest of the people in the company were unknowns. However, it wasn't a particularly successful company. While we were still at 1846 N. Wells, Fred Willard, Robert Klein and David Steinberg were all there and that was a wonderful company which we moved intact to the space we had then in New York. We were in Piper's Alley first, and then the other places, including That Steak Joynt which moved in around us. Once we moved to Piper's Alley, things were different and everything started getting better, although Piper's Alley became one big "head shop."

We opened Playwrights at the Harper Theater in Hyde Park in 1967, but it was a disaster. We did two shows, and it folded because it was so awful, it was embarrassing. That was Bernie and Paul and me trying to get together again under the auspices of a man who had taken over the Harper Theater. The first show was *Deer Park* by Norman Mailer that I directed, but I wasn't allowed to direct the leading actor because it was Paul Sills, and he was wrong for the part. We brought the Pivens back in for that and they stayed, and Mike Nussbaum got his Actors Equity card from that production, and he was wonderful. Bernie and I quit when it was time to do the second show, *The Cherry Orchard*. Paul directed the play, but it also wasn't very good, so the company folded.

Wells Street had some terrific restaurants in those days, including Paul Bunyan, located across the street from Barbara's Bookstore, which I named. Barbara Siegel and I were going together, and she said to me, "I don't know what to call the store." I said to her, "Why don't you call it Barbara's Bookstore?" She sold the bookstore when she moved to California in 1967, and someone else took over. Barbara's sister, Judy Curto, was our manager once I finally convinced Bernie, sometime in the mid '60s that I couldn't be both the artistic director and the manager any more because it was just too much for me.

My most vivid memory of the 1960s, other than Second City, was 1968, and, most of all, the Democratic National Convention. First of all, when the police got the protesters out of Lincoln Park at 11:00 pm and pushed them toward us, we could smell the tear gas. We saw kids getting beaten up across the street against the wall at Walgreens. One of our guys came down the stairs too far, and he got beaten up.

The confrontations seemed to stop where we were located on Wells, and it was a very bad time and quite difficult to see your friends being beaten up by the police both live and on TV. As for the Martin Luther King riots in April 1968, that was unprecedented, since we were closed down by the city for two nights because the riots were too near Second City. Wells Street and North Avenue were being patrolled by the National Guard with their rifles, and it was just a very, very scary time. So, 1968 was the worst single year I remember in the life of the country. (It also included such events as the killing of Bobby Kennedy, the My Lai disaster, and the election of Richard Nixon.) As a result of the year's events, we opened our strongest, most political show at Second City right during the convention, and it was called "A Plague on Both Your Houses." It was so angry that it wasn't funny enough. That was the last show I worked on at Second City and sold out my share before moving to New York in September 1968.

Business at Second City in Piper's Alley dropped again in 1969 because people started staying away from Wells Street, as well as from Second City. It needed a new audience which it hadn't found yet. The cast was new, including Harold Ramis, John Belushi, and Joe Flaherty, but the new audience still had to develop. In the mid-'70s, in a period of about three years, Saturday Night Live, SCTV, and Animal House all happened. As a matter of fact, in the first season of SCTV, even before it was syndicated in the U.S., Harold Ramis left after the first 13 shows to finish writing Animal House, and he came back occasionally after that. But, all three of those shows, in their publicity and their coverage of various kinds, made it clear that many of the people responsible for them came from Second City. Business at Second City changed in those years, and it became more of a tourist place. Happily, Second City became popular again, and it has remained very popular since then.

Exterior view of Second City, c. 1965.
(Courtesy of Second City).

Joyce Sloane

I grew up on the West Side of Chicago and attended Mason Elementary School. Although I was supposed to go to Farragut High School, I attended Marshall High School instead, using my aunt's address because it was located within the boundaries of the school district. We moved to the North Side when I was 16, and I enrolled at Senn High School. However, I stayed there only one week because I missed my friends at Marshall and was involved in many school activities there. Instead of staying at Senn, I went back to Marshall, and since my English teacher was in charge of the attendance room, she adjusted the records and got me back into all my original classes. Going to Marshall required me to travel each day from the North Side by "L" and bus, which I did it for two years from 1946 to February 1948.

I was involved in journalism at Marshall, serving as editor of the yearbook, and co-writing and producing the Class Night Show, which was great because practice for the show meant we were always rehearsing. After high school, my parents allowed me to travel for two years, and upon my return to Chicago, I made the decision to attend Roosevelt College. However, the environment at the school was disappointing because of my expectation that it was going to be a wonderful liberal college rather than a place for guys to attend to avoid being drafted to fight in the Korean War. There was no college atmosphere at Roosevelt, so my experience there wasn't positive and I didn't graduate. I stayed there for three years, but didn't like it and wasn't getting anything out of the college experience.

After Roosevelt, I found a job at the Furniture Mart on Lake Shore Drive. My cousin had taught me how to fill out a resume, and she said to me, "You have to lie on your resume. That's the only way to get a job." I was hired as a receptionist by a wonderful couple who owned a place at the Mart. They treated me like an "adopted" child, but just seemed to take over my life. The woman took me on buying trips and gave me a Dictaphone to take dictation, even though I said to her, "I don't know how to use this." She said, "You'll learn." Finally the situation became a little too much, and my parents were unhappy with the woman running my life and supervising who I dated. Finally, I decided to leave that job.

I got married in the '50s, and my husband (now ex-husband) was a circus producer. We produced the Christiani Brothers Circus and, in 1958, presented it on Chicago's lakefront at Soldier Field. We were the only circus other than Ringling Brothers to ever play there. When our circus came to town, we paraded down State Street with our elephants and other animals and it was a lot of fun. On another occasion, we took the circus to Los Angeles and had to move the entire show by truck and trailer. My husband and I flew out to the West coast, but during our trip, we learned that the circus was facing several crises. One was the fact that the truck carrying the elephants had been lost in the mountains. We did the show in California, it was a big hit, and we had a great time. Although there was some thought about us staying out there, I was pregnant at the time with our daughter, and wanted to go back to Chicago.

When we returned, I decided to get a divorce, but I needed to find a job because my daughter had been born. I had a "Dutch uncle" named Hal Zeiger, and he produced a show called *The Borscht Capades* with Mickey Katz and Joel Grey. My cousin, Jack Hilliard, who was a singer in the show, told Hal about my job search, and Zeiger said to me, "As long as you're staying home to raise your daughter, why don't you sell theater parties?" I didn't even know what that entailed, but I soon discovered that I could get an organization to sponsor a performance. Hal also got me connected with the Erlanger Theater, and I sold theater parties for their show

Once Upon A Mattress which became a big hit. After that, I received a call from Al Weisman of Foote, Cone and Belding to work for a show called *Mr. and Mrs.* with Marilyn Maxwell and Jackie Coogan. It was sponsored and produced by Johnson Wax, and Al wanted me to sell theater parties for his company. Although I still had a baby at home, I needed the income and accepted the opportunity.

I went to see Al, and he suggested that I should also contact Irving Seidner who was opening a little club on Wells Street. Irv sent me over to meet Bernie Sahlins, the founder of Playwrights at Second City, and during our meeting in early 1960, Bernie and I crawled through the theater that they were just building. We looked over the place and discussed the development of a strategy for making the place into a success.

The first show at Playwrights was going to be a production of Jules Pfeiffer's *The Explainers*. Bernie asked me to sell out the first week, but I didn't know that no theater opens with the entire first week sold out. I was so young that I did what I was asked to do, but I had a problem because there were two groups that wanted to buy out the opening night: the University of Chicago Cancer Research Foundation and the Travelers Aid Society Junior Board. I called Sheldon Patinkin, who partnered with Bernie, and he said, "It's not a problem. We'll make one of the shows a preview." We opened soon after, and that was the beginning of the original Second City which was located at 1846 N. Wells Street, north of the current location. After that, Bernie never thought that there was anything too difficult for me to accomplish. My next concern was that Sheldon and Bernie decided to leave Chicago: Sheldon went to New York to work with Leonard Bernstein; and Bernie went to England to work for Granada Television. I seemed to have the complete responsibility for the club because the founders went to seek their own fame and fortune. I had the title of associate producer, but didn't think that the credits had any real meaning.

After helping Second City get started in Chicago, I also worked to establish an alumni company at the Royal Alexander Theater in Toronto, Canada. I traveled to Toronto with a wonderful company of actors who included Severn Darden, Mina Kolb, Jack Burns, and Avery Schreiber. They were fantastic, and people in Toronto, who had never seen anything like them, responded favorably to the show. Nathan Cohen, a Toronto theater critic who was very positive about our show, said to me, "What a wonderful gift it would be to the city of Toronto to have a Second City here."

Our publicist, Chino Empre, also represented a deli in Toronto called Shopsies. In Toronto, you don't have a hot dog—you have a Shopsie. So, Shopsie decided to back us, and we opened a Second City there. At first, we were an amazing flop because unfortunately, we didn't have a liquor license in Toronto.

We had hired a local barrister who appeared to be capable of representing our interests, but he was unable to get us a liquor license. While that was going on, Bernie wanted to close the Toronto operation. But, one of our waitresses named Susie Sachs, who had also worked for us in Chicago, was living in Toronto, and was managing the theater, said, "What if we get some people to put some money into the place?" I said to Bernie, "What if we get some investors?" He said, "Okay." So, Susie was able to find a few people to make an investment in our operation.

Meanwhile, I was traveling back and forth between Chicago and Toronto. One day, I had a call from a man named Andrew Alexander. He wanted us to open at his place in Toronto. I said to him, "You're a little late because we already have a space, but thank you." Yet, when we wanted to conduct auditions in Toronto, I called him and said, "Andrew, could we possibly use your theater for the tryouts?" He was at the O'Keefe Center and he let us use it. As things turned out, Alexander now owns Second City in Toronto. He was also consulting at the Ivanhoe Theater in Chicago, so on my trips to Canada, we would meet either at the airport in Chicago or Toronto to have our business discussions. One time, I said to Andrew, "Do you know anybody who would like to invest some money into Second City in Toronto?" He suggested Jim Patrick, a terrific guy who was a young, self-made, Toronto millionaire. Jim put money into the place, we made a go of it, and he told us that he would back the show if Andrew Alexander ran the operation. We moved into the old Fire Hall, about a block from our original theater.

In the mid to late '60s, Second City was doing fine in Chicago, even though we weren't selling out every night. Business wasn't as big as it is now, and, in 1967, we decided to move to our current location in Piper's Alley. Although we were doing okay, we had some lean times, and it was hard keeping track of our operations in Chicago and Toronto. Things were good on both fronts and we had a great cast in Toronto that included Dan Aykroyd, and his partner, Valerie Bromfield, one the funniest people I had ever known. Gilda came to see us when we were playing the Second City touring company in Ann Arbor, told us she wanted to join our company, so, of course, we hired her. It was a wonderful company that also included Eugene Levy and Jane Eastwood. *Second City Television* (SCTV) is what made Toronto a hit, and it became like a cult show. The great John Candy worked in Chicago before he worked in Toronto, and when he came here, supposedly for a week or so, he had about 12 bags of luggage when I picked him up at the airport. By the mid-to late-'60s, you literally couldn't drive down Wells Street when Old Town became so popular, the traffic was bumper-to-bumper, and Second City was so successful.

Harold Ramis

In 1960, I was attending Senn High School, and we had moved to near Washtenaw and Granville in West Rogers Park. When Mather High School opened in 1960, students who had been attending Senn for a year or more had the choice of transferring to Mather or staying at Senn. I wanted to finish at Senn because my friends were there and I was really happy being at a high school with some diversity in its student body. I was also beginning to become very active in extracurricular activities, and I was a member of a four-year club known as the Ietas, which I mistakenly thought was a Greek letter. The high school also had one-year clubs, but when the Prestigians asked me to join during my senior year, I declined the invitation. I graduated from high school in 1962 and went to Washington University in St. Louis, Missouri.

In the early '60s, I became interested in playing a musical instrument and began going to the Old Town School of Folk Music for music lessons. My friends played guitar, I played the five-string banjo, and we used to perform for whoever would listen. In 1960, I was singing in the Senn High School chorus, performing in an all-city chorus at the Chicago Symphony Orchestra, and was an extra at the Lyric Opera. Before I went to college, I developed an interest in performing and did a lot of skits and shows at Senn, as well as being a member of the school theater group. Our little band was playing in coffee houses and hanging out at those places by the time I was 16 years old, and although I wasn't doing formal improvisation at that time, we were making stuff up just like the improvisational skits I would later do at Second City.

That same year, I got a work permit so I could get a job after school. My first job was at M. Hyman and Company, an underwear and hosiery warehouse at Adams and Franklin. I worked there with a friend of mine, but we managed to get fired after a few months because we were fooling around one day and knocked over a lot of merchandise that we had spent a week stacking up. My next position involved working with my brother for the *Chicago Tribune* as a messenger in their advertising order department. We delivered ad copy and tear sheets to the stores and ad agencies, and then brought completed copy back to Tribune Tower. During those high school years, I thought I wanted to be a doctor since I was a good student. I determined that I should go into medicine because, to my family, a doctor was the most respected person. And, one reason I went to Washington University was because they had a strong pre-med program. In fact, in my senior yearbook, there was a statement that my ambition was to be a neurosurgeon, not just a doctor.

When I was growing up, the big deal was to take the "L" downtown, meet under the clock at Marshall Field's, and go to a movie at the Chicago Theater, State-Lake, Roosevelt, Oriental, or Michael Todd Theaters and then, we might walk over to Art Institute. But, by the time I came back to Chicago after college, the action had shifted to Old Town, The Mother Blues club, Earl of Old Town, and Second City as the Near North began to develop into the center for entertainment for my generation.

As for politics, when I finished high school, we all were trying to look like John Kennedy, but when he was assassinated, we all started trying to look like Bob Dylan. So, it was *Camelot* when I entered college in 1962, and by the time I graduated, it was Abbie Hoffman, free speech, the Civil Rights movement, and the anti-war movement.

It was an amazing sea change in American life during my four years of college. In fact, when Chris Miller, Doug Kenny, and I later wrote *Animal House,* we were thinking of the way things were when we went to college. So, we took the revolutionary energy that developed in the '60s and based *Animal House* on a combination of Chris's experiences in his fraternity at Dartmouth, short stories he had written from which we took some of the names and incidents, Doug Kenny's writings about adolescence for The Lampoon, and a lot of personal anecdotal material from ZBT at Washington University and my brother and cousin's fraternity, Tau Delta Phi, at the University of Illinois..

I began at Washington University in 1962 and was able to go there because I received a four-year scholarship. Ironically, my friend Ira, who had talked me into applying there, didn't get accepted, so I attended Washington University by myself. When I got to college, I had the feeling that I was probably from the "wrong side of the tracks" because everyone had more money and all the Chicago kids were from either the North Shore or the south shore. I felt economically disadvantaged, but I joined a good fraternity (Zeta Beta Tau), made friends right away, and things were pretty cool.

Despite my clearly defined career plans, I gave up on pre-med within about two weeks after I started at Washington University. I decided that I just didn't want to study that hard, and thought that I had worked enough in high school and continued to work during the summer while I was in college. I kind of went crazy while I was in college and had a great time with all the freedom. When I received my undergraduate degree, I decided to stay at Washington University and try graduate school. That lasted one semester before I quit at the end of 1966. Then, I worked for seven months in a locked psychiatric ward at the Jewish Hospital in St. Louis and that was really interesting both from a political and psychological point of view. It taught me a lot about dealing with extreme behavior, and it really broadened my tolerance for difference as well as giving me a way of dealing with violence and irrational behavior.

In the summer of 1966, I went out to San Francisco, and as a result, I came back to the Midwest with very long hair, a whole new set of attitudes and habits, and a girlfriend. We got married in 1967, and, when we returned to Chicago, we lived at State and Walton. I didn't get a job until the wedding presents ran out and then I drove a Yellow Cab for a month but didn't like that work. So, I became a full-time substitute teacher in the Chicago Public Schools, and I

taught at Beethoven School at 47th and State for two semesters. When I was growing up, my family had its first grocery store at Lake and Hoyne. My grandfather owned the store, while my father was the junior partner. The store had an exclusively African American clientele, and I always felt comfortable in that world and wasn't frightened by it. Of course, it later became more challenging to be there since I was working on the West Side in April 1968 when Martin Luther King was assassinated.

I also became more interested in show business around that time and took 12 workshops in 1967 and 1968 at Second City with Josephine Forsberg. There was an opening in the touring company, but when she didn't select me, I stopped going to the workshops. I actually started teaching a workshop at the Old Town Players, which was at a church in Old Town. That was fun and, while I was still teaching, in 1967, I began freelancing for the *Chicago Daily News* working for Richard Christiansen. I was writing entertainment features, and he assigned me to cover movies on various locations. Christiansen also allowed me to review major rock and roll concerts like The Cream and The Doors and Jefferson Airplane, as well as the Joffrey Ballet, and Dick continued to print all my pieces in the newspaper. When I finished a second semester of teaching in 1968, I took my published stories to *Playboy* and got hired in the summer of 1968 as party joke editor at the magazine. After about two months, they moved me up to Assistant Editor and then, in a few more months, I became Associate Editor and stayed with *Playboy* for 18 months before leaving in 1970.

In 1968, Dick Christiansen called and said that a friend of his, Michael Miller, had become the new director of Second City. Dick asked if I would be interested in auditioning for Miller. So, I called Michael and he told me to come in on a Saturday night. To my surprise, my audition involved going onstage in front of a full house on a Saturday night in an improv set. I was told to just go up there and see what I could do. I think that I did well because when Michael formed a new touring company, he included me in it. The stage was ours on Monday nights at Second City, and we actually did very little touring. At that time, Bernie Sahlins and Joyce Sloane were around, but Sheldon Patinkin had already left. My company included Brian Murray, Joe Flaherty, David Blum, Jim Fisher, Roberta McGuire, and Judy Morgan. Then, in 1969, Bernie moved the entire Second City cast out and sent them to New York and made the touring company the main stage group.

For a while there, I was working 40 hours a week at *Playboy Magazine* at the Palmolive Building, and then I got into Second City's regular company six nights a week at the theater. I would finish at the magazine, relax for a while, get something to eat, go to the theater, do the show until 1:00 am, and repeat the schedule the next day. It was a killer schedule, but those two jobs were great. In the late '60s, after Abbie Hoffman was indicted with the Chicago 8, he used to drop in at Second City, going on stage and doing an improvisation of Judge Julius Hoffman with John Belushi playing Abbie Hoffman.

I remember that 1968 was an amazing watershed year for the whole country, and, in many ways, Chicago was the main focus for it and the stage on which much of that played out. I was only involved sympathetically in those events, although I did have very long hair and was definitely counter culture. The city was not a hospitable place for long hairs at that time, although that culture was unstoppable and my generation wasn't deterred by it. I remember going to a Joan Baez concert at the Auditorium Theater in '68 or '69, and feeling that once the concert was over, the entire audience was going to march together to City Hall and protest something, although I didn't know what it would be. That was what the times were like. During those years, I wasn't as much a political activist as a political synthesizer, and I was really building my career as a writer and/or performer.

People were really polarized, but we actually felt like something good was going to come of it. I think that those feelings were stirred by the empowerment of the presidency of John F. Kennedy, the shocking disappointment of his assassination, which led to a feeling of outrage, and then, the feeling that there were conspiracies going on like the Vietnam War and intolerable injustices. Also, we had the sense of our demographic strength. We were this huge generation which recognized our numbers and our power of collective action, both nonviolent and violent. We had the strong feeling that we could take over power in this country, especially in commercial entertainment. There clearly was an unstoppable youth market, and we thought that this would transform into American political as well as cultural life.

Interior view of Second City, c. 1965.
(Courtesy of Second City).

Interviewee Biographies

Robert Adamowski
Attorney and son of former
Cook County State's Attorney,
Benjamin Adamowski
pp. 154-156

Leonard Amari
Attorney and Owner, Amari
and Locallo
pp. 74-75

Jon Anderson
Columnist, *Chicago Tribune;*
former journalist, *Time* Magazine,
Chicago Sun-Times
pp. 40-41

Judge Marvin Aspen
U.S. District Court Judge,
Northern Illinois District
pp. 172-173

Kent Beauchamp
Former record promoter
pp. 308-309

Art Berman
Former Illinois State Senator
and Representative
pp. 152-153

Shelley Berman
Actor, comedian, movie
and television star;
former member of
Compass Players
pp. 198-199

Trudy Bers
Director of Institutional
Research, Oakton
Community College
pp. 72-73

Dick Biondi
Disc jockey, WLS-AM, WCFL-AM,
B-96, WJMK-FM, and 94.7 FM
pp. 266-268

Eric Bronsky
Model railroad enthusiast;
office manager
pp. 46-47

Edward M. Burke
Alderman, 14th Ward,
Chairman, Chicago City Council
Finance Committee
pp. 68-69

Truda Chick
Former elementary school
educator
pp. 20-22

Richard Christiansen
Former theater critic-at-large
and chief critic, *Chicago Tribune*
pp. 314-315

Joel Daly
Former news anchor, WLS-TV;
attorney; country music singer
pp. 282-284

U. S. Congressman Danny Davis
U. S. Representative, Illinois 7th
Congressional District
pp. 218-220

Leon Despres
Former Alderman, 5th Ward
pp. 158-159

Anna Marie DiBuono
Lifetime Chicagoan and resident
of Little Italy
pp. 54-55

Tom Dreesen
Comedian, television and nightclub
star; former opening act for Frank
Sinatra
pp. 194-196

Judge Richard Elrod
Cook County Circuit Court Judge;
former Cook County Sheriff
pp. 256-258

Robert Feder
Television and radio columnist,
Chicago Sun-Times
pp. 86-87

Rick Fizdale
Former Chairman, CEO and CCO,
Leo Burnett Company
pp. 252-254

John Gorman
Press Secretary, Illinois Cook County
State's Attorney
pp. 26-27

Jacky Grimshaw
Vice President, Center for
Neighborhood Technology; former
aide to Mayor Harold Washington
pp. 226-228

Jon Hahn
Former columnist, *Chicago
Daily News, Lerner* Newspapers,
and *Seattle Post-Intelligencer*
pp. 32-33

Al Hall
Former director of "Bozo" show
on WGN-TV
pp. 296-297

Glenn Hall
NHL Hall of Fame goalie for Chicago
Blackhawks and St. Louis Blues
pp. 104-105

Bill "Red" Hay
Chairman, NHL Hall of Fame;
former center, Chicago Blackhawks
pp. 108-109

Hugh Hefner
Founder and editor-in-chief of
Playboy Magazine
pp. 204-206

Ken Holtzman
Former southpaw pitcher, Chicago
Cubs, Oakland Athletics, and
New York Yankees
pp. 122-124

Reverend Jesse Jackson
Founder of Rainbow PUSH
Coalition; Presidential
Candidate
(1984 and 1988)
pp. 214-216

Walter Jacobson
Former newspaper reporter,
Chicago American; former news
anchor and political analyst
WMAQ-TV, WBBM-TV and
WFLD-TV
pp. 298-300

Bill Jauss
Former sports journalist,
Chicago Tribune,
Chicago Sun-Times,
Chicago Today
pp. 96-98

Marilyn Katz
Founder and President, MK
Communications
pp. 244-246

Johnny "Red" Kerr
Television broadcaster;
basketball star,
high school, college and
NBA; former head coach,
Chicago Bulls
pp. 132-133

Nick Kladis
Former basketball star,
Loyola University; part-owner,
St. Louis Cardinals
pp. 136-137

Judge Charles Kocoras
U.S. District Court Judge,
Northern Illinois District
pp. 64-66

Rick Kogan
Journalist, *Chicago Tribune;* WGN-AM
radio host; former journalist, *Chicago
Sun-Times, Chicago Daily News*
pp. 36-37

Bill Kurtis
Former television news anchor,
WBBM-TV; producer and program
host, A&E Network
pp. 302-303

Jim Landis
Former star center fielder,
Chicago White Sox; member, 1959
pennant-winning team
pp. 110-111

Richard Lang
Former college educator, Chicago
City Colleges
pp. 240-242

Joe Levinson
Jazz and popular bassist
pp. 200-201, 230-231

Ramsey Lewis
Jazz pianist and founder,
Ramsey Lewis Trio
pp. 306-307

Gene Mackevich
Senior Vice President, Salomon,
Smith Barney; Director,
Maxwell Street Foundation
pp. 60-61

Joe Mantegna
Theater, movie and television actor
pp. 326-328

Norman Mark
Radio host, KNWZ-AM, Palm
Springs, California, former journalist,
Chicago Daily News; former radio
and television personality,
WMAQ-TV, WIND-AM
pp. 236-237

Frank Mathie
News and features reporter,
WLS-TV, ABC-7
pp. 286-288

Erin McCann
Senior Investigator, Illinois
Supreme Court
pp. 50-52

James McDonough
President, McDonough Associates;
former Director, Chicago
Department of Streets and
Sanitation
pp. 168-169

Jo Baskin Minow
Civic leader
pp. 146-148

Newton Minow
Former Chairman, Federal
Communications Commission;
attorney, civic leader
pp. 146-148

Mike Nussbaum
Theater, television and movie actor
pp. 316-317

James O'Connor
Former Chairman, Commonwealth
Edison; civic leader
pp. 78-81

Sheldon Patinkin
Co-founder, Playwrights at Second
City; former assistant director
and manager, Second City;
co-founder, SCTV television series;
educator, Columbia College
pp. 330-332

Sandra Pesmen
Journalist and newspaper
columnist, *Lerner* Newspapers and
Crain's Magazine
pp. 90-91

Jerry Petacque
Attorney and sculptor
pp. 42-44

William "Billy" Petersen
Founder, Remains Theater;
television, movie and theater actor;
star, "CSI," CBS-TV
pp. 322-324

Dr. Charles "Arch" Pounian
Senior Consultant, Hay Management
Consultants; college educator,
former City of Chicago Civil Service
Commission Director of Personnel.
pp. 174-175

Mike Pyle
Former star center, Chicago Bears
pp. 116-118

Harold Ramis
Movie actor, writer, director
and producer; co-author,
Animal House movie;
former member, Second City
pp. 336-338

Ronnie Rice
Rock and roll musician and
singer; former lead vocalist,
New Colony Six
pp. 312-313

Jimmy Rittenberg
Owner, Mother Hubbard's
pp. 184-185

Jack Rosenberg
Former manager of sports,
sports editor, producer
and writer, WGN Television
and Radio
pp. 100-101

Carmen Salvino
PBA Hall of Fame bowler
pp. 128-129

Warner Saunders
Television anchorman,
NBC-TV, Channel 5; former
Executive Director,
Better Boys Foundation
pp. 222-225

Gale Sayers
NFL Hall of Fame halfback,
Chicago Bears
pp. 120-121

U.S. Congresswoman
Janice Schakowsky
U.S. Representative, Illinois 5th
Congressional District
pp. 76-77

Raymond Simon
Executive Director, Helen Brach
Foundation; former, City of Chicago
Corporation Counsel
pp. 162-164

Gary Sinise
Co-founder, Steppenwolf
Theater; theater, movie and
television actor; star "CSI-New
York", CBS-TV
pp. 320-321

Bob Sirott
Television anchorman, NBC-TV;
radio host, WCKG-FM; former disc
jockey, WLS-AM; former television
personality, WBBM-TV, WFLD-TV,
and WTTW-TV
pp. 12-15, 28-30

Joyce Sloane
Producer Emeritus,
former Associate
and Executive Producer,
Second City
pp. 334-335

Lee B. Stern
Owner, LBS Limited; member,
Chicago Board of Trade;
former owner, Chicago Sting
pp. 138-141

Bill "Moose" Skowron
Former star first baseman,
Chicago White Sox and New York
Yankees; member, eight
World Series teams and six
American League All-Star teams
pp. 114-115

Harry Volkman
Former weather man,
WBBM-TV, WMAQ-TV, WGN-TV,
and WFLD-TV
pp. 290-294

Clark Weber
Former disc jockey, WLS-AM
and WCFL-AM; Owner,
Clark Weber Associates
pp. 270-277

Joel Weisman
Attorney and media agent;
former journalist, *Chicago Daily
News, Chicago American*;
television host, WTTW-TV
pp. 238-239

Lois Wille
Former Pulitzer Prize
winning journalist, *Chicago
Daily News, Chicago Sun-Times,*
and *Chicago Tribune*
pp. 180-183

Harvey Wittenberg
Former general manager,
WLS-FM; former news writer
and reporter, WLS-AM;
former Chicago Stadium
public address announcer and
voice of Chicago Blackhawks
pp. 278-279

Bruce Wolf
Television and radio personality,
NBC-TV, Channel 5 and WLUP-FM;
attorney, former newspaper
journalist.
pp. 82-85

Steve Zucker
Attorney and sports agent;
owner, Zucker Sports Group;
former Chicago Assistant
Corporation Counsel
pp. 248-251